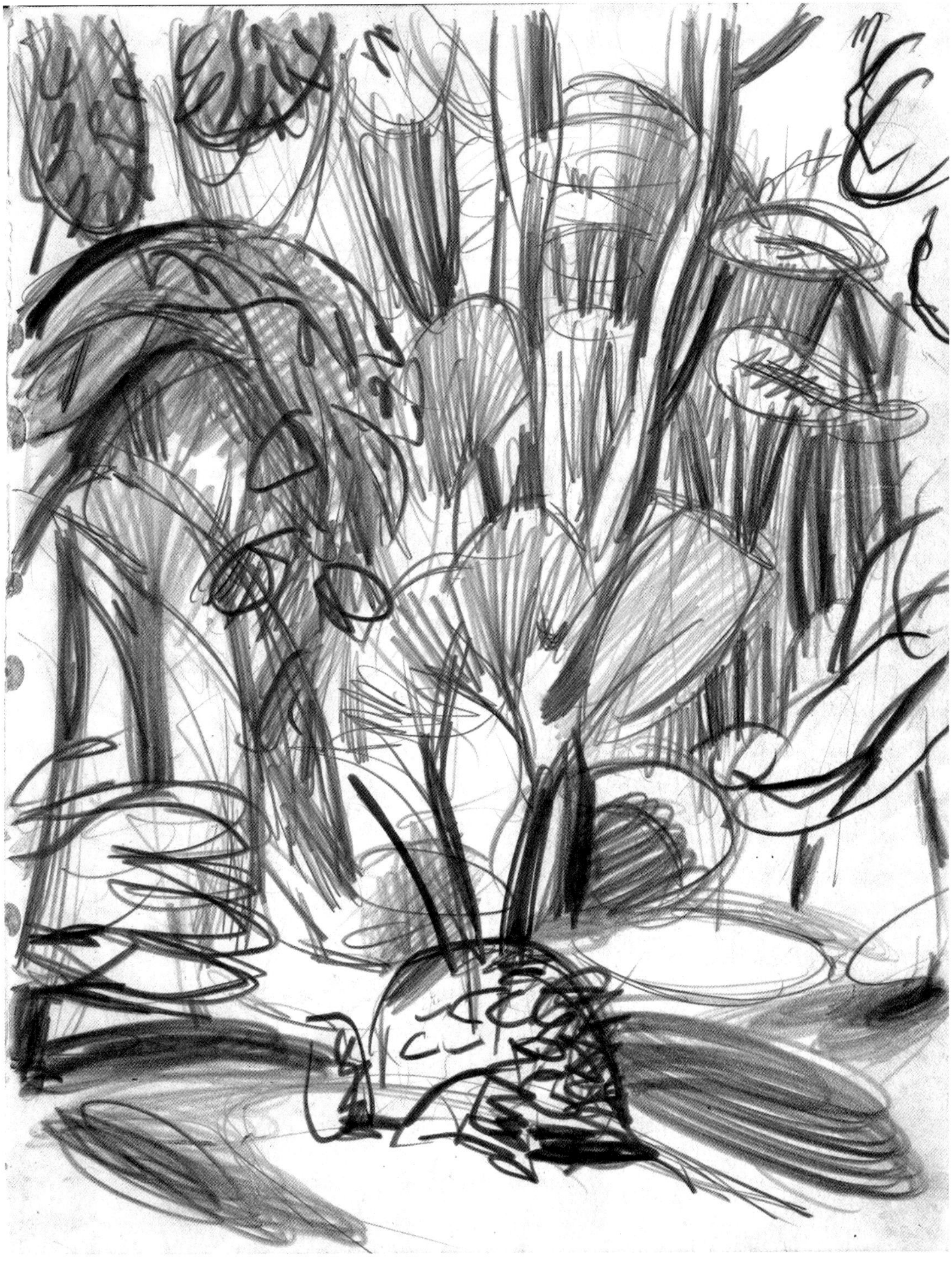

1 ‘Plant Stems II’ (nd, 1931–40). Pencil, 22.8 cm by 17.9 cm

William Gillies

Modernism and Nation in British Art

Andrew McPherson

EDINBURGH
University Press

Edinburgh University Press is one of the leading university presses in the UK. We publish academic books and journals in our selected subject areas across the humanities and social sciences, combining cutting-edge scholarship with high editorial and production values to produce academic works of lasting importance. For more information visit our website: edinburghuniversitypress.com

Cover image: *Trees on the Tyne, Haddington* (*c.* 1924) Oil, 55.8 cm by 64.8 cm
Cover design: www.paulsmithdesign.com

Edinburgh University Press Ltd
The Tun – Holyrood Road
12 (2f) Jackson's Entry
Edinburgh EH8 8PJ

Typeset in Bembo and Helvetica by
R. J. Footring Ltd, Derby, UK, and
printed and bound in Turkey

A CIP record for this book is available from the British Library

ISBN 978 1 3995 1834 5 (hardback)
ISBN 978 1 3995 1835 2 (paperback)
ISBN 978 1 3995 1836 9 (webready PDF)
ISBN 978 1 3995 1837 6 (epub)

Design direction by Sandy Wood, Collections Curator, The Royal Scottish Academy

RSA The Royal Scottish Academy

Contents

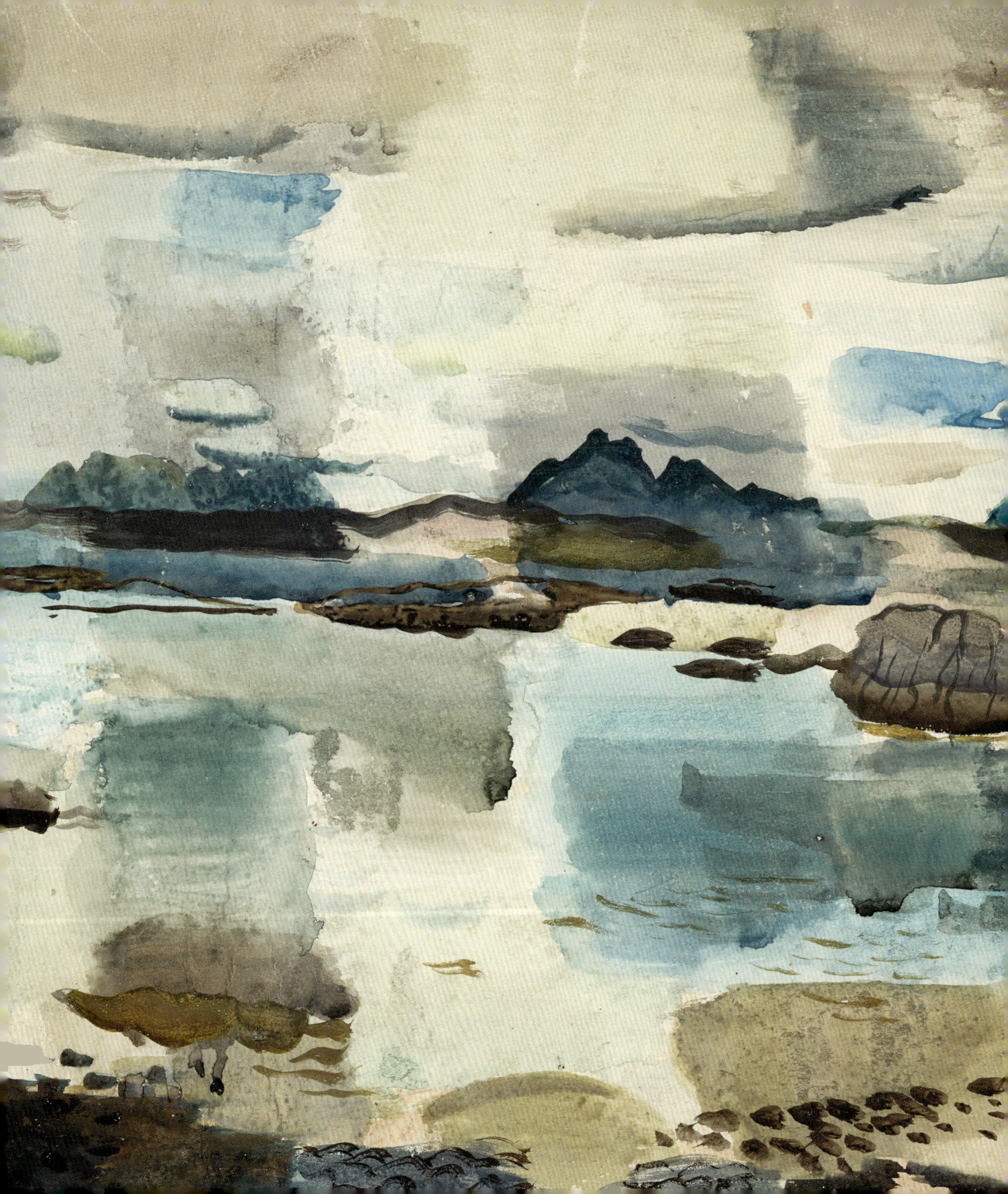

Abbreviations and Text Conventions

ACGB	Arts Council of Great Britain
AITD	auto-immune thyroid disease
anon.	anonymous
ARTUK	Public Catalogue Foundation <artuk.org>
BBC	British Broadcasting Corporation
bw	black and white
c.	*circa*, approximately or around
ce	catalogue entry number
ECA	Edinburgh College of Art
fc	full colour
GA	Gillies archive, Royal Scottish Academy of Art and Architecture
illus	illustrated or illustration(s) according to context
LWG	*The Life, Times and Work of William Gillies 1898–1973* (McPherson, in press)
NGS	National Galleries of Scotland
ni	not illustrated in this book
NLS	National Library of Scotland
PKF	Paul Klee Foundation
RSA	Royal Scottish Academy of Art and Architecture
SAC	Scottish Arts Council
SK	Joanna Soden and Victoria Keller (in reference to their 1998 volume *William Gillies*)
SNGMA	Scottish National Gallery of Modern Art
SSA	Society of Scottish Artists

Other textual conventions

[ ]	illustration number in square brackets
( )	year of written or visual work in parentheses

For the conventions used for the dates and formats for the titles of visual works, refer to 'Note on the Dates and Titles of Images' (p. 215)

Opposite:
Detail from *Skye Hills from [near] Morar* ([62] – see p. 91)

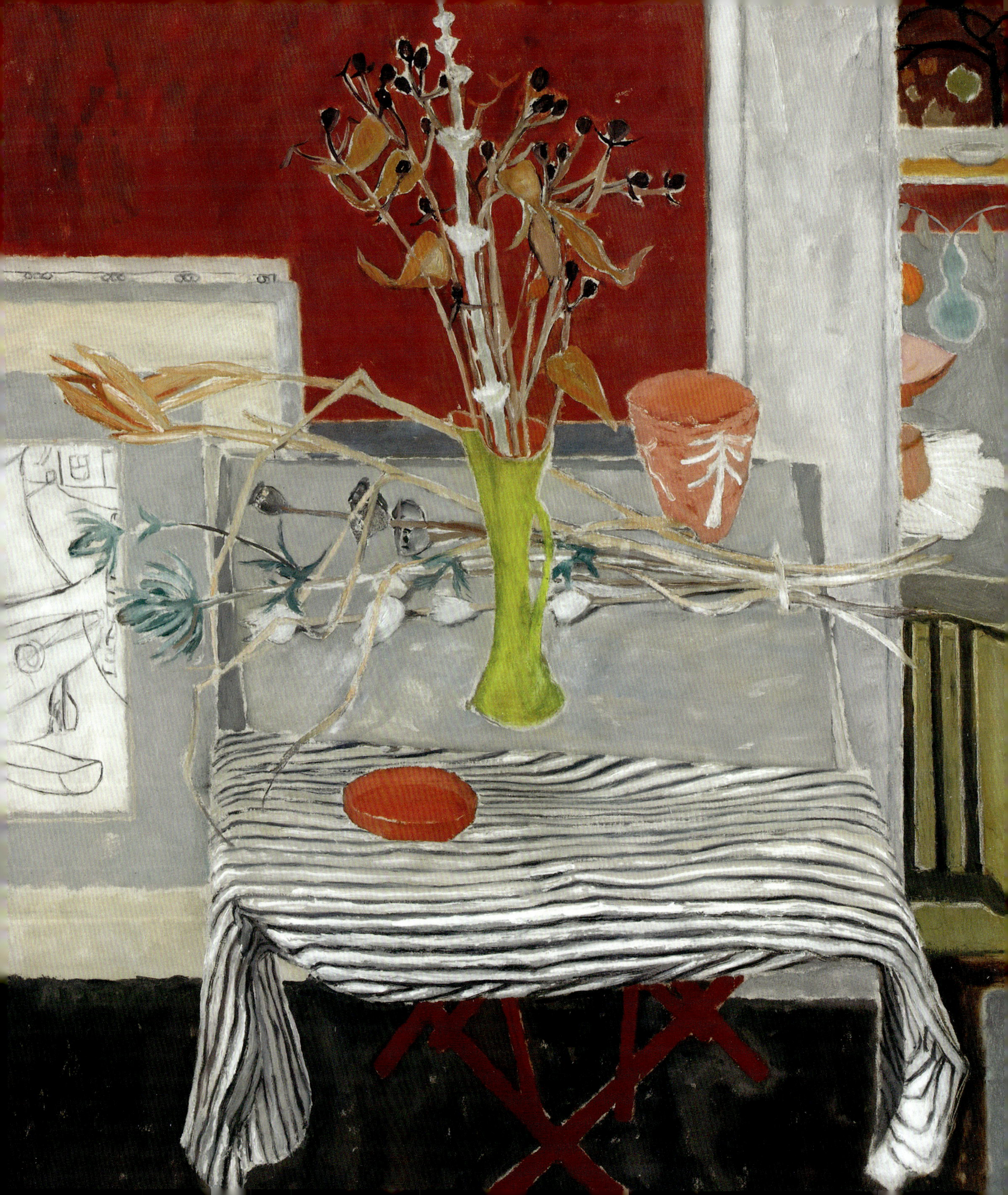

Foreword

by Gareth Fisher

President, Royal Scottish Academy of Art and Architecture

As it approaches its bicentenary, the Royal Scottish Academy (RSA) continues to support its academicians and emerging artists, and to promote, develop, collect and archive the visual arts in Scotland to make them accessible to a changing interconnected audience. Gillies furthered this mission when he bequeathed his estate, studio and papers to the Academy on his death in 1973. The ensuing years of cataloguing, research and curating culminated, in 1998, in a major RSA exhibition and monograph. *William Gillies* by Dr Joanna Soden HRSA and Victoria Keller was the first to give notice of the hitherto unsuspected extent of Gillies' engagement with contemporary British and European artists in the decades after the First World War.

The RSA's work on the Gillies collection and archive has developed an accessible resource that is becoming part of a digital world of archives that add value to each other. It has also become a blueprint for the extensive work on legacies across its membership of artists and architects.

Andrew McPherson saw the 1998 exhibition and found his way to the Gillies archive in 2006. Writing independently of the RSA, he produced a text in 2018 that throws startling new light on the artist and on major questions that were left unanswered in 1998. The RSA offered to make this text digitally available and to support the publication of a second, shorter, version it proposed the author should write. With the feedback of Honorary Academician Professor Murdo Macdonald, these versions were largely complete by the end of 2021.

This initiative, accompanied by an RSA exhibition due to open in December 2023 and tour in 2024–5, has led to a partnership with Edinburgh University Press to publish this book, and the longer *The Life, Times and Work of William Gillies 1898–1973* in digital and hard-copy form. Both books include extensive illustrations, drawn from the RSA's own holdings and from other collections. The author's Preface explains the differing emphases of the two books, but both works exemplify the RSA's mission to support the national conversation on the place of visual art in a changing world.

The RSA has not sought external financial support for these two publications, but has used the Gillies Fund (established and grown since 1973 from proceeds realised from the Gillies estate) to digitise and secure many of the images required for this ambitious publishing project. We are indebted to our Collections Curator, Sandy Wood, and his team for their support to the author and their work in amassing all the images and rights for the book; the project has been made possible by the RSA's ownership of the copyright in Gillies' work. We also wish to thank everyone whose in-kind and private support has made publication viable through the absorption of costs related to the location and reproduction of images.

We are delighted that this new partnership with Edinburgh University Press, which has been involved in printing many of our Annual Exhibition catalogues, has led to the publication of these seminal books on Gillies, which will reveal and reinterpret his life and work for generations to come.

Opposite:
Detail from *Still Life, Yellow Jug and Striped Cloth* ([102] – see p. 136)

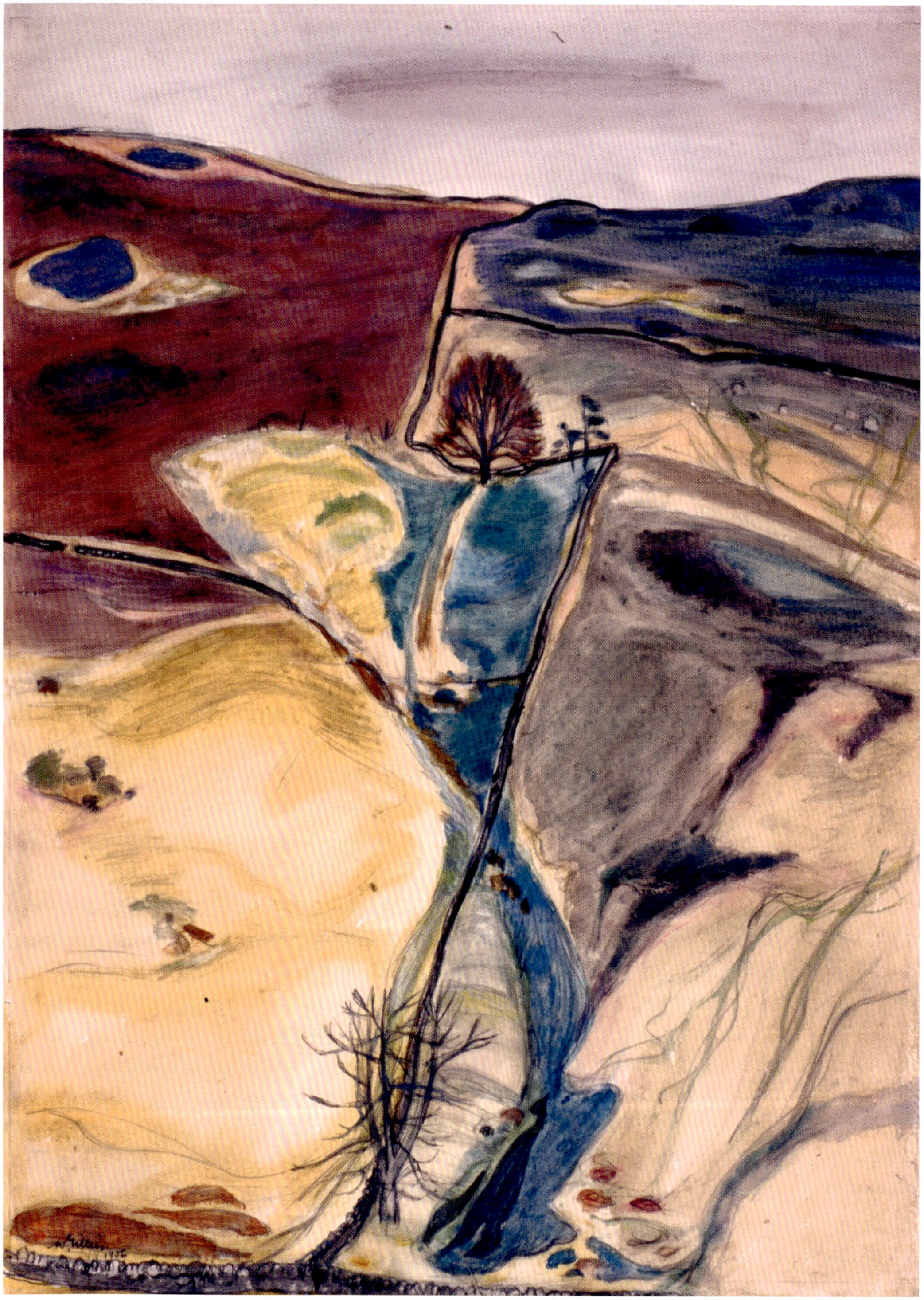

2 *Moorfoot Hills* (1956). Watercolour, 66 cm by 48 cm

Preface and Preview

This account of the life and work of William Gillies acknowledges for the first time the existential concern that lies at the heart of his painting and the modernist idiom through which it was expressed. It also challenges the received view that he was a countryman at heart, a painter of lyrical landscape who lived a serene bachelor life and produced his most telling work only when he abandoned the modernist distractions of his wayward early years to return to his childhood roots in the Scottish countryside.

The origins of this view lie, I shall argue, not in the truths of Gillies' life, which he kept mostly to himself, nor in any credible summation of his art. It originates, rather, in disputes over visual modernism and national identity in Scotland and England that were already under way at the start of the last century. These disputes extended into and beyond the 1950s, when the countryman view of Gillies first emerged, and the view itself is with us still, uncontested by Gillies in his own lifetime and widely accepted thereafter.

It was always, however, unfit for purpose both in its claims and in its omissions. It relies on a-historical stereotypes of countryside, town and city and on an unexamined assumption that only nationalists paint landscape. It does not explain the disturbing portraits of his mother and two sisters or the character and volume of some 400 still lifes produced over five decades but especially at times of existential crisis. It overlooks obvious questions about his life, times and changing reputation, his modesty, irony and silences, his bachelor status, and the legacy of his service in the First World War. It misses too the ways in which his idiom was shaped by his understanding of fundamentals of visual modernism and by a culture that he came to know in part through the fortuitous connections in Scotland of friends, mentors and relatives to various prominent figures of his age.

These figures include the author Sir James Barrie, the Norwegian artist Edvard Munch, Viscount Haldane the sometime Secretary for War and two erstwhile associates of Oscar Wilde. One was the millionaire and author Marc-André Raffalovich. He was Jewish and French by origin but naturalised British by the early years of the last century, when he established in Edinburgh a salon of the arts that continued as a node in the cultural life of Scotland and England until his death in 1934. The other was the Symbolist poet John Gray. Gray is regarded as the muse for Wilde's *The Picture of Dorian Gray* (1891), the novel that led indirectly to Wilde's imprisonment and death and to Gray's subsequent arrival in Edinburgh as a recently ordained Catholic priest and partner in life to Raffalovich. All these figures were material at some point to Gillies' life and work.

The hold of a 'countryman Gillies' on scholarship and the popular imagination is itself, therefore, a puzzle that requires an explanation. It has sentimentalised his life and allowed questions of national identity to distort accounts of the visual evidence. It has also diverted a wider potential audience from his works by obfuscating his engagement with the art of modernist contemporaries in Britain and mainland Europe. This engagement was of its time and place but was distinctive in any context, at times a matter of life and death, and in several respects unique.

Gillies is an unrecognised part of the story of modernism in Britain. His art is rooted in the modernist critique of the tradition of academic painting in which he was raised, and it responds to the alienation and uncertainty of an age that had found the machine and was losing God. From his earliest years, he was confronted recurrently by issues of sanity and violence. These led him, I argue, to embrace the freedom and variety of the modern movement and to reconfigure elements of traditional painting in novel ways to articulate his being in a conflicted and unstable world.

That said, he is not easily pigeon-holed, fits only a canon of misfits, for he was an eclectic who cared little for reputation. He was also a truly original, assiduous and outstanding painter in watercolour. These are not features that bring a modernist artist immediately to mind. What does sound more pertinent, however, is his confessedly obsessive commitment to work and experiment, especially in oil but also in watercolour. There, his coaxing of form from formless wash was arguably generative, animating his grasp of human perception and abstraction and of ways to evoke idea and form in both watercolour and oil.

William Gillies: Modernism and Nation in British Art is the shorter of two books that are closely related products of an enquiry that began in 2006 and developed into the present attempt to explain and supersede the existing orthodoxy. It is a condensed, and accordingly restructured, version of a longer book, *The Life, Times and Work of William Gillies 1898–1973*, but is complete in itself. It does not require reference to the longer book. The longer book carries the same illustrations but also provides end notes, unlike this shorter book, and fuller ancillary listings. Readers of this shorter book who want a fuller statement of the arguments and evidence, and a fuller account of the persons, events and circumstances of the time, can explore the thirteen chapters of the longer book, using its indexes and bibliography, the list of nearly 1,000 works by Gillies it considers, and search-terms of their own choice from the text of this book. The sources of quotations in this text can also be found in this way. The few references I do give here are mostly prompted by considerations of courtesy and copyright. The 'Note on the Dates and Titles of Images' explains my dating of Gillies' artworks (and why sometimes the multiple dates are similar).

Towards the end of both books, I thank by name the persons who gave so generously of their time and support, many through the precious institutions that sustain creation and enquiry – the centres of learning, teaching and making, the libraries, galleries, museums and archives, the associations of artists, and the treasure of an open World Wide Web. But I do wish to acknowledge from the outset the persons most intimately involved but whom I never met: William Gillies himself, his sisters Janet and Emma, his mother Emma Gillies (née Smith) and members of his extended family, especially William Ryle Smith, 'but for whom'. Gillies communicated almost solely through his painting, leaving others to get him right or wrong and to decide for themselves whether the truth of the matter has any bearing on what they take from his work. Had he not left his estate to the Royal Scottish Academy, had the Academy's curating of the bequest under Joanna Soden and colleagues not been exemplary, we could only glimpse now all he gave us to see.

Andrew McPherson
Hogmanay 2022

THE DEATH OF THE QUEEN.

HER LAST MOMENTS.

DIES SURROUNDED BY HER FAMILY.

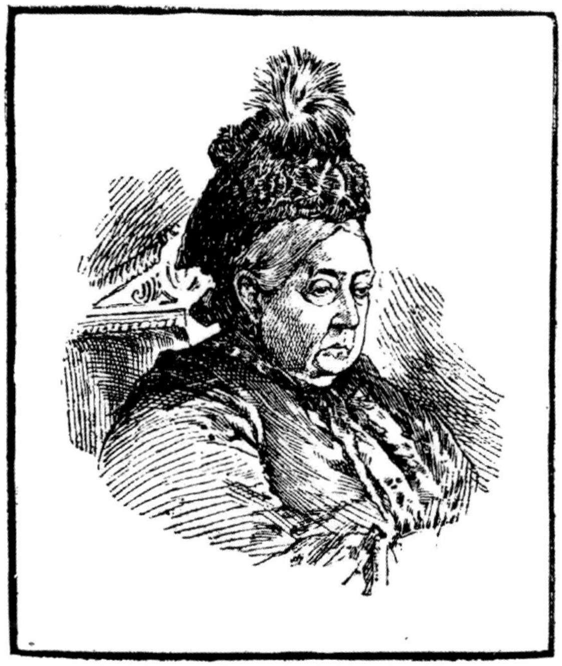

3 *The Death of the Queen* (1901). *Edinburgh Evening News*, Wednesday 23 January

I was born in Haddington in September 1898. My first recorded use of the pencil occurred in 1902 [1901?], I've been told. Queen Victoria had just died and the newspaper carried a large portrait, a line-engraving, I suppose, as an act of homage to her. I got hold of a pencil and repeating the words

Dead, Dead

systematically completely blacked her out.

Gillies speaking, around 1970

Films of Scotland and Scottish Arts Council (1970) (author's bracketed correction)

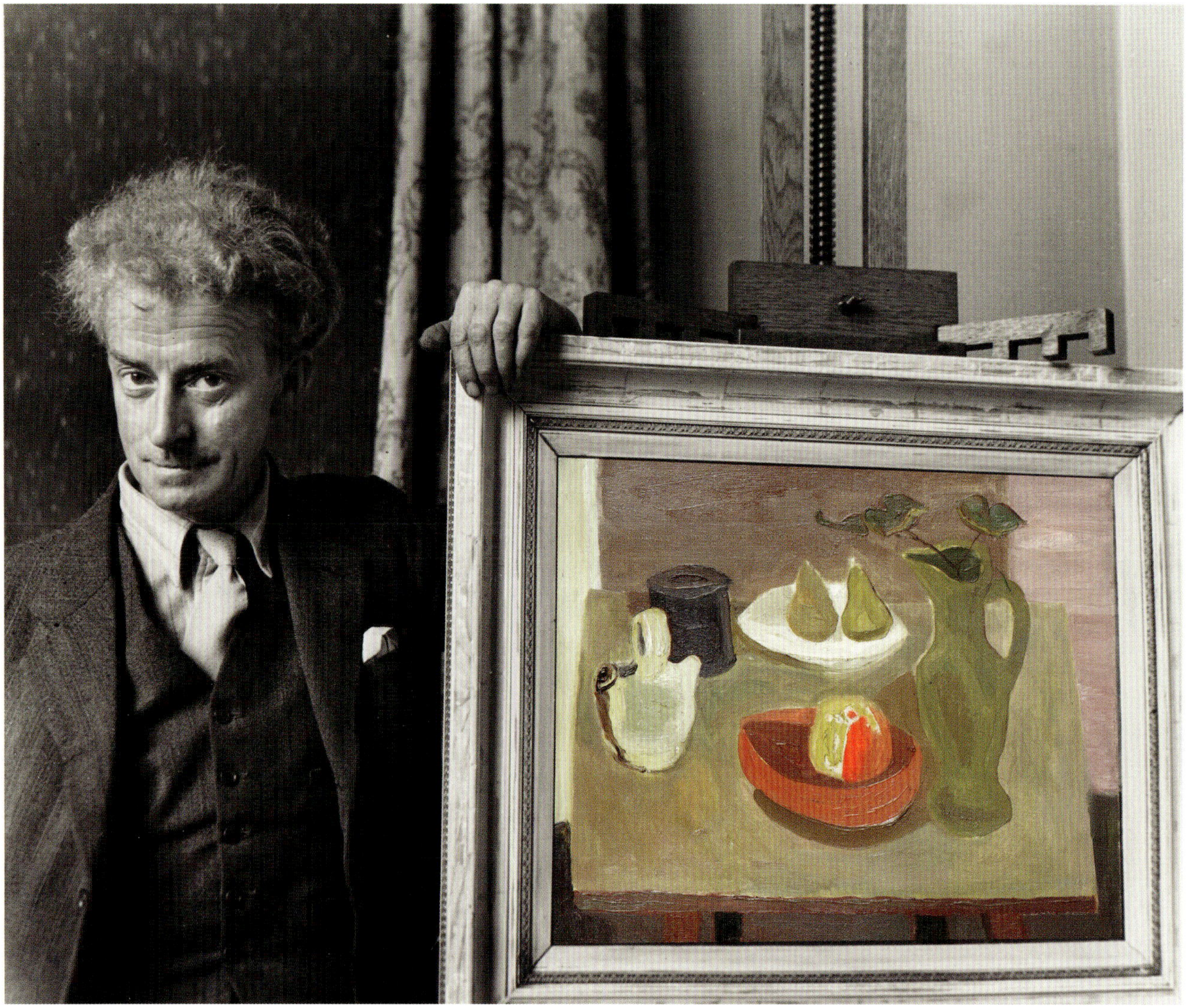

4 Gillies in 1949, with *Apple on Red Platter* (1951, *c.* 1949)

[He] used to find it very difficult to speak.

Wilhelmina Barns-Graham, student of Gillies

(Barns-Graham 1994: 10–11)

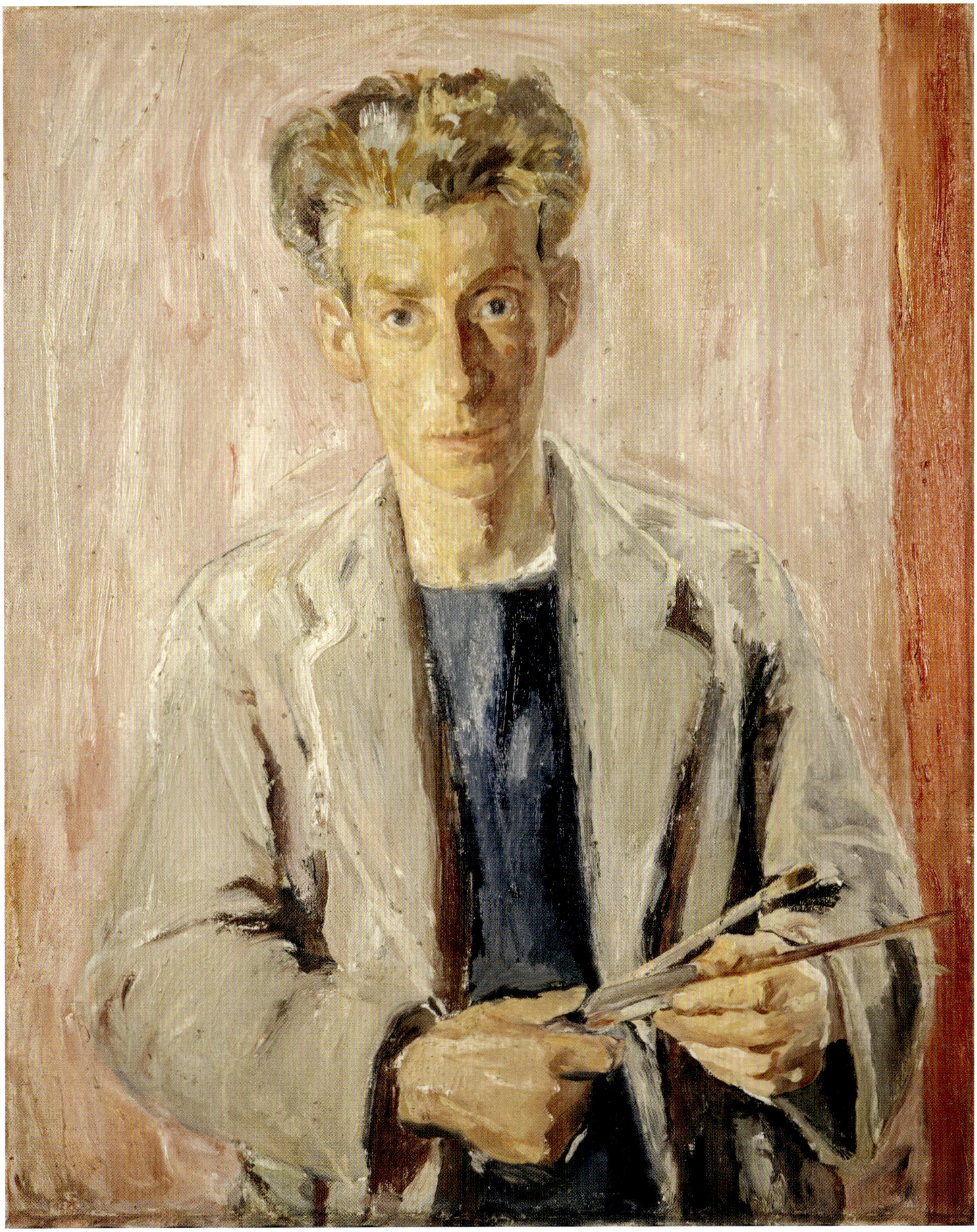

5 *Self-Portrait* (1940). Oil, 86.9 cm by 71.4 cm

[O]ur picture, not only of the external world but of the moral world as well, overnight has undergone changes which were never thought possible. With the World War a process began to become apparent which has not halted since then. Was it not noticeable at the end of the war that men returned from the battlefield grown silent – not richer, but poorer in communicable experience? … A generation that had gone to school on a horse-drawn street car now stood under the open sky in a countryside in which nothing remained unchanged but the clouds, and beneath these clouds, in a field of force of destructive torrents and explosions, was the tiny, fragile human body.

Walter Benjamin (1936)

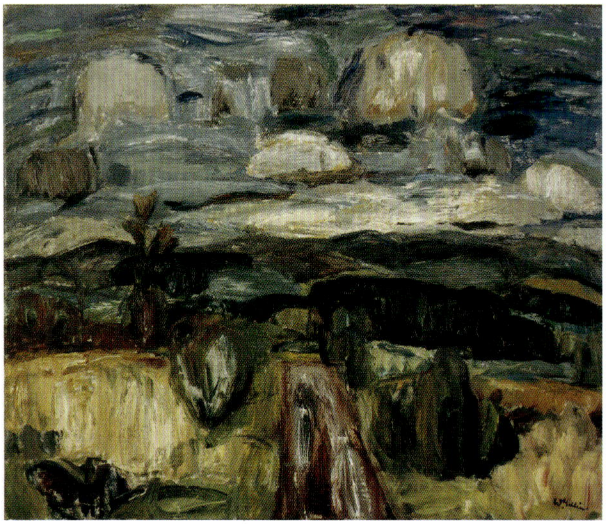

6 *Near Durisdeer* (*c.* 1932, *c.* 1933). Oil, 63.4 cm by 76 cm

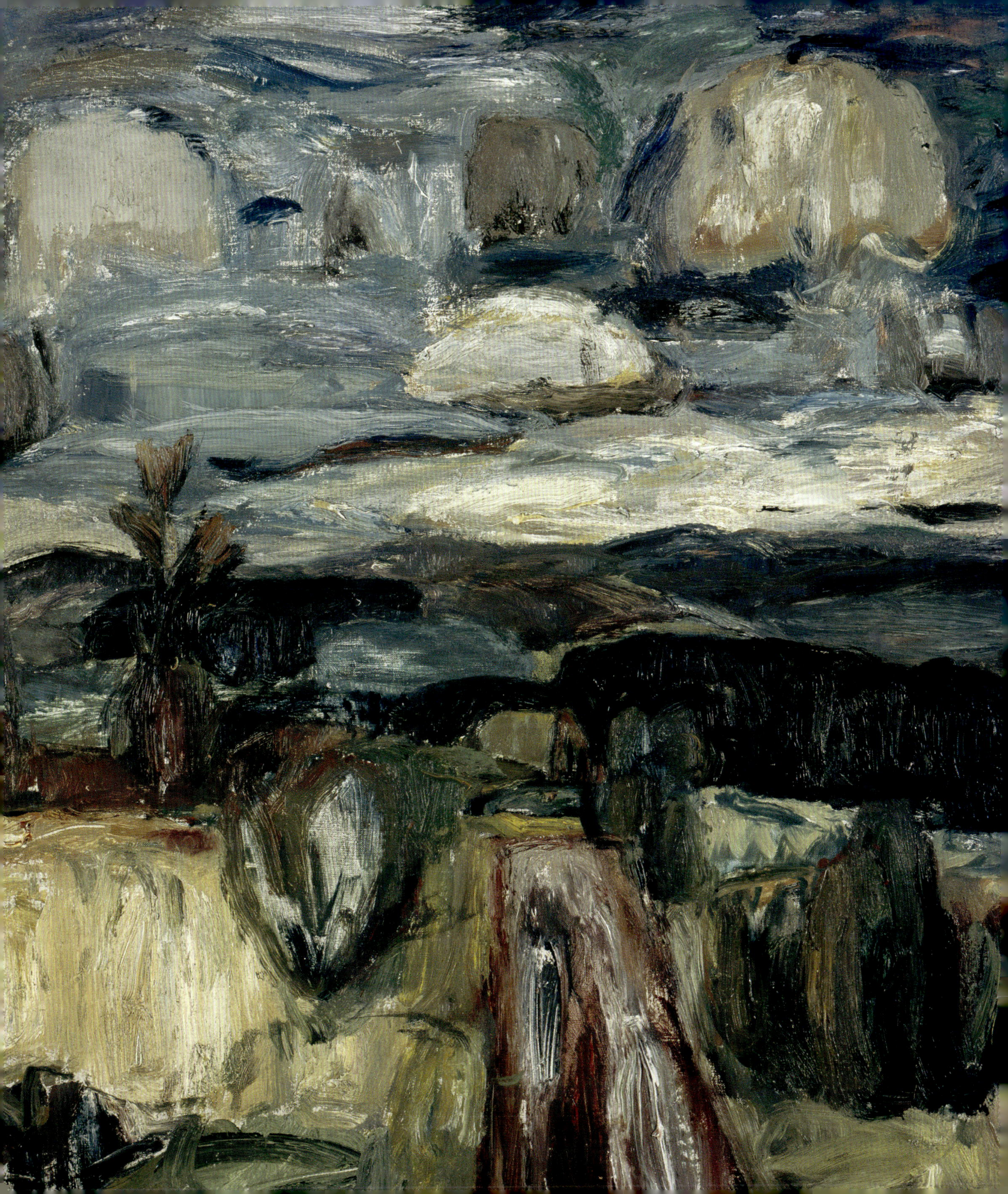

No soldier who has fought ever entirely overcomes his disrespect for the Staff. David Jones is one in whom forty-five years after the war that disrespect is still vital and fructive … [H]is point is that to make art one must hurl oneself into it, get down into one's material, roll in it, snuff it up: know it, in fact, the way troops know fighting, rather than the way the Staff conjectures about it:

> *'Ars is adamant about one thing: she compels you to do an infantryman's job. She insists on the tactile. The artist in man is the infantryman in man … all men are aboriginally of this infantry, though not all serve with this infantry. To pursue the analogy, this continued employment "away from the unit" has made habitual and widespread a "staff mentality".'*

Which is to say that the artist is overweighed by critics, reviewers, discussants, conjecturers, manipulators. *'Today'*, Jones concludes, *'most of us are staff-wallahs of one sort or another'.*

Paul Fussell (1975)

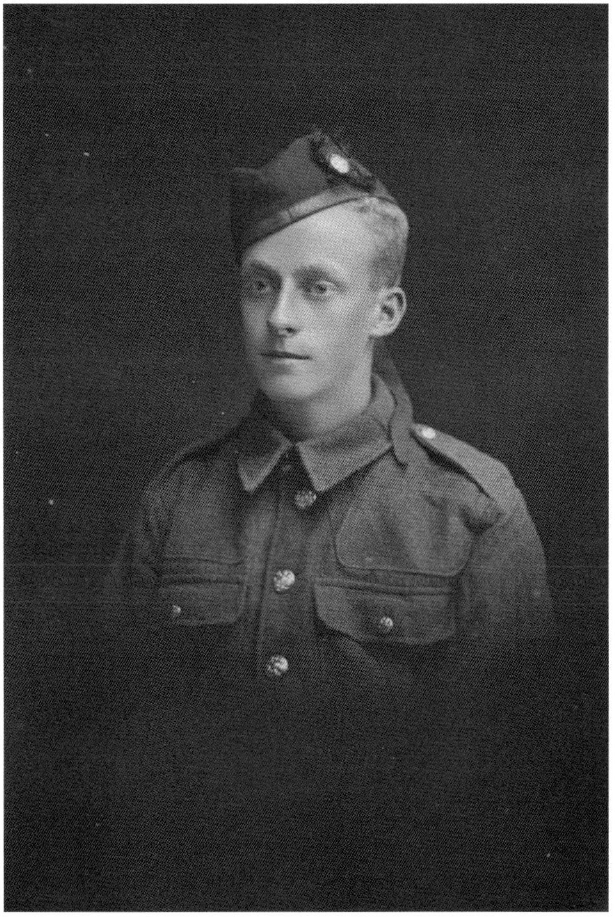

7 Gillies in the uniform of a private in the Scottish Rifles (1917)

Extracts (in italics) from an essay by David Jones (1958) and from Paul Fussell's (1975) comments (non-italic) on Jones' essay; Jones' emphases; author's brackets and italics.

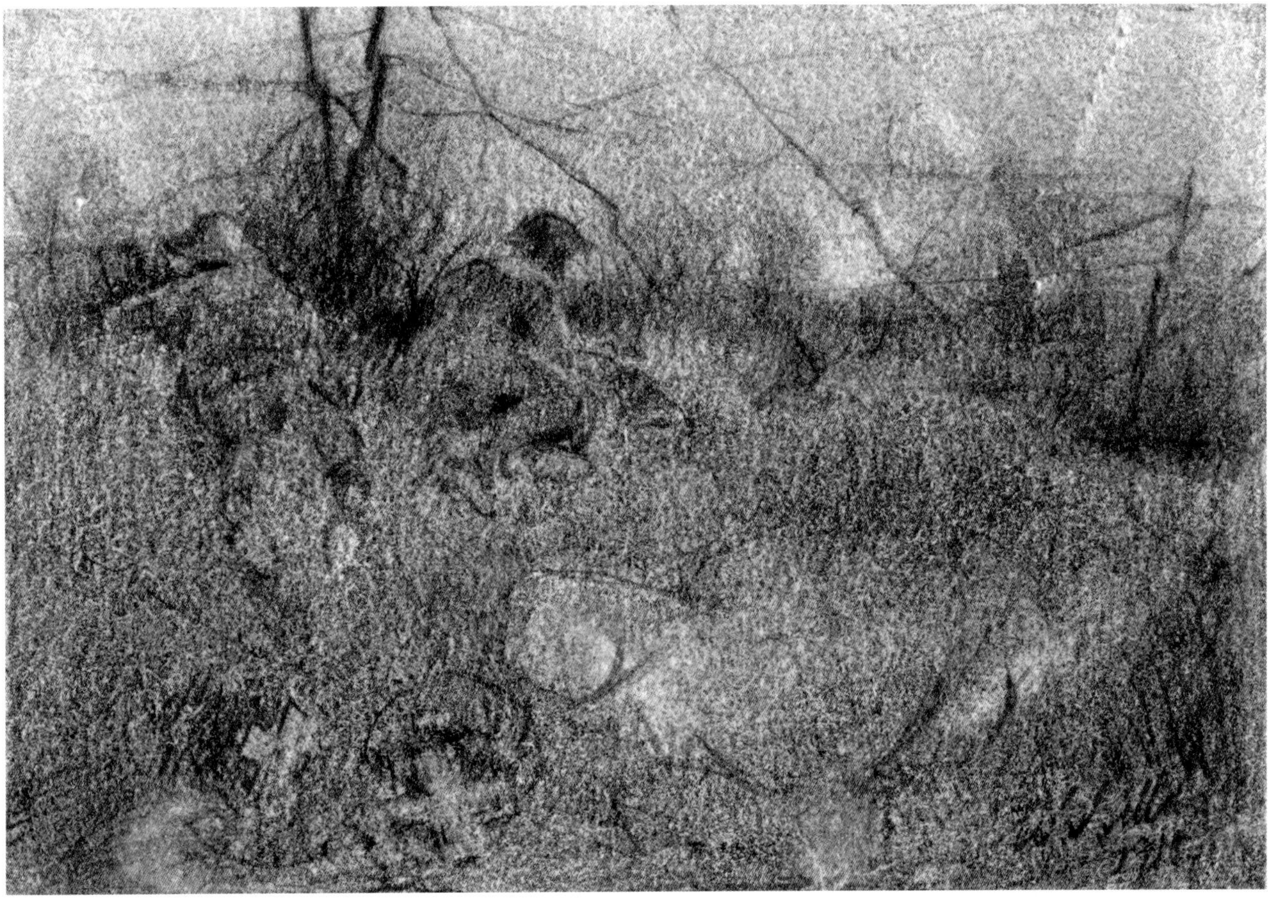

8 *Our Post Behind Our Wire* (1918), 'meant to be Lawton and yours truly'. Pencil, 9 cm by 12.7 cm

At least then he [the artist and infantryman] will know, by direct contact, the nature and depth of the entanglements to his immediate front. Which is more than they know at H.Q. for all their revised maps. The contactual is essential. You have to have been there.

David Jones (1958)

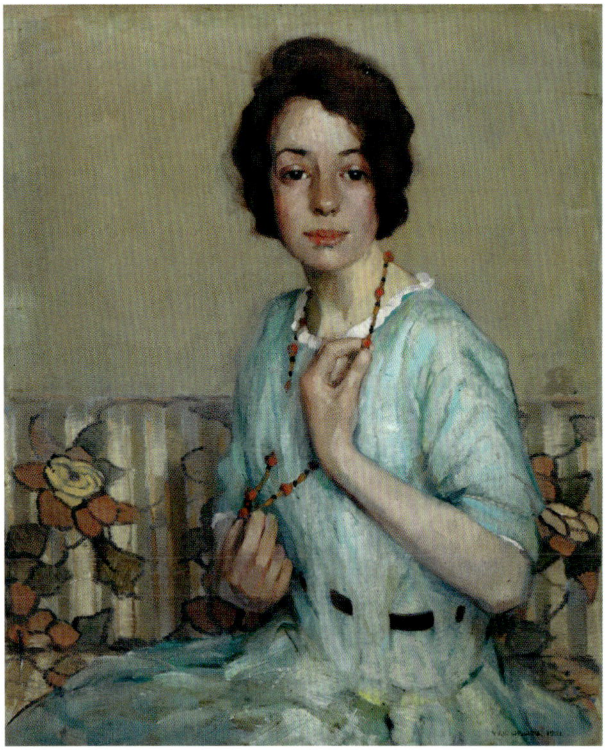

9 *Portrait of Emma* (1921). Oil, 76.2 cm by 63.8 cm

Gillies' father finally died in July 1921. Whilst Emma was sitting, therefore, the principal cause of her adolescent trauma was either lying upstairs incapable or was lying the other side of town freshly interred ... How, we may ask, could Gillies have thought to create such a work in these circumstances and discover in his sister the 'gentle prettiness' that others have remarked?

LWG, Chapter 9, and SK (1998, 48)

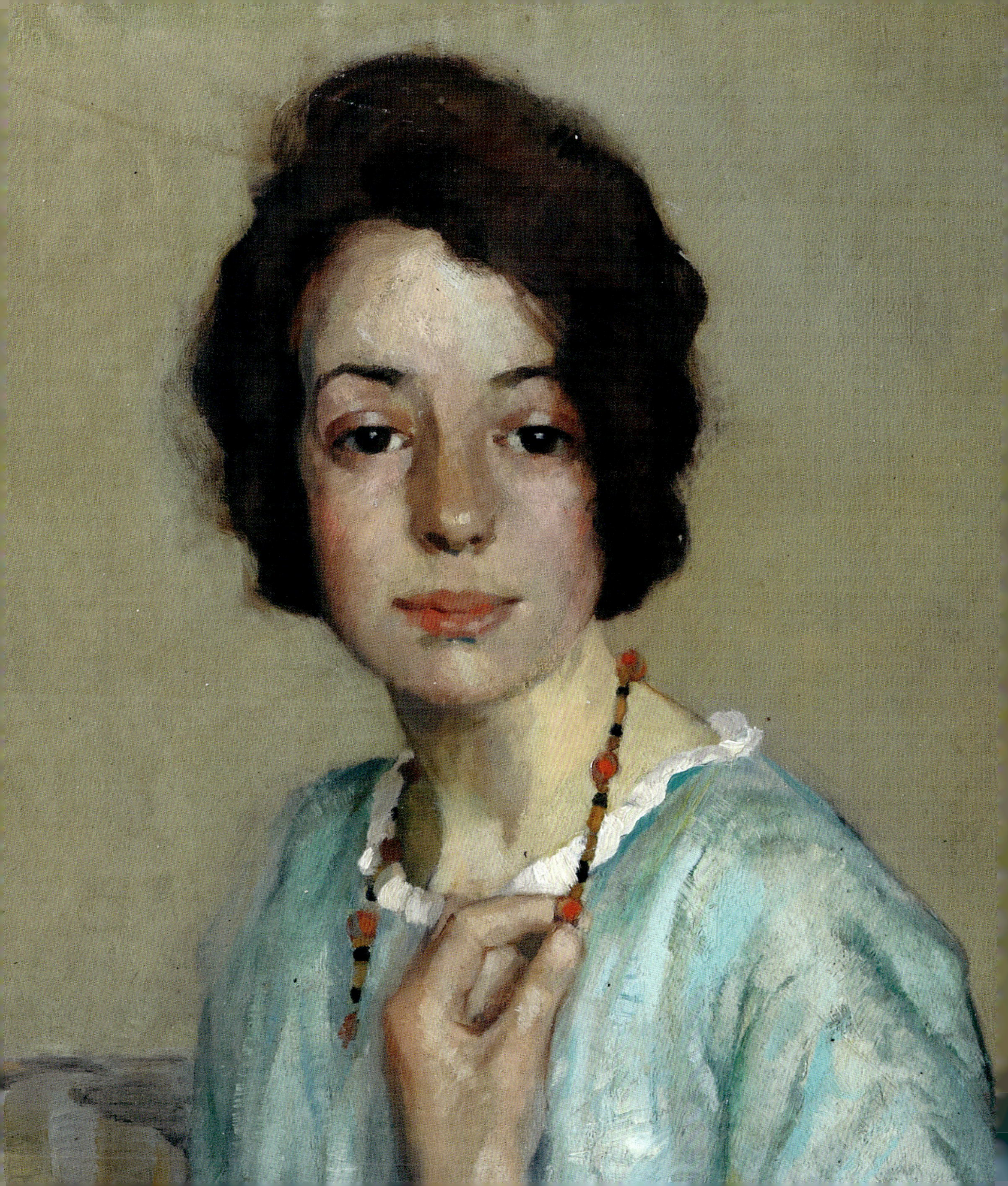

Life and Death, Violence, Irony, Sanity and Sex

Gillies rarely spoke in public about his life. He kept it from the world, even tried for a time to keep it from himself. There were secrets to hide, persons to protect, things he had encountered beyond the compass of everyday experience. The one time he did talk at any length was in *Still Life with Honesty*, a short film that accompanied an exhibition in 1970 of his life's work. He did not reveal then, or ever, so far as I know, that death ran deep in his life. Nevertheless, he could not help but begin his remarks with the tale about Victoria, reciting 'Dead, Dead' as he systematically blacked her out [3].

The story of his first recorded use of the pencil gave him a light-hearted opening to the film, but also one that was appropriate to the modernist this infant became – the regal authority of the nineteenth century duly despatched at the start of a new century in which artists would reject the authority of tradition and find art even in defacement. The more important point for us, however, is the irony that gives his tale its humour, for it also animates the person and is a clue to much else. Gillies' irony is pervasive. It helps explain both his habit of silence and his modernism, for it is, I claim, the response of a person who was disabled by prevailing narratives, who found that the stories that served the persons around him excluded his own experience.

Like Benjamin's war veterans, Gillies had seen as a child the transition from horse to internal combustion engine. At the end of his teenage years, he had returned from war silenced by the unanticipated realities of the Front. Thereafter he was sceptical, I argue, of all that was taken for reality back home, sceptical of all big ideas and of all hierarchy that lacked the authority of hands-on experience.

Gillies' irony and isolation are those of the infantry private. To really know, you had to have been there, to be, like David Jones, one of the stunned fraternity of survivors. These disablements he eventually turned to advantage through his six decades of involvement in the Edinburgh College of Art (ECA). In this he was helped by his first encounters, there and in Paris, with the modernist critique of the prevailing view of the artist he knew from texts and teachers of his adolescent years, the artist as expositor of a divinely created and benign universe having mankind at its apex. This was not the only Victorian belief to be challenged by modernity nor the only form the challenge took. For many, the war itself was the culmination of a new, urbanising way of life, regimented yet fragmented, one that degraded empathy, identity, understanding and hope.

The other main source of his existential isolation was friends and family. They, too, confronted him with things that could never be captured in traditional, mimetic works. His student *Portrait of Emma* (1921) [9] was painted in circumstances that were the very antithesis of the 'gentle prettiness' (SK 1998, 48) he discovered in his younger sister.

Gillies' mother had been born into a family that was torn apart by alcoholism and sexual transgression, and he and his two sisters were in turn to be traumatised by their father's drinking and violence. Around the age of thirteen years, his mother had left her birthplace in the mill town of Kirriemuir for the Hilltown, an industrialising area of the city of Dundee. Several years later, she went to a job at the lunatic asylum in the county town of Haddington, east of Edinburgh. She lived in the asylum for thirteen years and worked there until her marriage to John Gillies in 1894. His abuse of her and their three children began around 1905 and continued until a stroke in 1920 disabled him.

Gillies' direct contact with mentally fragile adults dates probably from the time of his earliest memories, around 1903, when it appears that his mother was providing annual respite care, accompanied by her children, for two women classified as lunatic. It continued through his late infant years, when his father began to suffer what appear to have been paranoid episodes, described by Gillies as 'very violent fits of temper with very unfair suspicions of the rest of the family'.

These did not abate during Gillies' teenage years, years in which a partially recovered patient of the asylum (a so-called 'melancholic' or depressive) lodged for a time with the family. Several years later, and within weeks of Gillies' repatriation in 1918 with injuries from the Western Front, the wife of his maternal uncle William, the most influential mentor of his childhood years, was found by their son, hanged by the neck in their family home in Broughty Ferry. Gillies never forgot the 'long hours' he had already spent in William's library and his first encounters there with a range of traditional and contemporary painting, Scottish, English and international.

Later, in his early professional years, between 1927 and 1935, three friends from his first exhibiting group died young. William Crozier died accidentally but one of the others, William Munro, died by his own hand as, most probably, did the third friend, David Gunn. The latter's death was around the time of the attempted suicide and early death of Gillies' younger sister, Emma, in a psychiatric hospital in 1936. Then, on a February evening in 1943, the young author and mother Ann Scott-Moncrieff walked into the sea at Nairn and was never seen again. Her husband, the author George Scott-Moncrieff, was one of Gillies' most sympathetic interpreters. The couple had entertained Gillies in their home and George had lived with the Gillies family for some weeks after the Scott-Moncrieffs sold that home to Gillies and his sister Janet in 1939. Meanwhile, from the early 1930s onwards, Gillies was also witness to the long-term decline of one of his closest friends, the homosexual artist Harold Morton, who survived until 1965 in and out of psychiatric care.

In her final extremity in 1936, Emma Gillies had wrongly believed that she herself was mad and had compared her symptoms with those of her father, by then fifteen years dead. She was, in fact, not the Victorian 'hysteric' that her professorial consultant diagnosed, but an unrecognised victim of a thyroid vulnerability that she and her sister Janet inherited from their father. For some years, Gillies had no way of knowing whether the condition would eventually take him too, for in 1935 it had also claimed his friend and colleague S. J. Peploe when Peploe was all of sixty-four years old. Gillies, in addition, will almost certainly have witnessed the condition and ultimate fate of Evelyn Read, the first wife of Herbert Read, who was the Watson Gordon Professor of Fine Art at the University of Edinburgh, 1931–3. Evelyn was 'bloated from … thyroid deficiency' (King 1990, 104) when Read deserted her in 1933. For several years thereafter, she turned for support to Lily Harvey Wood, wife of a close friend of Gillies, before she, Evelyn, was permanently consigned to mental institutions.

In the light of all this, we can be virtually certain that Gillies was aware of the potential implications of genetic inheritance for his own sexuality. Indeed, at a time when friends in their thirties were marrying, his closest female friend was Margery Porter. Seven years younger than Gillies, she was Peploe's niece and the daughter of a medical doctor. The medical advice of the time counselled against marriage and reproduction if the family line carried the thyroid dysfunction then known as 'exophthalmic goitre' or Graves' disease. Both Gillies and Margery were potentially at risk. But it was meningitis that killed Margery in 1948, ironically around the time that oral treatment was becoming readily available for the condition that had already taken Peploe and Emma.

One learns virtually nothing from earlier monographs on Gillies of this unremitting pulse of untimely and arbitrary death. He remained silent to all intents and purposes, and someone destroyed or lost most of the family evidence. He also kept quiet about his experience in the First World War. Or, rather, he tried at first to do so. In 1931–2, however, the example of Munch's painting of the traumas of his own life persuaded Gillies to acknowledge the legacy of his own two sources of trauma – family and war – and so to open himself to the trials of the world around him as the prospect of war returned.

In *Still Life with Chagall Print* (1933) [10], a Jew unmasks beside a barely discernible black vase made larger by its forward placement. This and other works around 1933–4 (including illus [11], [34], [45], [46]) mark the start of his resolve to open himself to others and to find more thereby within himself. In attempting this, he broadened his engagement with modernism beyond his first direct encounter with Cubism in Paris of the 1920s, to explore what he could also take from Expressionism, abstraction, symbol, the naiveties of child art, the phenomenology of Paul Klee and the latter-day *belle peinture* of the French. The results emerge cumulatively across the full range of his work, in portraiture, still life and landscape, as he worked over the following thirty years to make out (discern, show, affirm, own) his being in the world and, through this making, to end the silence of his isolation.

The Countryman: Political Context

The fiction of Gillies the countryman emerged from cultural-national resistance to metropolitan condescension towards the arts in Scotland during the first six decades of the last century. These were years in which questions of a national art and its place in the modern world shaped major developments in the governance of the arts in Britain and Northern Ireland. The questions assumed a particular importance during the two World Wars, and at times in the years between, becoming matters of national purpose and morale that involved governments and directly affected artists' prospects and standing, even their very survival.

This did not end with the ending of the Second World War. The founding of the Arts Council of Great Britain (ACGB) in 1945–6 under the guidance of Lord Keynes embedded hierarchical assumptions about the importance of a nation's art in expanded arrangements for the support of the arts on the mainland of the United Kingdom. Northern Ireland was given an independent body for the governance of the arts in 1942, but not Scotland. Keynes dismissed the Scots who wanted a similar body as 'bagpipers' and allowed only a

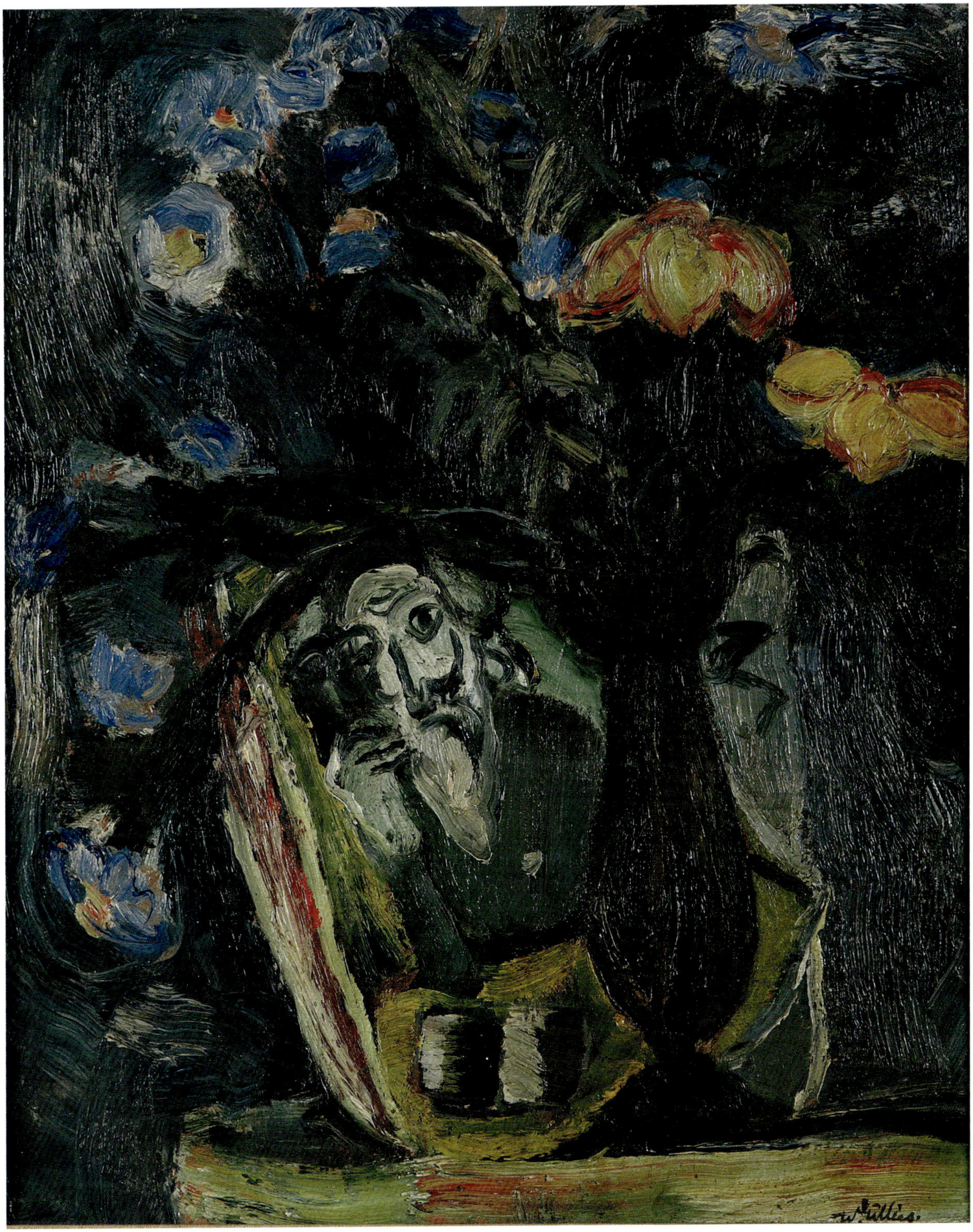

10 *Still Life with Chagall Print* (1933). Oil, 56 cm by 45.5 cm

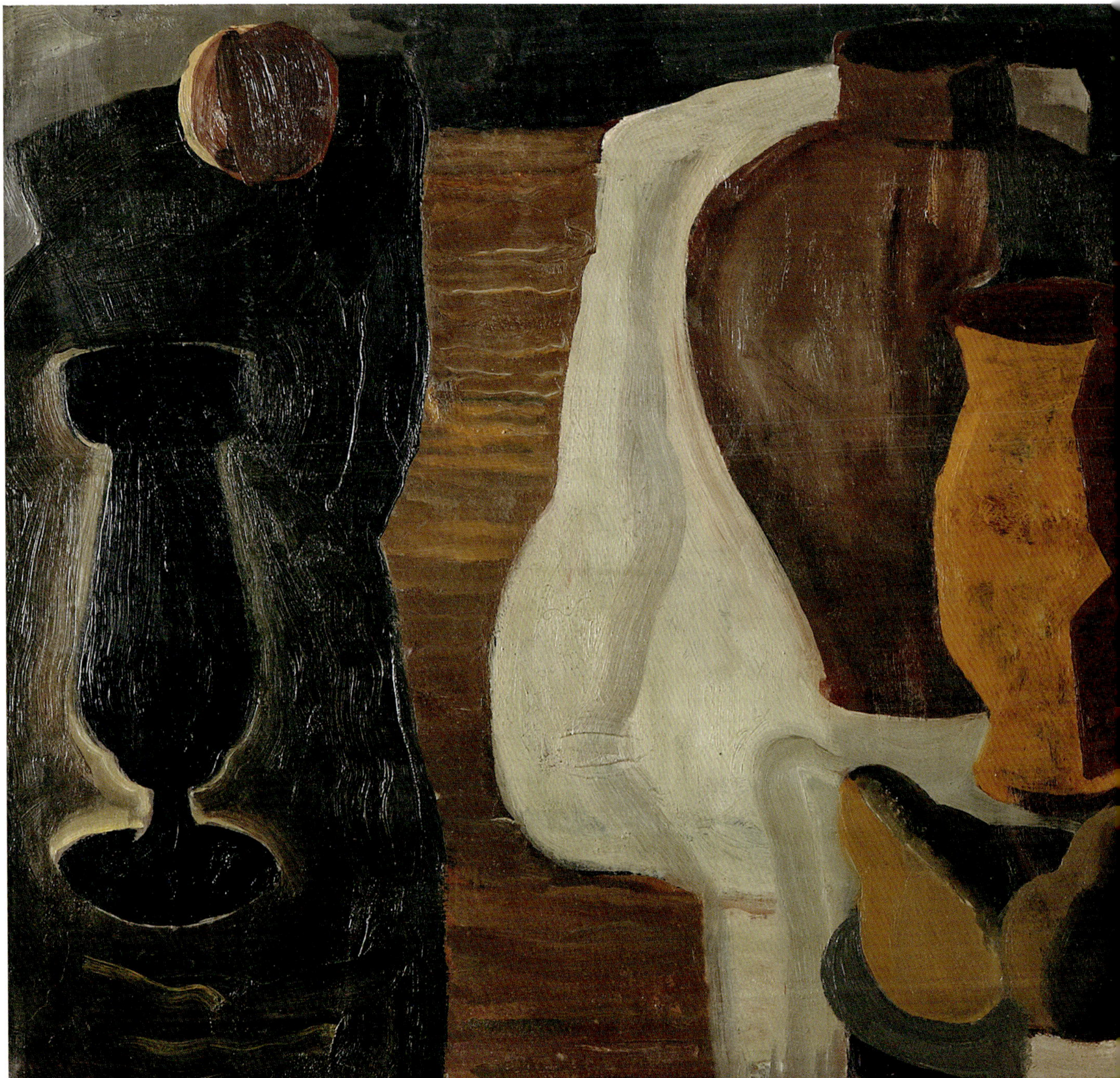

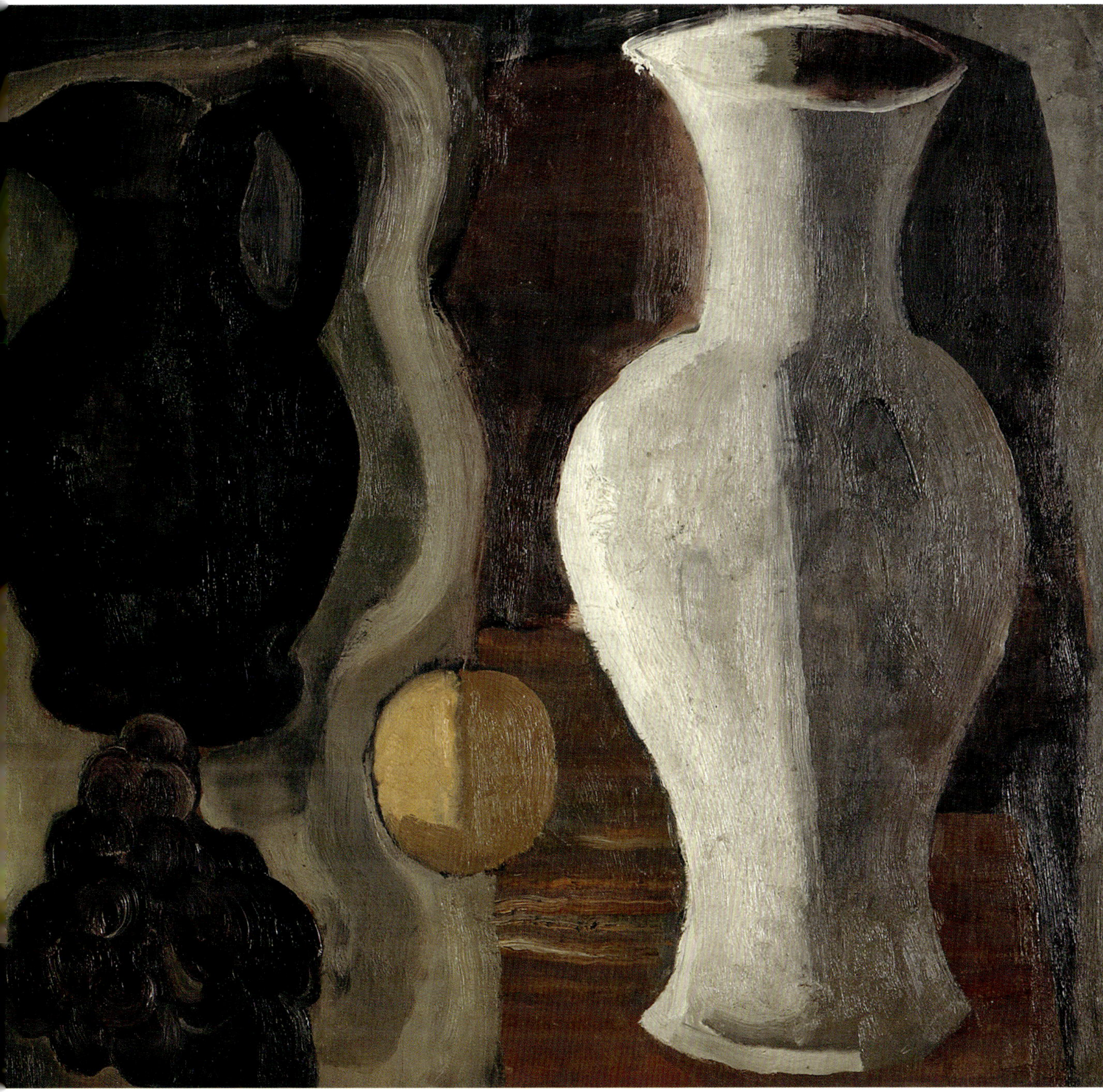

11 *Still Life with Black Jug* (1933). Oil, 56.5 cm by 127.1 cm

Scottish sub-committee of the Council with a limited executive autonomy that was itself reluctantly conceded. Likewise, Kenneth Clark (later Sir Kenneth, and himself of Scottish origin) found the Scots he dealt with 'really *odious*, so noisy and tactless'. Clark was a long-time colleague of Keynes on the body that preceded the Council, the first chair of the Council's arts panel and, from 1953 to 1960, the third chair of the Council itself.

The ACGB soon stimulated the growth of a symbiotic cultural economy of publicly funded patronage, privately operated galleries and freelance critical leadership, all centred on London and offering new opportunities for exhibition. Other than the chances to exhibit, however, Gillies wanted none of this new world of cultural promotion, or of the cultural-national reaction it provoked in Scotland among those who saw it as an extension of a long history of metropolitan indifference.

His main concerns were with the consequences of the new forms of patronage for practising artists – with the sharp end, if you like – and, at the other extreme, with questions of life and death that had faced the youth of his generation and his close family in particular. Confronted recurrently by the arbitrariness of fate, he worked for much of his life to reconcile the vulnerability of the human condition with the transcendental potential of human awareness. But he rarely explained himself except through his art and so became a pawn in the cultural politics of his day.

Visual modernism challenged national schools of painting in ways that divided opinion within Scotland and England and divided Scotland from England. At issue was whether to resist a change that was driven by continental artists, and especially by those of the School of Paris, or else to adapt in some way or to concede altogether. Could one go modern and remain British? And what was so good about British anyway, whatever British was?

Before the First World War, the Vorticist artist Wyndham Lewis had wanted to 'Kill John Bull with Art'. After the war, but in similar vein, Hugh MacDiarmid, poet, communist and nationalist, urged that Scotland could escape English domination only by conceding that Scottish culture was so degraded by English colonisation that it should be disowned in favour of a modernism that was international, unsentimental and distinctively un-English. MacDiarmid was nothing if not combative, and unsparingly so. He anathematised all of the English and most of his fellow Scots as well, alienating many of the nationalists among them but also finding followers.

Gillies, however, allied himself neither with the several Scottish artists attracted to MacDiarmid, nor with any group or emergent avant-garde in England. In the 1920s he exhibited annually in Edinburgh with the 1922 Group, a dozen or so young friends from the ECA. Thereafter, he showed regularly with several established Scottish societies but also periodically in London, beginning in 1928. In the twenty-four years between then and his featuring in Herbert Read's 1951 book *Contemporary British Art*, his co-exhibitors in Edinburgh and London included at some point most of the well-known British modernists of his generation and many of his major European contemporaries.

Between the two World Wars, his eclectic promotion of European modernism in Scotland marked Gillies out as a modernist and rebel. But Scottish perceptions of him changed in the aftermath of Keynes' rebuff. In the 1950s and 1960s, cultural nationalists found a nation in his landscapes, alleged expressions of a primordial national sensibility that could be pressed in aid of Scotland's claim to sovereignty over the promotion of its expressive arts. What was called Gillies' 'sense of place' (in England, sometimes elided with a sense of the 'spirit' of a particular place, or sense of its '*genius loci*') was held to be uniquely Scottish and collectively shared.

Among the contributors to this argument were two doctors of philosophy of Edinburgh University. Robert A. Lillie was a knowledgeable semi-professional philosopher and an able pianist and performer. A bachelor of fragile health and moderate independent means, he amassed by far the largest private collection of Gillies' works. Thomas Elder Dickson was a trained artist, psychologist and school teacher. He published the first monograph on Gillies in 1974 and was Vice Principal in charge of administration at the Edinburgh College of Art from 1949 to 1967. He also lectured there on the history of art.

A third contributor was George Scott-Moncrieff, widowed husband of Ann and, following her example, a convert to Catholicism. He came from a long-established, diversely distinguished and well-connected family but struggled to maintain an adequate income from his writings alone. In 1939, he published the first illustrated article on Gillies. Later, in 1953, he promoted an exhibition of his works that established the countryman persona firmly in the public mind as an antidote to MacDiarmid, communism and Picasso. Gillies objected in private to some of the detail of Elder Dickson's several accounts of his life and work but said virtually nothing in public about the wider political and cultural project to which Elder Dickson, Scott-Moncrieff and others annexed his work.

Two proximate goals of the cultural-national claim to sovereignty were an independent arts council for Scotland and a new national gallery in Scotland with powers, already available to the Tate in London, to buy and show the work of living artists. By the mid-1950s in England, however, younger modernists were abandoning the touchstone of nationality and turning from the School of Paris towards the new worlds of Pop Art and American Abstract Expressionism. In this context, Gillies began to appear multiply irrelevant to those who thought that modernism in Britain was necessarily metropolitan, that it could not exist in north Britain and that any modernist there with any sense would soon gravitate south. Gillies' Scottish domicile and village home, his evident debt to French masters of his teachers' generation, his appropriation by the cultural-national cause and his silence on the matter came to look like allegiances that modernism now disowned.

Thus, neither the cultural-national nor metropolitan positions, though mutually opposed by 1960 on the imperative of a national sensibility, would dispute that Gillies was a countryman and, by virtue of that, a patriot or nationalist as well. This view of Gillies is still widely shared, though only as an assumption that both sides of the divide have left undisturbed, the one because it matters to them, and the other because it licenses an effortless indifference and matters only that Gillies and his idiomatic modernism should not.

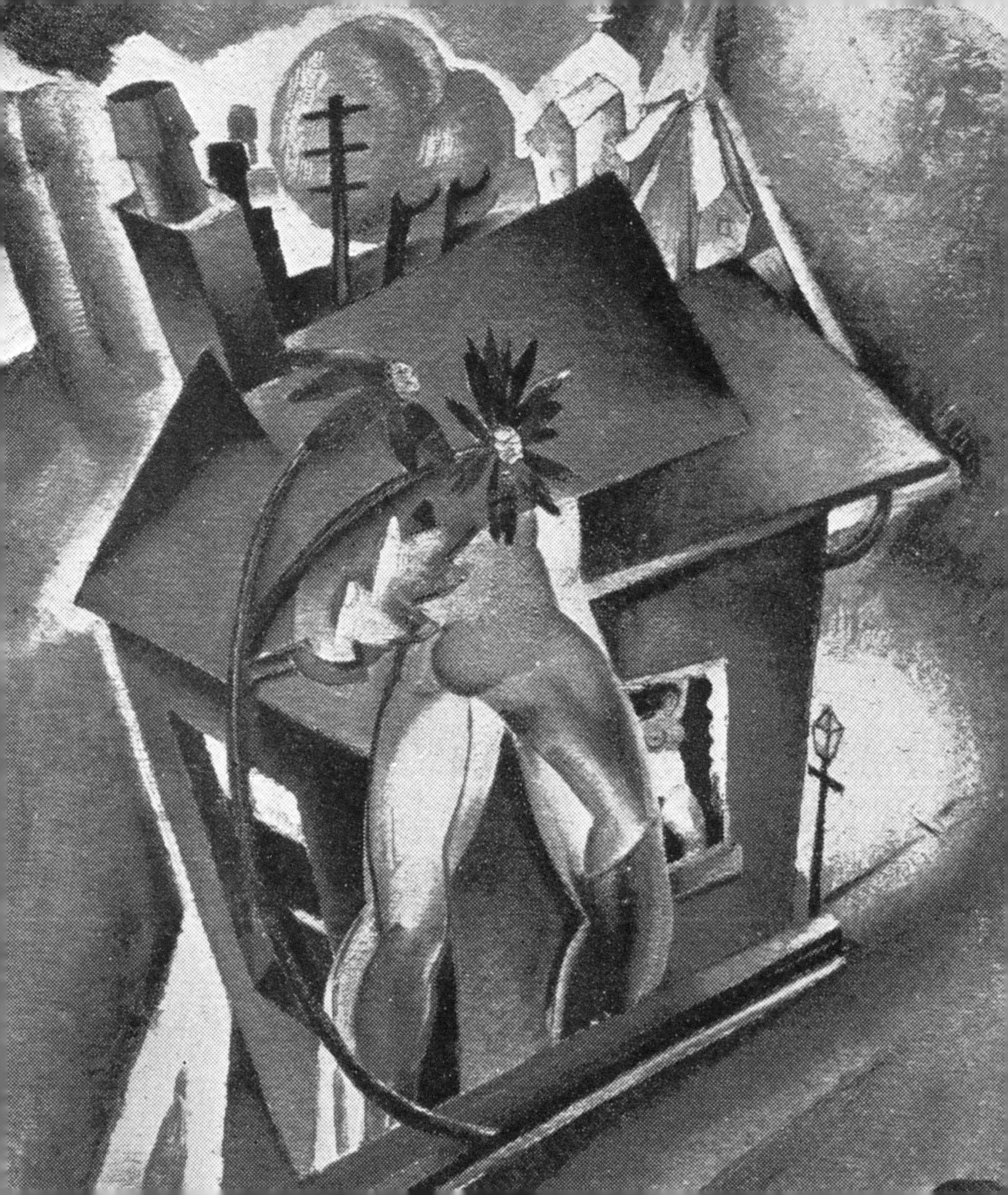

Kailyard and Kin

Gillies' mother stands in middle age outside her birthplace and family home in Kirriemuir [12], a town where realities mingled with fictions, and a symbolic epicentre of the cultural struggle for Scotland's soul in the years between the two World Wars. Gillies was caught in this struggle for much of his life, empathising with his immediate and wider family but unable to subscribe to the kailyard (sentimentalist) narrative that sustained many of them in their diaspora.

Mrs Gillies' father, George Smith, ran the Temperance Hotel for the Total Abstinence Society. He drank himself to death there in 1870 when she was six years old and he was forty. It was also there that, within three years of his death, Mrs Gillies' mother bore a half-brother, David Mitchell, to her eight children. Four months earlier, she had married the father, John Mitchell, the head hostler of the hotel. He was barely closer in age to his wife than to her eldest son. The departure to Dundee of most of the eleven members of the newly composed Smith/Mitchell family soon followed, and further dispersions ensued from there.

By the time this photograph [12] was taken, Kirriemuir had embraced the fictional identity enshrined in the sign above Mrs Gillies' head. The fiction was created by a childhood friend of her elder brother, William Ryle Smith. A few doors from the hotel was the W. B. Mills toy shop, library and publishers. It drew the young J. M. Barrie to the street and sparked his interest in theatre and literature. During Mrs Gillies' years in Dundee and in the lunatic asylum in Haddington, the popularity of Barrie's early novels, drawing on his mother's memories of pre-industrial Kirriemuir,

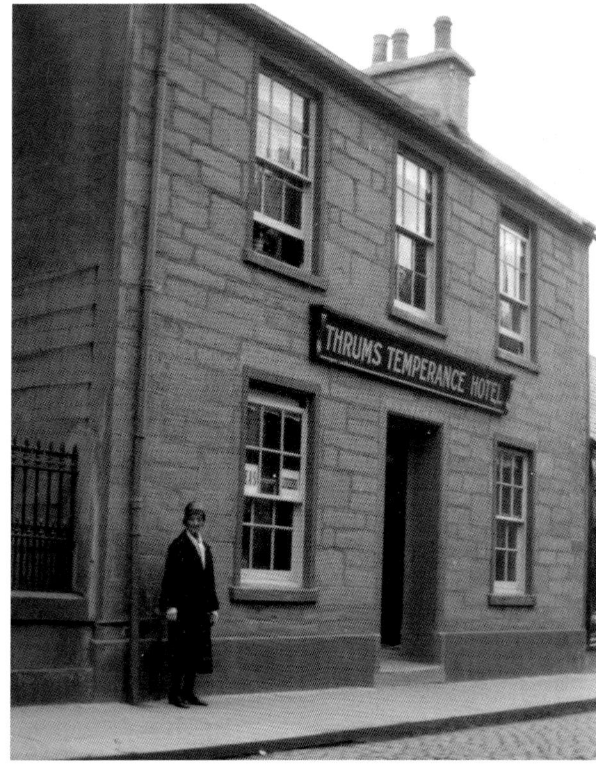

12 Mrs Gillies outside her birthplace in Kirriemuir (*c.* 1930)

brought thousands of visitors to the town and transformed 'a bit of obscure earth into a spot where pilgrimages are made'.

Barrie called the town 'Thrums', after threads used by handloom weavers when the principal industry of the town and its hinterland was still conducted in cottages and farms; and he set this fiction firmly in his own mother's lifetime, before what he called the 'giant' arrived to mechanise the industry and wake the Smith children with its early-morning summons. In later life, Mrs Gillies' side of the family would understand themselves through the example of Barrie's life and through his stories of the birthplace they shared. Over some sixty years or more, they and their children would make regular visits to 'Kirrie', a place they

Opposite:
Detail from *From Another Window in Thrums* ([15] – see p. 25)

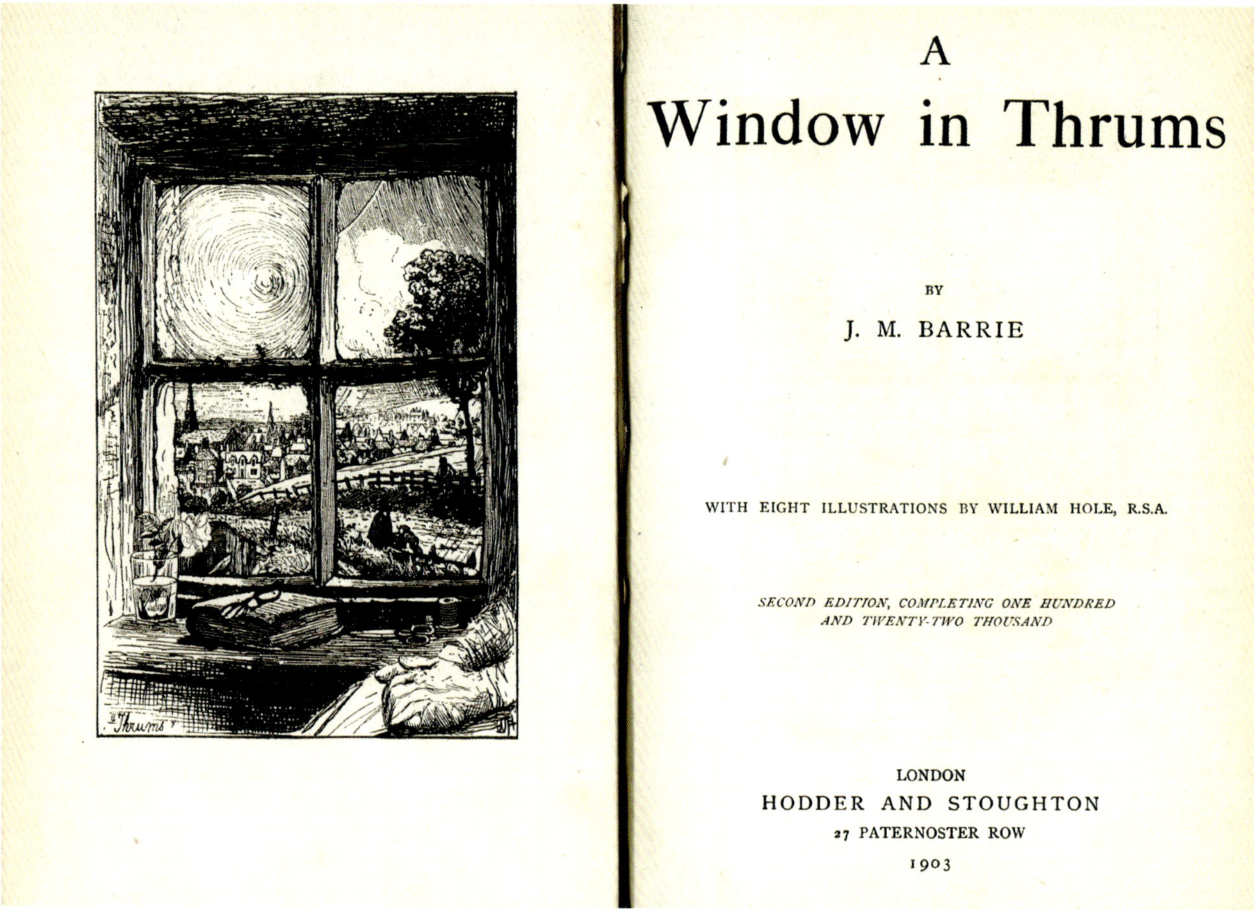

A

Window in Thrums

BY

J. M. BARRIE

WITH EIGHT ILLUSTRATIONS BY WILLIAM HOLE, R.S.A.

SECOND EDITION, COMPLETING ONE HUNDRED AND TWENTY-TWO THOUSAND

LONDON
HODDER AND STOUGHTON
27 PATERNOSTER ROW
1903

13 Frontispiece of the compendium edition of *A Window in Thrums*, by J. M. Barrie (London: Hodder & Stoughton, 1903). Given by Gillies to his sister Janet, Hogmanay 1930. Passages therein from the Bible are marked in her hand

had scarcely known except through stories told by others. Many of these visits were orchestrated by Mrs Gillies' brother William. He was custodian of a family Bible, reputedly a lifelong friend of Barrie, and Uncle Jolliboy to the Gillies children. But only one visit to Kirriemuir by the adult Gillies is known. He took his mother there in 1946, probably to attend to William's grave and newly erected headstone.

Like much landscape painting of the time, Barrie's early novels conveyed a surrogate rural life to an urban British population long since detached from it in all but memory. In the 1920s and 1930s Barrie's allegedly sentimental (kailyard) evasions of contemporary realities were roundly condemned by the modernist critique associated with MacDiarmid and his project for a Scottish Renaissance. His poem 'Frae Anither Window in Thrums' (1930) is over 1,000 lines. But it will have been the painting by MacDiarmid's associate, William McCance, with Barrie's fictional window in its title, that caught Gillies' eye [15].

It was through the eponymous window that Barrie's central character, a mother called Jess, watched the life of the community go by [13]. The McCance Thrums is not like Barrie's, public, solidary, traditional, sceptical of change, credulous of gossip, moral but also moralising. It is, rather, an empty Futurist townscape lit only by gas. There is no public life, no mutual social control. A naked female profile can be glimpsed through the lighted window that gives onto a voyeur. A couple burst out and upwards. They too are naked and there is a suggestion of copulation. An outsize flower is almost the only organic feature in a desolate scene. Its incongruity speaks of the flowering that Thrums inhibits with its suppression of the carnal impulse. There could be no Scottish Renaissance here.

This other Thrums would make uncomfortable viewing for any family unmade by the carnality that made them, and Gillies revisits this disquiet in his family portraits of the 1930s. Though the family dispersed on its departure from the town, it was held together morally by the support the five sisters were able to lend each other's families and by the life that William Ryle Smith (Gillies' Uncle Will) made out of the opportunities he found in Dundee. There, a mix of industrial wealth, patronage and demand for graphic skills from its shipbuilding and publishing industries was fuelling the city's artistic life and provision of courses. Beginning as a coach-builder, and later studying art in Leipzig, Uncle Will emerged as a fully-fledged teacher of Drawing (art) and an exhibiting member of the Graphic Arts Association in Dundee. Thereafter, he guided his much younger half-brother into school teaching through the pupil-teacher system and sent at least one of his own two sons to George Watson's College, an independent day school in Edinburgh.

Uncle Will remade his life, and the lives of others, through cities – Edinburgh, Leipzig and Dundee. In 1910, he set the eleven-year-old William Gillies on a similar path. In the years immediately following, he introduced him to drawing, graphic design, watercolour, journals of contemporary art, exhibitions in Edinburgh and Dundee, and the pupil-teacher ladder to art college and professional qualifications in school teaching. No less important was what he showed of himself, a man who was creative and caring, who would rather interest himself in the well-being of his nephew and nieces than terrorise them, and who would share his time and interests coevally with his pupil. It was to prove Gillies' introduction to the indissoluble connections in his own life between painting, sociability, teaching by example and 'profession' in its broadest sense of witness – an introduction that is itself witnessed by the joint initials of uncle and nephew on the watercolour *A Corner of Kirrie* (1912) [ni], made on a visit to Will's birthplace from his home in Broughty Ferry.

When Uncle Will arrived in Haddington in 1910 for the first of a succession of summer holidays painting in the town, Gillies was about to start his secondary education in the town's Knox Institute, having been awarded one of just seven county bursaries for a level of schooling accessed by perhaps only one-in-seven of his age peers. This early success was an outcome of a major break his parents had made with their own parents' ways of life. In the mid-nineteenth century, Gillies' paternal grandfather, an earlier William Gillies, had a prosperous tailoring business in Haddington with twenty employees

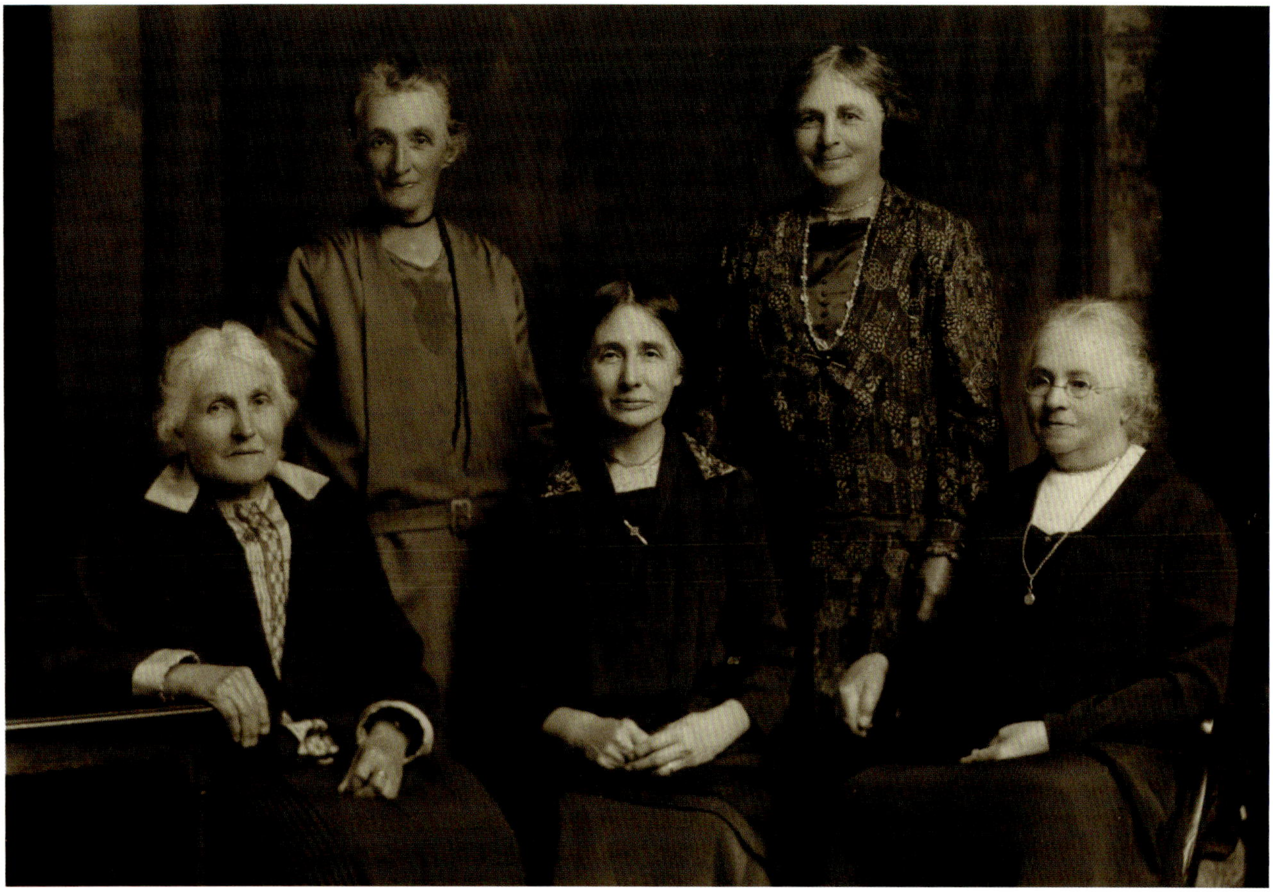

14 The pre-1947 welfare state: Mrs (Emma) Gillies (back left) and her four sisters, (clockwise) Margaret, Mary, Elizabeth and Georgina

and help from several of his children. Among them were Gillies' father John, and Gillies' uncle Peter Gillies. But railways and cheap grain imports weakened the town's commerce, parts of which migrated to Edinburgh. The resultant decline of the family business saw John and Peter postpone their respective marriages for years until John left tailoring for a tobacconist's shop he acquired from a close relative.

The two brothers then married within months of each other in 1894, limited the size of their families, and opened to their children the prospects of employment offered by an expanding education system that was siphoning the young of a depopulating countryside towards the towns and cities. There were already teachers and pupil-teachers on both sides of Gillies' family, and a graduate marine engineer. Peter's only child graduated in Mathematics from the University of Edinburgh, and Gillies was the male Dux (leading boy) of his school in 1916.

In making this change, Gillies' parents had adopted a further twentieth-century practice when they burdened themselves with a loan in

1900 to buy a newly built, semidetached villa in an expensive part of town. This move shaped from the start the youngsters with whom Gillies mixed and, arguably, the way he was treated at school. The friendships he remembered were exclusively urban. His only countryside friends were the teenage children of local elites whom he met only later, when they came to the Knox Institute in Haddington from further afield. When younger, he played with friends from a wider social mix of town families. But we can exclude all possibility of the habituating daily contact with the rural cycle like that known to Gillies' college contemporary, the abstract artist William Johnstone. He was raised on his father's farm and called himself a countryman, something never recorded for Gillies.

Elder Dickson attributes Gillies' allegedly primordial sense of Scottish landscape to his innocence of eye, to his absorption in early childhood of sense impressions of the natural world that in turn fed a developing intuition unmediated by the ideas of the social world. The trope borrows from eighteenth-century Associationist philosophy via the poet William Wordsworth. It is also invoked in *The Innocent Eye* (1933) by another farmer's son, Herbert Read, whom Elder Dickson assisted during Read's time in the Edinburgh chair of fine art.

Such claims are inherently difficult to verify but there is nothing to suggest that they could anyway help to explain Gillies, and much to suggest they do not. Gillies' discovery of the countryside coincided with his learning from adult artists how to paint and picture the world. His memories of childhood are eclectic, sociable and centred on the town. They do not depend on alleged oppositions between urban and rural or between artefacts and nature. The countryside does figure but only as part of a wider experience of the world that comprehends humanity and its works. There is nothing that privileges landscape that would not also privilege still life and portraiture. Some seventy works are known from his pre-college years. They reflect his time with mentors and the demands of school examinations. Also striking is the recourse to styles suitable for multiple reproduction and done with an eye to a future in graphic design, should school teaching fail.

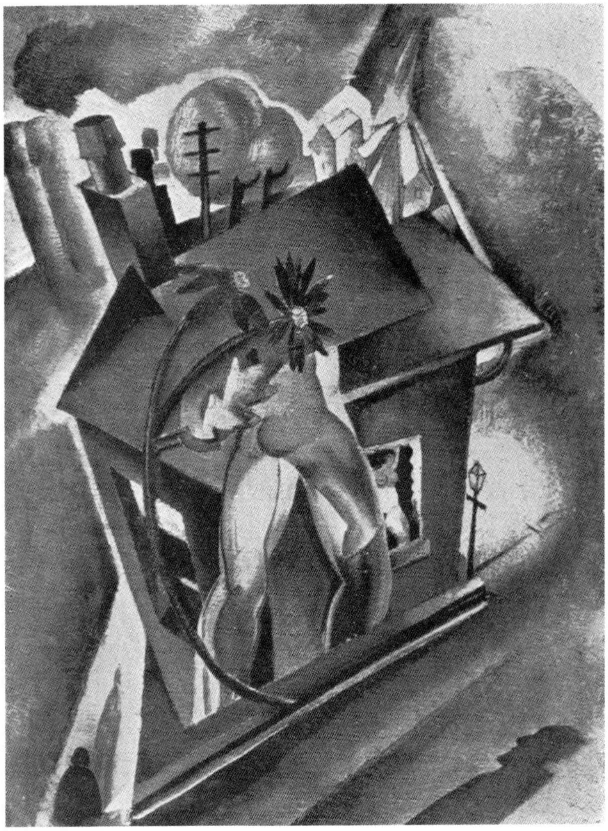

15 *From Another Window in Thrums* (1928), by William McCance. Oil, 60 cm by 46 cm

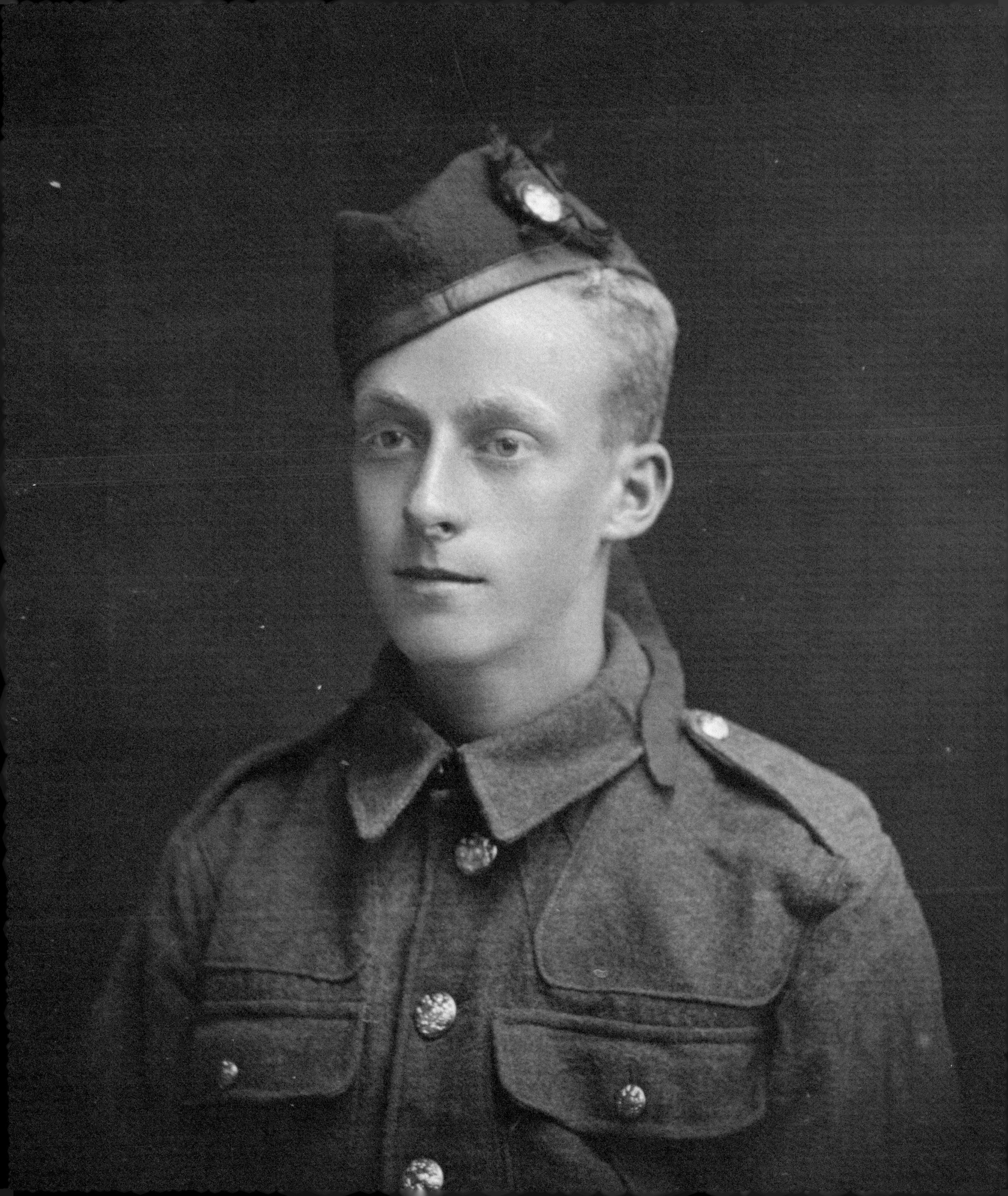

The Theatre of War

There was another fiction in Gillies' life, another mentor and another conjunction with a major figure and narrative of his times.

R. A. Dakers was editor of the *Haddingtonshire Courier*, a larger-than-life extrovert and competent amateur artist who worked in oil and exhibited on occasion at the RSA. From around the age of fourteen years, Gillies joined him on frequent painting trips around the county, and also in Dakers' studio, where he learned some basics of oil technique.

R. B. Haldane was the local MP, a Liberal and a philosopher of German Idealism. Frequent travel in Germany had alerted him to the threat posed by Prussian militarism to Britain and its Empire. As Secretary for War in 1906 he had the support of Dakers against Parliamentary opposition to his scheme for an officer reserve fed by cadets from Britain's secondary schools. An officer cadet force was formed in Haddington's Knox Institute in 1907, funded in part by a campaign featured in Dakers' *Courier* [18]. Dakers helped Haldane prepare his speeches, even sketched him smoking one of the Kaiser's cigars [16]. Thus, the schoolboy Gillies was to learn his oil painting from an extrovert who was a mouthpiece for the statesman who reformed the British army and conferred with the Kaiser in person.

But was that all Gillies learned in the hours he spent with his mentor? In 1906, Dakers had commended Haldane's Hegelianism to his readers:

> We need better thinking laid to the roots of our patriotism, something tending in the direction of silence and willing personal sacrifice … Cadet corps do a … service to the State by … disposing the mind of youth towards service which the manhood of any nation is necessarily always liable to perform.

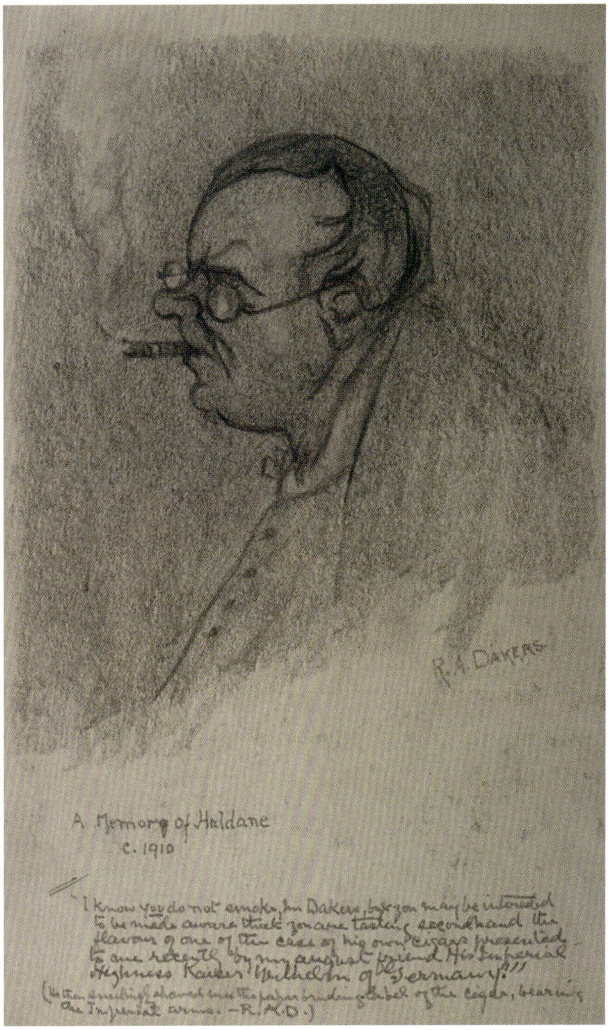

16 *Sketch of R. B. Haldane* (*c.* 1910), by R. A. Dakers. Pencil, 27 cm by 20 cm. The writing below reads, in part '"You [Dakers], … are tasting second-hand the flavour of one … of his own cigars presented to me recently by … His Imperial Highness, Kaiser Wilhelm of Germany!"'

The cadets were soon marching through Haddington, bayonets fixed and pipes skirling, to be told by Haldane himself that the survival of the nation rested on them. Pressure? What pressure?

Opposite:
Detail from Gillies in unform ([7] – see p. 8)

Someone, probably Dakers, put Gillies to making the *Roll of Honour* [19] in 1915. It is no ordinary roll that remembers the dead. No deaths are recorded and virtually no space is left for additions. Like the concert party of *Tipperary* [17], it was a means of recruitment, to boost the number of volunteers when conscription was the looming alternative. Not just anyone's conscription but also Gillies' own. As he inscribed the names with no distinction between living and dead, he could but wonder how his own fate might shortly be dissembled. It was his first consequential experience of image, reality and fiction, of the disjunction between private experience and public narrative. Indeed, as the soldiers of *Tipperary* were waved from the stage, did they even own their own experience? He would not know it at the time, but he had stumbled across one of the generative questions of modernism itself and would soon face it again.

Gillies was conscripted on leaving school and was called up on 5 April 1917 after two terms as a student of the ECA. By this time, almost a third of the volunteers among the alumni and students of the College had been wounded or killed. His service with the 10th Scottish Rifles (Cameronians) lasted 720 days. When his draft reached France in January 1918, the battalion had twice suffered huge casualties (at Loos in 1915 and at Ypres in 1917) and had meantime been remanned and retrained. Gillies was one of hundreds of new arrivals.

He was overseas for roughly 200 days and in front-line trenches near Arras for sixty-nine. On thirty-eight of these, the battalion was engaged in offensive hostilities or was the object of explosive shelling or attack by gas. In just over six months it sustained 674 casualties or well over three-quarters of its typical fighting strength. The majority of these occurred on just three days, on 28 March 1918 in the German Spring Offensive, on 27 May, and on 26 July, possibly in the French Ardennes.

Gillies' experience of war was therefore fairly standard: periods of routine activity and waiting punctuated by occasional violence that was brief but overwhelming. He survived because, early in each of the three engagements, he sustained a moderate disablement, by bullet, by gas and by severe damage to an ankle. These injuries probably saved his life by taking him from the front line. But they did not shelter him from knowledge of the carnage he had escaped. The 7th Cameron Highlanders beside him in March 1918 fared worse. Their history cannot properly be told because they were virtually annihilated, mostly by shelling and flame-throwers. In the six most exposed platoons only one man survived.

But 'Who dies if England live?' Rudyard Kipling's rallying call was Haldane's philosophical Idealism taken to its logical extreme. When all their men were gone, remanned regiments did still live – in the name, the roles and the traditions that could motivate, and often still did. The individuals alone were different. By 1918, however, the infantry private was not unnaturally sceptical of such ideas. Social expectation enabled but it also destroyed.

Gillies' generation had been raised to respect God, King, Country and Empire and to manifest courage, honour, service and sacrifice. What they actually faced was the impersonal, attritional, mechanised killing of members of one supposedly civilised nation by members of another. Technology displaced individual heroism. The infantryman, in particular, was unmanned by

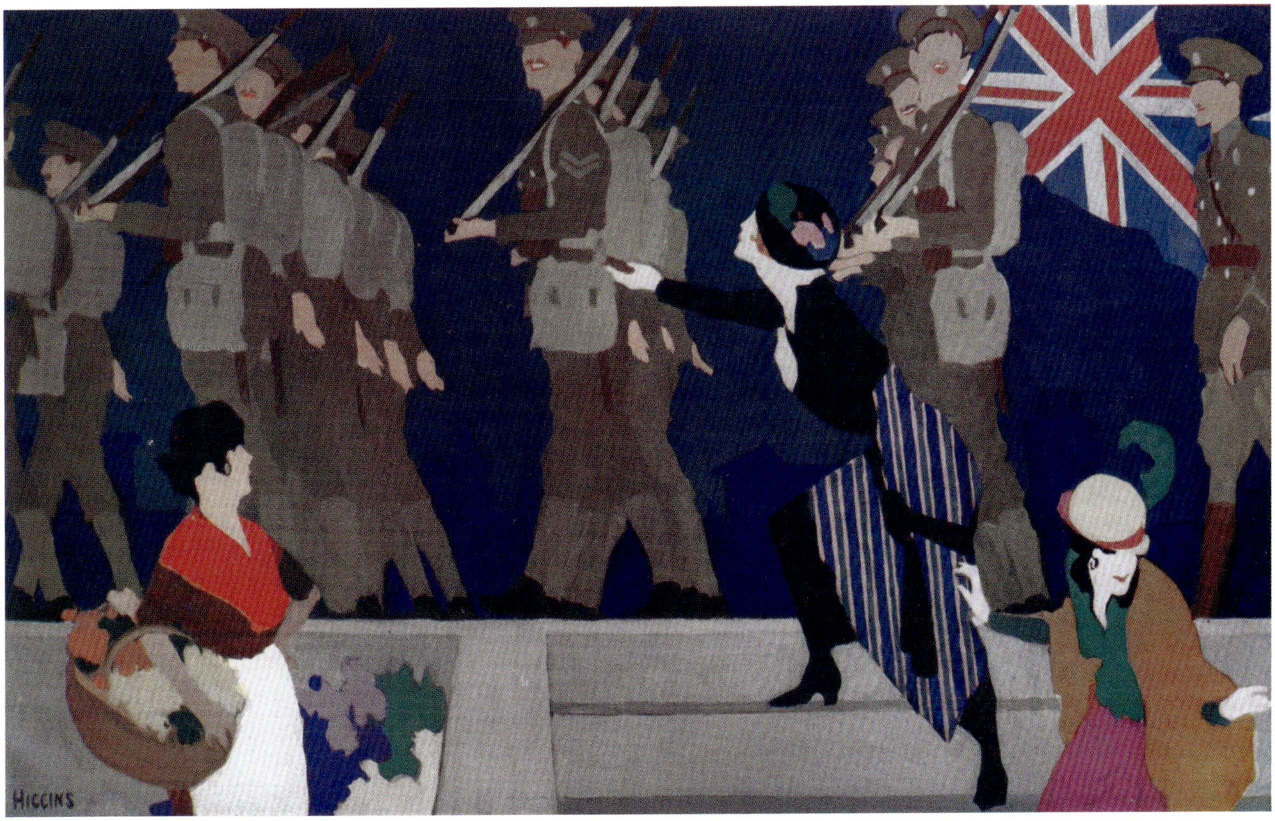

17 *Tipperary* (*c.* 1915), by Reginald Higgins. From *Colour* (May 1915, p. 14), a journal Gillies read while still at school

this new reality. It forced him into a humiliating passivity to which the only alternative was gallant but futile attack. The resultant gap, between the new experience of conflict and the imagined war of yesteryear, the war that those back home still imagined, was to leave veterans with a lasting sense of isolation from civilian life, and loyalties towards survivors and dead alike.

There is no reason to think that Gillies was exempt from the common experience. He rarely spoke about the war and did so only with difficulty. He opted for a strategy of suppression, talking of his time in the infantry as two 'wasted' years that should be 'subtracted' somehow from his life. But the war was there, nevertheless, in many manifestations. Some border on the pathological, like his hoarding of army greatcoats and his aversion to hospitals, even to visiting close friends there. Yet a sense of indebtedness to friends was always in his mind when he did say something about his life. It is one aspect of the memorialising habit of a man who was condemned by memories of war to live with death in a continuous present.

When war returned in 1939, time, in the words of Wyndham Lewis, 'bent back on itself', and Gillies fled the bombs. It bent back on itself

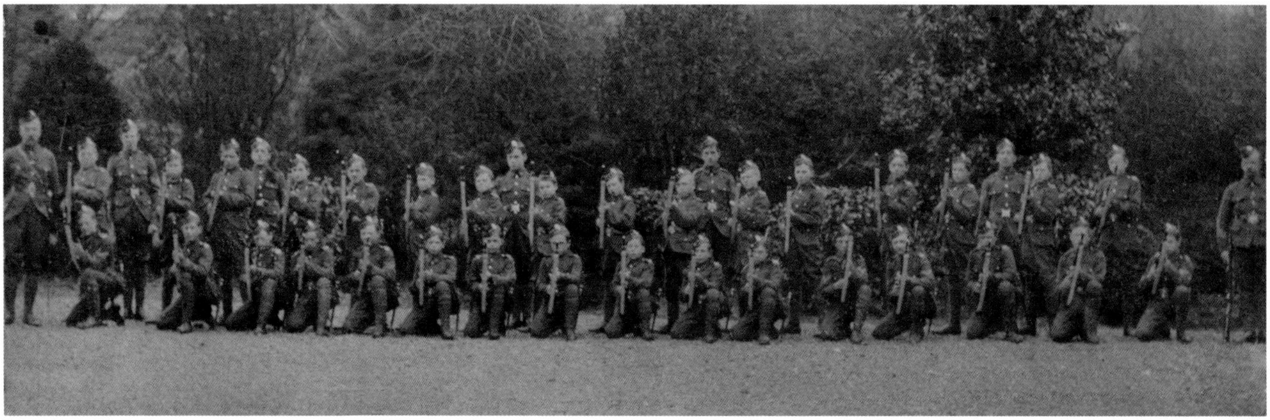

18 Knox Institute cadets (1907). Gillies' cousin William is in the back row, seventh from the right

again with the arrival of the nuclear age. In *Aldermaston Hadeans* (nd, *c.* 1960) [22], lines of young men in uniform are sheltering or immured in their 'earthy *patria*' (David Jones' term for the infantryman's natal home). The date on the work is indistinct, but the first protest march on the Atomic Weapons Research Establishment at Aldermaston, supported by the Campaign for Nuclear Disarmament, was in 1958 [21], forty years on, almost to the day, from the launch of the German Spring Offensive of 1918.

Aldermaston Hadeans is an extraordinary image. The processional lines are reminiscent, not only of remembrance and protest [20, 21], but also of the line of pilgrims in Goya's *The Pilgrimage to San Isidro* (1819–23) [ni], which is painted in similar, sombre ochres with desperate, skull-like faces. Gillies knew this work, from his copy of Ahdémar (1941), where mutilated bodies from Goya's graphic series *Disasters of War* also assaulted his eyes – from pilgrimage to protest, from dismemberment to remembrance. I have not seen *Aldermaston Hadeans* but otherwise have no reason to doubt the auctioneer's attribution to Gillies.

Occasional outliers like this are a feature of his work, and other works at this time speak of apocalypse. *Ferniehirst* (nd, *c.* 1959) [23] is painted in blazing red and orange, the woods, in the words of the artist and critic Martin Baillie, 'sprung like some black beast upon the hills, two fields of ploughed earth gleaming like gouts of blood'. *Sunflower* (nd, *c.* 1954) [25] places its distortions of nature in the imagined landscape of *Ferniehirst* [23]. The thorn hedge in *The Little Hut, Eddleston* (1958) [24] is its own distortion, disfiguring a familiar landscape under a lurid sky.

College

Gillies was one of 100 ex-service personnel who (re-)enrolled at the ECA in 1919. But they were not the only presence. The names of 100 more were lodged within the memorial that gives onto the sculpture court in the College, and the names of 10,000 more in the National War Memorial on Castle Rock that overlooks the studio windows of the College. There were also more than 100

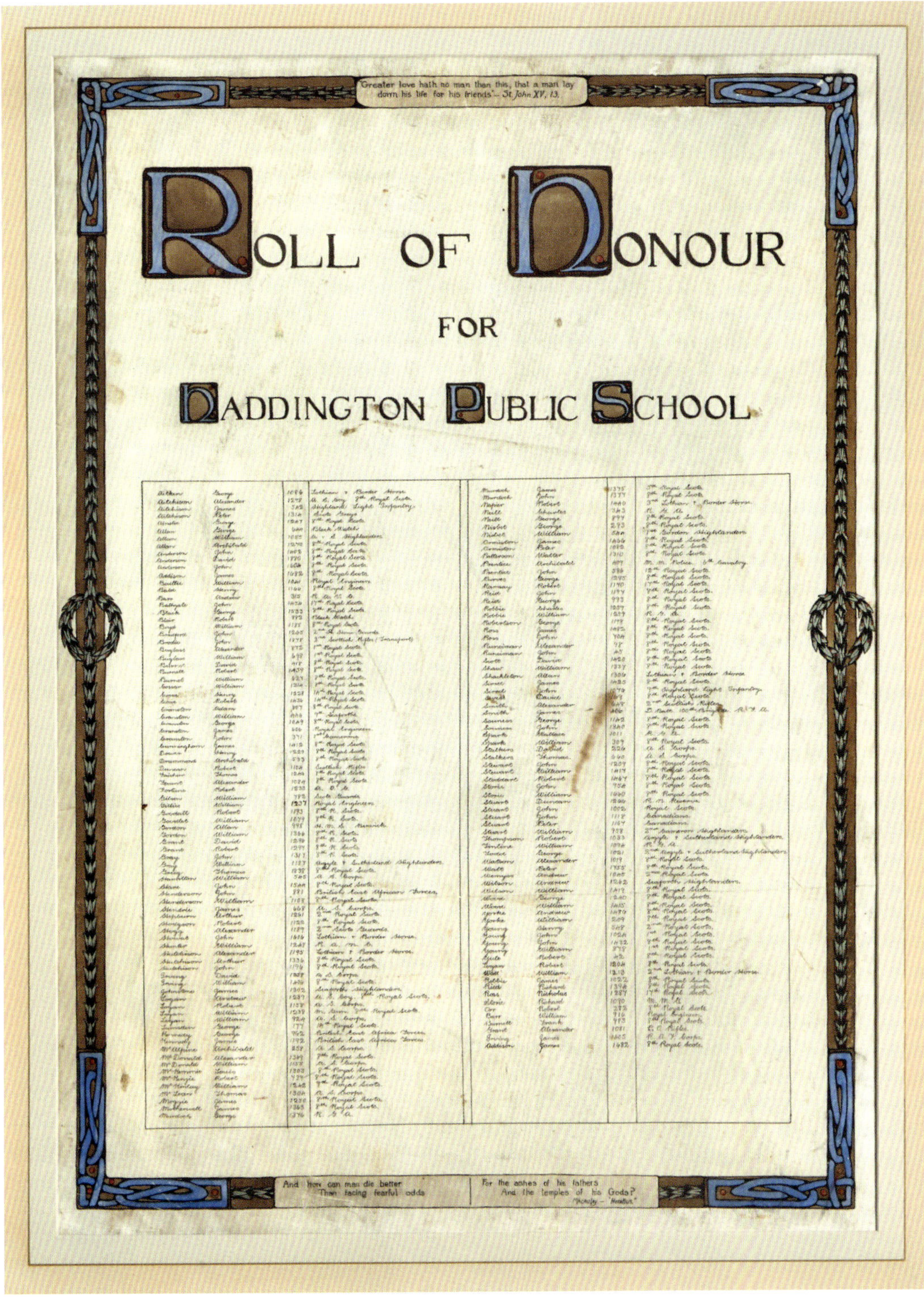

19 *Roll of Honour for Haddington Public School* (1915). Ink, watercolour, gouache, 75.5 cm by 54.5 cm

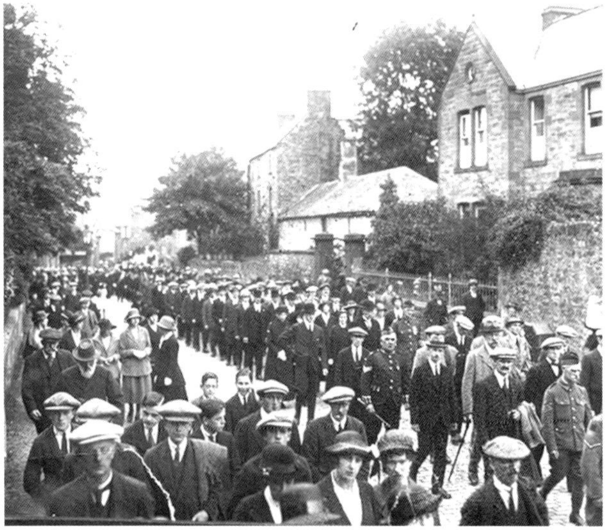

20 The War Memorial procession in Haddington (1921)

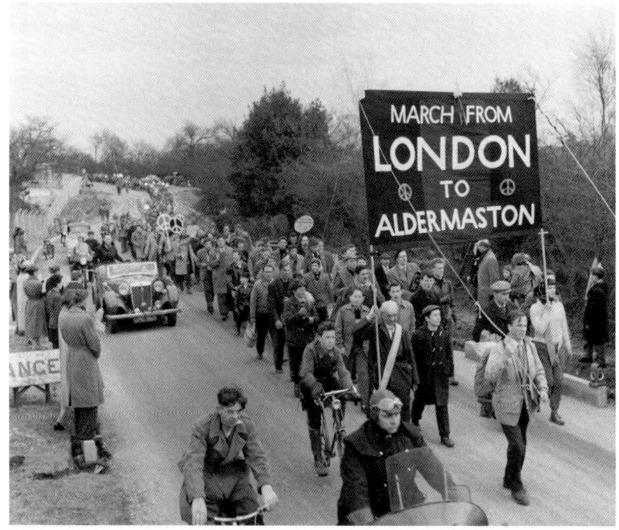

21 Anti-nuclear protestors march on the road to Aldermaston (1958)

recorded on the memorial in Haddington. Its dedication in 1921 filled the street as far as the eye could see [20]. The war also had a continuing presence in the life of the College. Staff and students contributed for a decade to the design and execution of local memorials, and of the iconic National War Memorial to which Gillies himself made a small contribution.

What was more peculiar to Gillies, however, was that the circumstances of his personal life, for thirty or more years after his demobilisation, fuelled the existential legacy of his time in the infantry. Untimely death, whether through illness, accident or suicide, was never far away, and its incidence was arbitrary. The death in 1930 of his close friend, the artist William Crozier, is illustrative. Always at risk from his haemophilia, Crozier died within hours following a fall in the studio he shared with fellow artist William MacTaggart. In these respects, his life and death were civilian replications of Gillies' daily situation at the Front.

The black vase shown both in *Still Life with Chagall Print* [10] and in *Still Life with Black Jug* [11] first appears in the aftermath of Crozier's death. The death would seem even more arbitrary because Crozier was the outstanding student of his generation. Gillies took over his share of the studio and, more important, was nominated by Peploe and his fellow Colourist Francis Cadell for the Society of Eight, a prestigious exhibiting society. For the eight years that remained of the Society's life, Gillies' membership allowed him to show large numbers of works of his own choice. For a modernist in Edinburgh, that freedom was invaluable but it would likely have been Crozier's but for his fall.

We do not have to see Gillies as a perpetual victim of war to claim its effects endured. The search for fraternity was another legacy of conflict he later turned to advantage. The instinct of David Jones after the war was to seek a form of fraternity that was viable in its simplicity, and he found it

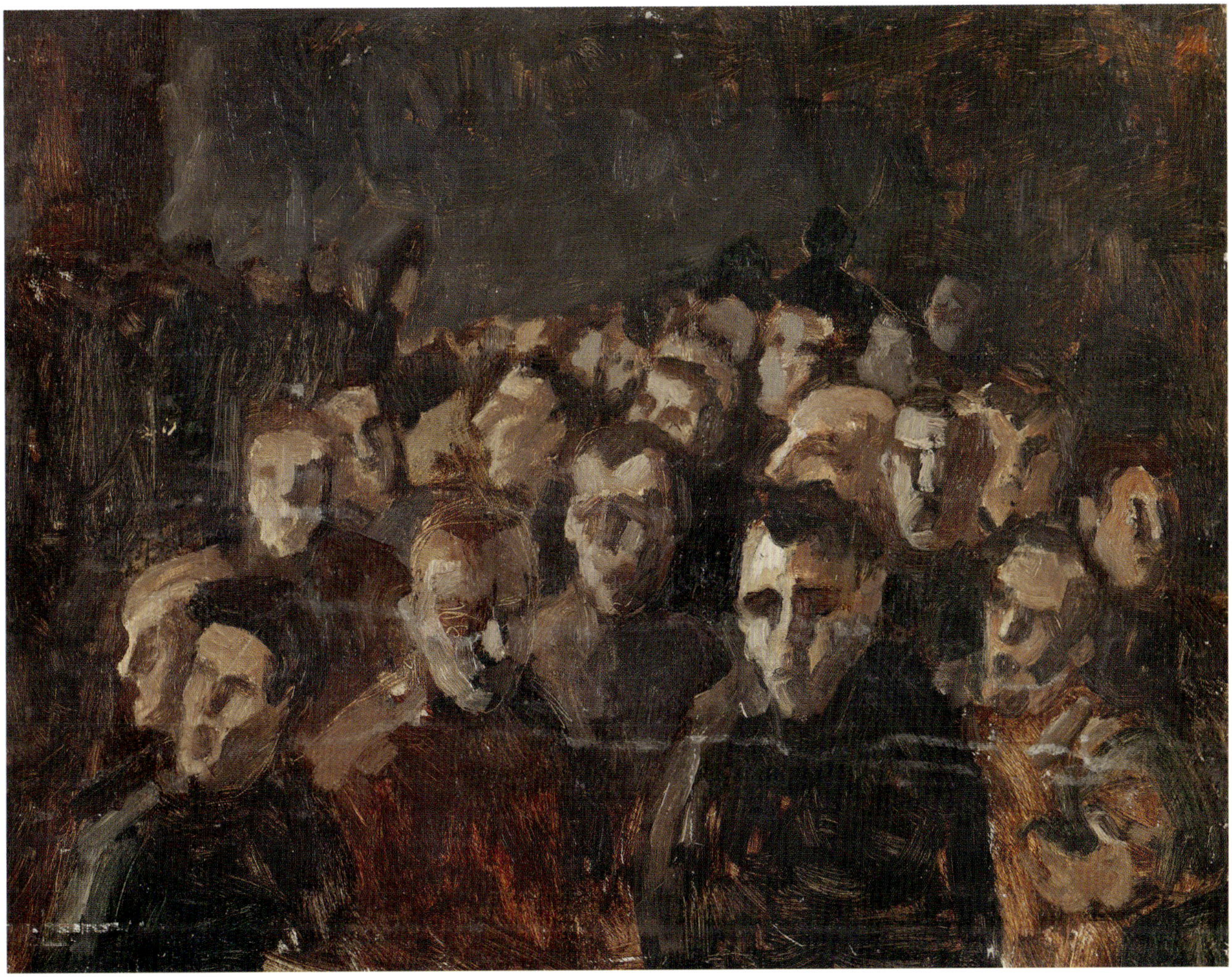

22 *Aldermaston Hadeans* (nd, *c.* 1960). Oil, 50.5 cm by 62.5 cm

for a time in a country community of artists and craftsmen formed around the Catholic sculptor Eric Gill. Gillies, I think, sensed a possibility for something similar in the weekend painting trips he organised immediately on his return to the ECA in 1919, and in the extended annual camping and painting holidays with friends and colleagues from the College that developed out of these weekend forays. Painting became a sociable activity, a mitigation of veteran isolation, a seamless sharing, not just of the practicalities and times of relaxation, but also of subjects, sketch-books, ideas and styles – the canvas of the painting and the canvas of the tent. Throughout his life, this reputedly shy and private man thrived on sociability, but only among the trusted and like-minded.

With Gillies' first sorties into the world back home, a world that a schoolboy had once thought

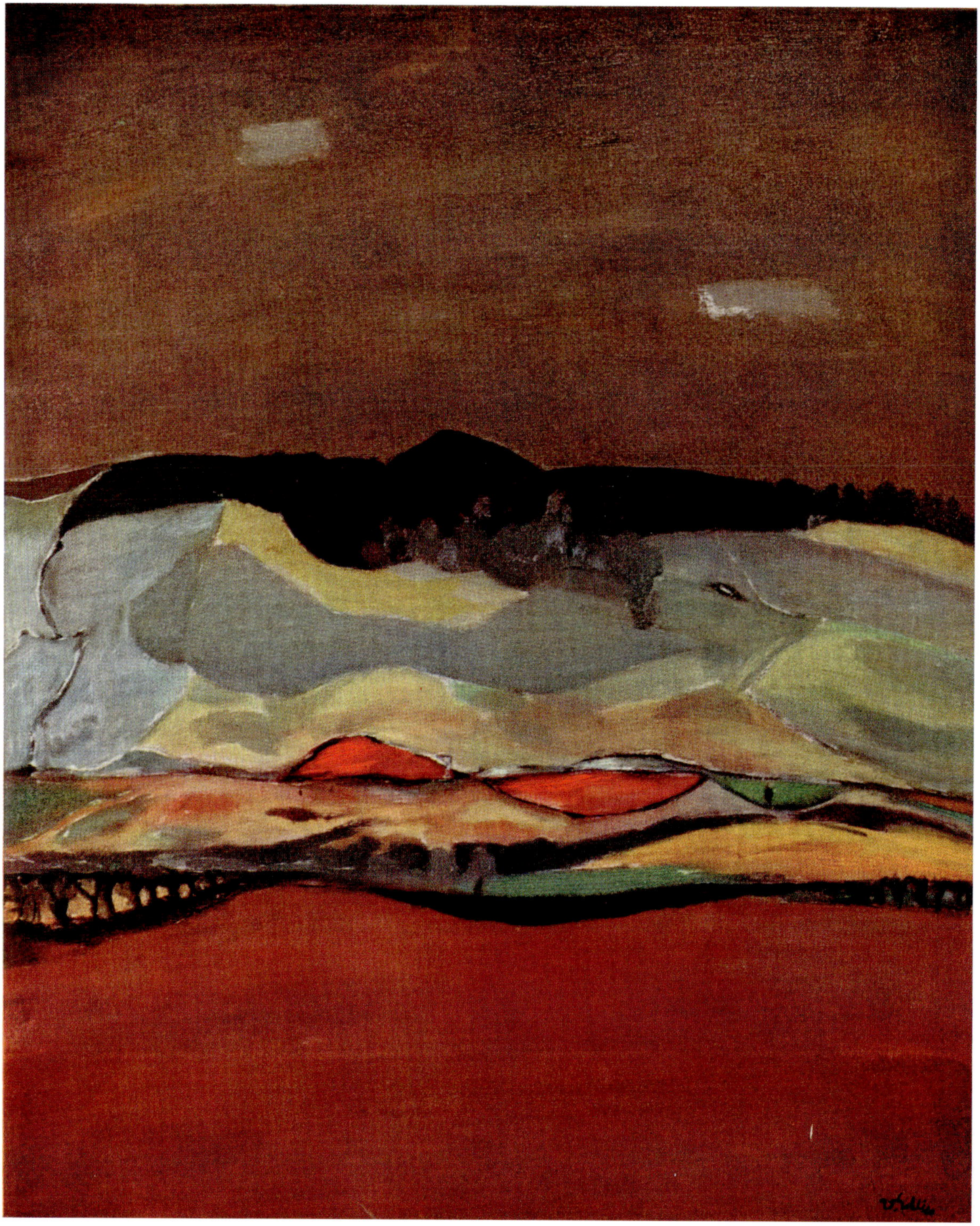

23 *Ferniehirst* (nd, *c.* 1959). Oil, 84 cm by 69 cm

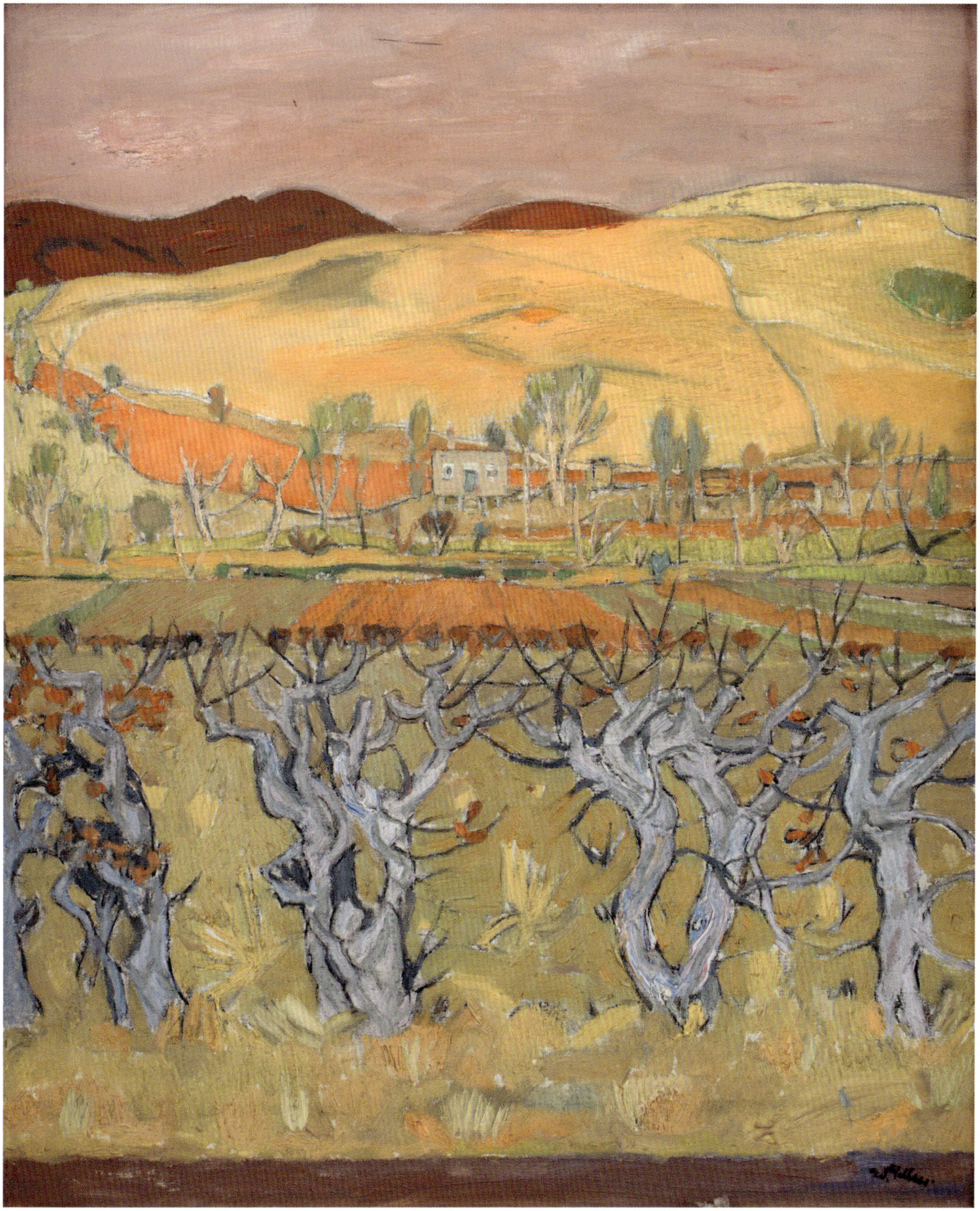

24 *The Little Hut, Eddleston* (1958). Oil, 77.5 cm by 64.5 cm

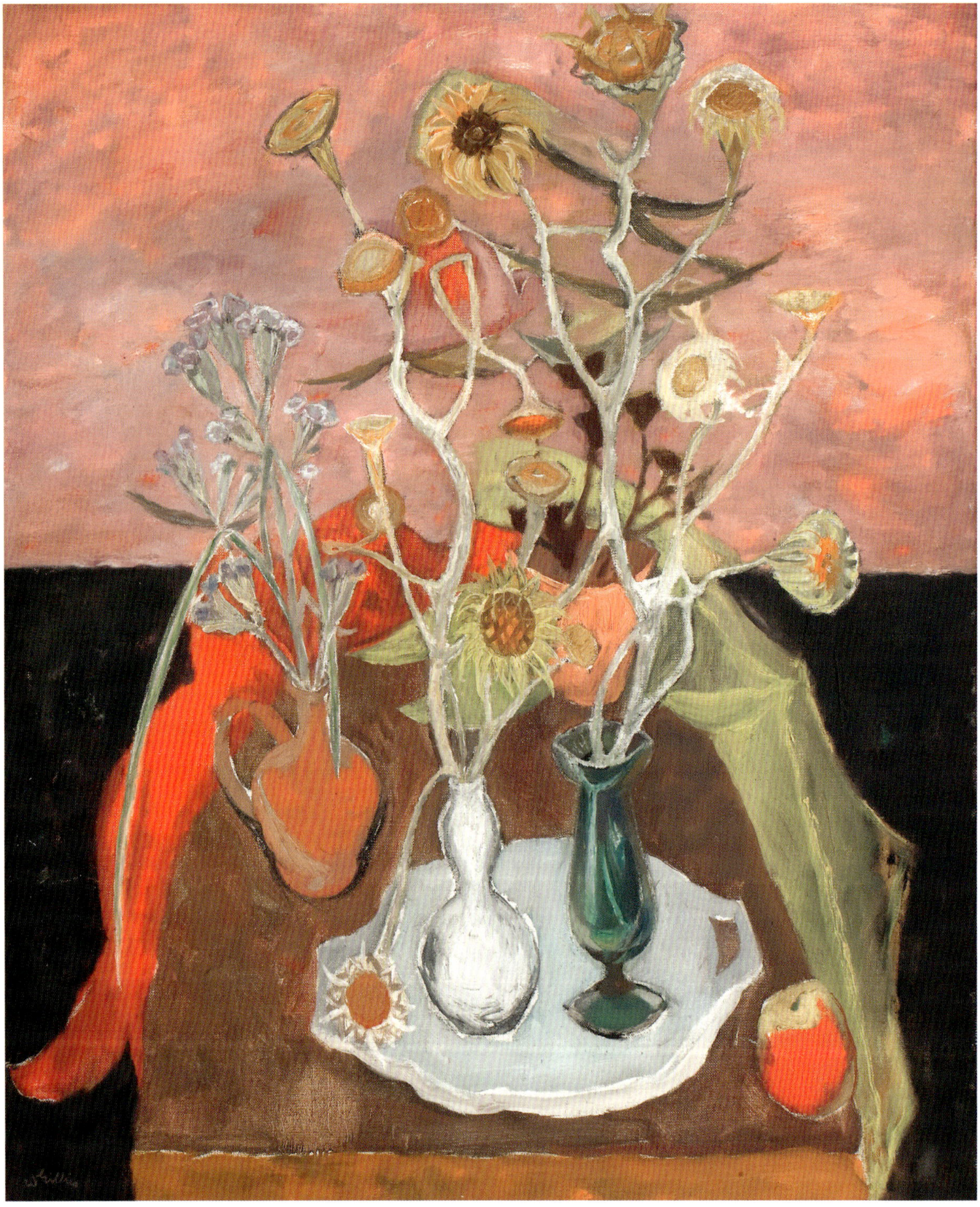

25 *Sunflower* (nd, *c.* 1954). Oil, 91.7 cm by 76.5 cm

familiar was approached anew. College, it might be said, became the place that most closely approximated that earthy *patria* where an infantry, ill-served by elevated discourse and obsolete maps, could try to get to the truth of a terrain only they could really know once war had changed it. Contact with the earth was essential. Touching and looking, drawing and painting, was the only way to do it. Everything else was staff-wallahs and propaganda.

The ECA gave Gillies a traditional training founded on drawing, tonality and finish, and on an understanding of materials and technique, all of which were realised through studies of still life and the human form to the complete exclusion of landscape. With one possible exception (*Figure Composition* (*c.* 1922) [ni]), works that survive from his student years do not explicitly refer to war. They are, rather, the response of a student to the ideas, styles and subjects of his teachers. On his own admission, Gillies tried to carry on as before and took things from everyone. Where Dakers and Uncle Will had once filled his horizons, now it was David Alison, who was indifferent to colour but emphasised tonal harmony; and contrastingly, as Gillies said, the 'exciting' David Sutherland, with his modernist sympathies and 'brilliant' handling of broken colour.

By the time of *Portrait of Emma* (1921) [9] and *Life Study* (1922) [131], it was clear that little would hinder his progress, and certainly not technique. He could represent more or less anything he pleased and was the outstanding student of his year. The College funded a postgraduate year and then, in 1923–4, a further year in which he, Crozier and William Geissler worked for four months in Paris under the cubist artist André Lhote, and afterwards toured in northern Italy.

'A Charter of Liberty': Early Years

Much has been made of the consequences of Gillies' time with Lhote and much of it is wrong. It does not help that Elder Dickson misreported what Gillies told him about his reaction to Lhote's methods; nor that Elder Dickson conflates Lhote's brand of 'synthetic' cubism with Cubism as a whole; nor that he describes Gillies' response to Cubism as years of alleged obsession broken only, but irrevocably, when Gillies encountered Munch in 1931–2.

A person in a better position to judge was one of Gillies' closest friends from his student days onwards. Henry ('Harry') Harvey Wood, husband of Lily, had been a fellow student of Gillies at the ECA. He then lectured in English in the 1930s under the Edinburgh Professor Herbert Grierson, before running the British Council in Scotland throughout the 1940s. He also made a vital contribution to the success of the City of Edinburgh in capturing (and retaining against English opposition) the new international festival of music and drama first mounted in 1947 with funding from the Arts Council of Great Britain and other sources.

By deconstructing traditional mimesis in its early ('analytic') years before 1914, the Cubism of Picasso and Georges Braque had prepared the way for a new understanding of everything that had gone before. Lhote was a synthetic cubist who advocated a new approach to the composition of paintings with recognisable subjects. His system developed the dynamic of line and curve latent in the composition of traditional works. He enhanced form through simplification, that is, by 'abstracting' (removing or reducing) mimetic detail and brushwork. Gradations of thinned

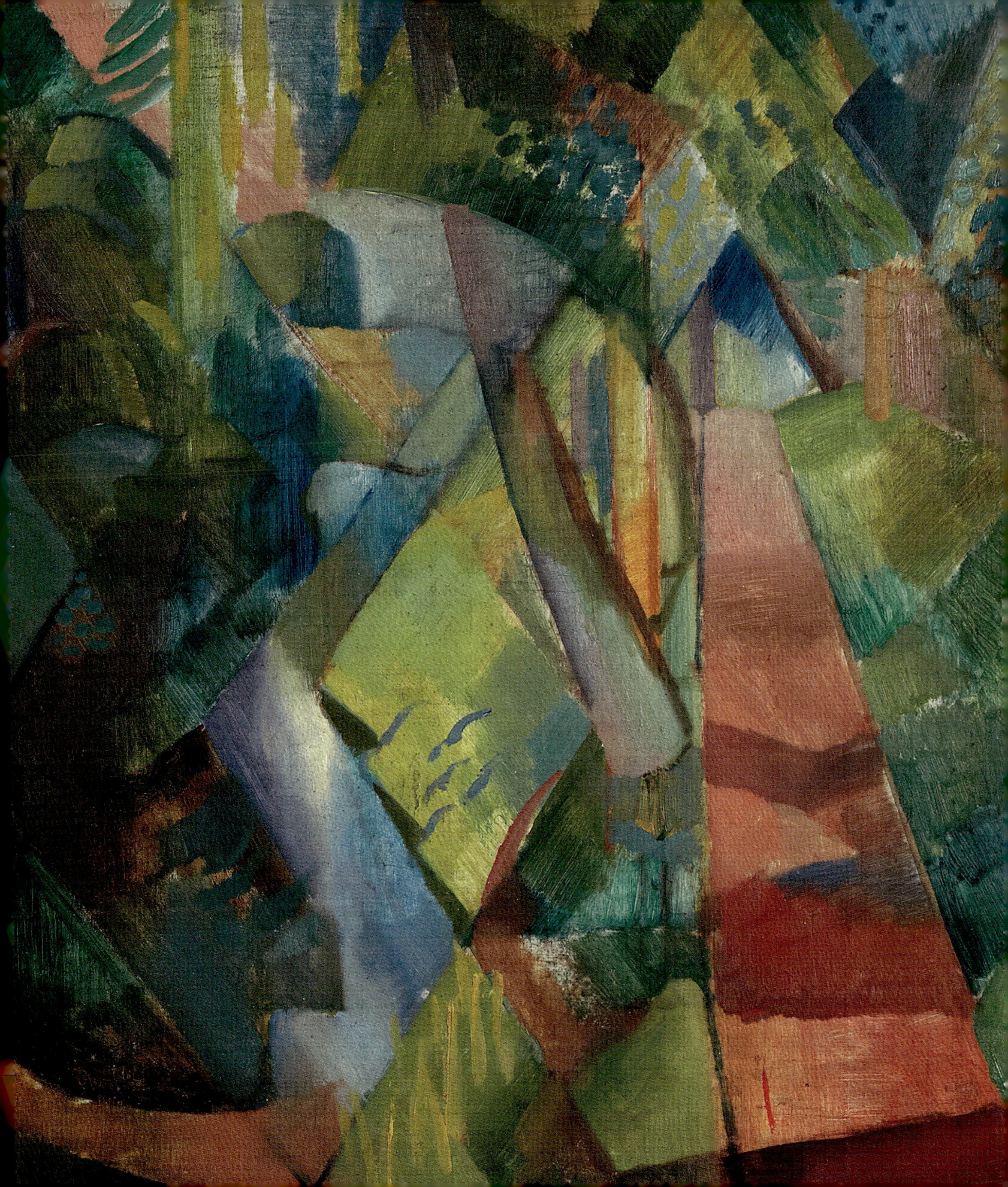

colour, dispersed with more regard to colour theory than to mimetic authenticity, could then smooth the *passage* (travel) of the eye across the surface with the aim of delivering to mind and eye a more unified and cogent experience of light, colour, form and space.

This was, indeed, one way of making pictures and Gillies could do it standing on his head. Lhote thought he and Geissler rarc talents who were already producing exemplary art to an Academy standard. But such works were not, as was commonly claimed of Gillies' landscapes from the 1920s, a product of obsession or imprisonment by system. What Gillies took from Lhote was, in Harvey Wood's words, 'not so much a permanent influence as a charter of liberty' that licensed 'free and unprejudiced experiment on his own'.

Gillies returned to Edinburgh in 1925 for a part-time appointment at the ECA after an intervening year of school teaching in Inverness. There followed a series of ten or more oil landscapes, mainly of trees over water, that explore the ideas of Lhote, but also of Lhote's close associate at the time, Robert Delaunay. *Trees on the Tyne, Haddington* (*c.* 1924) [136] and *The White Lodge* (1926) [27] have an affinity with *Les Fenêtres Sur la Ville no. 3* (*2ème motif, 1ère partie*) (1912) [26], one of Delaunay's celebrated '*Fenêtres Simultanées*' series of 1912–14.

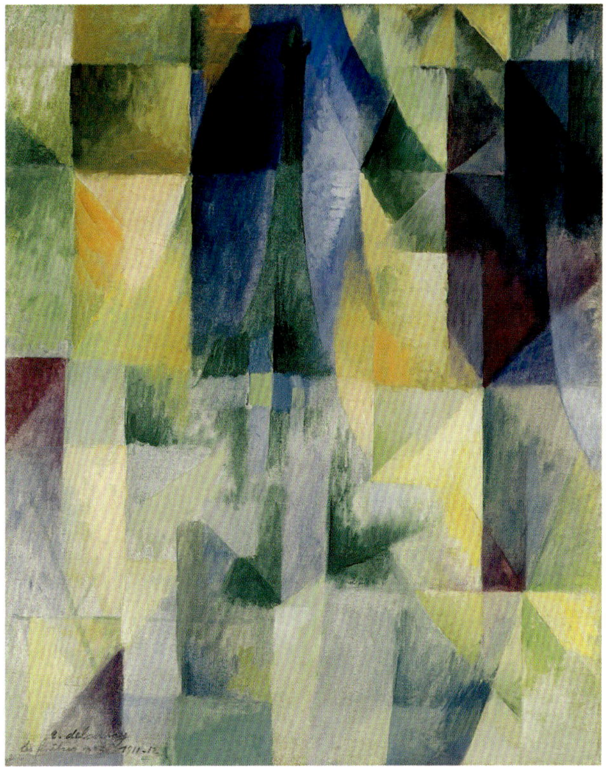

26 *Les Fenêtres Sur la Ville no. 3* (*2ème motif, 1ère partie*) (1912), by Robert Delaunay. Oil, 79 cm by 64.5 cm

Gillies' series, however, cannot be evidence of obsession or capture, for he was also painting in other ways in the mid- to late 1920s, using oil and watercolour, a variety of landscape subjects (trees, buildings, coastal, extensive inland) and a looser style which gave brushwork and mass precedence over thinned paint, *passage*, planar composition and abstraction of form. Nor is this variety evidence of a potentially disabling segmentation in his work, for example reserving cubist tropes and oil for urban subjects, or watercolour and looseness for empty landscapes, water and skies. Rather, it is the beginnings of what is, indeed, experiment, and systematic at that, because most combinations of these subjects, media and styles are found among the eighty or so Gillies landscape paintings known to me from 1924 to 1931.

Harvey Wood also tells us that Gillies returned from Paris 'more excited about Derain than about Lhote'. André Derain had been a Fauve ('untamed' user of strong colour) and an adherent of early Cubism but was now combining traditional landscape with a late-cubist emphasis on

Opposite:
Detail from *Trees on the Tyne, Haddington* ([136] – see p. 185)

mass, tonal contrast and simplification. From the outset, however, Gillies could happily paint in a cubist mode that was not obviously indebted to Lhote, Delaunay or Derain. *A Highland Farm* (nd, *c.* 1925) [134] is an effortless reconciliation of cubist plane and decoration with the frozen forms, limited colours and contrasting tonalities of winter. In *Autumnal Wooded Landscape* (1925) [135], by contrast, cubist abstraction discovers growth and movement in forms that open to us a scale of time that lies beyond our everyday sense of moments, days and season.

Gillies did, nevertheless, take things of consequence from all three artists. In the long term, Lhote's precept of a balance (*équilibre*) between concrete and abstract was combined with conflicting elements of mimesis in Gillies' exploration of coexistent potentials in the mundane. In the short term, the precept helped him meet the demand of London critics for attention to 'architectonic' form. *The Beeches* (1928) [28] is a fine example of such painting, in the manner of Paul Nash. Shown at the Modern English Water-Colour Society in London, such works won him a larger and more varied show there and pleased the critic who thought he was 'intelligently adapting Continental principles of design to the native impulse'.

Derain gave Gillies the confidence, once he had the exhibiting outlet of the Society of Eight, to measure his response to critical stricture and imperatives, whether of 'native impulse', Surrealism or abstraction. When confronted by Munch in 1930–1 he would respond, but in his own, un-Munch-like, way as he developed his own expressionist forms and reached his own conclusions on abstraction in the mid-1930s independently of English artists like Ben Nicholson. Nicholson scorned Derain and was pushing for complete, non-figurative abstraction, but Delaunay again would help Gillies in reaching his own position. *Trees and Coppice* (1928, *c.* 1928) [29] is a brooding marker of his growing independence of Nicholson and Nash, of the direction he would take and the questions he would pose.

Finally, while there is in his inter-war paintings little of the monochromatic geometry of Cubism's early, analytic, years, its broken, angular forms would resurface in his still lifes of the later 1940s, when he returned to existential issues after the war to come. Gillies' cubism was never uncritically embraced and never wholly discarded.

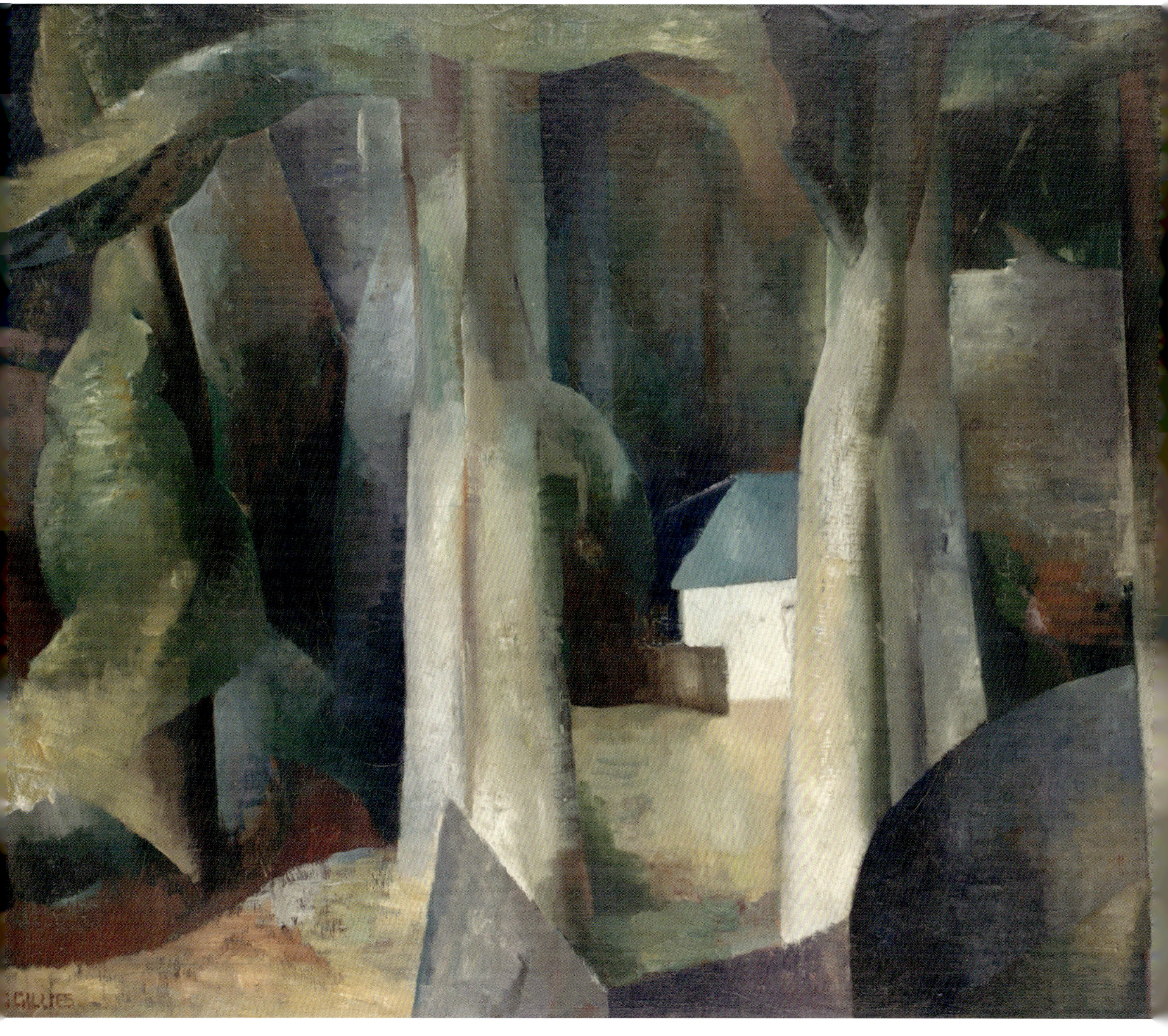

27 *The White Lodge* (1926). Oil, 83.5 cm by 104 cm

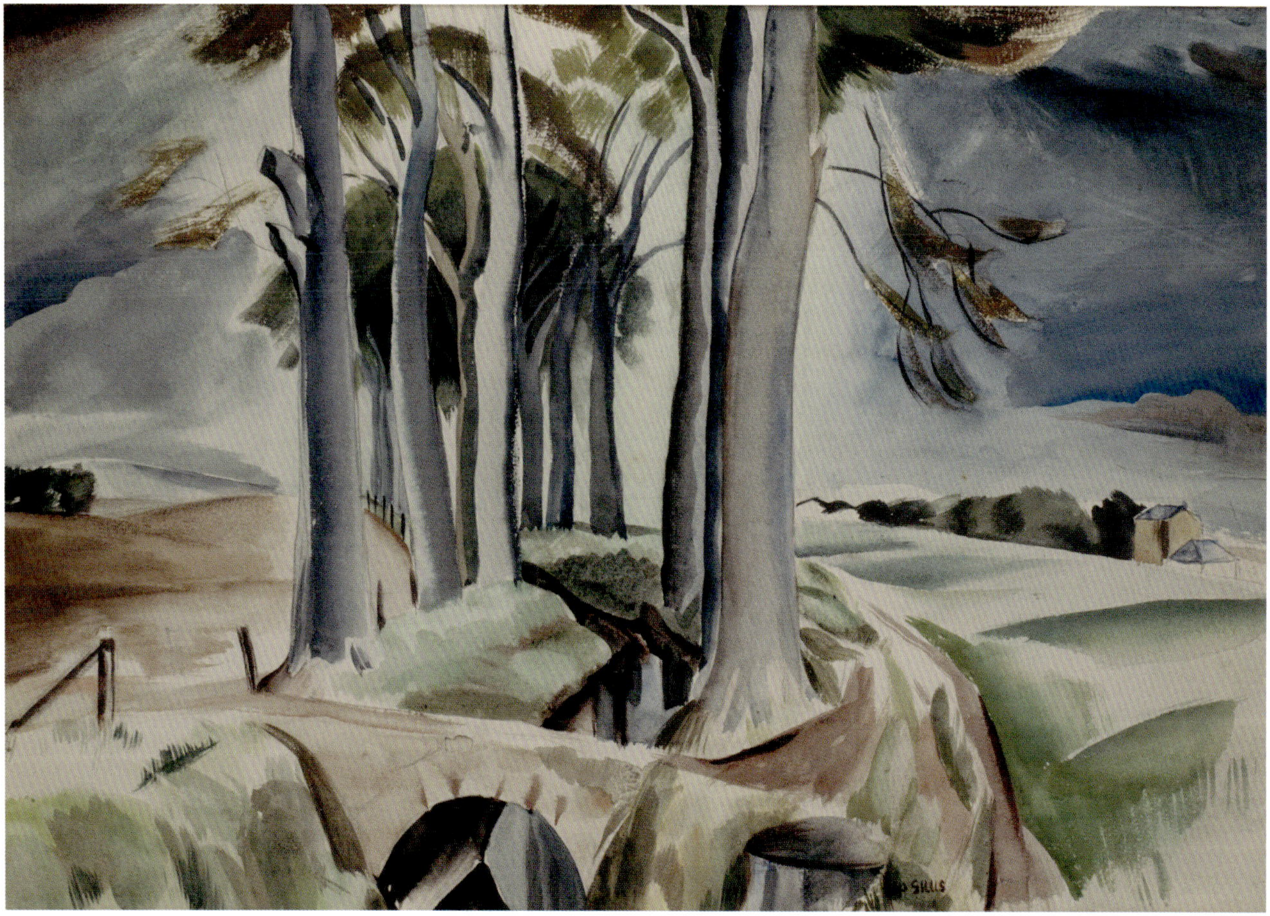

28 *The Beeches* (1928). Watercolour, 28.5 cm by 42 cm

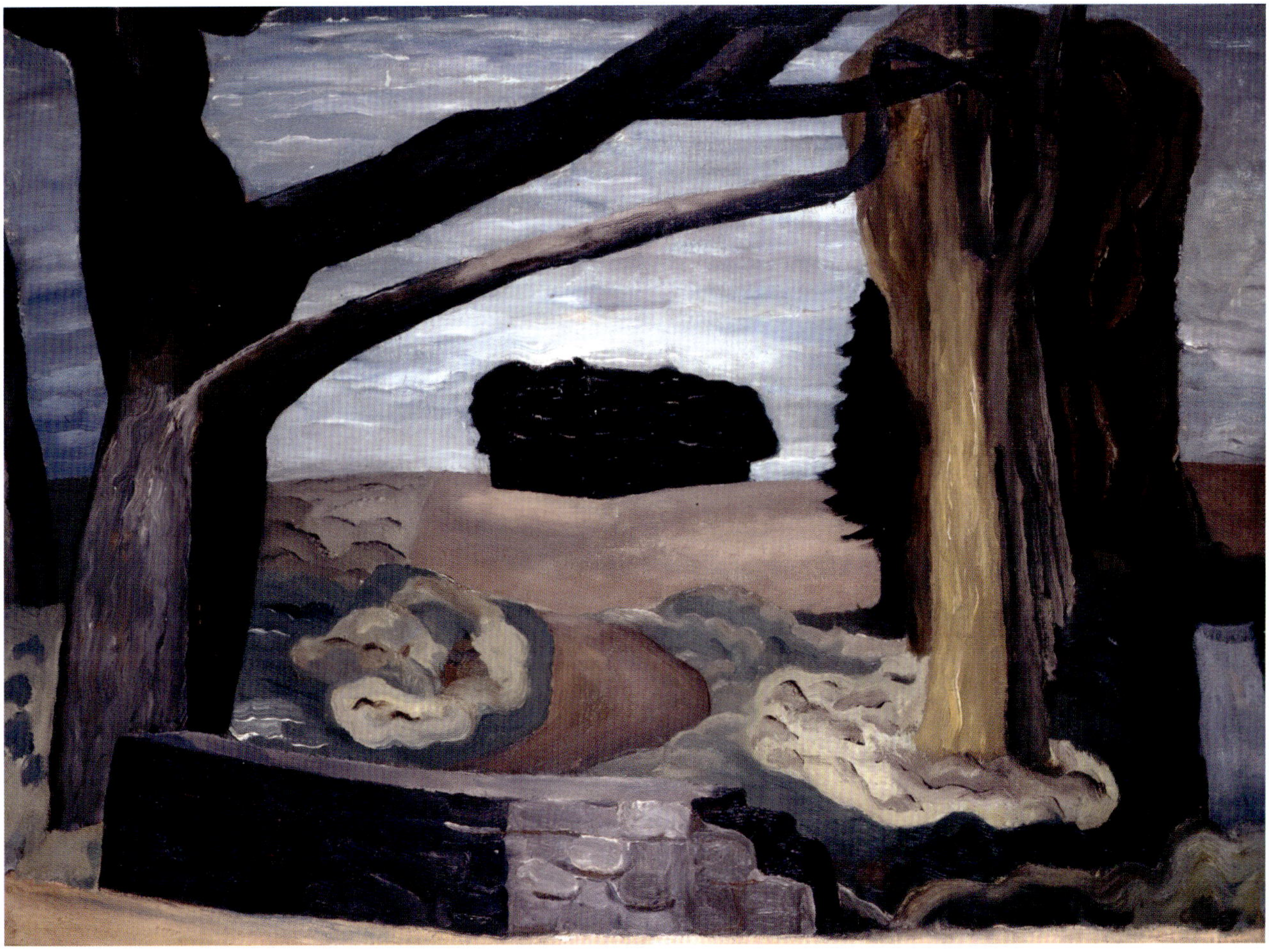

29 *Trees and Coppice* (1928, *c.* 1928). Oil, 89 cm by 124 cm

Bohemian Edinburgh

When Oscar Wilde was convicted of gross indecency in 1895, the word 'homosexual' had only recently been coined to describe sexual orientations that were increasingly apparent in the culture of the *fin-de-siècle*.

As mentioned, living in Edinburgh from around 1905 until his death in 1934 was Marc-André Sebastian Raffalovich. His *Uranisme et Unisexualité* of 1896 anatomised homosexuality. Raffalovich was a self-declared enemy of Wilde, having won from him the affections of John Gray, the probable model for the principal character of Wilde's *The Picture of Dorian Gray*. Fearing they would face Wilde's fate, Gray and Raffalovich fled overseas when Wilde was imprisoned. Gray trained as a Catholic priest at the Scots College in Rome and was sent to the Cowgate, at that time a central Edinburgh slum that housed part of the city's Irish-Catholic population. Raffalovich converted to Catholicism, had an audience with the Pope and followed Gray to Edinburgh. There he made no secret of his proclivities or past while rescuing Gray by largely funding for him the construction of St Peter's Roman Catholic Church and Presbytery in the genteel suburb of Morningside, well towards the southern outskirts of the city.

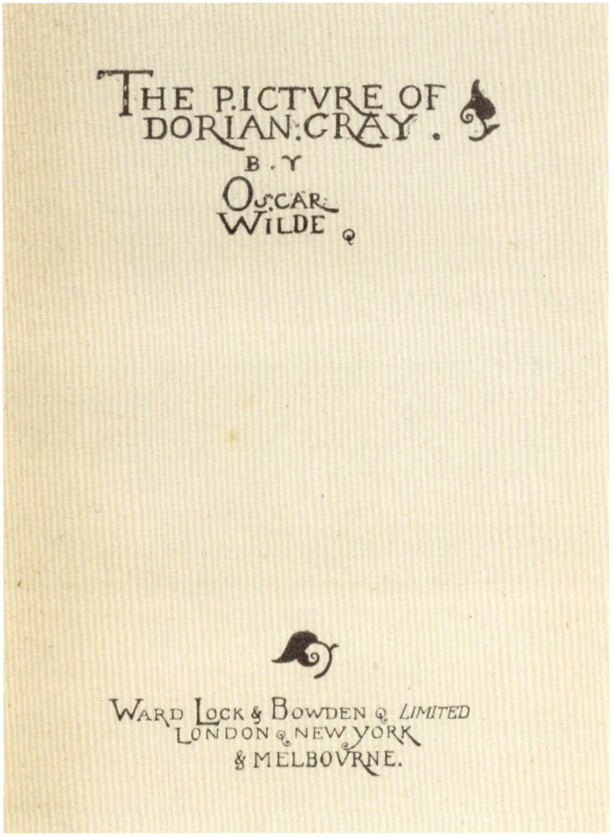

30 Title page of the first British edition of *The Picture of Dorian Gray* by Oscar Wilde (1891)

Father (later Canon) Gray duly fulfilled his charge. He also co-hosted with Raffalovich the salon of the arts in the latter's nearby home. Its axis of refinement, Catholicism and homosexual apology attracted a variety of minority interests and tastes, and also scores of young men of various, and sometimes insecure, sexual orientation. Most were socially well connected, and they included many of Gillies' friends, colleagues and students. Among them were Willy and Denis, the sons of S. J. Peploe and cousins to Margery Porter, Harry, the son of Henry Lintott, who had taught Gillies, Hew Lorimer, a Catholic convert and son of Robert Lorimer, architect of the National War Memorial, Harry Harvey Wood and, from an older generation, two of Gillies' ECA Principals, Morley Fletcher and Hubert Wellington, both of whom again were Catholic.

For thirty years, the Raffalovich salon was the centre of high cultural life in Edinburgh and a node in the cultural life of Britain, with links to the highest levels of government and society, the

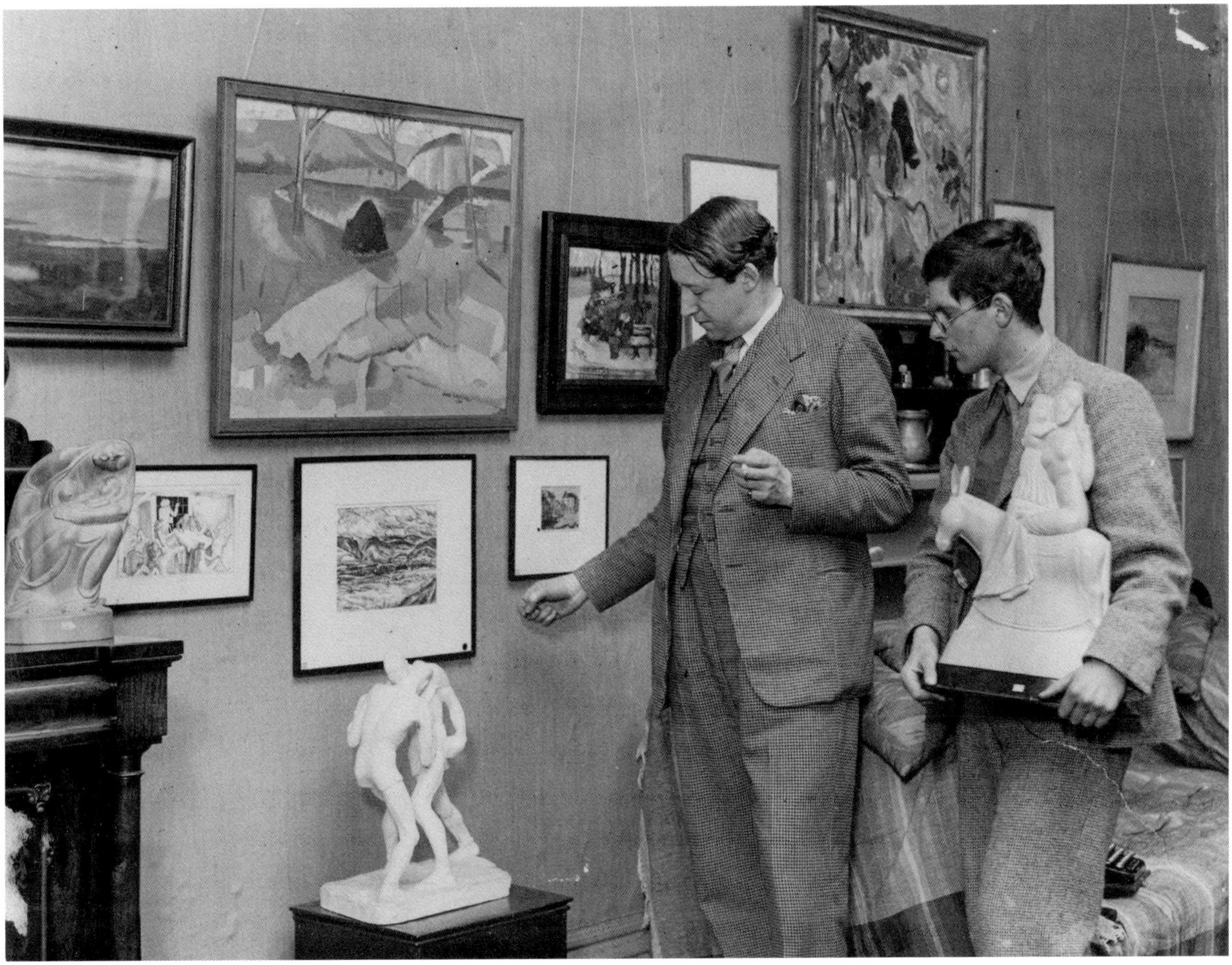

31 David Cleghorn Thomson (left) and Ruthven Todd in the Garret Studio, Edinburgh, 1935. Behind them is Gillies' *Landscape with Road and Sun* (nd, *c.* 1935) – see detail overleaf

elite colleges of Oxford and Cambridge, and two generations of Bloomsbury artists, writers, critics, bibliophiles and publishers. It was also a perennial subject of Edinburgh gossip that found in the ambivalent celebrity of its *habitués* a confirmation of the equation, common to other capitals in Europe, of modernism in the arts with decadence in private life. Intellectual Edinburgh loved it, and not just for the champagne and *frisson,* nor only for the weekly presence of Lady Margaret Sackville, a poet, Catholic and anti-war activist. Her long affair with the widowed Prime Minister, Ramsay MacDonald, set the gossips' tongues wagging on his visits to Edinburgh.

The salon also offered a living rehearsal of some fifty years of literary and visual modernism,

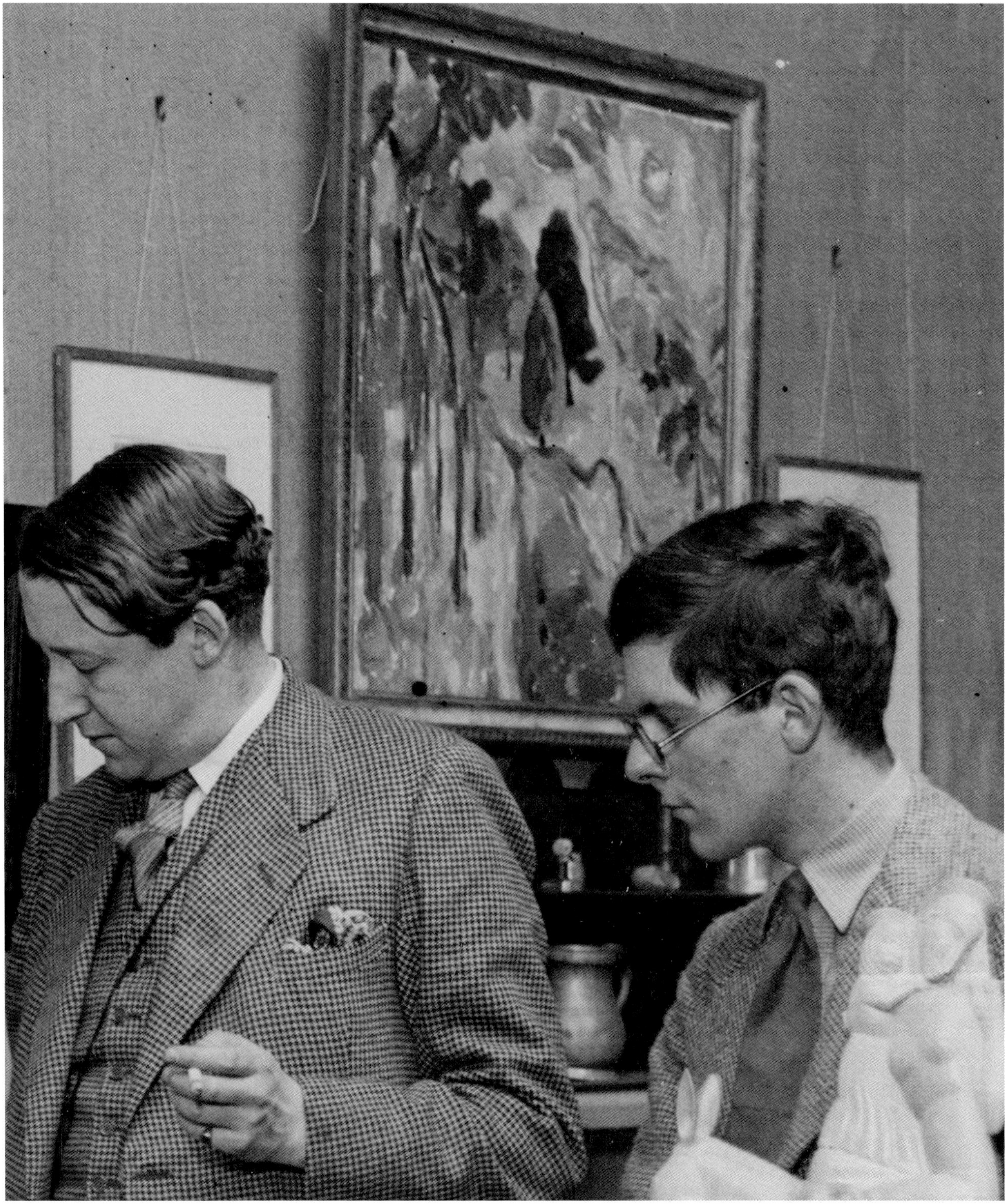

from French Symbolist poets and painters, the Paris of the Ballets Russes and the London of Burne-Jones, Whistler and Sickert, to Post-Impressionism, the verse of Eliot and Yeats, and the epicene aesthetic of the Bright Young Things of the 1920s. These privileged young men, and some women, were satirised in the novels of the Catholic convert Evelyn Waugh which drew on his Oxford circle of friends. We shall meet several notable figures from this circle again: Kenneth Clark (Director, National Gallery), John Rothenstein, another Catholic convert (Director, Tate), David Talbot Rice (Professor of Fine Art, University of Edinburgh) and David Lindsay (earl, scholar, government minister and leading figure in the governance of visual art in Scotland and England after 1945).

The display of Gillies' *Landscape with Road and Sun* (nd, *c.* 1935) [ni] in the Garret Studio founded by David Cleghorn Thomson [31] links Gillies to the networks and energy of this scene. During its brief life, the Studio functioned as a national hub for all the arts in Scotland and some of its politics too. The multi-talented Cleghorn Thomson had not long been sacked from his post of regional director of the BBC in Scotland. His offence was insubordination certainly, probably cultural-nationalism, possibly his homosexuality as well. He was a Raffalovich regular and a former contemporary at Balliol College, Oxford, of Waugh's friend and fellow Catholic, the novelist Graham Greene. Greene too was lunched by Raffalovich.

The precocious young poet Ruthven Todd [31] wittily described Cleghorn Thomson as 'a cross between a bookmaker and a provincial Oscar Wilde' (the gay Cleghorn Thomson had founded the periodical *The Scottish Bookman*). In his teenage years, Todd was himself plied by Raffalovich with champagne and the drawings of Aubrey Beardsley. Later, as assistant-secretary to the International Surrealist Exhibition in London in 1936, a position he achieved through the good offices of Herbert Read, he almost suffocated Salvador Dalí at the opening by screwing down a diver's helmet over his head.

Gillies knew them both, Cleghorn Thomson through the Society of Scottish Artists (SSA) and his support of the 1922 Group, and Todd as one of a group of students at the ECA. Also in this group were Norman Reid, who later followed Rothenstein as Director of the Tate, and three British modernists in the making, namely William Gear, Margaret Mellis and Wilhelmina Barns-Graham. Gillies encouraged them to show alongside him and other European modernists at the SSA, the Garret and the Fine Art Society of the University of Edinburgh, a joint venture with the ECA. In 1937, he also took three of them (not Reid) to the Exposition Universelle in Paris. Mellis and Barns-Graham also knew Cleghorn Thomson through the Garret and through their friendship in Edinburgh with Martin Lindsay, son of A. D. Lindsay, Master of Balliol. The latter had been tutor to Cleghorn Thomson in his time at Balliol and invited both women artists from Edinburgh to enjoy the hospitality of the Oxford college.

The new information on the family thyroid condition provides an explanation for Gillies' lifelong bachelor status that is independent of sexual orientation. Even so, the totality of evidence cannot decisively arbitrate what has become a tacit default assumption that, because Gillies lived his entire adult life as a bachelor with his mother, he too must have been gay. None of the many judgements of his contemporaries that

I know or know of, including that of an openly homosexual member of the ECA, subscribe to such an assumption. The more pertinent question, however, concerns what Gillies took from Raffalovich circles.

Much of the answer is implicit in the Eric Gill statue *St Sebastian* (1920) [32], an image of a contemporary homosexual icon, modelled on his own torso by a manipulative Catholic sculptor who equated the love of God with sexual penetration and was facing a court action for bankruptcy when he asked Raffalovich to commission it. Gray and Raffalovich prayed before it and Raffalovich reproduced it on cards he sent to young men struggling with their own sexual orientation. Gill also made two nude male acrobats as part of his contract, and a 'fleshly statue' for Gray, who kept it under wraps in the Presbytery. In Cleghorn Thomson's Garret Studio, male simulacra wore boxers' shorts [31]. He collected images of boxers into the 1970s in the same scrapbook as cuttings of church figures whom he admired.

Whether in everyday life or in more studied artistic activity, there are few acts of self-expression that are not mindful of some measure of discretion or awareness of others. Wilde tested the boundaries to the point of self-destruction. Raffalovich always knew that he, too, was giving others the material to bring him down. He protected himself through connections in high places and his daily attendance at St Peter's, but also through the protections offered by the codes of symbols and signifiers, comportment and costume, cosmetics and coiffure, through which extrovert gay identity at once concealed and showed itself.

Familiars of the salon were conversant with the sacred and profane, impatient – some of them – with the necessity of covert identity, but

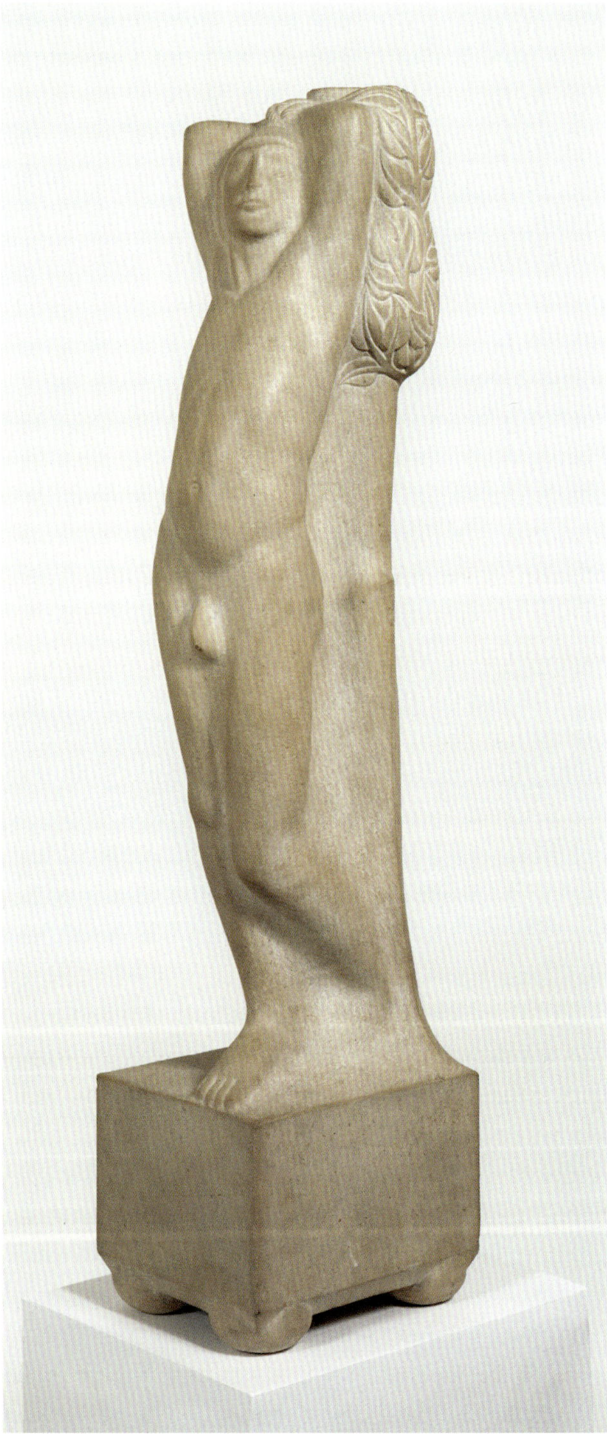

32 *St Sebastian* (1920), by Eric Gill. Hoptonwood Stone, 100.5 cm by 20.2 cm by 24.7 cm (56 kg). Carved for Marc-André Raffalovich

attuned – many of them – to life as theatre and to symbol as a mode of self-expression. This accommodation was there in the reinvention of the two most prominent lives, and there also in stone, the sacred in the fabric of St Peter's, the profane within the oratory of the salon itself. There the 'relaxed sensuality of the saint's languid pose' received the devotions of the two hosts while their well-lunched, and sometimes embarrassed, guests awaited their return.

The accommodation was also there in the compromise marriages made by homosexual men in the attempt to escape the sense of guilt and the risk of blackmail or suicide consequent on legislated intolerance. From 1931 to 1936, Gillies' homosexual friend Harold Morton was embroiled in a covert triangular contest with another of his close friends, the artist William MacTaggart, for the affections and hand of Fanny Aavatsmark. She was the young friend of Munch who brought his paintings to the 1931–2 exhibition of the SSA. Fanny and suitors all suffered, and Harold continued to suffer after MacTaggart married Fanny.

Such marriages were not unique to homosexual men. Heterosexual partners in marriage could also live a fiction and suffer as a result, or so persuade themselves. In 1933, after two years professing the case for modernism, the poet and war hero Herbert Read abandoned Edinburgh, his wife, his child and his chair, to elope with Margaret Ludwig, a young Catholic musician he met through Raffalovich. This confirmed for the gossips the equation of modernism with decadence that Munch had invited when showing them his *Bohemian Wedding* (1925–6) [ni] and the vigorous, yellow, full-frontal, naked virilities of *The Bathers* (1915) [ni].

Gillies painted for the Raffalovich circle when he decided to open himself to the world. The discourse of this circle too was rooted in an alienation from a dominant narrative, had also to navigate ways to show, conceal and survive. And so, just as he had raided the techniques of his college teachers, he raided this culture too for its tropes and stories, and whispered his own predicament to an audience attuned to confession by signifier and symbol.

Portraits

Sisters Emma and Janet (nd, *c.* 1931) [33] is the last portrait Gillies painted of his family before the Munch exhibition opened late in 1931. The impression it gives, of sisters isolated one from the other, is thought by some to result from poor composition. I think it is the subject of the painting and its strength. By this time, the family business had been sold, Emma was over-working as a student of pottery at the ECA, Gillies was still on a part-time, annually renewable, 'pittance' of a salary, and Janet (Jenny), now an assistant cashier in the office of an Edinburgh lawyer, was the main breadwinner. Emma was dependent, arty and feisty, but stressed, whereas Janet, five years her senior, was established, religious and independent. So, Gillies places Janet to the fore, shows her full face, gives her handsome features made stylish with plucked eyebrows, a flawless skin, lipstick and a wave in her coiffure. The hair is gold and the dress too, with a collar that opens to below the throat. This is the oldest sibling, the breadwinner, the golden woman.

And then we have *Portrait of Jenny* (*c.* 1933–4) [34]. It is the only single portrait Gillies painted of his elder sister, and the largest of any exhibited portrait up to that point. Janet is barely recognisable as the woman we last saw portrayed with her sister [33]. In the space of two years, he has aged her by more than twenty and savaged her face with impasto that has been roughly worked by knife. He has also given her a Catholic identity, 'as if she were a medieval Virgin Mary surrounded by her attributes' (SK 1998, 61). But why?

Gillies owned a book of anti-Nazi, anti-militarist images by the German artist and satirist George Grosz. Many are unsparingly brutal. It was published in 1930. In 1933, a reported 800 persons attended a meeting in Edinburgh to protest against Hitler's policy of rearmament and his persecution of minorities, among them German Catholics as well as Jews. It was chaired by Archibald Kennedy, Earl of Cassillis and friend of Raffalovich. The principal speaker was the Chief Rabbi of Edinburgh, Salis Daiches. His student son, David, had an interest in literary and visual modernism that anticipated his later academic career and had already caught the attention of Harvey Wood, and probably of Herbert Read as well.

This was also the year in which a growing hostility in Edinburgh to its Catholic minority first made national headlines. Sectarian demonstrators invaded conventional sites of performance – cinema, and later conference hall and church – and claimed their own performance space in violent incidents in the city centre. Nor were the Raffalovich sites spared. His garden was vandalised, a broadcast from St Peter's Church was sabotaged and demonstrators at the Presbytery, it is alleged, threatened Father Gray with castration.

Familiars of Raffalovich and Gray drew the parallel with events in Germany. One of these was the novelist and Catholic convert Compton Mackenzie. He also remarked a parallel with the Protestant expulsions of Belfast Catholics that he had witnessed at the time of partition in Ireland, 1920–3. Sophie, the sister of Raffalovich, was married to William O'Brien, the member of the British House of Commons whose earlier agitation for the reform of land tenure in Ireland became a model for nationalists in Scotland. One of these nationalists was George Scott-Moncrieff. He had been counselled by Father Gray some years before his conversion to Catholicism. George too saw Nazis in the Edinburgh mob.

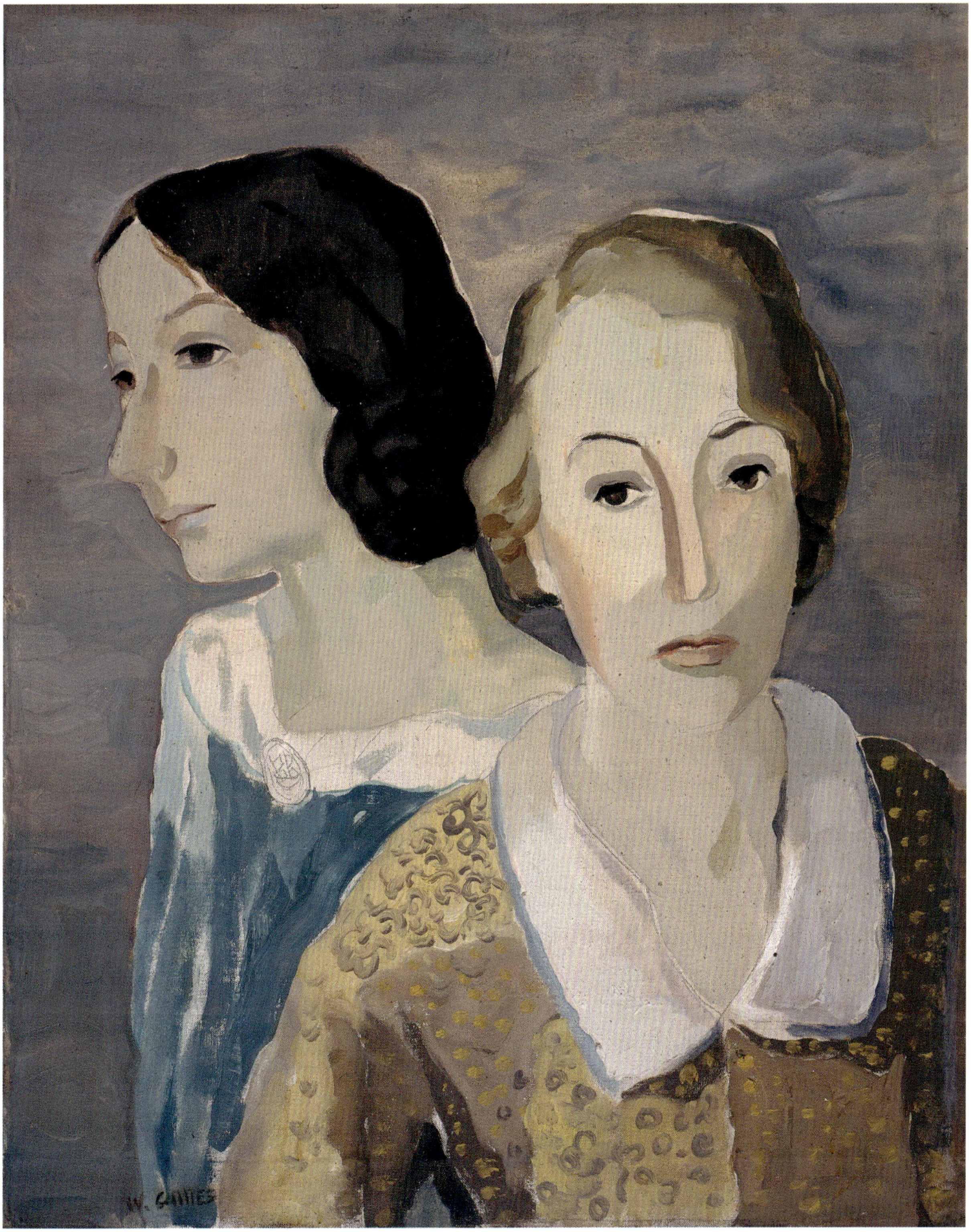

33 *Sisters Emma and Janet* (nd, *c.* 1931). Oil, 76 cm by 60 cm

I suggest, therefore, that the impulse that led to *Still Life with Chagall Print* [10] in 1933 contributed also to the ambition of *Portrait of Jenny* [34]. As the son of a family with its own diaspora, Gillies was identifying himself and his sister with the vulnerability of minorities at a time when the international situation was renewing his own sense of vulnerability to death from the air, a vulnerability made graphic in one of his Grosz cartoons [86]. But why a sister, and why Janet?

The thyroid vulnerability inherited by Janet and Emma is now known as auto-immune thyroid disease (AITD). In the early 1930s, Janet developed symptoms of what was very probably the variant of AITD commonly known then as myxoedema but now as Hashimoto's thyroiditis. The symptoms of this form of hypothyroidism (under-activity of the thyroid gland) have been treatable since the late nineteenth century.

The colours of Janet's face in the portrait, yellowy cream and white with a blush of pink, show the very peaches-and-cream complexion that eventually characterises many afflicted with Hashimoto's thyroiditis. This may be coincidence, especially because this feature is usually not apparent in the early stages of presentation. If Gillies were not responding to what he could see in his sister, then either he was preternaturally prescient or the coincidence is remarkable. If it is a response to what was before him, then we can understand the image in part as consoling and therapeutic in intention.

Gillies confronts Janet's future unblinkingly but comforts her with the thought that she, like the Virgin Mary, also inhabits a world that is both corporeal and spiritual. Her body now is dematerialising, an effect he achieves by the proximity of the tone and colours of her uniformly rendered costume to those of the wall behind. All we can see of her physicality is her full face, the seat of her spirituality, and her hands, the agents of her labours in this world.

To emphasise these, Gillies paints them larger than life. Janet's hair has also changed, no longer coiffured but scraped back, receded and gender-neutral. What we can see of it is now given the tints of her costume and diminished further by the tonality it shares with the wall. The head is in effect reverting to a skull. It floats, almost, as another icon among the objects that surround her. Then, to complete the union between Janet's spiritual being and these attributes, he repeats in them the tonalities and colours of her face. However aged or ill Janet may be, the implication is that the qualities of her worldly being are intimations of the divine. It is a version of the transfiguration for which the Christian hopes on the Day of Judgement, an idea that may have been prompted by a recent work of Gillies' colleague, John Duncan [40]. Gillies will certainly have known it, and probably Janet and Mrs Gillies too, for it was shown in Edinburgh in 1930 and reproduced in the same publication as *Sisters Emma and Janet* [33].

Gillies respected the religious beliefs of Janet and Mrs Gillies but did not share them, which begins to explain why he anchors these effects in the mundane world by placing symbols at three corners of the picture. Here is the black vase again – a *memento mori*, I suggest – a counsel to spirituality that is to reappear at significant junctures in his work. With the passage of time its harebells have wilted. Then, placed in contrast at the bottom right-hand corner, are living things, flowers in a vase, but set on a table that is, again, funereally dark.

Opposite:
Detail from *Portrait of Jenny* ([34] – see p. 55)

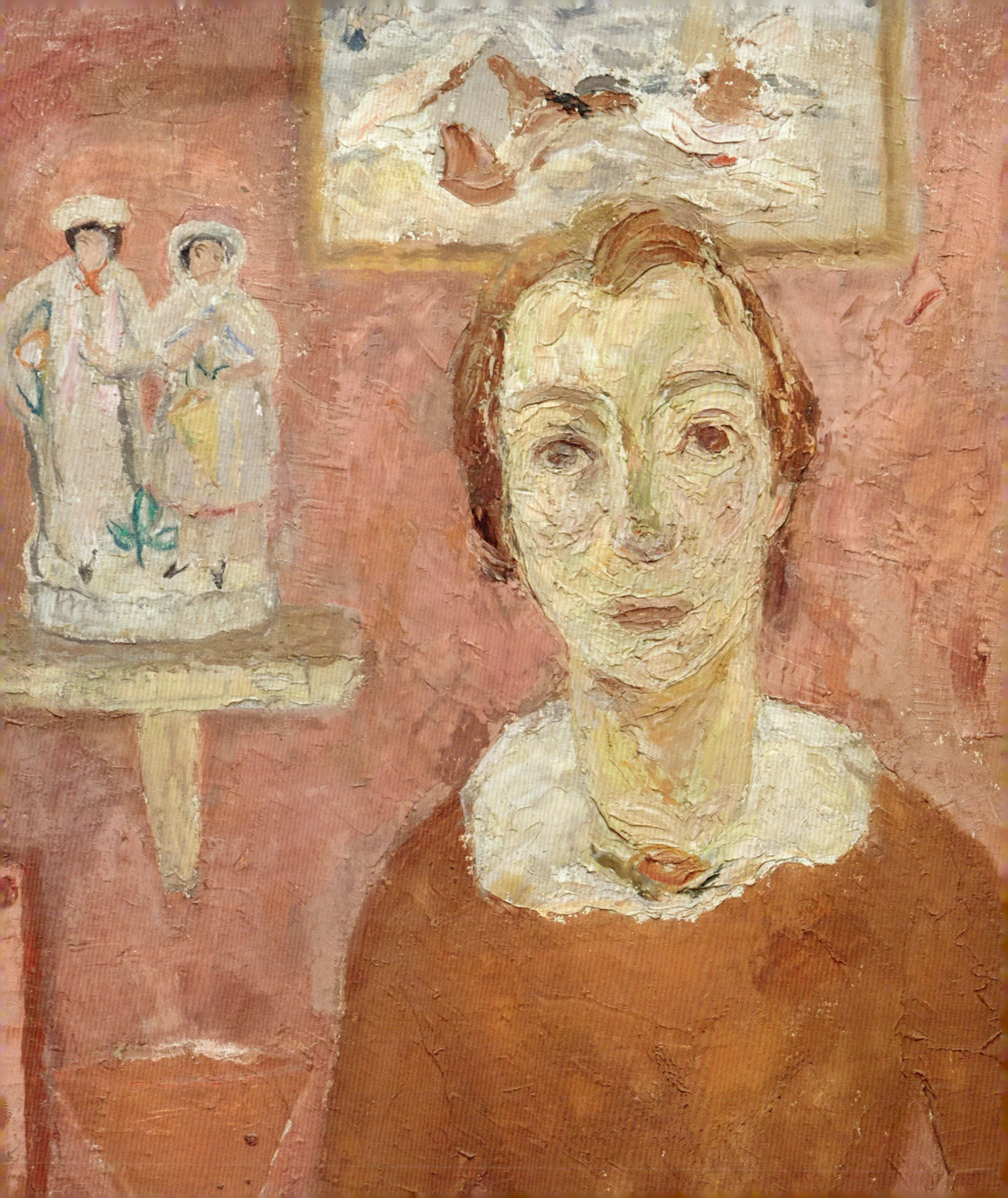

Opposite these living things is, I assure the reader, a symbol of the profane, the wally dug. Well known in Glasgow, Amsterdam and other sea ports, such dogs were commonly given to male clients who, in buying the ceramic for an inflated price, received, at no further cost, the carnal services of a woman who could thereby comply with a local ban on soliciting. Wittily, the dog is not fully admitted to the picture but peeps in around the edge. Above it is a pottery figure of the sailor himself. Elder Dickson tells us that it bears the legend 'Ready and Willing'. This is true of the surviving Staffordshire figure that Gillies used but he has omitted the sexual double-meaning.

My further suggestion, then, is that the sequence of symbols, scanned downwards from the top left-hand side, can be read as a narrative of 'decline and fall' in a world where spirituality and flesh contend. This contest supplies the title of Waugh's celebrated first novel and the theme of many 'Catholic' novels, among them Compton Mackenzie's *Sinister Street* (1913). The latter is one of two works on which aesthetes of the post-Wilde generation modelled their own life choices. The other was Proust's *À La Recherche du Temps Perdu*, first translated by Charles Scott Moncrieff, a Catholic and homosexual of Rabelaisian exuberance (Findlay 2014, 3–5). Charles was uncle to George of that name, had spent time in Edinburgh, and was also known to Raffalovich.

More specifically, the decline and fall, I suggest, is that of Herbert Read. One starts with a second piece of pottery, an ageing couple whose arms are linked. This is a long-established relationship, a marriage. Below, two objects, a slim volume and a small terracotta beaker, are Read's former lives, the book his verse and criticism, the beaker his earlier post in ceramics at the Victoria and Albert Museum. Then comes the sailor 'Ready and Willing'. The motto originally celebrated the bravery of those serving in the Crimean War. Read was decorated for bravery in 1918. For Eric Gill, the motto signified the unbridled sexual activity he equated with religious experience. And below the sailor is the final act of the Fall.

One can, then, think of the painting as an attempt by Gillies to find common ground with Janet; a place of multiple meanings where rapport (trust and empathy) could be maintained despite the struggles of flesh with spirit and of scepticism with faith; a shared expression through which the incompatible beliefs of separate beings could accommodate each other, literally inhabit the same space.

I do not mean that Gillies' purpose was to tell Read's story; rather, that the Read scandal presented itself to Gillies at a time when he and his closest friends were exercised by the exigencies of sexual and artistic expression. Read's was a specific instance of a predicament that could be formalised into an open-ended language of symbol and figuration. Through such works, Gillies could explore the dilemma he himself faced. Read believed that his failing marriage inhibited his creative life. Grierson believed that the modernist Read did not have to resign his chair in order to keep his Catholic lover. How different would the story of modernism in Britain have been had Grierson's counterfactual been the outcome, and how different Gillies' life and work had Gillies followed the examples of Read or Ben Nicholson and left his family?

As he pondered his own possibilities of independence, I suggest, Gillies was similarly exercised by the implications of his mother's ageing and his

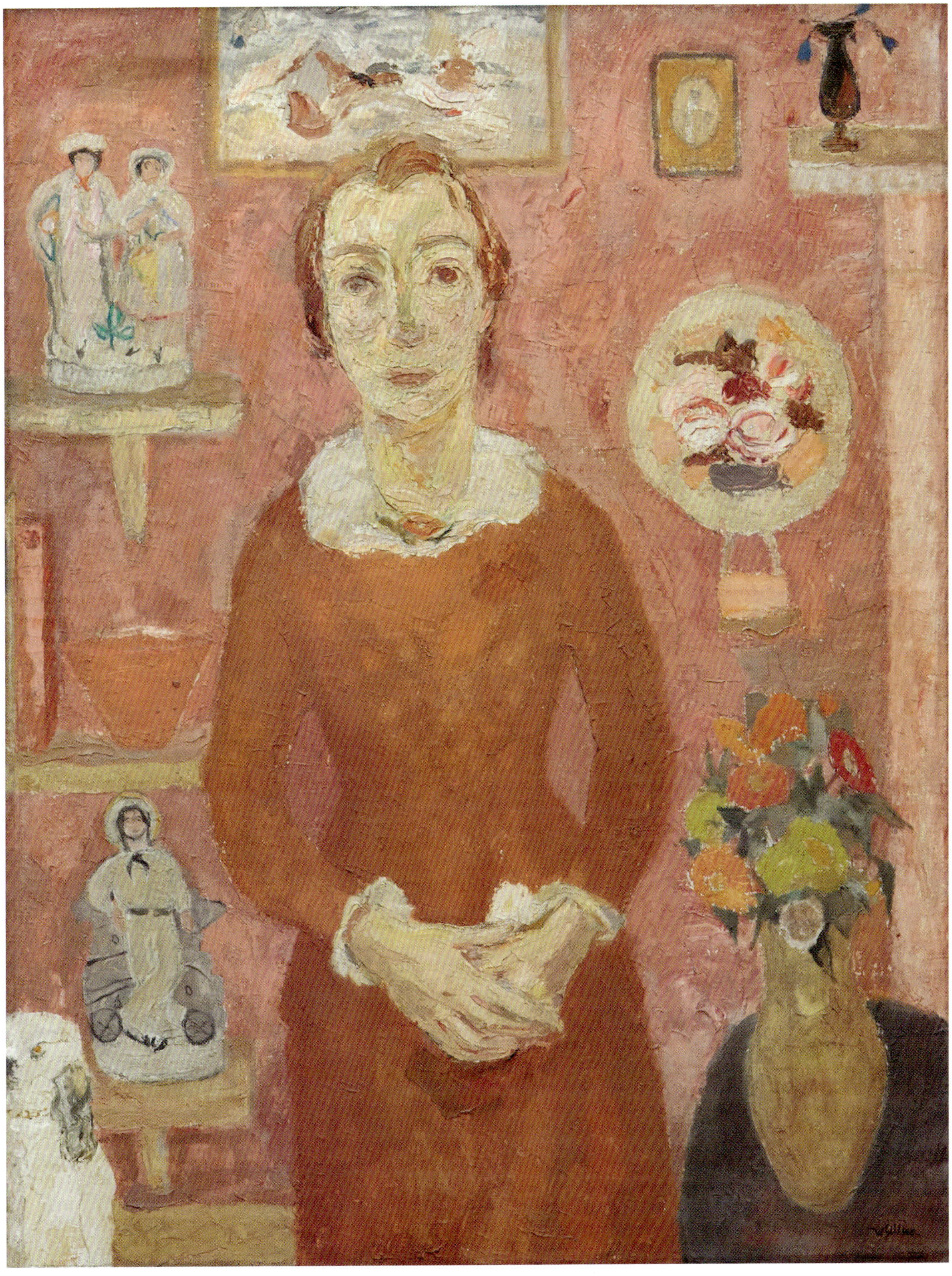

34 *Portrait of Jenny* (*c.* 1933–4). Oil, 115 cm by 90 cm

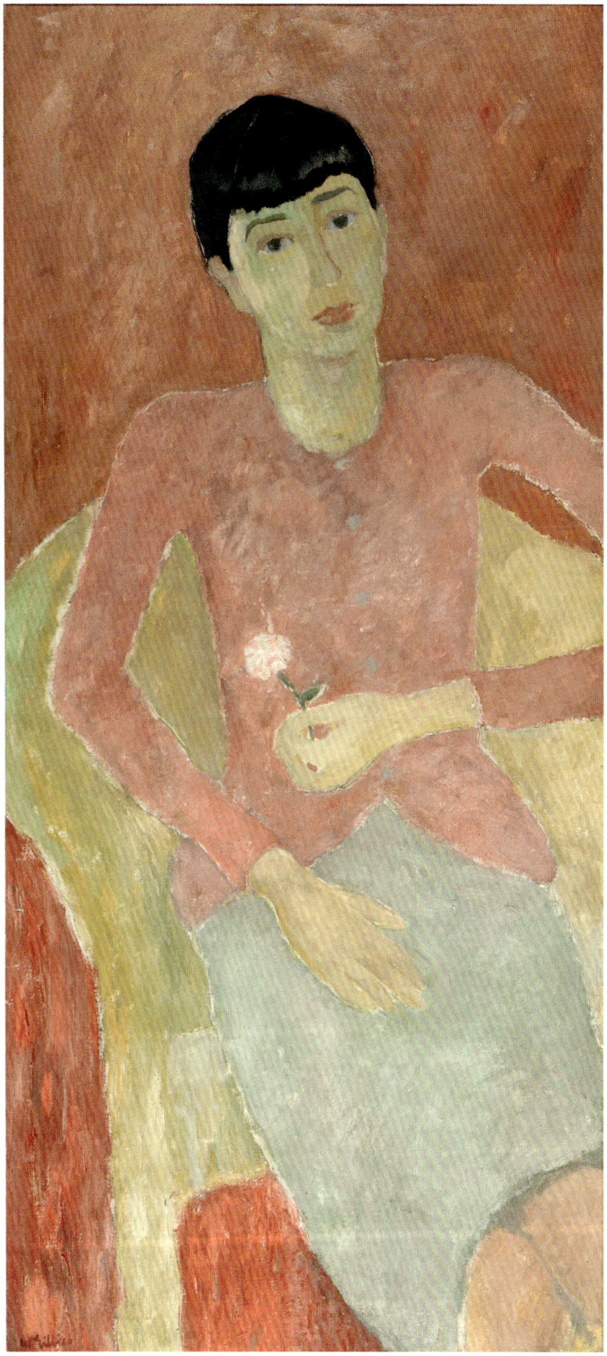

35 *Marjory Porter 1* (nd, *c.* 1935). Oil, 129 cm by 58.5 cm

sister's ill-health, and he expressed this dilemma in terms of objects dear to them. The ceramics belonged to Janet but he and Emma would know that Read regarded craft pottery, like the old Staffordshire flatbacks, as precursors of modernism, an art in which the craftsman 'strays unconsciously into a realm of purer forms … [and] blunders into beauty'. Thus, they had the potential to articulate Janet's world of meaning with Emma's and his own.

Whether or not this is to overinterpret, I maintain that the symbols are neither randomly assembled nor assembled by criteria that are purely visual, without wider signification. There is also, moreover, a clear ordering of objects in the right-hand array. Linking the *memento mori* at the top with the vase of living flowers at the bottom, Gillies has inserted the tapestry with calendar attached. A long iconographic tradition suggests a reading of the right-hand array as the task God gives humankind to use the finite span of years (the calendar) that separates life (the living flowers) from death (the wilted harebells in the black vase) to weave into our life and labours the creation in which God is manifest (the tapestry).

In much Christian piety, the salvation of the soul is assured when God is accepted into a life. Whether or not Janet was aware of the way in which the story of the Fall is told in the left-hand array, the tapestry and calendar could speak directly to her of the equation of female piety with domestic virtue, an equation she may also have known from verses inscribed in a Smith family Bible in the Gillies estate [170]. And, in the Protestant tradition in which she was raised, good works in this world offered some assurance of salvation in the next.

Margery Porter (the correct spelling of her name) was a friend of Gillies for sixteen years or more. The pink (carnation) she holds in *Marjory Porter 1* (nd, *c.* 1935) [35] must surely dispel any remaining doubts that Gillies used symbols. The power of symbol, however, lies not only in an agreed single meaning but sometimes also in an ambivalence or plurality of association. We must also remember Gillies' sense of humour and love of role-play, his hamming his own personality with students, his allowing others to mistake him for the college janitor.

If this awareness of role and fiction goes back to the darker side of army life, his embracing it arguably goes back to the lighter. There is humour in role-distancing. On his return from the Front, we see him in hospital (ni), with boisterous posture, denying to camera the role of invalid enjoined by the special uniform the army obliged convalescents to wear. We see his nurses too, changed out of their nursing uniforms and into improvised gypsy costumes, surrounding a pantomime witch who looks, under the make-up, very like Gillies. He acted in College home-movies [37] and loved the masquerade of the College Revel, when costumed students and staff inverted the hierarchy of the College with cabaret, parody and impersonation.

The emotional charge of *Marjory Porter 1* lies in the contrast between the meaning of the pink and the virtual inscrutability of the rest of the work. Margery is expressionless and, but for her exposed knees, ageless too, anywhere from her late teens upwards. And are her lips naturally red, or is that lipstick she is wearing? The overall impression is of vulnerability and innocence, or even resignation. It is hard to be sure. The pink itself is also uncertain. It has an iconographic

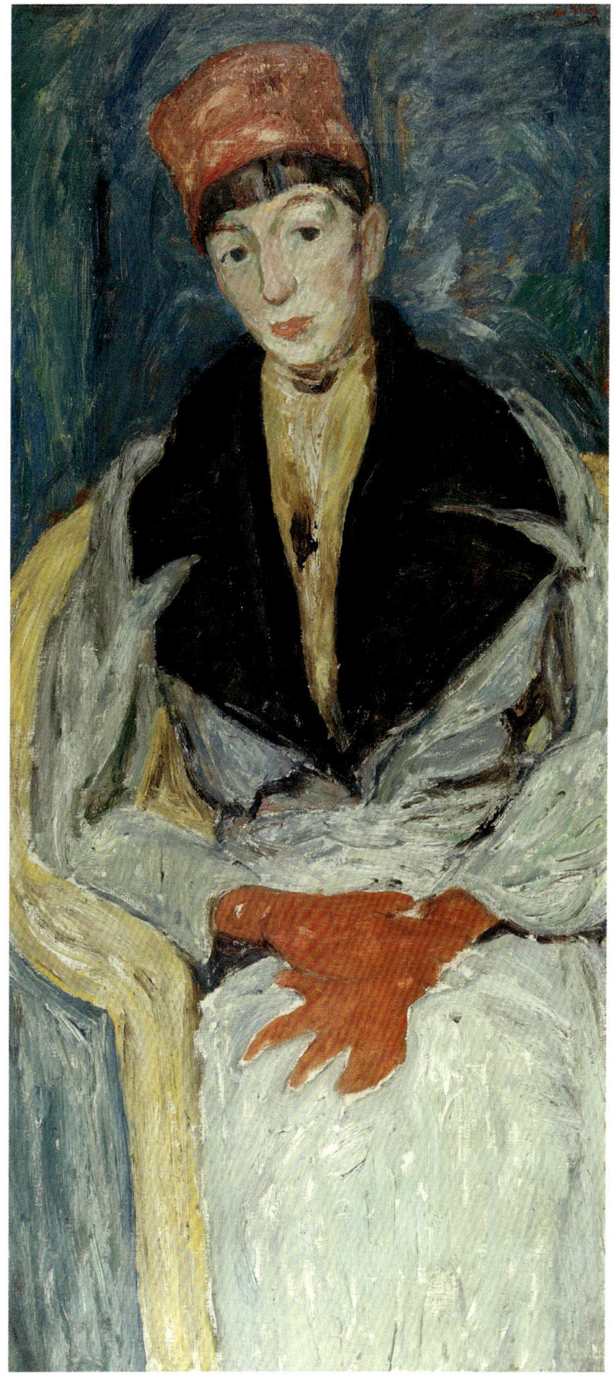

36 *Marjory Porter 2* (*c.* 1935). Oil, 130 cm by 59 cm

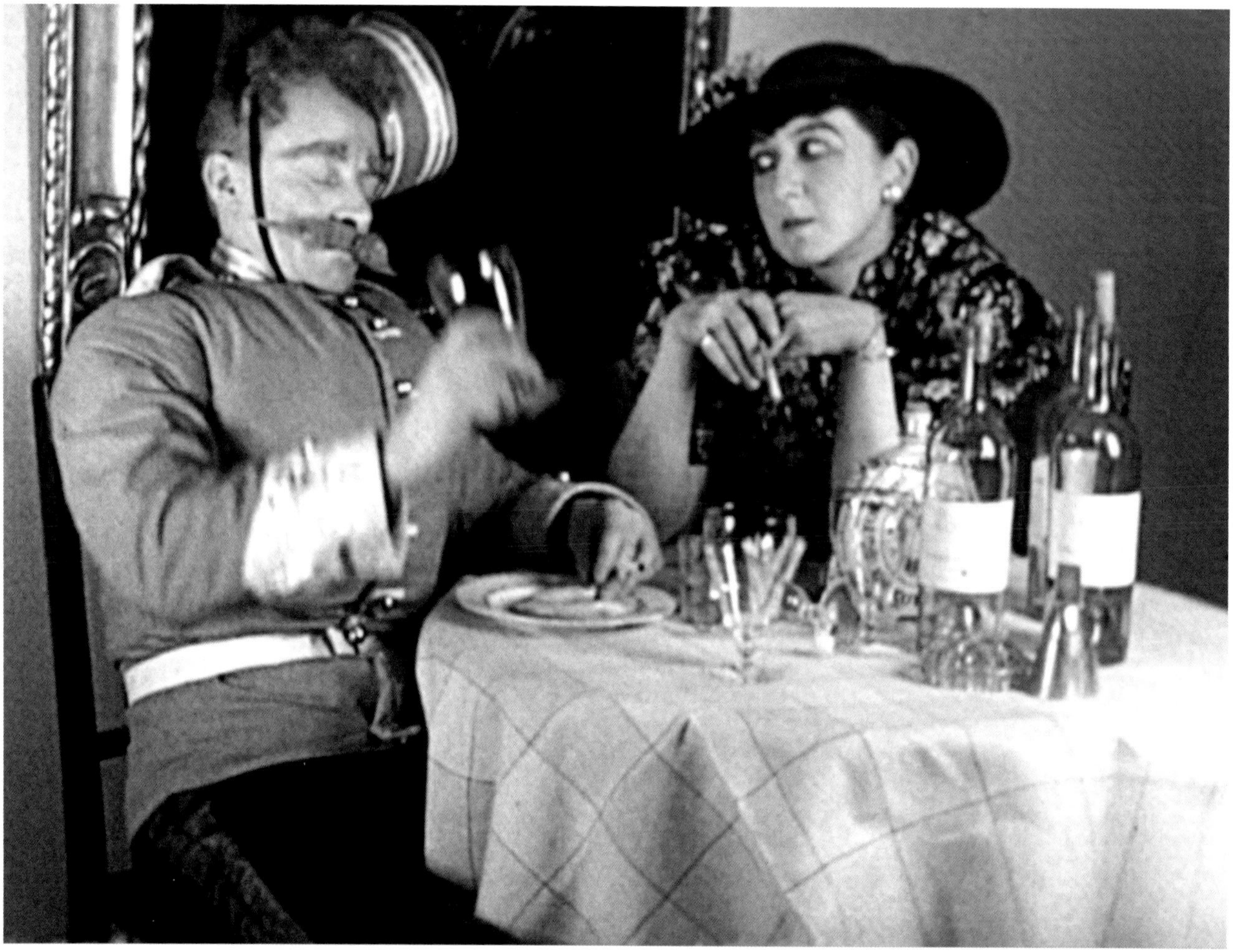

37 Veteran and vamp: Gillies and Margery Porter in *Parisian Café Society* (1938). Amateur film by unknown maker

history as a symbol of betrothal. But Margery was a girlfriend of Harvey Wood before he married Lily. Is Margery awaiting her lover or has she been left with her flower unclaimed? The pink can also symbolise undying maternal love, the sort of love that might be attributed to a mother who could not let go of her son. The Virgin Mary again, or Mrs Gillies?

Contrasting with this work are two virtually identical portraits of Margery. *Marjory Porter 2* (*c.* 1935) [36] shows a mature and stylishly dressed woman whose town-coat with astrakhan collar now covers her knees. This time there is no doubt that Margery is adult and assured. Munch had shown in Edinburgh a full-length portrait of a woman of similar age and sophistication on a canvas of similarly distinctive proportions (*Lady [Woman] in Grey*, 1924–5). Her coat too was grey and had a large fur collar. But there may also be references here that were closer to home.

Gillies paints the hat and gloves in the scarlet of the fallen woman. When Evelyn Read wanted to exact public revenge on her unfaithful husband in 1932, she bought brightly coloured clothes to disrupt the sedate *sub-fusc* (dark formal suits) of the platform party in Leeds that gave him an honorary degree. Herbert Read was particularly angered by the bright red of her gloves.

We do not have to regard Margery as fallen of course, or jilted, but merely complicit in games Gillies was playing. Indeed, there survives a College home-movie from 1938, *Parisian Café Society*, in which Gillies plays drunken soldier to Margery's vamp [37]. And did he tell her, as he painted her gloves scarlet, that one of the stories in *A Window in Thrums* (he had given Janet a copy of the 1903 compendium edition) tells how the possessive Jess finds a woman's glove in the suitcase of her bachelor son and realises at that moment that she (Jess) has lost him to a younger woman? Gillies appears to paint one of Margery's gloved hands clumsily. Her fingers are spread wide and distorted, a contrast with the hand that so delicately held the pink. But is this clumsiness? And, if so, why did he repeat it in the second version of this work, *Marjory Porter 3* (*c.* 1935) (ni), to give us something more like blooded talons?

Financially, Gillies was probably in a position to offer marriage by 1933, but we do not have to assume any such premeditation or outcome. Margery was younger and things may have developed in and around his studio in ways that neither of them had initially expected. Thus, the pink and the gloves may originally have been playful. But playful complicity can itself become a form of courtship, a prospect of deeper complicities to come. Had the relationship progressed no further, Gillies could have painted over the pink and shown all three works in Edinburgh. But he did not. He kept all three, along with a preparatory drawing as well, and none was shown in Edinburgh while Margery and her parents still lived. This is most unlike the Gillies of the 1930s and it marks the three Porter portraits off from even the most personal of Gillies' portrayals of his family, all of which were exhibited in the capital.

Gillies shared his understanding of life and art with Emma and also owed much of it to her [38]. She, in turn, owed much to him. Pottery saved her but ultimately hastened her death. The effects show in his work for at least the next twenty years, and he probably never forgot.

When a second stroke incapacitated their father in 1920, a pact was made among the three children that Emma would run the shop while Gillies went through college, and then Emma would get her turn at something. She could have had this when Gillies graduated in 1922. But she stayed in the shop for his postgraduate year, then for his year abroad, then during his year in Inverness, and then for several years more while he established himself at the ECA on his meagre pittance. She started her course in pottery at the ECA only in 1929, the year the family moved to Edinburgh. She graduated in 1932 and then went to the Royal College of Art in London to study under William Staite Murray. He was an associate of Ben Nicholson in the Seven & Five Society (later '7 & 5') and reputedly the foremost studio potter in Britain.

Pottery saved Emma, for a time, because she hated the shop. Her father's abuse had left her with a phobia of men, her main customers. The stress activated her AITD. In Emma, this manifested as Graves' disease, a form of thyroid over-activity, for which the drug treatment that

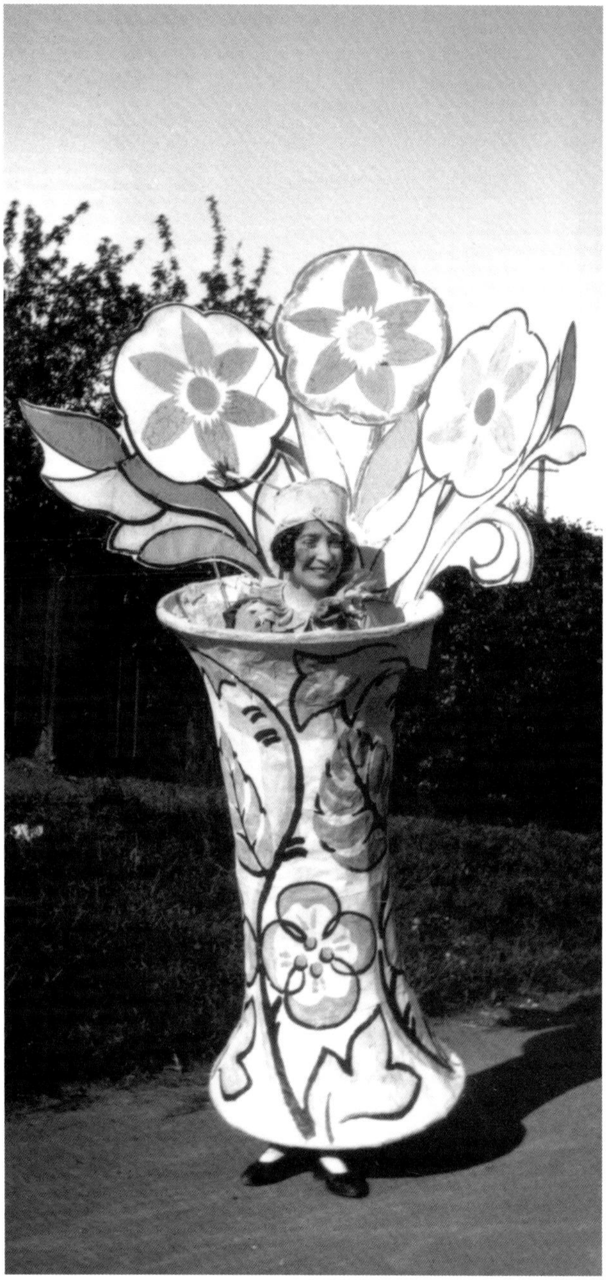

38 Emma Gillies in parade costume, around 1928

replaced thyroidectomy became widely available only in the 1940s.

Emma found pottery through the activities in Haddington and district of the Scottish Women's Rural Institute. This was a new sorority of suffragettes, rural workers, graduates, medical doctors and campaigners for peace and other causes. Associated actions extended to civil disobedience, which sometimes was violent and criminal. The Institute established rooms near the shop, where Emma could meet like-minded radicals, and taught skills formerly the preserve of men. Its founder, Catherine Blair, was a local farmer and suffragette who made and taught pottery, challenged Haldane's opposition to universal female suffrage, practised civil disobedience and publicly defended the tactic. Emma had found a role-model and profession. The support of Uncle Will and his friend the artist and potter Henry Wyse, followed by her success at the ECA, restored the self-confidence her father had destroyed.

Staite Murray, however, appears to have undone all this. Certainly, Emma felt undermined by his Buddhism, his guru disdain of formal teaching, his acolytes and favouritism and, above all, by what Emma experienced as his sexual harassment, 'following her around', she said, 'like an old dog'. Her defence was to work harder but to miss classes, despite his offer to help her prepare a gallery exhibition of her own. But at what price? For Emma, a price was already being paid in the reactivation of her condition. She refused the offer, returned home ill and never recovered. Late in 1934 she was admitted to hospital weighing under six stone and able neither to eat nor to walk, only to crawl. In the ensuing fifteen months of her descent into seeming madness, the family was misled by the misdiagnosis of 'hysteria' and

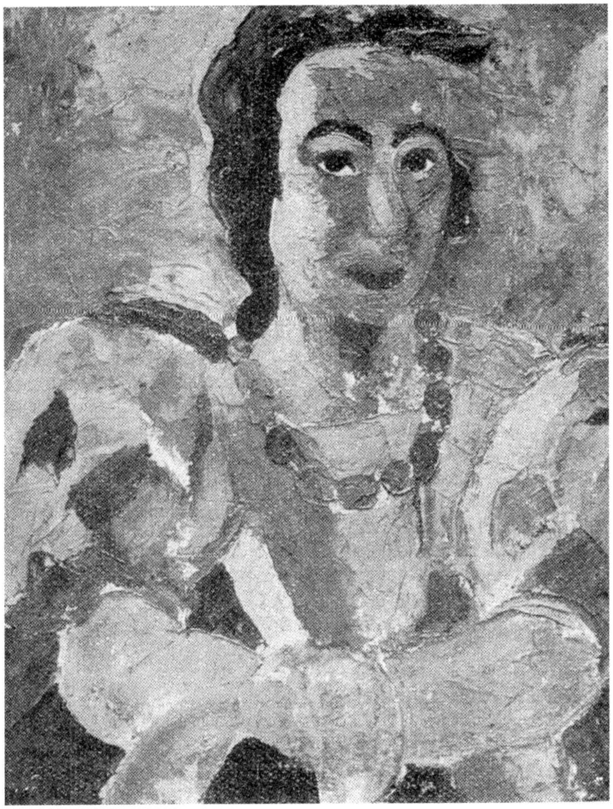

39 *Portrait [of Emma]* (*c.* 1933–4). Oil, dimensions unknown

believed that she could pull herself together if she tried. Only within days of her death was a tell-tale goitre noticed.

In 2012, a cupboard in the ECA that had formerly been used by Gillies and had been locked for over a decade was reopened. It contained over 200 pieces of Emma's work. During her lifetime, it is possible that Gillies was never fully aware of the cost to Emma of her years of sacrifice on his behalf. In times of remission, she was popular, productive and exuberant, sharing his sense of humour and love of Revel. The purely naturalistic *Emma* (nd, *c.* 1931) [140] was probably painted in such a period. *Portrait [of Emma]* (*c.* 1933–4) [39] is closer to *Marjory Porter 2* [36] in its shared enjoyment of transformation of identity by dress. The work is untraced but was reproduced in *The Listener*, whose critic found in it 'the dignity and impressiveness of early Florentine painting'.

It was bought by Mary, one of the five formidable daughters of Herbert Grierson, President of the Fine Art Society of Edinburgh University. Mary (Molly) Grierson was herself married to an academic at the University of Leeds, where Evelyn Read sported her gloves. All the Griersons were involved at some point in the Raffalovich salon, and Herbert Grierson especially, along with others of the Arts Faculty professoriate. Among them was the composer Donald Tovey. He gave Barns-Graham singing lessons and gave concerts with Read's lover, Margaret Ludwig.

Family Group (nd, *c.* 1932–7) [41] was probably painted in the unhappier times to follow. It, too, is known only through a black and white photo and press report. It was large, around six feet square, and 'brightly' painted with a background in red. Mrs Gillies is clearly the matriarch and Janet a commanding presence. The diagonal of their heads deepens the implication of inferiority forced on Emma by the height and position of her chair. Her knees are high and she must turn to conform to the direction of gaze of the group. The contrast between her wide-open eyes and Janet's narrowed gaze is a further diminution. One is reminded of the functional paralysis that by the summer of 1934 had left her able only to lie in bed or crawl (to a low chair?); and reminded also of the family's harsh but mistaken opinion that her condition was owing to a failure of will.

The original title (long mistaken but here restored) is important for the question it invites – what sort of family is this and what sort of group? And why did Gillies show it in 1937, so soon after the death of his sister? My preferred answer is that it is a conflicted work that flows from the same concerns as *Portrait of Jenny* [34] but now with the added awareness of Emma's vulnerability. I think it may draw on John Duncan's *Out of Great Tribulation* [40], a work that Gillies undoubtedly knew, and probably Janet and Mrs Gillies too. Duncan was a Symbolist but also an 'inveterate experimenter' (Wood 2016, 56) who encouraged an interest in Cubism at the ECA, where he was a colleague of Gillies. His title refers to the Book of Revelation. 'The Great Tribulation' was also a name by which the Great War was known. Duncan's themes are war, death, redemption and peace (see also the discussion of [45]). The three androgynes are posed in quasi-military line-array as they are transfigured on the Day of Judgement.

By analogy, then, *Family Group* [41] consoles Janet and Mrs Gillies with the prospect of salvation, and acknowledges their delivery from the tribulations of the family. But it also expresses the despair of a war veteran and sceptic over the inability of humanity to protect its own from arbitrary death – and now, with the misfortunes of both his sisters, from arbitrary illness as well. The two main sources of existential trauma in Gillies' life – family and war – are beginning to converge.

Interior (1938) [42] (which at one time was mistakenly known as *Family Group* (1937)) is the most ambitious work Gillies ever made and an important one for the argument. First shown in 1938, it has hitherto defied explanation, or been avoided, or been explained in terms that are false or trite, or blind to the questions it poses.

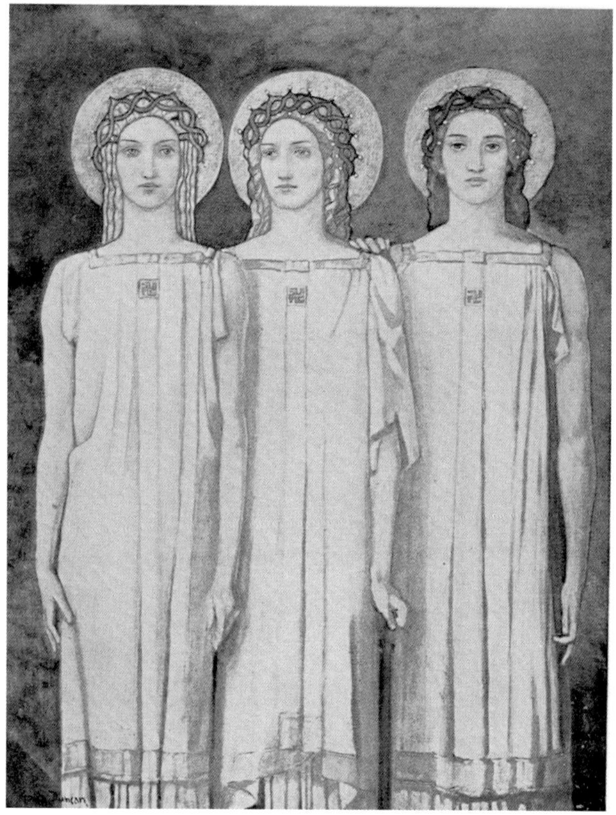

40 *Out of Great Tribulation* (nd, *c.* 1930), by John Duncan. Medium and dimensions unknown. From a volume in which *Sisters Emma and Janet* [33 above] was also shown

For example, how did Gillies get into this picture? He tells us: by painting himself in a mirror positioned between the two rooms. And what is he doing? He shows us: painting what he sees. But both answers are false. With his feet at the base of the mirror he has to be standing seven feet tall with his nose touching the mirror. He cannot see into the two rooms and there is nothing on his canvas. If this were a mimetic image from a single viewpoint at a fixed point in time, the work that conveys the reality of what he sees could not

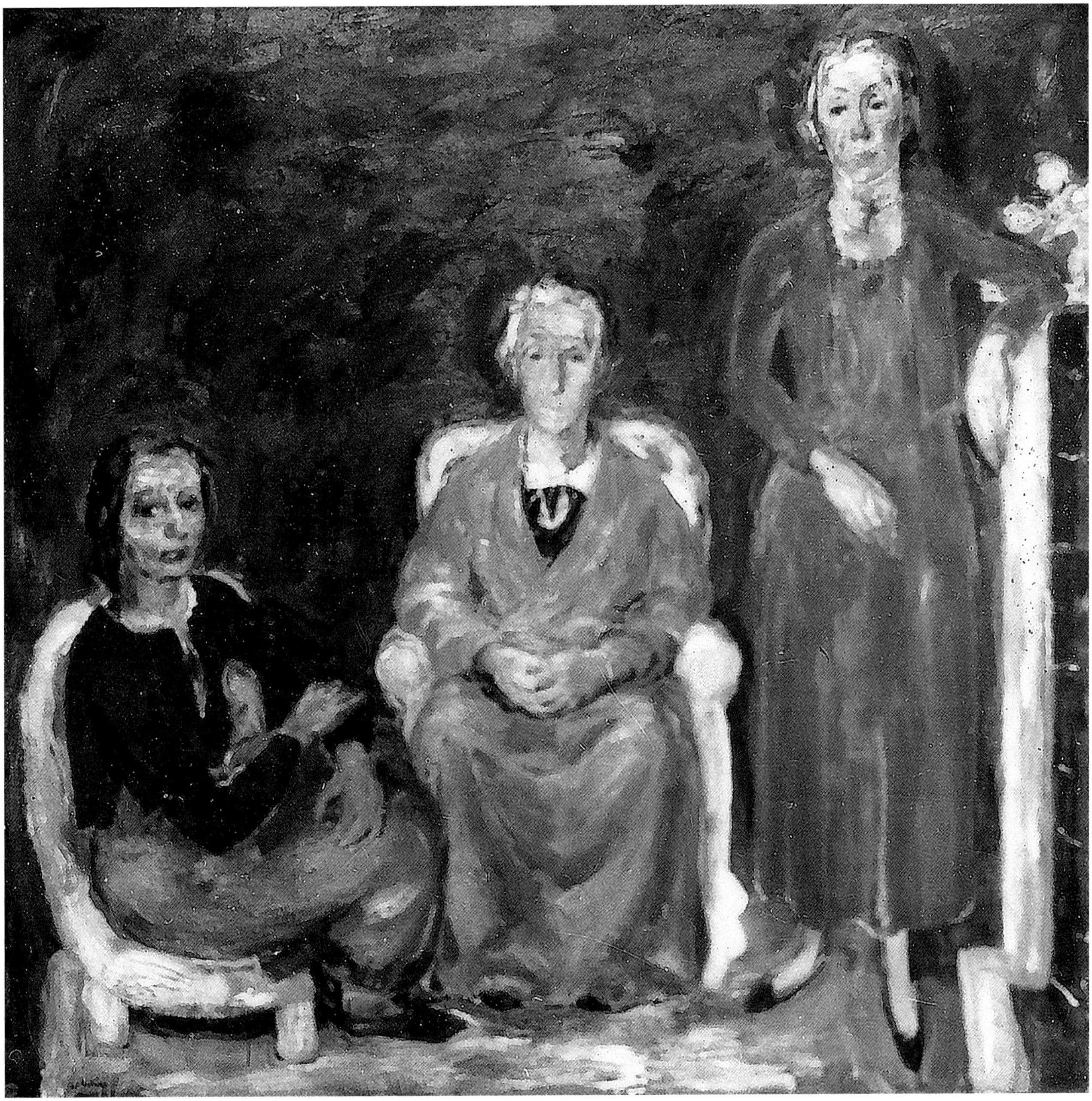

41 *Family Group* (nd, *c.* 1932–7). Oil, dimensions unknown

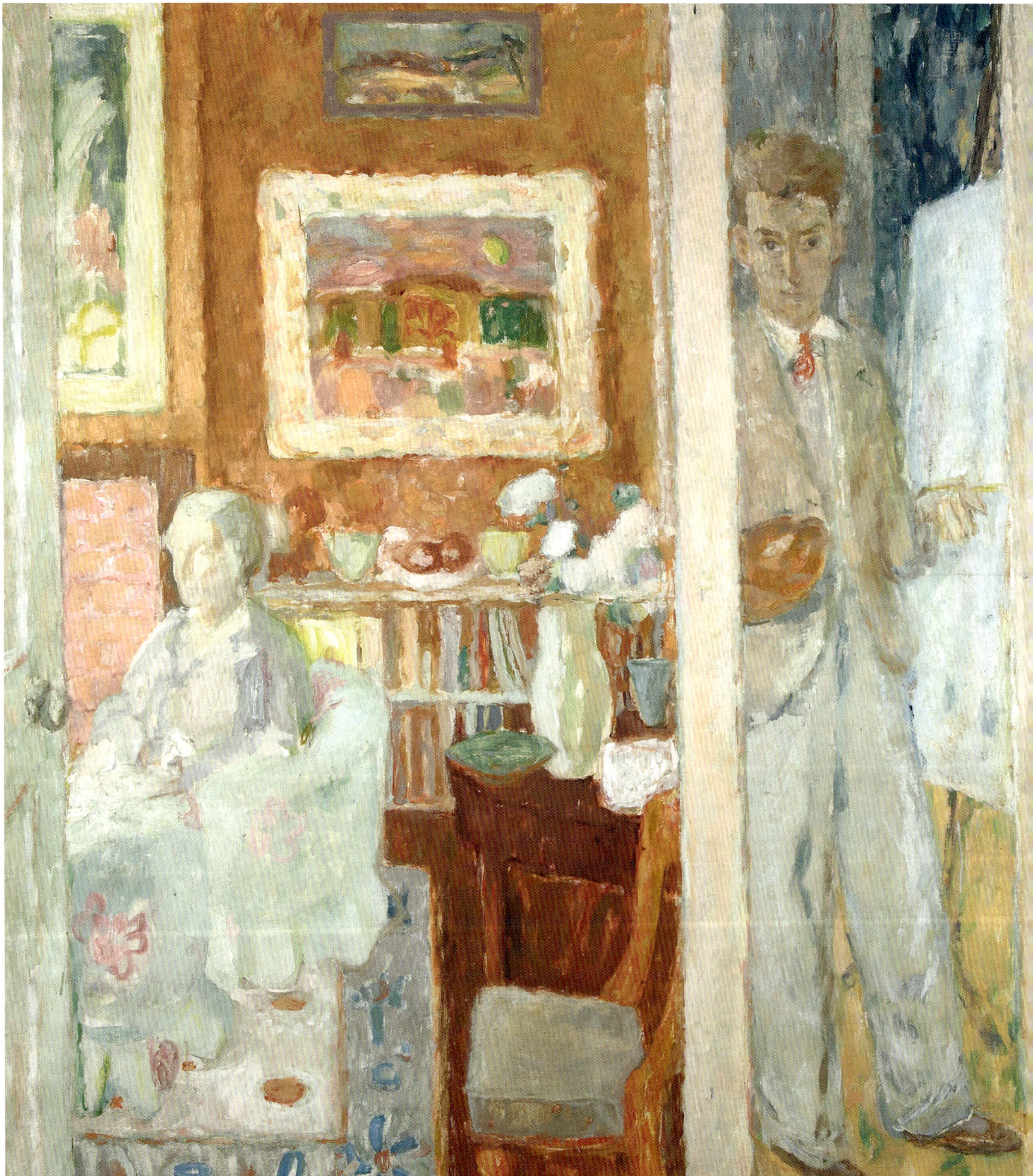

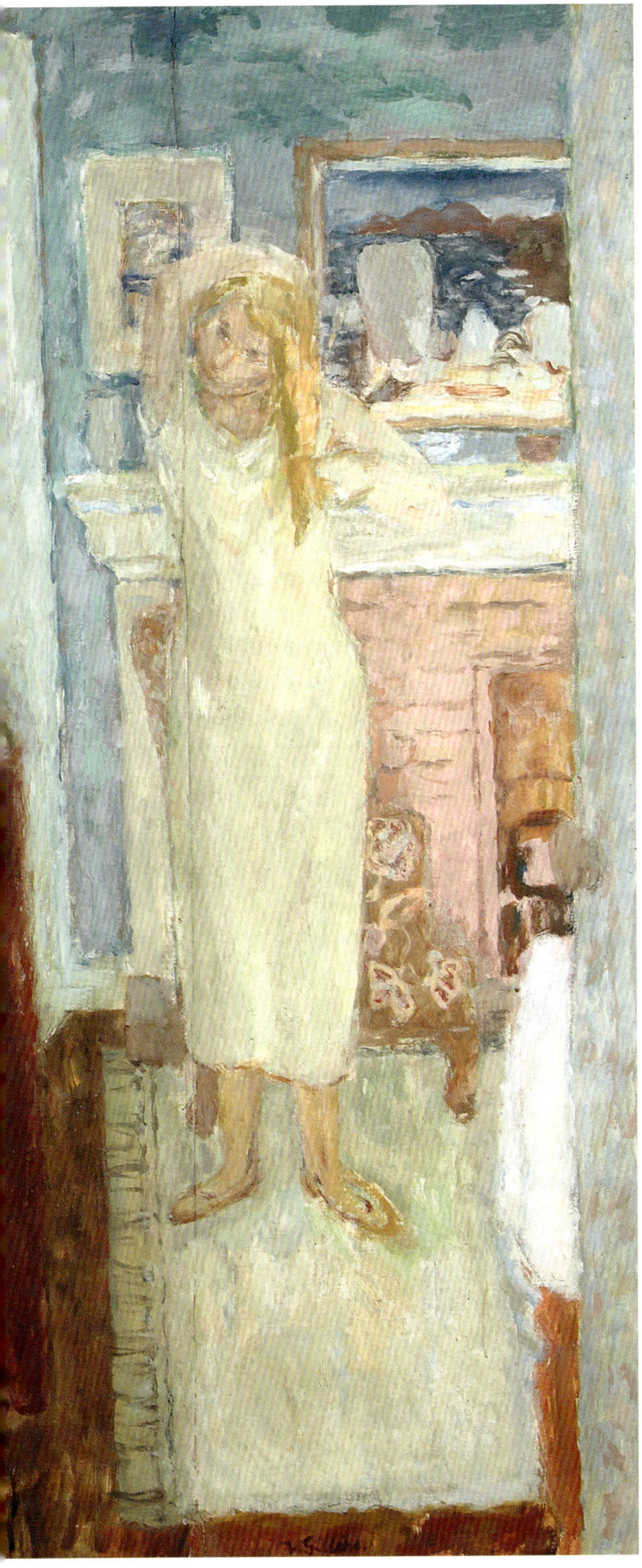

exist. *Interior* contradicts itself. That this has never been remarked in print suggests that something – neglect, perhaps, born of condescension – has obscured this deployment of a cardinal element of modernist critique.

Unremarked also, at least until 2006, is his signalling Velásquez' famous use of a mirror in *Las Meninas* (1656) to explore the conundrums of mimesis. Across the full range of his work, Gillies conveys his hallmark sense of the otherness of mundane realities by novel combinations of mutually inconsistent elements of mimetic representation. He said only that *Interior* was an homage to the French artist Pierre Bonnard. Perhaps, but only up to a point, and it is also much more.

And why is Gillies in this picture? He has been lurking just outside the frame, so to speak, since the early 1930s. But here he is now in person, a disruptive presence in a space that defies spatial logic. And who is that person to the right in the picture? When we last saw Janet eleven months ago on the walls of the SSA, she was not looking too well [34]. Her hair was short, her dress middle-aged. Here Gillies bends time back. We know one internal reality is referenced on 1938 or thereabouts because the landscape behind Mrs Gillies' head is *Autumn Moon* (1934, *c.* 1934–7) [84], a work that itself manipulates the elements of mimesis (discussed below). But he also drops Janet's age by twenty years, restores the golden locks her aunt Margaret remembered from Janet's childhood, and strips her dress to reveal suggestions of the physical being within the slip, distorting time to address identity.

42 *Interior* (1938). Oil, 127 cm by 173.5 cm

And what is Mrs Gillies doing here? Gillies himself occupies a cold, blue space with tonally equivalent creams; Janet similarly but for the pink of the fireplace. But Mrs Gillies herself is cold and blue amidst the warm colours of the room. Red dominates blue in our foveal imaging. If anyone is departing the substance of 1938 reality, it is she.

In sum, Mrs Gillies is real but insubstantial. Janet is substantial but unreal. And Gillies is both real and substantial but an impossible presence in an impossible work. We can resolve these conundrums, I suggest, if we take the 'Interior' of the title that Gillies originally gave the painting to be his subjective self, and the painting to be a concrete analogy for the imagined moments of its conception.

He approaches this in three ways. First, the central panel he occupies is the most realistically painted (in traditional terms) of the three. The canvas on the easel recedes whereas the rugs in the two rooms have right-angle corners, as though tilted up to lie flat against the picture surface. And photos show that he did, indeed, sometimes paint in jacket and tie.

Second, the most realistically painted objects in the two rooms are not Mrs Gillies or the Janet figure, but works by Gillies himself. These objects are mimetically painted, although the originals are not (illus [80] and [84]). In similar vein, the (non-picture) objects in Mrs Gillies' room require only a frame around them to turn them into Gillies still lifes. With brushes poised, we might say, he is about to make Janet and Mrs Gillies more real too by painting them in a way that gives meaning and signification precedence over the superficialities of mimetic representation, by having elements of figuration and visual signifiers interact across a total picture-space that is itself a signifier by virtue of its incommensurable spatial components.

Third, Gillies' panel flouts the spatial expectations created elsewhere. In order to 'reach' Gillies, one must scan across boundaries that separate the more traditional reality he gives himself from the more symbolic version of reality that he will create in and from the rooms on either side. To find a reality in the painting as a whole, the panel reminds us, we must accept the contradictions of mimesis. Its only indisputable (warm) realities are his whispered subjective self (the head) and his means to express this (the palette).

Turning to the subject matter, in the edition of Barrie's *A Window in Thrums* that Gillies gave Janet, there is an illustration of Jess, the ageing mother (hands and lap only) [13]. She is lit by a window, like Mrs Gillies, apparently, in the left-hand panel. Through it, Jess sees the life of Kirriemuir go by. The memories this stirs supply the main content of the book. This content, however, is contained within a narrative framed, not by Jess, but by a person of education, the widowed teacher who visits regularly, and often lodges with the family. He is utterly in sympathy with the moral fabric of the family's life and history. His role, however, is not to live in the bygones of Kirriemuir or submit unquestioningly to its values and beliefs. He is there, rather, to shape it into a narrative for a wider audience more acquainted with modernity. The position of Barrie's narrator, then, is analogous to the position that Gillies adopts in the middle panel – in the household, yes, but not of it, an observer as much as a member, with a job of 'representation' to do.

Others have remarked that the triptych structure frames the three family members like saints. Some see isolation in this framing, others domestic harmony. But the separate rooms have a further religious reference. The popularity of the Thrums novels owed much to what they could offer diverse readerships, including one that was devoutly Christian. In the volume that Gillies gave Janet, two passages are marked in the ink that Janet used. One is a quotation from the Bible that is read aloud by one of Barrie's characters: '"In my Father's house are many mansions; if it were not so, I would have told you. I go to prepare a place for you."'

Thus, the separate rooms ('mansions') occupied by Janet and Mrs Gillies are also a reminder of the Bible's assurance that the place one occupies on earth has its counterpart in heaven. And this in turn reminds us of the theology enshrined in Victorian verses pasted into a Smith family Bible, a theology of the sanctity of place and family based on the mother/daughter relationship and on daily life as witness [170]. It was arguably this assurance that Gillies had in mind when painting *Portrait of Jenny* [34] and *Family Group* [41].

It may also explain why he paints the Janet figure here so much younger than his two most recent images of her, dresses her in a white slip and gives her long golden tresses. By restoring Janet's youth, he is able to express a mother/daughter relationship that would have been impossible to convey pictorially had he given the younger woman the age he gave Janet in the two earlier portraits (by the late 1930s, it can be difficult to distinguish Janet from her Aunt Margaret in a photo). 'You are still a wee fair haired girl to me yet, Jenny', Aunt Margaret told Janet when Janet was in her early sixties and nearing death. And this is what Gillies makes her too.

Barrie made the white pinafore of his mother's girlhood a symbol of her youth. He said he could think of her in no other way. But white also signifies purity and devotion. It is yet another 'beautiful female dressed in white', the spectral White Lady in Walter Scott's *The Monastery* (1821, 235–6), who speaks verses inscribed in a family Bible that Aunt Margaret gave Janet. Also golden-haired and dressed in white are the three transfiguring androgynes in *Out of Great Tribulation* [40]. As the body dematerialises before the judgement throne, illness and infirmity hold no sway.

There are many things, therefore, that Janet and her mother could take from the allusions in *Interior*. Indeed, Gillies may well have done enough for them to infer that he, too, thought he had a place reserved in heaven, was again visualising his home as an accommodation of disparate beliefs. Persons who know much more about art than Mrs Gillies or Janet did have concluded that he, too, is occupying a room.

Gillies was aware of course that few persons who saw *Interior* would be privy to such associations, that many would view it through secular eyes, and many bring other associations to it. He must also have known that the Janet figure hinted at the erotic. The artist Ian Fleming saw *Interior* as 'Gillies Between Domesticity and Vice'. Others have jumped to the conclusion that the Janet figure is in her bedroom even though Gillies tells them and shows them it is a living room.

But the erotic is a problem only for those who think it evidence of an emotional deficit, of an adult Gillies tied to the apron strings of his mother. This misses a key point. He was, I argue, prepared to risk, indeed to invite, the erotic interpretation of the younger woman. His concern for his own, conflicted, position as artist and son is increasingly evident in the portraits and still lifes

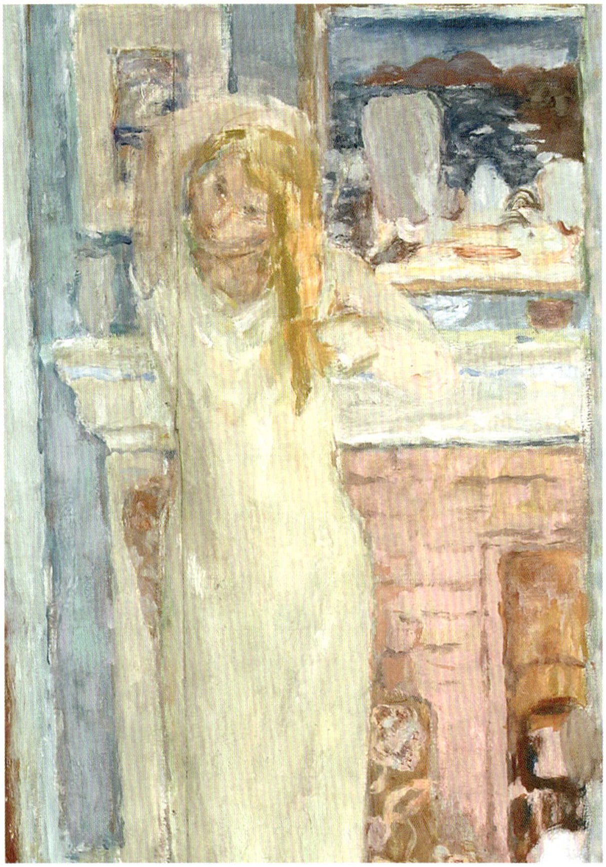

43 Detail from *Interior* (1938) [42]

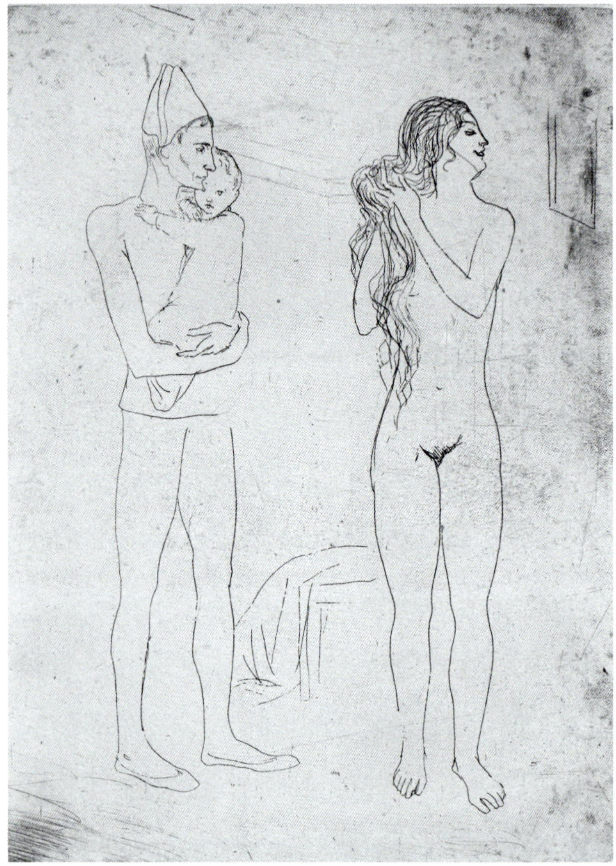

44 *La Toilette de la Mère* (1905), by Picasso. Etching, 23.5 cm by 17.8 cm

of the 1930s. *Interior* takes it further, and back to Velásquez, by making the artist's act of creation a further subject of the work.

The image of Janet [42, 43] has antecedents also in paintings and etchings that Picasso made in 1905–6. *La Toilette de la Mère* [44] appears in a book Gillies bought in Paris in 1927 (Raynal 1922). Picasso regarded such works as a way to remake a woman's image of herself and bend her to his will. He also regarded the artist's stare (the *mirada fuerte*) as synonymous both with sexual possession and with the artist's gaze. And he was passionate about *Las Meninas*. Gillies' approach to portraiture was less predatory, more empathic, honest but implicitly therapeutic, pointing his sitters towards unrealised potentials that gave hope for the future. But he does make a satyr of himself in *Interior*, or so it seems to one critic (Macmillan 1998). Gillies wanted, I suggest, to intensify the reference to the act of creation, the *mirada fuerte*.

I also think that he was not unhappy with this whisper of a satyr self. For why, with a fantasy figure, stop at one? Why not plural associations for the Janet figure, an 'apparition' like Scott's

White Lady, ambivalent and protean? And why should Gillies (whatever his sexuality) not risk the inference that he faced the prospect of caring for his mother while a partly dressed woman brushed out her hair in the next room? Her golden locks would never be mistaken for the black crop of a Margery Porter. And those who knew him would know that Janet did not look like Janet.

But let us say further that, for Gillies himself, there was indeed a Janet in the white shift, and a Janet who was in her early twenties, a spectral memory, or a reincarnation as a healthier self, such as Emma had wished in her own extremity. And let us also say that there was a time when another figure dominated the Gillies household, not the Father whose house had many mansions, nor the 'Faather' with which Emma teased Gillies once he was the oldest male, but the father who abused them. The Janet, then, that we now see in the right-hand panel is the Janet of around 1918, when she left Haddington for Edinburgh because she could no longer tolerate her father's behaviour. And Gillies portrays her at a moment of vulnerability, partially clothed in another room, absorbed, like Picasso's mistress Fernande Olivier, in her own sensuousness, but prey to the predatory gaze.

We can, if we want, acknowledge the erotic in this too. But we do not have to believe that John Gillies' abuse extended to the sexual in order to credit this reading. It is enough that Janet should appear vulnerable as Emma herself had also been. Emma sacrificed herself to make Gillies' own acts of creation possible. But Gillies had been powerless to prevent his father's abuse and had afterwards failed to grasp the full extent of the damage that had been done by his father, by his own submission, ignorance or absence, and by his pursuit of a career that, in its early stages, had extended Emma's time in the shop by up to five years.

There was not only grief to be assuaged, but guilt as well – his own guilt and perhaps his mother's too. Mrs Gillies no longer occupies the place he had given her in *Family Group* [41]. She is instead displaced to the margins and looks unknowingly out of the window, like Jess with her Thrums memories, but turned away from events in the home that she had, Gillies said, 'wonderfully' held together. He, too, is uncomfortable, in the central position once occupied by his father. In adopting his father's position, he assumes his guilt and positions himself between two flawed alternatives, the gendered modernism of Picasso and the evasions of gendered Kailyard sentimentality.

Interior [42] explores human constructions of the social world, the fictions that sustain, destroy and redeem. It is also another window on Thrums, prompted in its confessional symbolism by Munch's own confessions, and painted with an eye, not only on Bonnard and Picasso, but also on the forensic voyeur who accompanied McCance to this place in the slipstream of MacDiarmid [15].

Still Lifes of the 1930s

In Gillies' *Still Life with Portrait Postcards* (*c.* 1934) [45], the Chagall print [10] lies on the table. Above it stands the black vase but now in the place it was given in *Portrait of Jenny* [34]. A drooping poppy replaces the harebells. There are flowers, too, but erect and living, in the off-white jug on the table. They may be anemones but they could be white poppies, the symbol of the Peace Pledge Union, formed in 1934 at the time this work was painted. In 1926, the Women's Rural Institute in Haddington arranged to host members on a peace march from Edinburgh to London. In Gillies' estate is a satirical novel by the gay peace-movement activist Laurence Housman. Like John Duncan's painting [40], its title, *Trimblerigg, A Book of Revelation* (1924) also references the final, apocalyptic, book of the Bible (and finale to the novel too). The marchers in 1926 wore white, as did those who nursed Gillies in 1918–19, as did another nurse, Gillies' aunt Margaret, who had moved back to Leith from Northumbria by the time this work was painted. Red poppies are remembrances of war. White is peace, healing, nurture, virtue. Black is death. To the left and rear of the white vase is a dark pot or pots. Dark tones push lighter colours forward, enhancing the emblems and embers of life.

Poppies, and one of them white, certainly appear in *Poppies in a Yellow Vase* (1934, *c.* 1936?) [46]. So, in effect, does Gillies. Several years before *Interior* (1938) [42], he is already exploring signifiers for his own being in space-time. The work contains an image of itself, and a suggestion of further, mirrored, recessions of that image in the truncated blue rectangle in the painting on the easel. It is as though the artwork were an endless, mirrored exchange with the artist's perception of the external world, and the repetition of the image were a signifier for someone condemned by memories of war to live in a recurrent present of appearance alone.

Opposed mirrors void light and exclude the observer. The mimetic artist, the artist as mirror, cannot be or become, at least not visually. But for Gillies now, in the aftermath of Munch and Klee, art must renew light, must bring the sensory self-affirmation that Fussell (1975) describes (see opposite [7] and [8]); in Klee's terms, must put the artist back in the frame to find, or else to make for themselves, the artwork that makes sense of retinal reception. Gillies attempts this in *Interior* (1938) by relocating the mirror to his external world – the mirror now his ousted jailor, his canvas now his memory and imagination, his way to escape and become. Hyman (1994) spoke of the visionary quality of *Near Durisdeer* (*c.* 1932, *c.* 1933) [6]. Other paintings of this time such as *Still Life with Chagall Print* (1933) [10] and *Dark Tree* (1934) [55] also have this quality, going beyond mimesis and its implication that time is an infinity of static partitions where the hare never reaches the tortoise.

The existential thread in the still lifes of the 1930s is the only communality I can find among them, probably because landscape was a greater preoccupation at the time and Gillies had come to still life initially because he had been told to teach it. It is difficult to generalise, however. While there are records of fifty still lifes painted between 1925 and 1939, only twenty-seven survive as known works or images, and only fifteen images can be dated to a two-year period or less. Only five years in this period are represented by more than two works or images. No single artist or influence

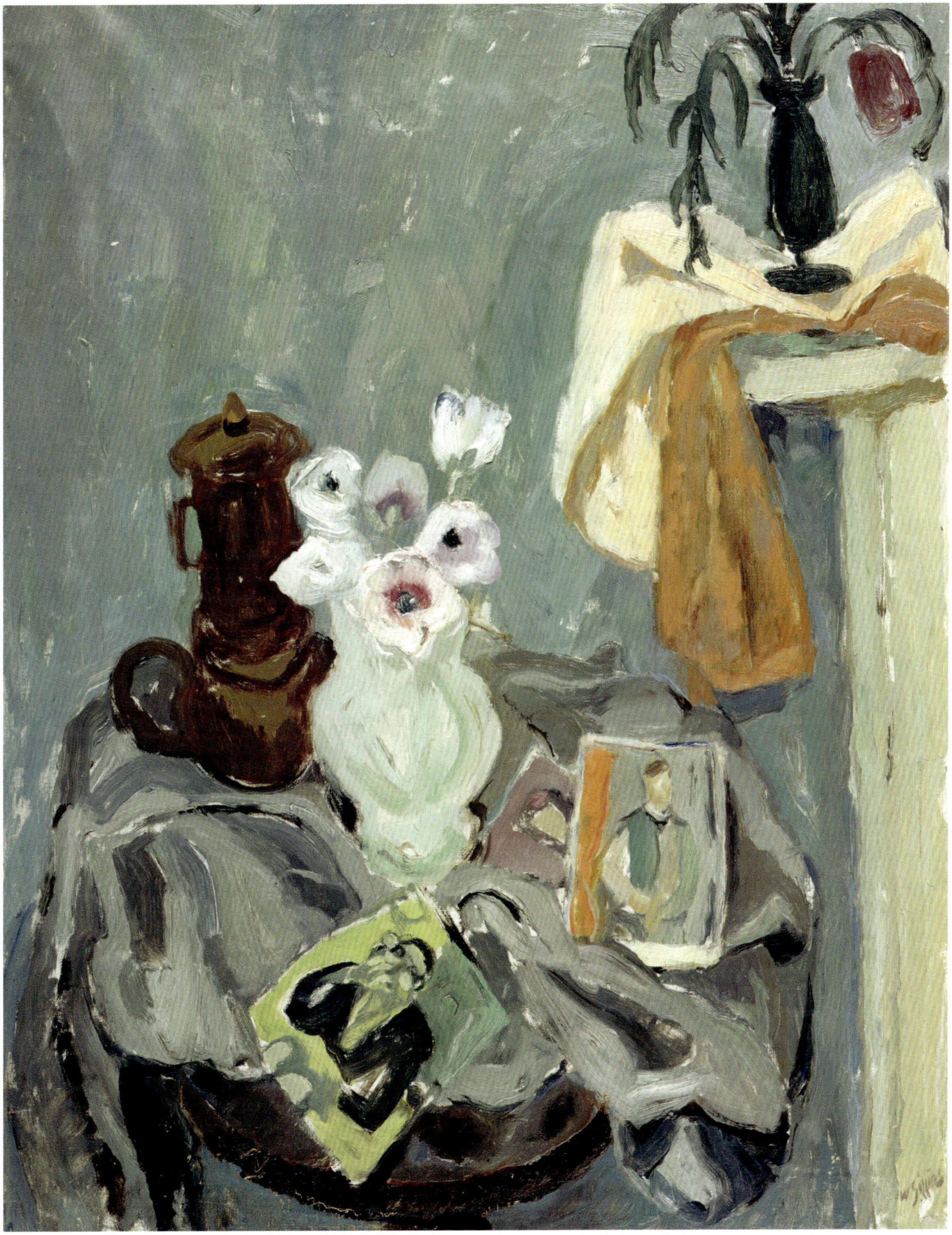

45 *Still Life with Portrait Postcards* (*c.* 1934). Oil, 82.6 cm by 65.9 cm

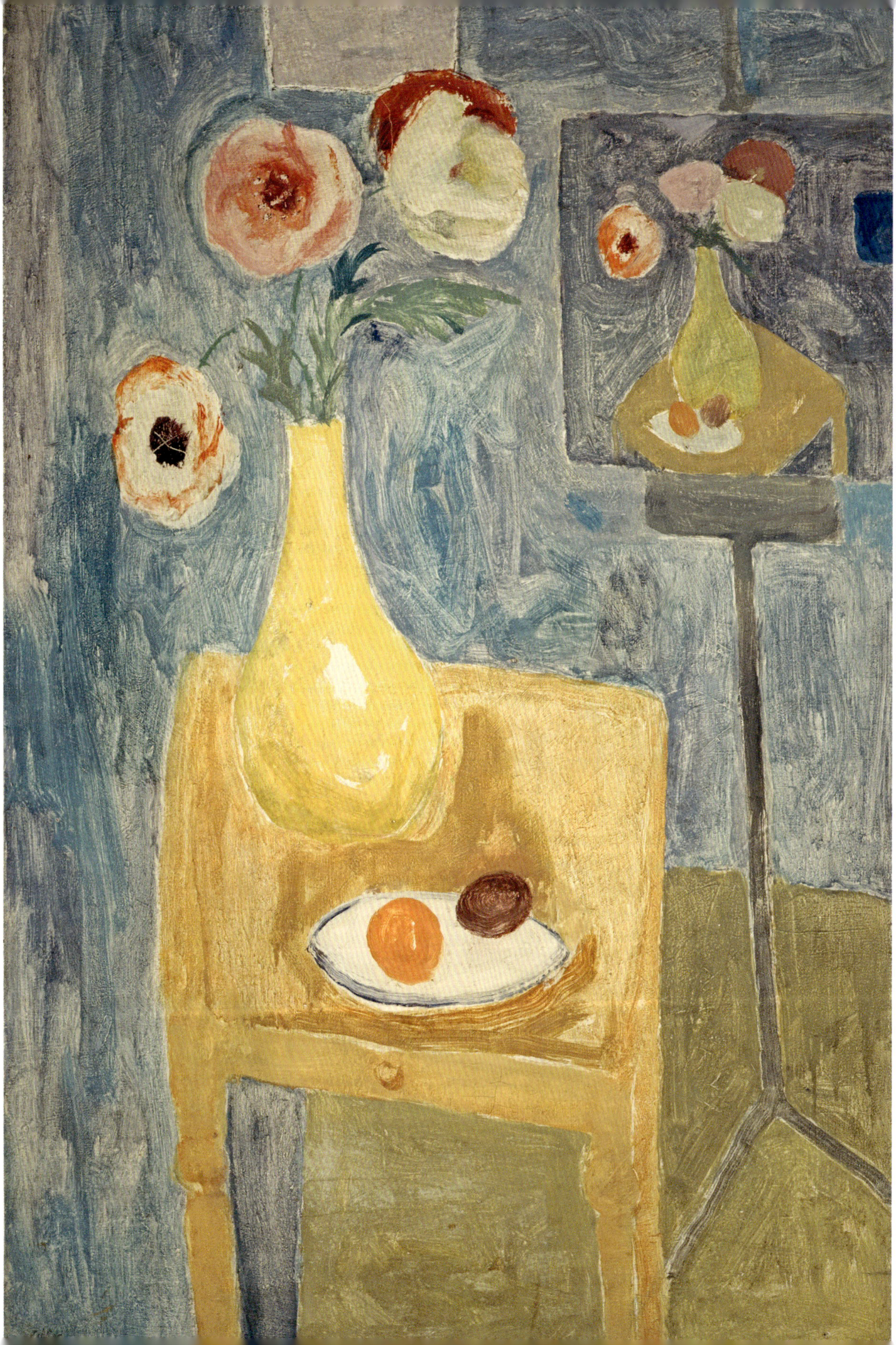

dominates and, at any one time, he paints in more than one way. *Still Life with Black Jug* (1933) [11], for example, has only one, less impressive, companion (in *Two Pots, Saucer and Fruit* (1933, *c.* 1933?) [ni]) even though the artist, Georges Braque, whose work the painting evokes, was an invited exhibitor at the SSA in 1935.

What does register, however, is the impact of the death of Emma and, more speculatively, of Crozier too. The black vase is not seen before Crozier's death but it appears also in *Still Life with Black Jug* (1933) [11] and in eight works that followed shortly after, including two prompted by the wedding of the Scottish artist Robert Heriot ('Peter') Westwater. What at first seems incongruous in a present for his colleague suggests that Gillies may initially have intended the black vase as a black armband of respect. Westwater knew Crozier and had sat to Gillies for his portrait. Gillies was close to Crozier, having spent time with him abroad. He also owed to Crozier's fate his larger studio, a shared library and, arguably, the incalculable advantage of his annual exhibitions at the Society of Eight – all occasions to acknowledge his passing.

Emma's death registers in two ways. First, he paints a small number of turbulent flower-pieces in the manner of his friend Lily McDougall. She worked in an adjacent studio (and had painted a portrait of Lady Margaret Sackville). Hitherto, virtually the only flowers Gillies had painted were secondary to the overall composition and symbolism of his still lifes. But the flowers now are the sole subject of these new paintings, filling the frame, providing the occasion for their charged brushwork and colour. Their affinity with McDougall's works, however, is not a sufficient explanation for the change, for he had known hers long before the first of his new flower paintings appeared.

Second, ceramics made or decorated by Emma begin to appear in his works, again for the first time. With its happy yellow backdrop, *Poppies and Cretonne Cloth* (*c.* 1937–40) [48] borrows from the *bonheur* of the French artist Henri Matisse. The terracotta dish is Emma's but its visual contribution is minimal. It is there solely as a memorial but is almost wholly private.

The blues of a companion piece, *Studio Interior and Red Poppies* (1939) [49], are cooler and its imagery more accessible. Gillies unmasks here, draws back a screen to reveal a truth *bonheur* conceals. The poppies stand in some disarray. One is blooming and upright. Another bends under the weight of its head and a third bends yet further. If there is a fourth, it has lost all signs of life and registers as a poppy only because it shares the vase with others.

These are, I suggest, the Gillies family in their several stages of life, and Emma, who now is lost to them. For Emma has an overt presence in the painting too. It shows a lower left-hand section of *Family Group* [41]. Emma, now three years dead, sits alone, approaching her end, a presence in their grieving. The red poppy had by now been a symbol of remembrance for two decades. In its allusions to family and war, *Studio Interior and Red Poppies* (1939) [49] marks the convergence of the two main sources of existential crisis in Gillies' life. Then, with the return of war, and time bending back on itself, he does for himself what his portraits had always tried to do for others close to him. He paints the sole, solitary *Self-Portrait* (1940) [5, p. 5, and detail on p. 76], facing down memories of the past and the prospect of exophthalmos that stares him back.

Opposite:
46 *Poppies in a Yellow Vase* (1934, *c.* 1936?). Oil, 91.5 cm by 61.5 cm

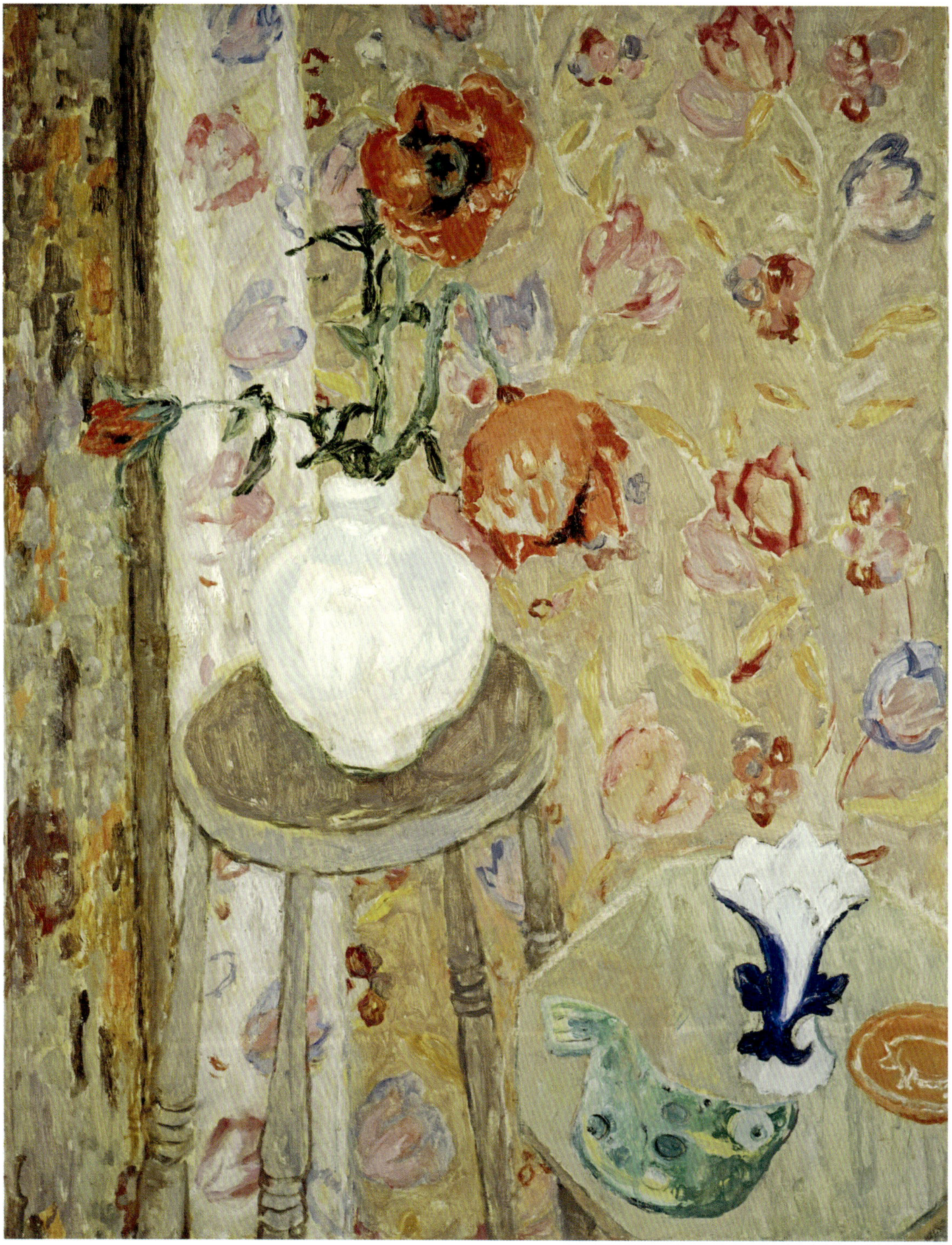

48 *Poppies and Cretonne Cloth* (*c.* 1937–40). Oil, 91.5 cm by 71 cm

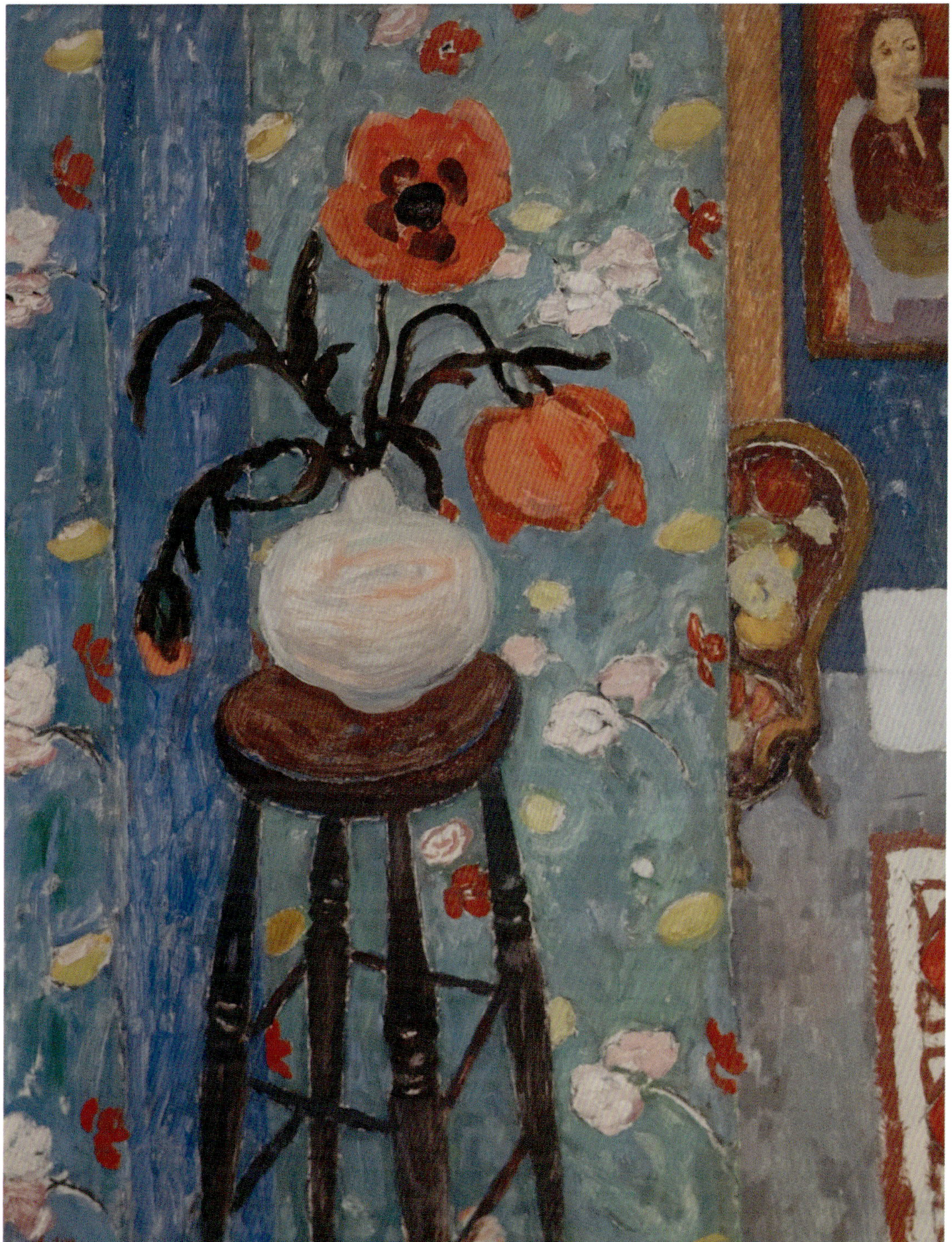

49 *Studio Interior and Red Poppies* (1939). Oil, 76 cm by 61 cm

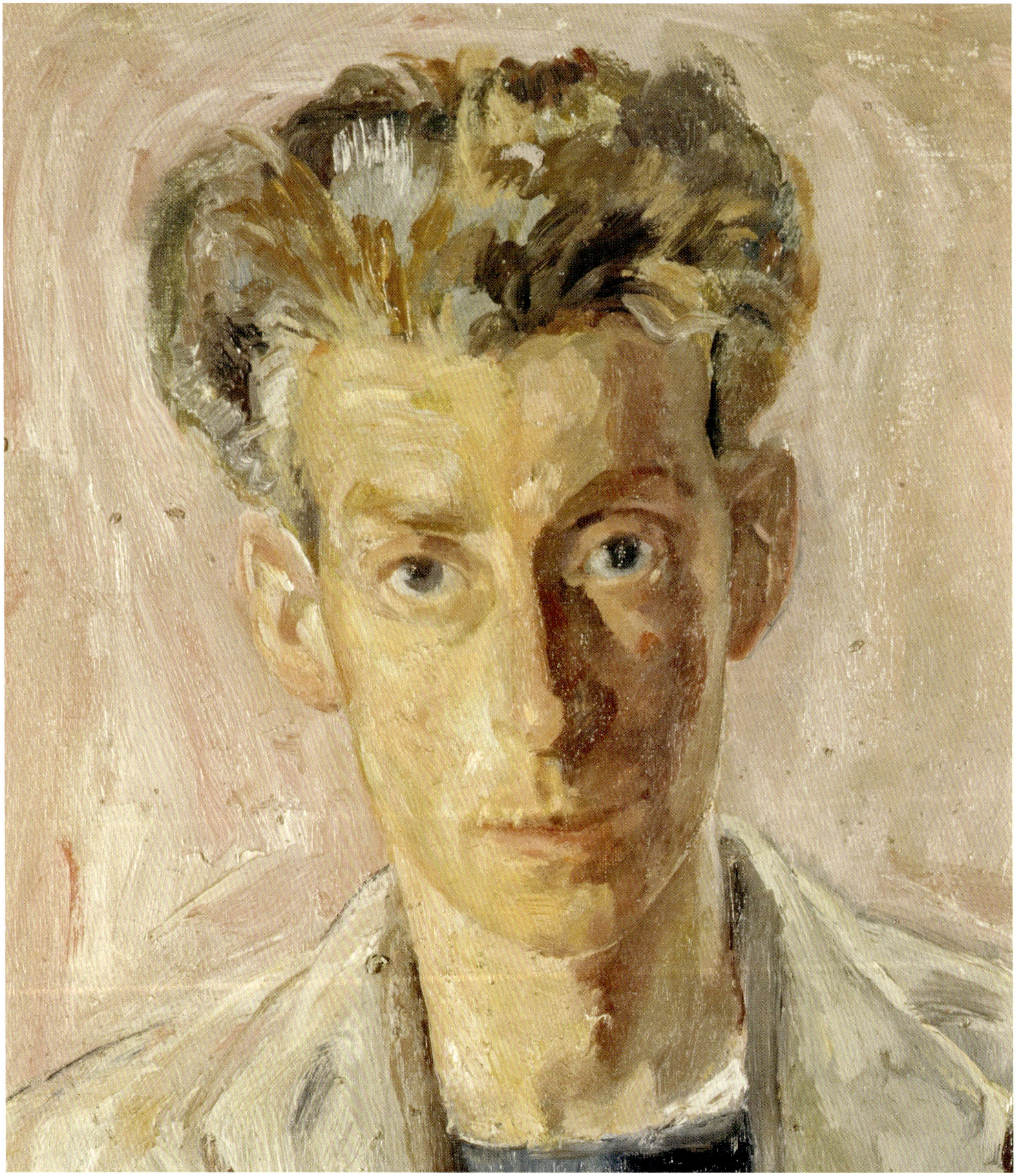

Detail from *Self-Portrait* (1940) ([5] – see p. 5)

Opposite:
Detail from Janet and Emma Gillies (right) c. 1933 ([176] – see p. 222)

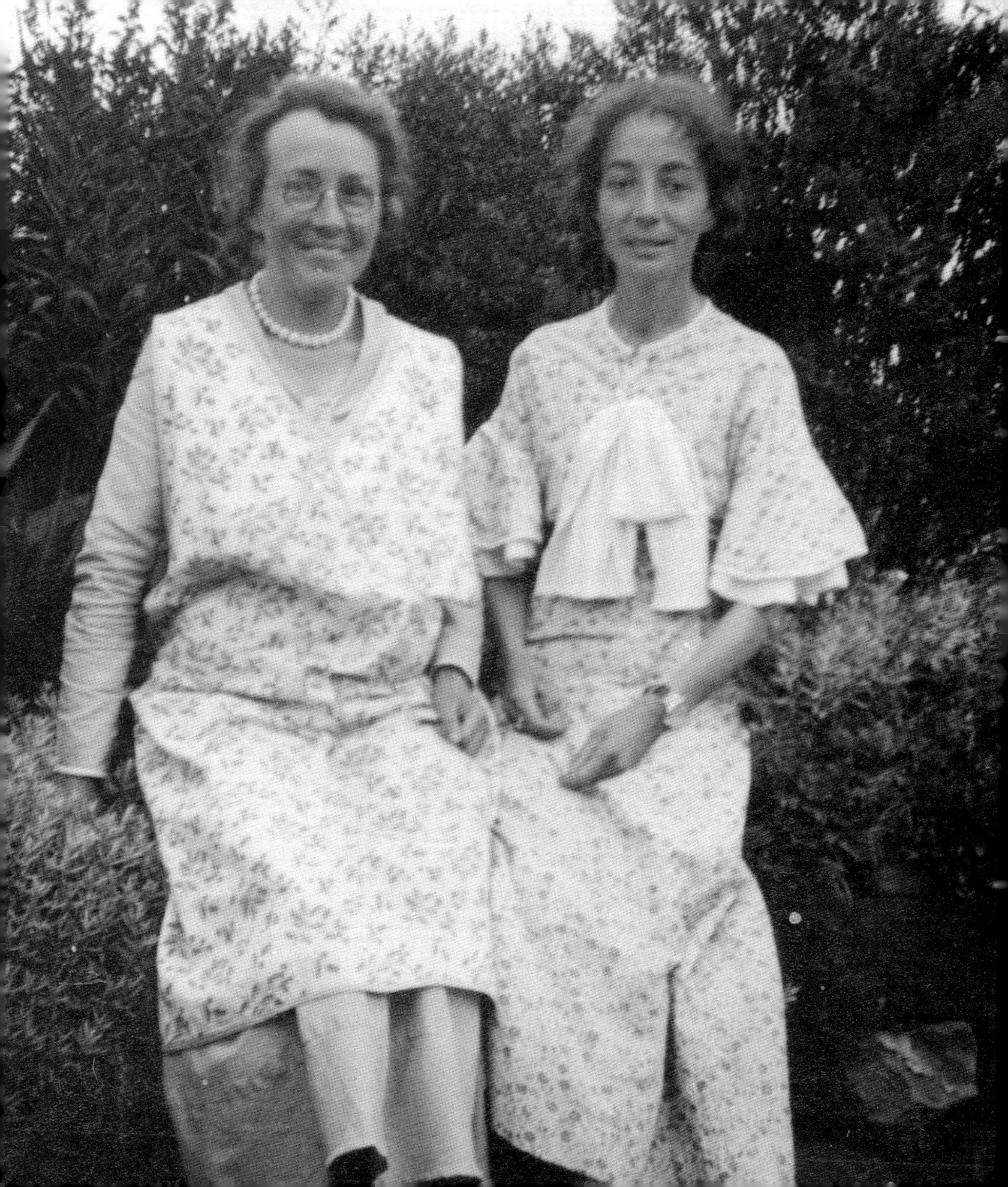

Landscapes of the 1930s

The large *Winter Landscape* (nd, *c.* 1933) [50] shown at the Society of Eight in January 1934 was probably painted in 1933. It was long known, wrongly, as 'Storm over East Lothian'. The place is immaterial, however, because it is clearly in the territory of *Near Durisdee*r [6] in its composition, brushwork, treatment of mass and sky, and use of the indeterminate – that is, of the extent to which it is open to more than one response to its mimetic elements.

These are new and challenging works. Indeed, *Winter Landscape* [50] and *Cramond* (1934) [54] stumped the critics in 1934, as did all the oil landscapes Gillies showed that year at the Society of Eight. His texture and colour were 'thick, massed and seemingly unrelated and perverse'; in several works, there was a 'lack of design, of any coherence in any parts of the painting'; and his forms were 'notable for their extraordinary fluidity, a sense of imminent disintegration into their component atoms'.

What was going on here? It was not Munch, at least not on the canvas. Munch never painted like this, nor did any contemporary of Gillies I know. Munch sent only four landscapes in 1931–2 and they were tame affairs. One presence in *Winter Landscape* [50] is Derain, seen here in the massing of forms. Another, especially in the lighting, may be the watercolour landscapes of two English early Romantic artists, Samuel Palmer, whom Gillies is later known to have rated, and John Cotman. Beyond that, the only help we have is Gillies himself.

Around 1960, Elder Dickson put it to Gillies that his style had at one time been 'loose', and asked him when he first felt 'the need for more definite formal organisation'. Gillies found this 'an impossible one': 'I have realised all the time the need for definite formal organisation but sometimes it is disguised by loose handling. It depends on what is to be expressed.' Elder Dickson never used this answer in any of his writings on Gillies. The idea of a critically aware Gillies conflicted with his thesis of obsession, of a wayward young countryman in the grip of non-native exemplars until he returned in 1939 to the countryside south of Edinburgh as 'an animal returns to its drinking place' (Elder Dickson's words).

All is not lost, however, for Gillies also shows us the truth of his reply. Latent in *Near Durisdeer* [6] and *Winter Landscape* [50] is a form of organisation he would soon make his own when taking liberties with mimesis: three or more horizontal strips that could variously correspond, as the need arose, to foreground, middle distance, far distance and sky. These provide a structure within which indeterminate combinations of mimetic elements can work their effects.

In *Winter Landscape* [50] we do not know where we are, except perhaps in a war zone. The perspective does recede but it is not clear where or by how much. This effect is achieved by colour, by the assumptions about light that come with colour, tone and contrast, and by the effect of these on the interpretation of forms. The lighting is English early Romantic, the yellows and creams of the immediate foreground brightened by the storm-drenched sky.

But is that the immediate foreground? Conventional perspective changes tonally as it recedes but here the relation between tone and perspective is disrupted by the lighting. The middle distance is pushed towards us by the darker tones that outline it. Detail should diminish with

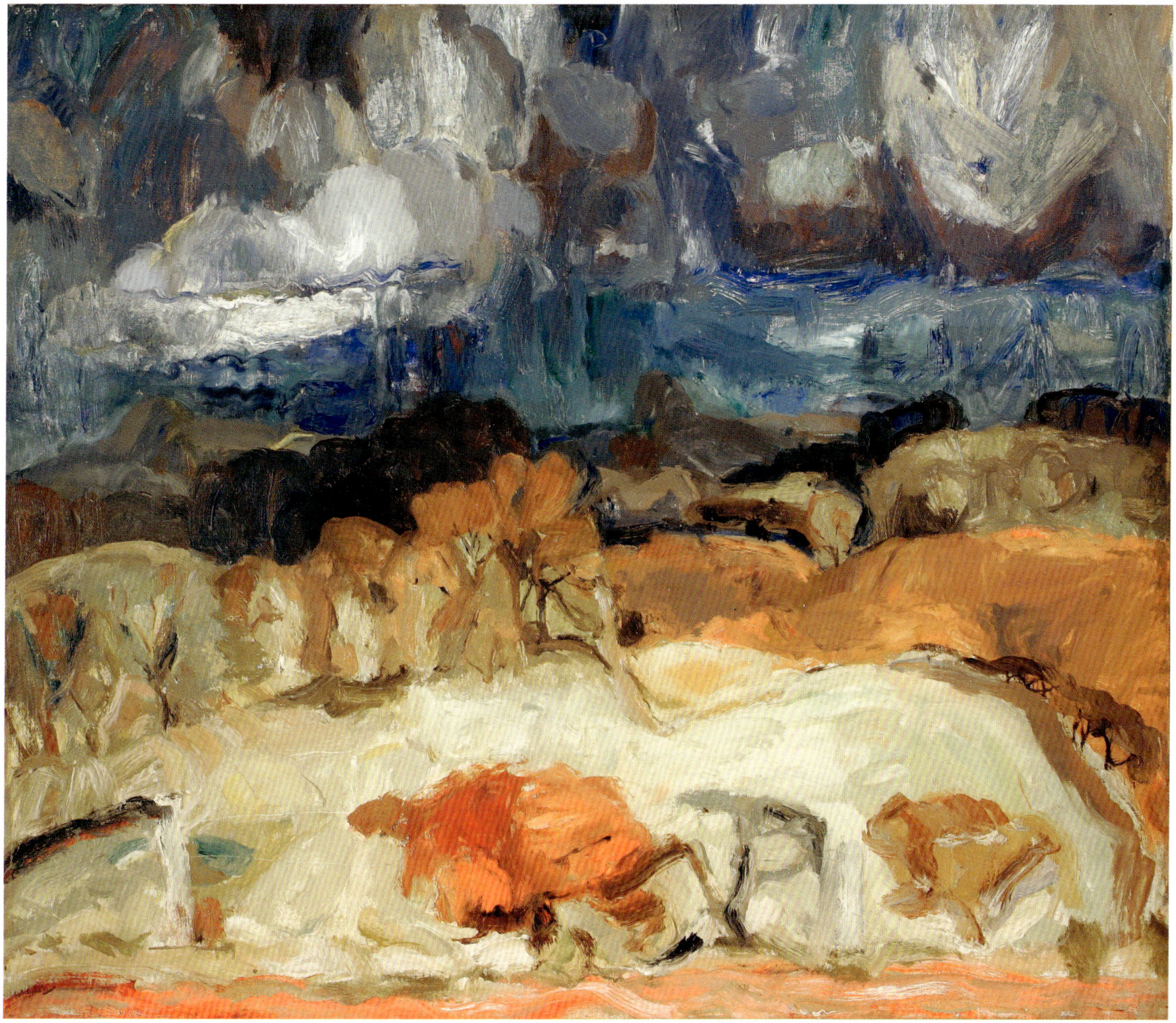

50 *Winter Landscape* (nd, *c.* 1933). Oil, 85 cm by 101 cm

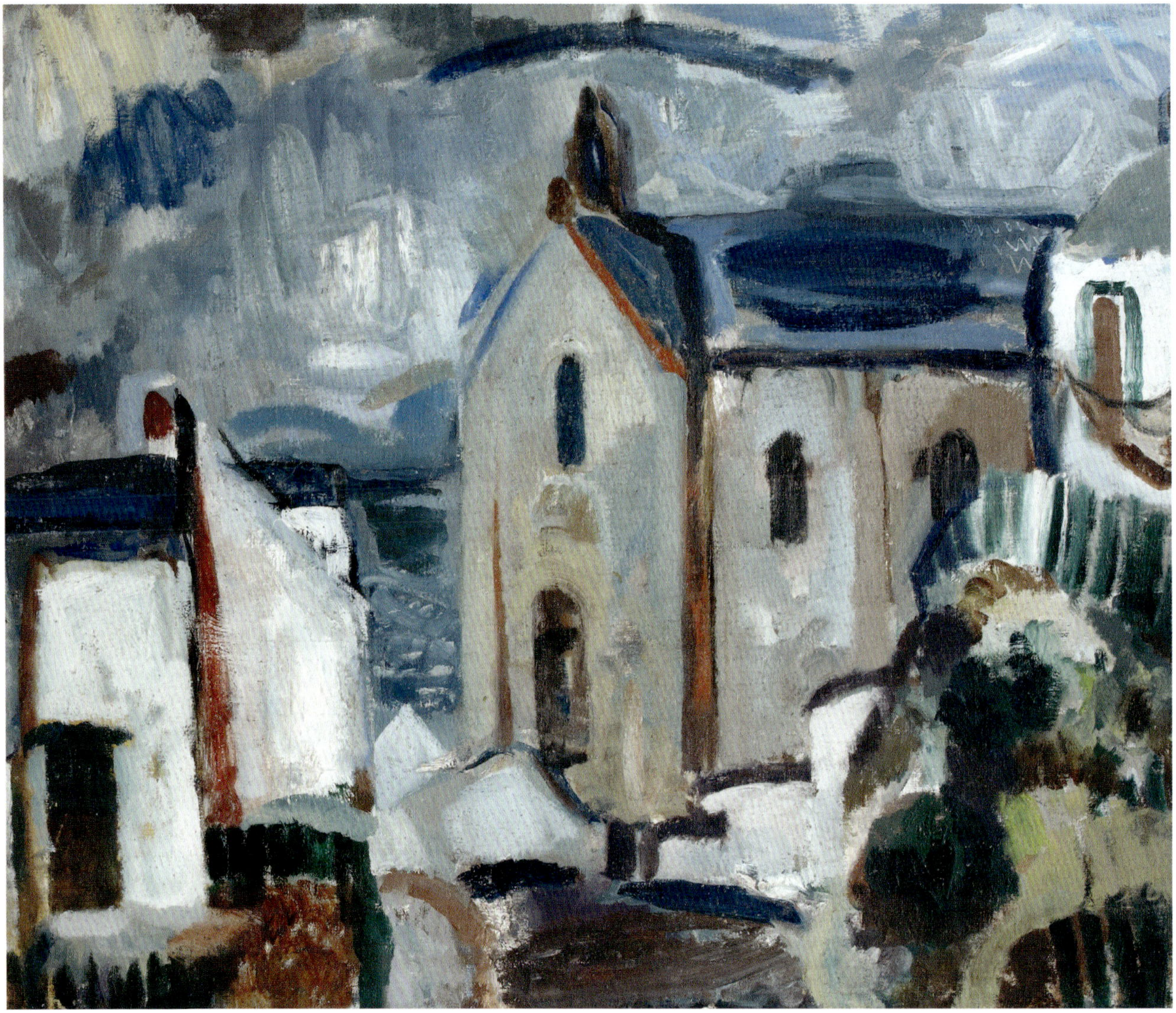

51 *Gardenstown* (*c.* 1932, *c.* 1930–2). Oil, 76 cm by 90.8 cm

recession, but what are those things ranged across the bottom? Colour tells us that two might be trees, sharing their reddish hues with the clearer-formed trees on what may be a bluff above. If so, their trunks are obscured by a closer foreground, indicated by the pinkish strip across the base of the work, and we must be overlooking them from a higher viewpoint; very much higher, it seems, if that is a second row of trees starting near the bottom right-hand side and curving in towards the apparent bluff following a brown strip that might either be a path or a delineation of an extended contour of a bluff. If the second row were a hedge, however, the reading of contour,

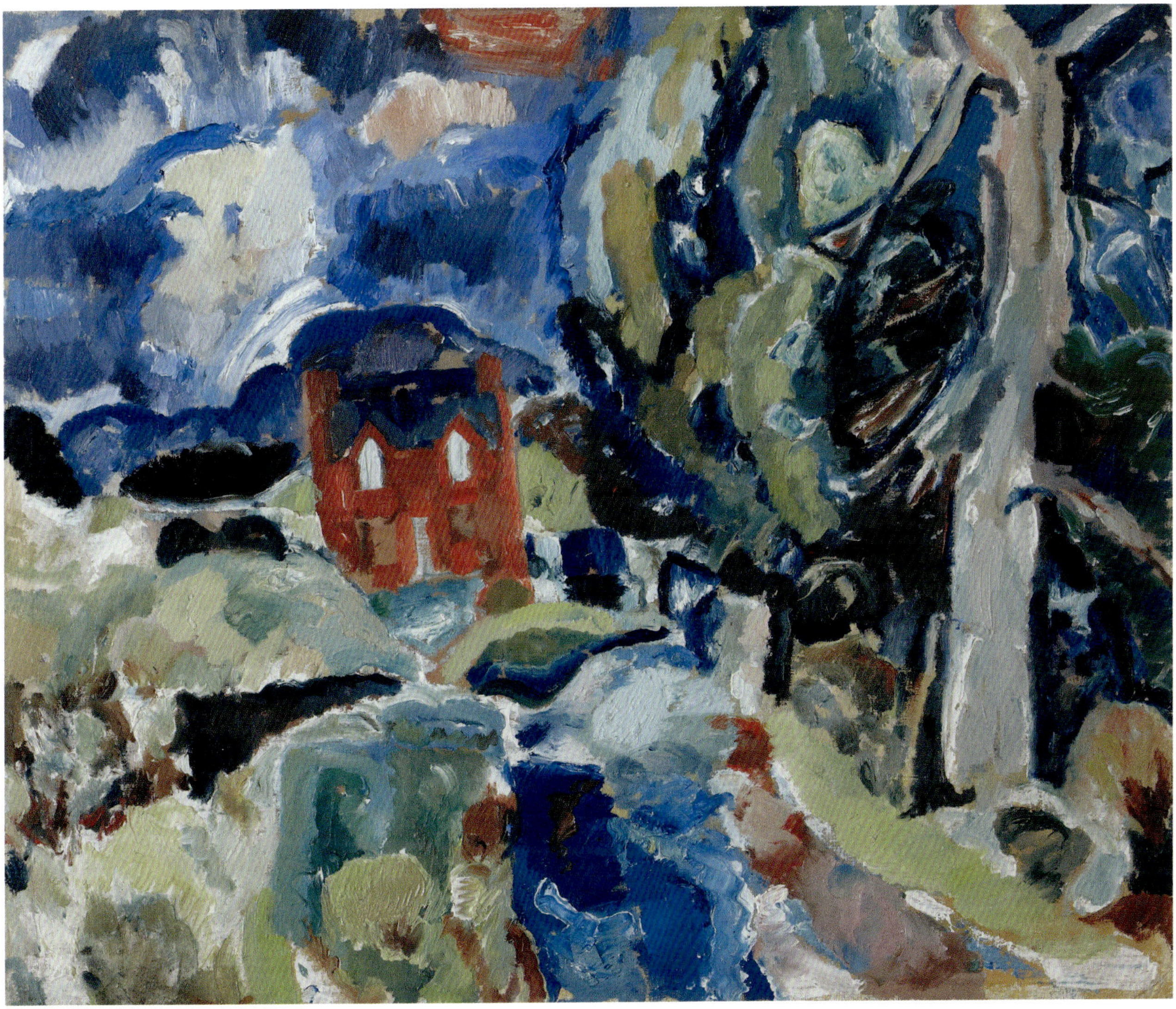

52 *The Red House, Durisdeer* (*c.* 1934). Oil, 76.7 cm by 90.2 cm

perspective and form is changed and a further incidence of indeterminacy is encountered. Earth and variegated sky jointly elicit apprehension of form and attribution of meaning.

This is typical Gillies, and the critics were superficially right. But what they did not see was that indeterminacy was also a tool. For Gillies, indeterminacy became a means of seeing beyond, of finding alternative potentials in a world in which he would otherwise be trapped by the continuous presence of the past. In *Winter Landscape*, we again see Benjamin's force field of 'destructive torrents and explosions'. But we also see Gillies turning to advantage that anxiety, over the logic of light

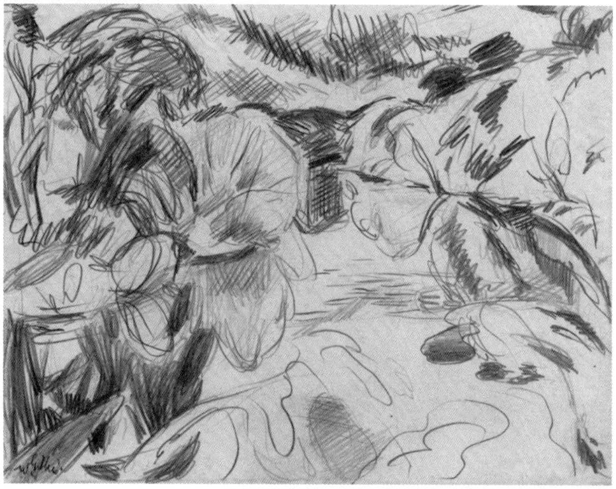

53 *River at Cramond* (nd, *c.* 1933). Pencil, 17.7 cm by 22.7 cm

and colour, that every forward infantryman has felt when trying to read the forms of an uncertain landscape at that moment of greatest danger and heightened perception, when dawn returns light to No Man's Land and the Stand To Arms sounds.

Our Post Behind Our Wire (1918) [8] tells us that Gillies knew such moments. Oddly, we have both posts and wire at the base of *Winter Landscape* [50]. We recognise these, not because they can be read unaided but because he has, unusually and perhaps unintentionally, given the game away in this case by drawing the handle of his brush horizontally through the wet paint. A barely visible line connects what become two posts, making a wire fence of them and the scraggy remnants of a hedge, not trees, out of the other forms. Thus, a single gesture can transform the reading of a work, but only if it is not over-determined.

Gillies' use of indeterminacy is a visual equivalent to what the English early Romantic poets knew as 'negative capability', an ability to relax everyday parameters of perception and cognition and thereby to open oneself to experiences that lie beyond. In *Winter Landscape* [50] the truth is in its initial impact, not the sense of a place or a *genius loci*, but a cosmological vision of a world shaken out of normal parameters of experience by something that permeates earth and sky alike.

The same alliance of permeating force with attention to formal organisation is clear in works like *Gardenstown* (*c.* 1932, *c.* 1930–2) [51] and Untitled View of the Cleish Hills (nd, *c.* 1932) [83]. *Cramond* (1934; nd, *c.* 1933) [54] has a prior drawing [53], and *The Red House, Durisdeer* (*c.* 1934) [52] and *Dark Tree* (1934) [55] have companion watercolours [ni]. Indeed, a number of oils of this period, 'loose' or otherwise, are studied replicas of watercolours. This is not an expressionism of obsession or of splashing paint about.

In January 1934, the Mayor Gallery in London showed twenty-five works by the Swiss artist Paul Klee. Under an arrangement broached two years earlier by William MacTaggart and Herbert Read, the works then came in December 1934 to the annual exhibition of the SSA. Norman Reid always remembered Gillies' delight on seeing them in Edinburgh. Work by Gillies and his former student John Maxwell was shown in the same room. So, too, was that of another student, Margaret Mellis, flanked by Picasso and Derain. Downstairs, Reid himself and William Gear were hung with Matisse, Dalí and Picasso again. To involve students in this way, to introduce modernism by means of example and shared activity, was typical of younger artists like MacTaggart who now controlled the exhibitions of the SSA.

Around this time, Gillies and Maxwell painted half a dozen works in response to Klee. But

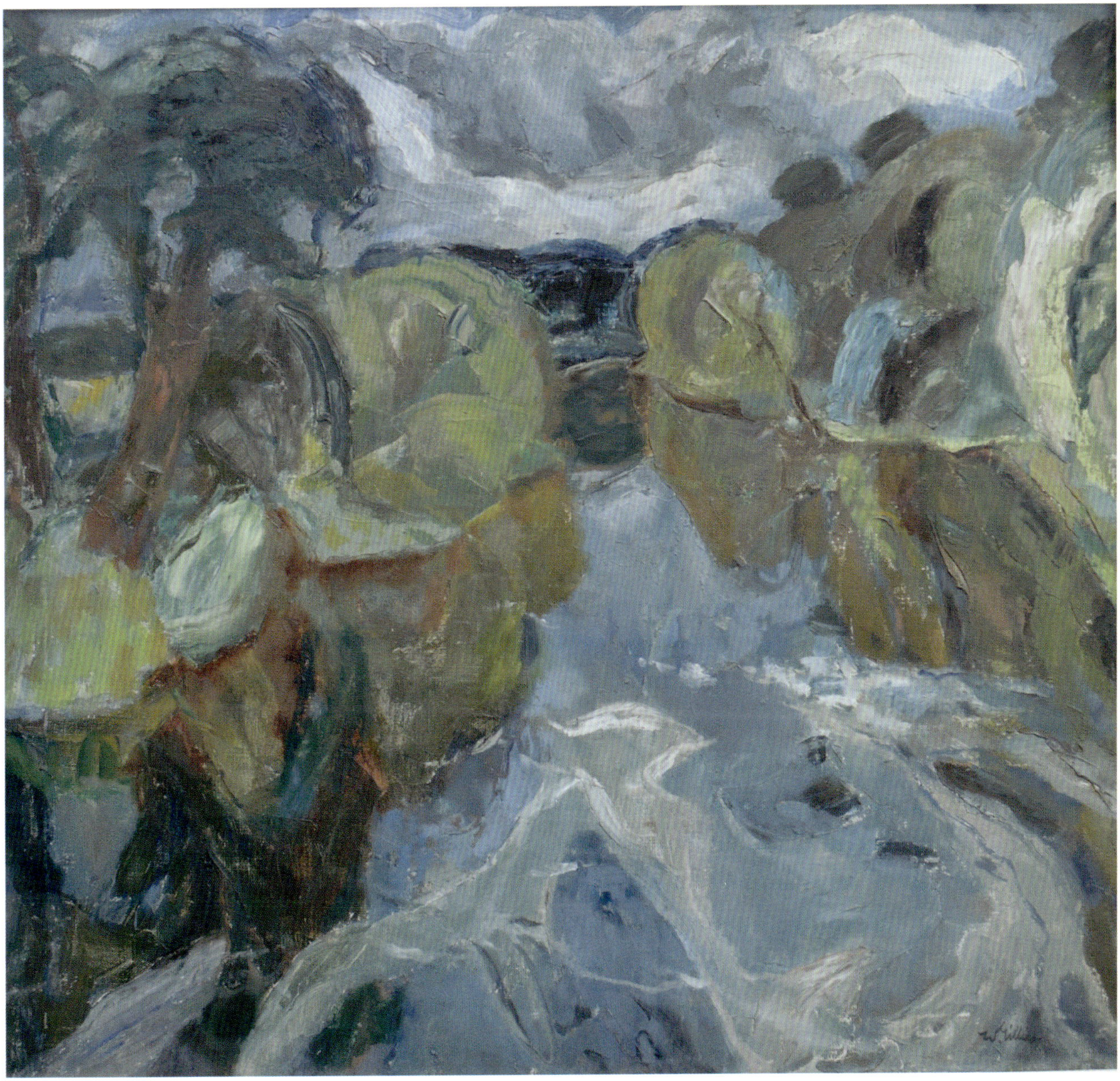

54 *Cramond* (1934; nd, *c.* 1933). Oil, 71 cm by 76 cm

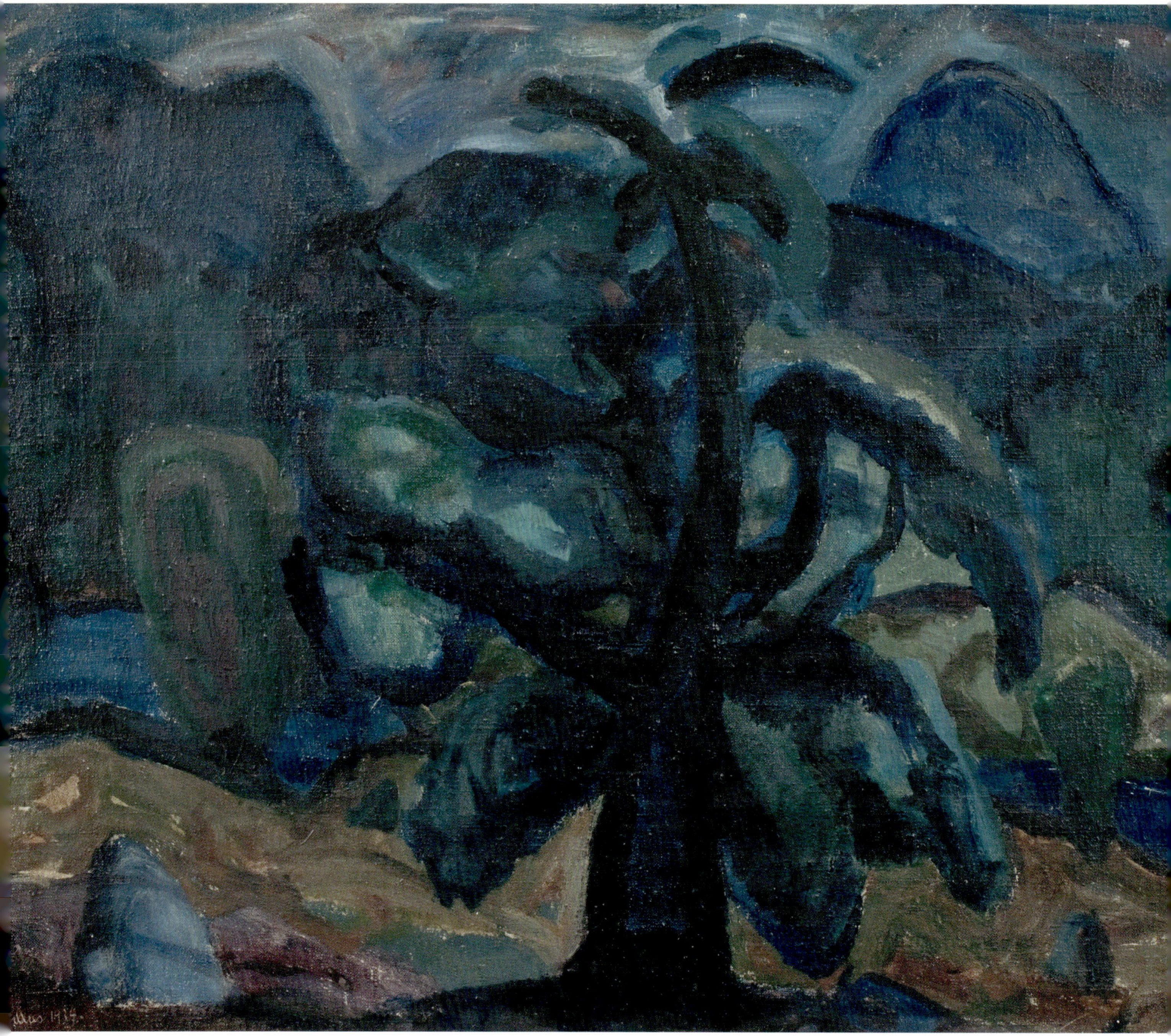

55 *Dark Tree* (1934). Oil, 61 cm by 76.5 cm

Gillies' interest almost certainly pre-dated the Edinburgh exhibition, possibly by years. Among Klee's exhibits, there is at first sight no obvious precursor to Gillies' large *Harbour* (1934, *c.* 1934) [58 and 64], shown at the Society of Eight only weeks after the Klee opening. But it has a lineage in Klee's *Reisebild[nis]* (1918), reproduced here from a book Gillies owned, published in 1920 [56]. Also in the book is Klee's *Kairuan* (1914) [61], a possible precursor to Gillies' *Skye Hills from [near] Morar* (*c.* 1931) [62]. These works of Gillies are neither pastiche nor those of an artist gripped by a single obsession, whether with Cubism, Munch or Klee. But they are part of an evolving understanding of idiom and of how pictures work.

Klee partitions *Kairuan* [61] and similar works from Tunisia into a grid brushed through mostly in light washes. Typically, only a minority of the rectangles contain anything approximating figuration, so the eye is left to interpolate instinctively across the indeterminate and empty areas. In *Skye Hills from [near] Morar* (*c.* 1931) [62], Gillies adapts this device to convey the passing quality of light under a changing sky. What shimmers in Kairuan is broken by clouds in Morar. Indeterminacy and mimetic suggestion combine to elicit that important first response.

They also open the interpolating eye to the interdependence of signifiers and context. Wavy lines, or even just repeated strokes, that in one area signify form and rock become form and aqueous ripple in another area, and form and vaporous sky in a third. Later, *Rocks and Sea* (*c.* 1935) [72] would take Gillies further towards a kind of abstraction in which mark-making and colour predominate. In such cases, mimesis is reduced to multi-referential ciphers whose unity of colour and form can now contribute a new dimension of rhythm and association in their own right no matter where they are contextualised in pictorial space.

These works of the mid-1930s engage with another of modernism's core concerns, the instability and sources of meaning itself. Meaning was not exhausted by Plato's essence of a thing like a carnation, or by its associations, or by signifiers like wavy lines. Signification also depended on context (in the case of landscape, the sky, sea, land, far distance and so on). And how was context to be indicated, if not by its contents or by its association with other contexts (for example, sky on top of sea on top of land)? The question threatened a fruitless regress, again into a place where all light disappeared.

By way of an answer, *In Arniston* (1935) [60] brings *Kairuan* [61] north, to the county of Midlothian. It can be read as a search for the lowest common denominator among colour, gesture and form to which figuration can be reduced but still yield an image that can signify or move – as a way of showing what is lost or gained at the point where mimesis first registers or vanishes. *In Arniston* [60] becomes a landscape only when the positioning of the blue triangular area, with its title on white, prompts the eye to see it as sky and cloud and, by extension, to see the other areas of colour as landscape elements.

Unlike the wire in *Winter Landscape* [50], however, the position of this blue area is clearly intended. Since painting *Winter Landscape*, Gillies had seen, certainly in Edinburgh at the SSA in 1934, but perhaps earlier that year in London too, an exhibit of Klee's that uses a similar device to similar effect. *Drohender Schneesturm* (1927) [63] (*Approaching* or *Threatening Snowstorm*) attracted adverse attention in both cities. The mystified

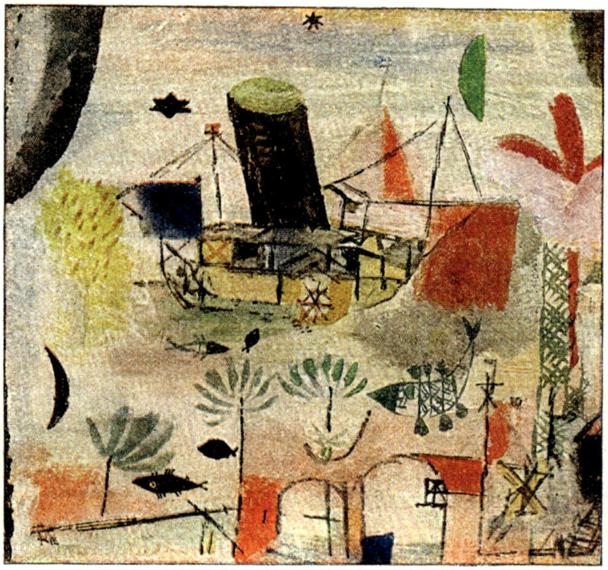

56 *Reisebild[nis]* (1918), by Paul Klee (1918, 150). Watercolour, dimensions unknown. From an image owned by Gillies

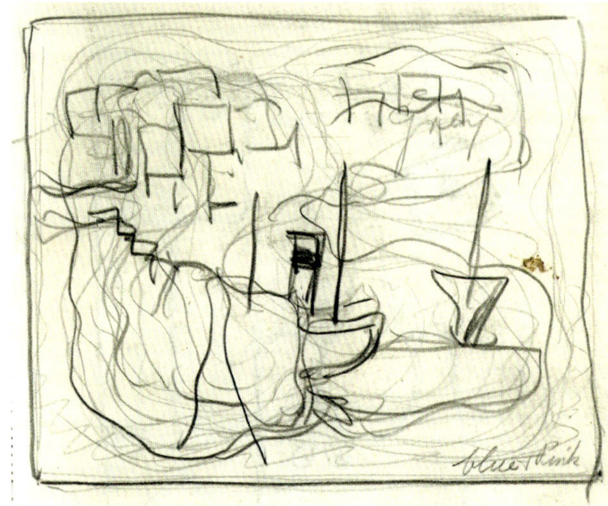

57 Sketch for *Harbour* (1934, *c.* 1934) [58 and 64 below] (*c.* 1934). Pencil, 9 cm by 12 cm

critic of *The Times* likened its overlapping quadrilaterals to aerial photos of prehistoric cultivation. Writing in *The Scotsman*, Gillies' former teacher, David Foggie, talked about square snowflakes. He was no less derisive on finding they were a town. A town or city is still a received interpretation. But a reluctance to suspend mimetic expectation misses much of what this work could show Gillies of Klee's radical reformulation of colour, line, form and perspective as reflexive creations of being in a world of space-time – of being in a world that could be represented, but never fully apprehended, by units of measurement that are static and discrete.

The 'circumflex' line (^) that tops the drawing presents mimetically as the apex of a pitched roof and thereby shows the power of a single sign (or is it figuration, or both?) to animate a construction with meaning. The blue triangular area of *In Arniston* [60] does this too. But *Drohender Schneesturm* [63] goes further. It explores the source of this effect by asking how one would experience the world if the visual component of perception (the 'circumflex' line) were detached from the conceptual (the noun, 'roof', and its predicate, 'pitched'). This question in turn invokes the 'prior' parameters of experience proposed by the philosopher Immanuel Kant, in particular, the human capacity to individuate the self in space, time and agency from retinal and other sensory experience and to articulate sensory reception with ideas when reaching judgements about (as distinct from 'knowledge of') the external world and how to act in it.

There is no single context or orientation from which Klee's line-drawing can be read consistently

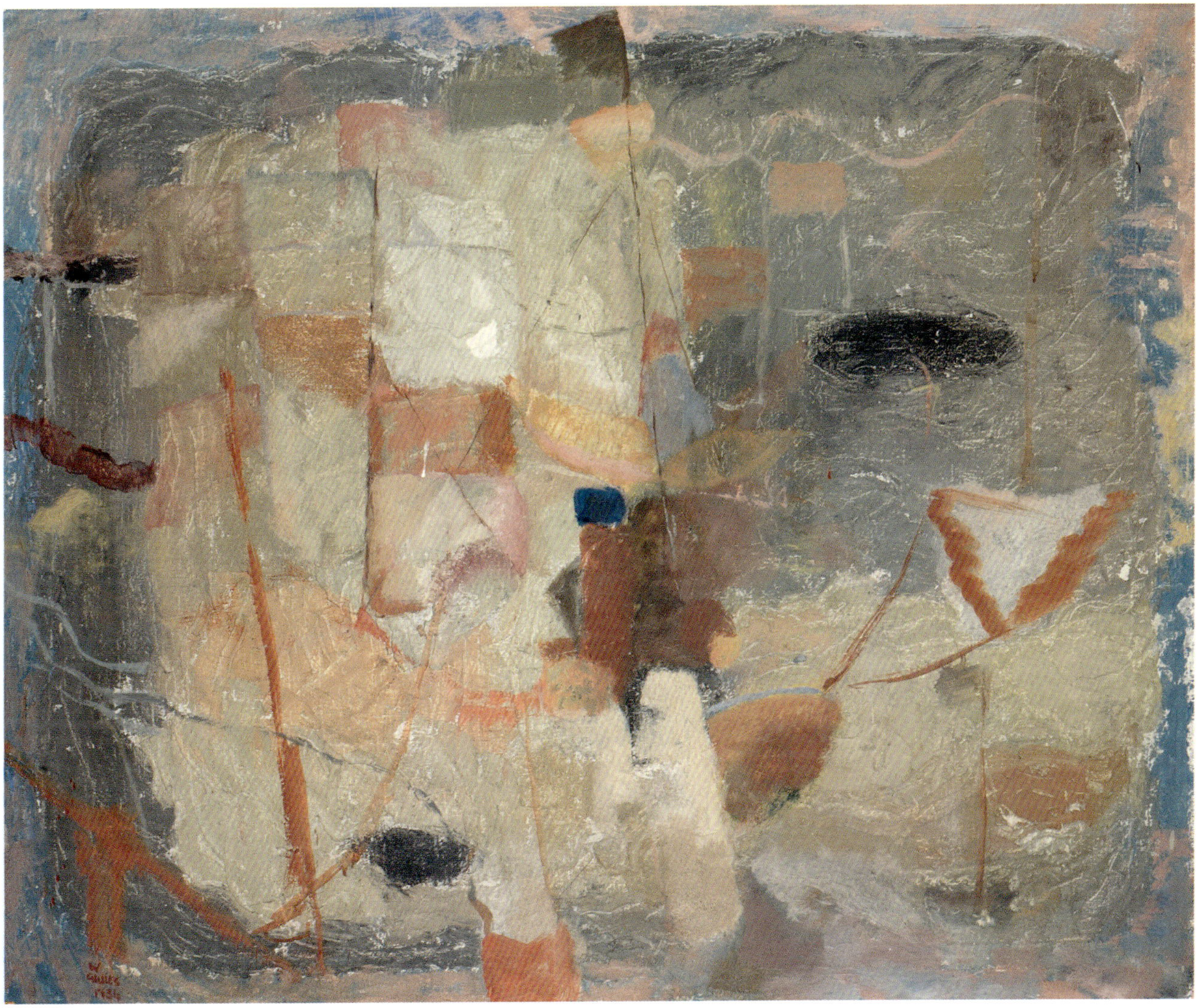

58 *Harbour* (1934, *c.* 1934). Oil, 83.8 cm by 101.6 cm

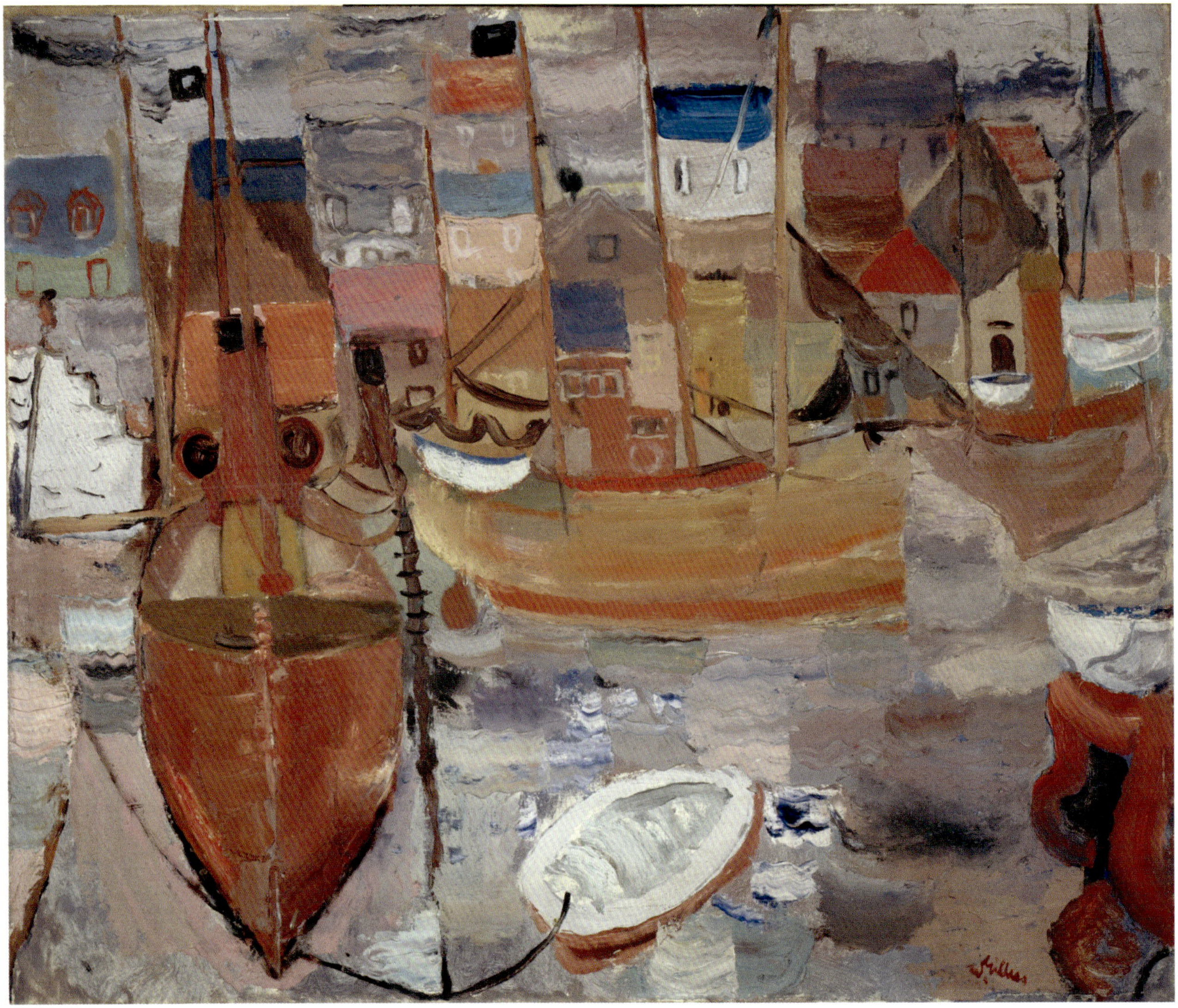

59 *The Harbour* (*c.* 1934–7). Oil, 76.5 cm by 91.5 cm

in mimetic terms. It is not wholly the architect's elevation implied by an apex, or a ground plan (which would deny the apex), or a set of exploded cross-sections of three-dimensional buildings, or an instance of perspectival recession from a single point of convergence, or anything else. And enough of its horizontals and verticals depart from their 'true' orientations, as fixed by its paper and framing, to keep our mind and eye open and uncertain. (Indeed, on first seeing the original, a recent acquaintance, with an experienced eye but no knowledge of Foggie's jibe, surprised me with their view that the entire construction was itself accelerating towards them.)

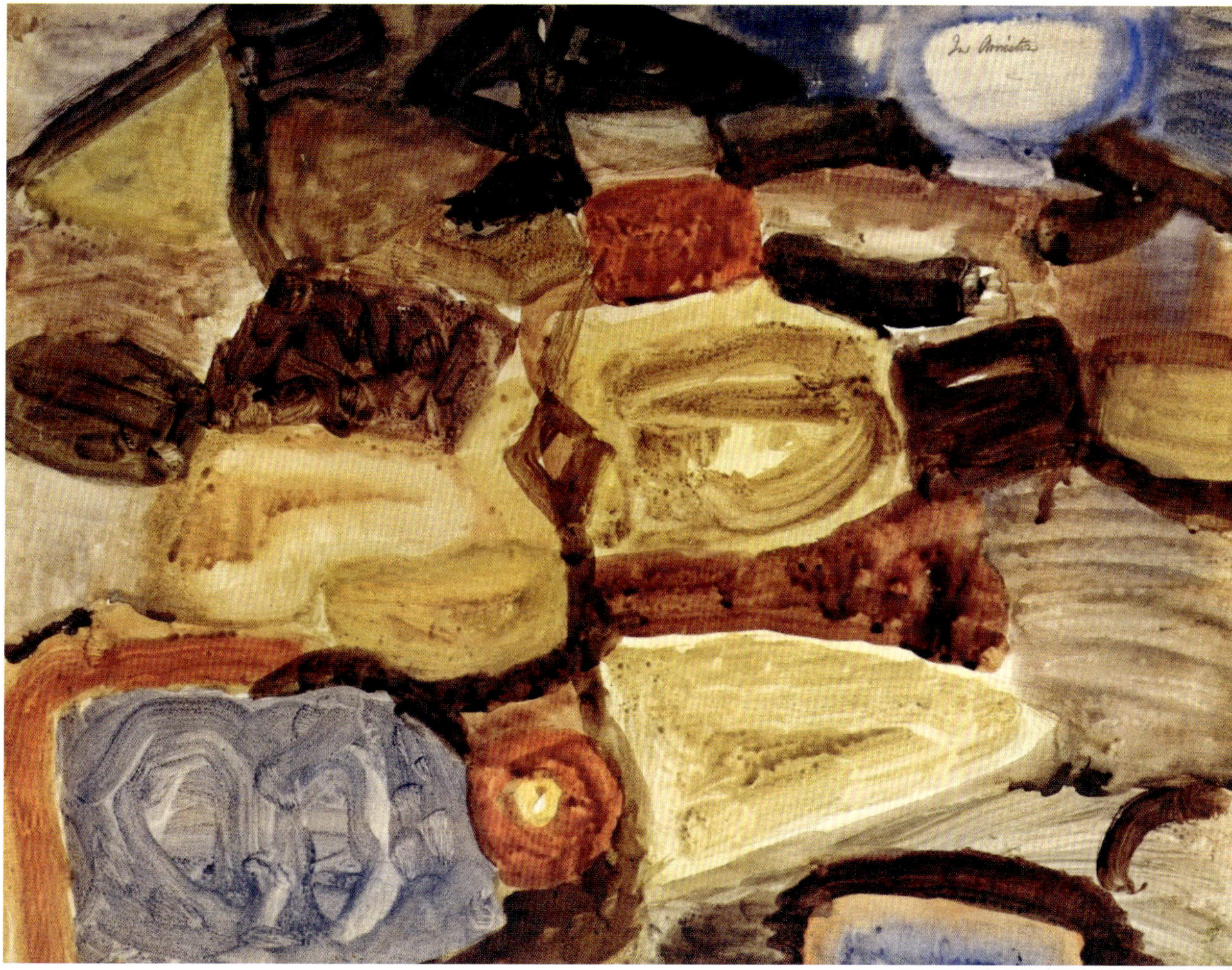

60 *In Arniston* (1935). Watercolour, 48 cm by 62 cm

So why is one so persuaded by the 'town'? A necessary part of the answer, paradoxically, lies in a title that mentions the storm but not the town. It tells us how we must individuate our 'self' in and from the retinal in order to see the apex as apex. We are 'outside' and looking at an elevation, outside but not airborne and looking down at a ground plan or prehistoric fields. It is the idea of the approach of the storm that enables us to see the drawing as a town, not a town that tells us that something here is a snowstorm. Indeed, nothing here presents as such.

Klee is also clear that this logic applies to the artwork but not to the real world. In the artwork, the idea of a town is sufficient for us to see the drawing as a town. Uncertainties are allayed by associations of linearity with the urban. Association trumps judgement. In real-world

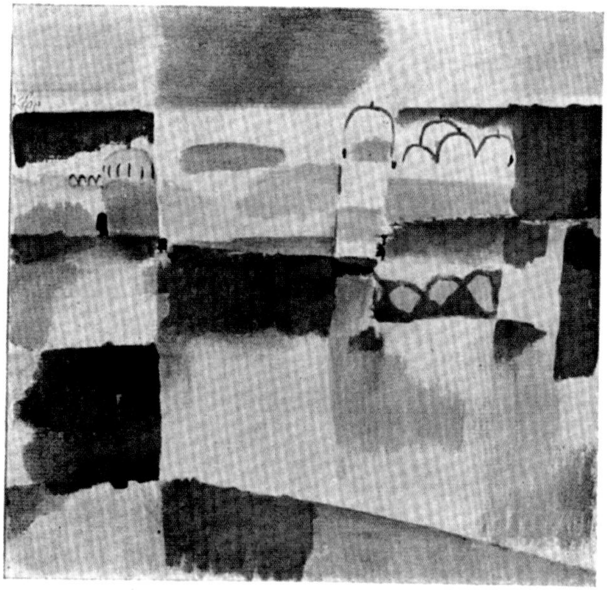

61 *Kairuan* (1914), by Paul Klee (1914, 38). Watercolour, 22 cm by 23 cm. From an image owned by Gillies

judgements, the idea of 'town', though vibrant with associations, is insufficient. 'Approaching' or 'Threatening' implies space and time, but there is no tonality in the work that indicates the planes, volumes and recessions through which we experience space-time. For this we need light, the light that brings tone, reflects off surface, refracts into colour, affirms the ideas of town and snow experientially. No matter how suggestive the quadrilaterals of the artwork or denotative its title, one cannot, in the real world, experience form as an individuation of something from nothing.

The snowstorm comes from the title and as an idea alone, not from our retinal reception of the artwork. By blowing flecks of red and blue in varying densities and degrees of overlap across the white paper support, Klee creates the impression of an emerging light with potential for tonal variation and colour – hovering, one might say, just beyond the edge of (re-)cognition. (The effect is more nuanced in the original and tends to be differently experienced, both from one individual to the next, and according to viewpoint and the area of the work itself. In print and digital reproduction, however, a merging of the flecks into grey is sooner and more commonly experienced as distance from the image increases.) Wherever or whatever this snowstorm is in the work, it is unrelated to the line drawing and has no form or identity, either of its own or in any effect on, or by, the town. It could be everywhere, somewhere or nowhere.

In the real-world situation implied by this artwork analogue, the retinal receptors would not yet have found an idea around which form and associations could be perceived. Similarly, if and when a snowstorm, or darkness for that matter, enveloped the person, retinal reception would be blanked and real-time perception of a town converted into a construct articulated by ideas, associations and memories of perception.

In Klee's snowy north in 1927 (*Drohender Schneesturm*), urban associations were linear. In the shimmering light of Tunisia in 1914 (*Kairuan* [61]), the distinctive remembered forms were not the apex but the curves that top Arab arches and domes. In the half-light of a Flanders dawn in 1918 (*Our Post Behind Our Wire* [8]), every scrap of retinal data, pregnant with possibility, would be measured anxiously against idea and enemy. As a matter of life or death, *a priori* capacities to judge space, time, causality and agency would be called into question – capacities that almost no one but philosophers, physicists and some psychologists had thought to analyse formally since the Edinburgh philosopher David Hume had persuaded Kant that observation alone could not

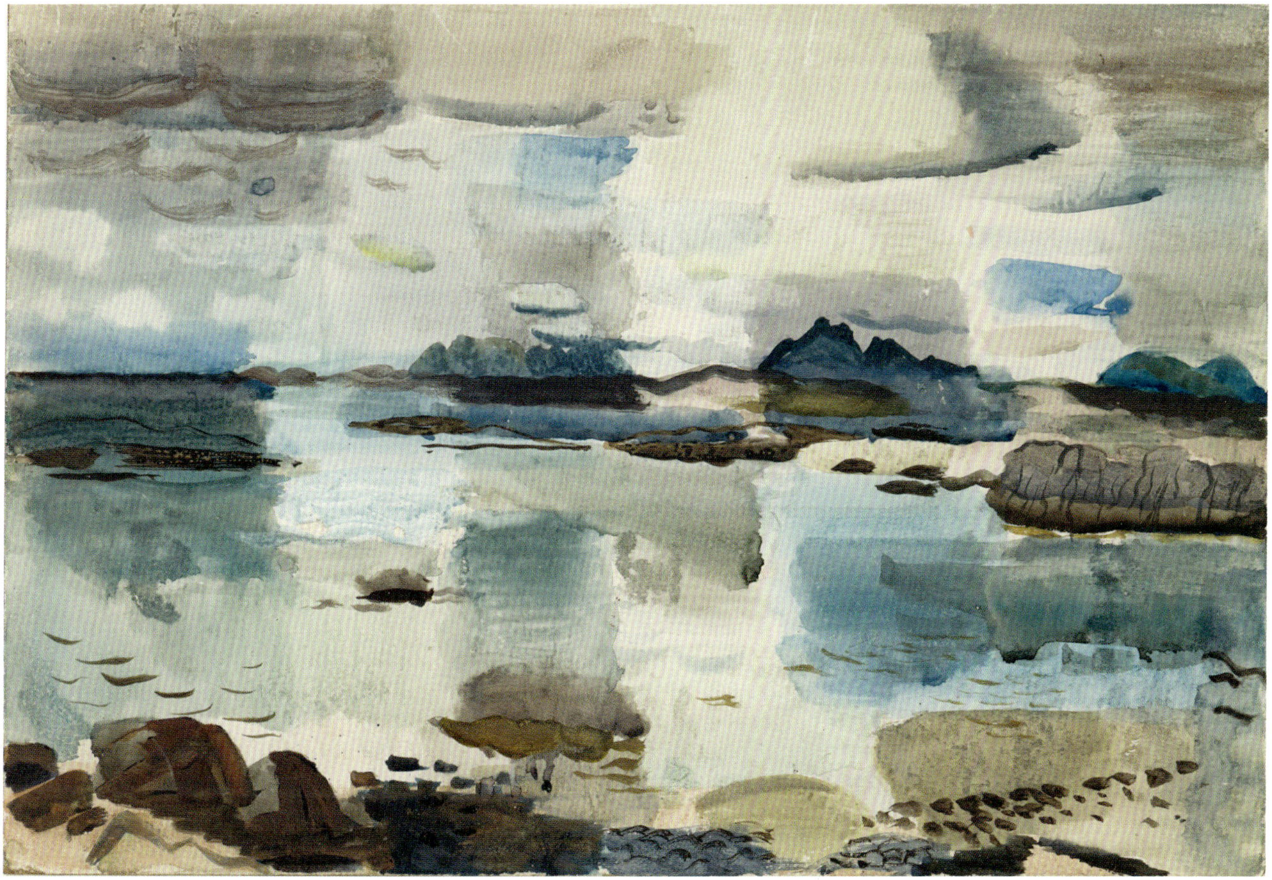

62 *Skye Hills from [near] Morar* (*c.* 1931). Watercolour and gouache, 37.6 cm by 55.8 cm

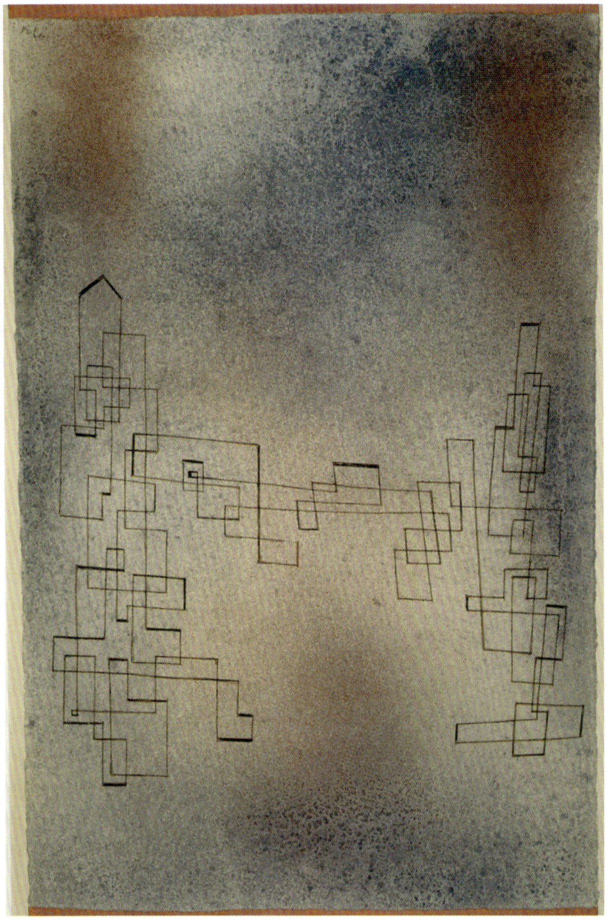

63 *Drohender Schneesturm* (1927), by Paul Klee (1927, no. 291). Watercolour and coloured inks, 49.9 cm by 31.6 cm

establish a true knowledge of all that is, and that human inference and judgement were exactly that, human and fallible. But this was something, I suggest, that the infantryman in Gillies had absorbed experientially and could recognise later in Klee.

Edinburgh knew *Drohender Schneesturm* well. Foggie mocked it. The secretary of the SSA defiantly bought it for himself. In 1935, Gillies could see it again, in Cleghorn Thomson's Garret Studio; and in 1952 it came to rest in the National Galleries of Scotland. There was much that Gillies could take from its provocations and paradox. Like Klee, he reassembled components of perception in novel ways. Unlike Klee, he retained, and scrambled, elements of mimesis to do work that Klee did with titles. The evidence for Klee's influence is almost entirely visual. But that is not a fatal shortcoming. Gillies never spoke about the mechanics of what he found in any major artist. And the evidence is cumulative, extending for some twenty years after *In Arniston* (1935) [60] and other abstracts of the mid- to late 1930s.

In 1934, Ben Nicholson proposed that the 1935 exhibition of the 7 & 5 in London be purged of all figurative painting. Gillies described most of the oils he showed at the Society of Eight in January 1935 as abstracts. *Harbour* (1934, *c.* 1934) [58 and 64] was one. In effect, it reunites the two components of perception that *Drohender Schneesturm* separates. Gillies superimposes a

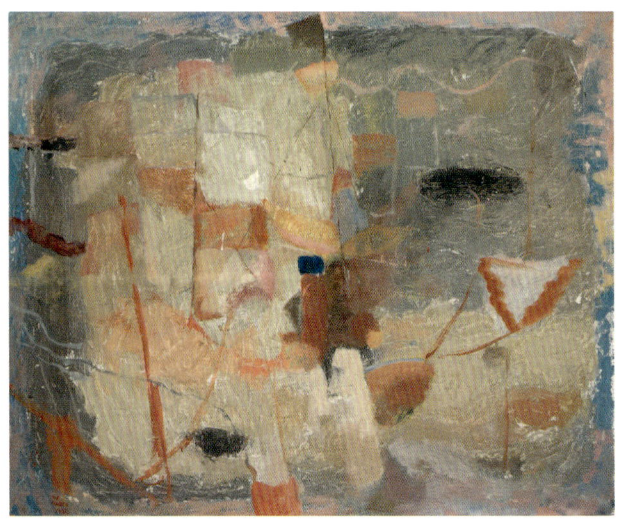

64 *Harbour* (1934, *c.* 1934). Oil, 83.8 cm by 101.6 cm

Opposite:
Detail from *Untitled* ([68] – see p. 95)

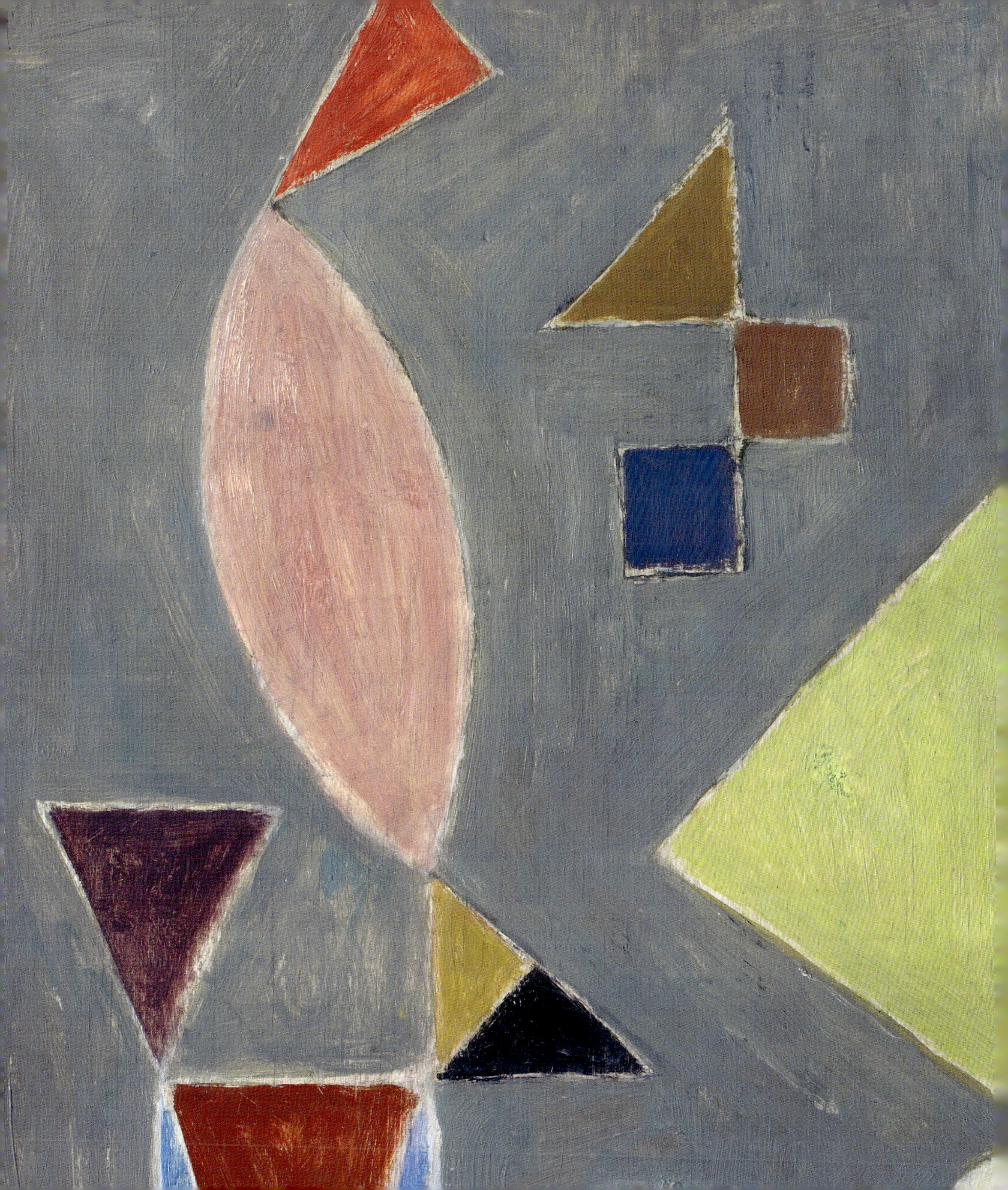

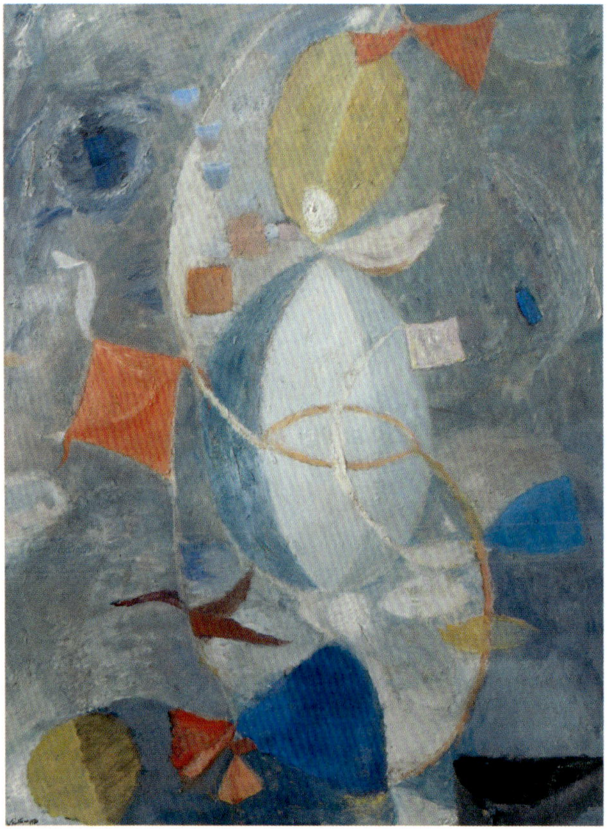

65 *Ascending* (1936). Oil, 98 cm by 74.6 cm

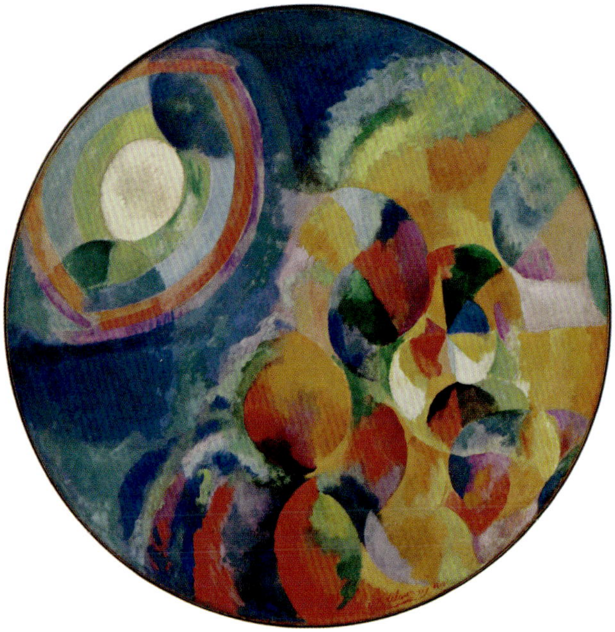

66 *Simultaneous Contrasts: Sun and Moon* (1912–13), by Robert Delaunay. Oil, 134.5 cm diameter

construct (idea) of a harbour over the tonality and colour that emerge when light reflects and refracts. In the darker area, the forms are obscure, and the emergent colours – *Drohender Schneesturm's* blue and pink – are muted. In the lighter area, the construct of harbour becomes visually clearer. Tilted horizontals and verticals, taken from masts and walls, interlock as rectangles and triangles. Colour now affirms the potential of planes to convert light into form. Wavy lines, some incised, re-enact sea in bodily movement. The funnel from *Reisebild[nis]* [56] unites retinal reception with idea in an analogue for a real-world subject (harbour) and plural ways to experience it – in Klee's terms, a 'coming into being' of human apprehension, a dawning of idea, the invisible made visible through the artist's extensions from a single point of grey.

Gillies chose eventually to position his abstraction closer to works like *The Harbour* (*c.* 1934–7) [59] and *Achgarve* (*c.* 1937) [82], but not, I suggest, before his own essays into the would-be separation of retinal reception from idea. In January 1935, *The Scotsman* described *Two Reds* (*c.* 1934) [ni] as 'two entirely inchoate arrangements of coloured surface, in which the repercussions of the one colour on the other constitute the motive'. The work is untraced, as are others that prompted similar critical reactions in the late

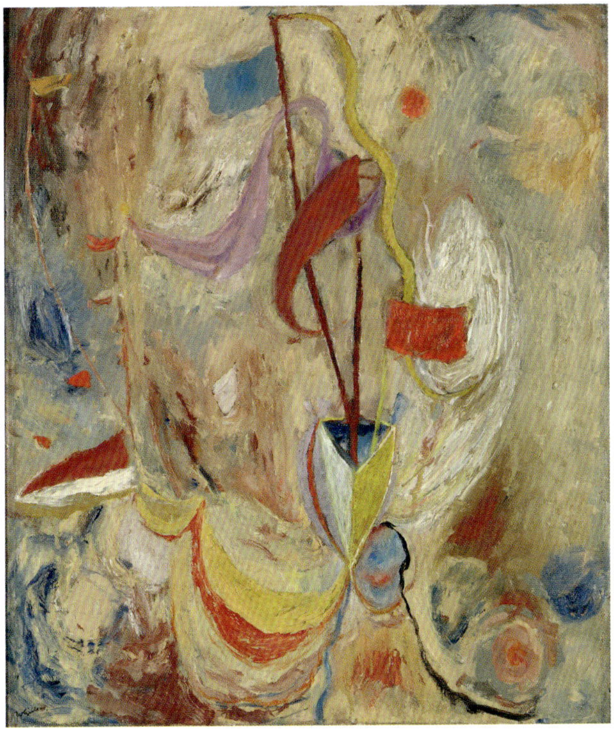

67 *Flags and Bunting* (*c.* 1935). Oil, 76.2 cm by 65.7 cm

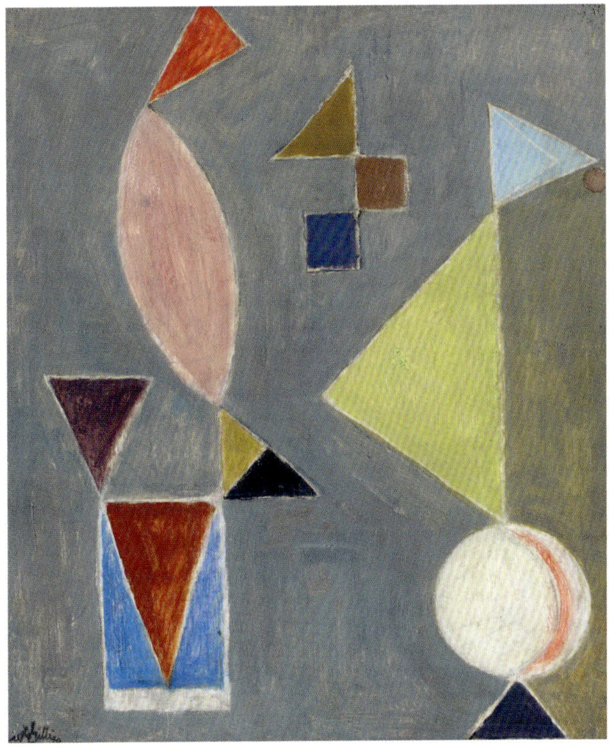

68 *Untitled* (*c.* 1935). Oil, 61 cm by 50.7 cm

1930s. The merits and nature of any such attempt must therefore remain uncertain.

However, there survive two Gillies abstracts that attempt to convey the reciprocal, cognitive component of perception implicit in the line-drawing and title of *Drohender Schneesturm* [63]. Unusually but tellingly, one of these abstracts, and possibly both, follow Klee in relying on the title of the work to unlock their meaning. 'Approaching' entails movement in space and time; another of Klee's Edinburgh exhibits was titled *Hovering Before Rising* (1930) [ni]. Gillies attempted cognate ideas in *Ascending* (1936) [65] and in a work currently known as *Untitled* (*c.* 1935) [68] but that was possibly first known as *Balanced* (*c.* 1934). Its elements, a critic said, were 'certainly not in a state of stable equilibrium'. But Klee thought of form itself as a finite balance of opposed forces of which gravity was only one; and he regarded the forms of Euclid's geometry as artworks already in their own right, plastic realisations of mathematical axioms that are abstract and invisible but nonetheless real. When shown in London and Edinburgh, the carved, geometric reliefs that Ben Nicholson had started to make gave a further currency to these questions of plasticity and abstraction and made this a pertinent issue for Gillies to explore. Does balance have any meaning or existence in a world that is purely abstract and where time does not flow?

Prompted by the thinking of Klee's colleague Wassily Kandinsky, Robert Delaunay's claims for

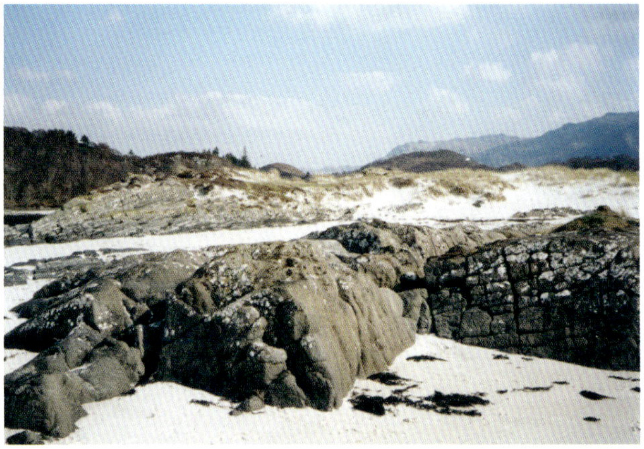

69 Morar Beach around 1998

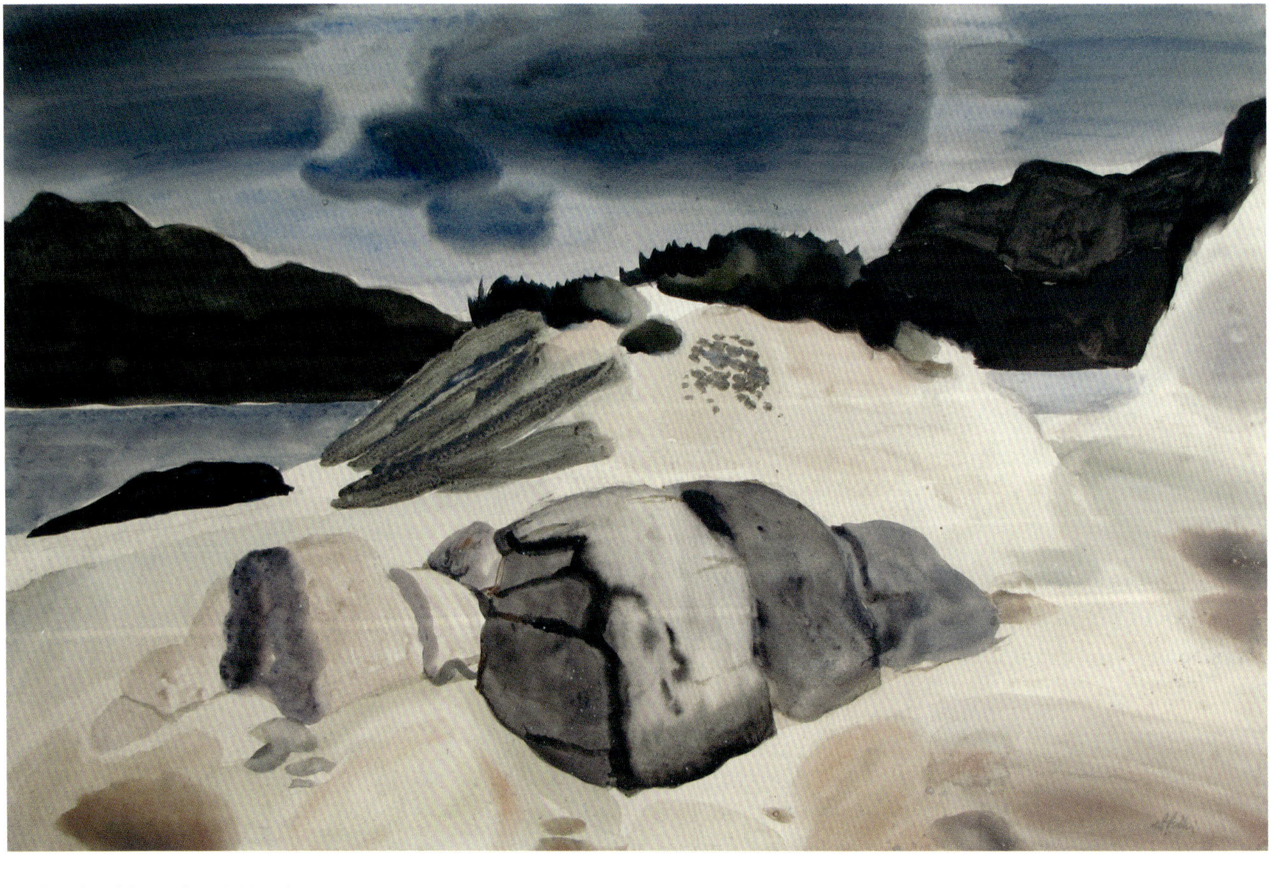

70 *Rocks, Morar* (*c.* 1933–4). Watercolour, 37 cm by 56 cm 'simultaneous' colour had earlier offered another way forward. In 1913, Klee translated Delaunay's essay on light into German. It was a key moment for all three artists and also for Bonnard and others. At issue were the parameters of all imaging and meaning, not only in artworks but in all the exchanges of life – a broader issue than whether to go abstract or to fall in behind Ben Nicholson's 7 & 5.

In arriving at his own position in the mid-1930s, Gillies looked not so much to London as back to Paris in 1913. He knew Kandinsky's work and spoke of its interest. *Ascending* (1936) [65] again draws on Delaunay, especially the series that includes *Simultaneous Contrasts: Sun and Moon* (1912–13) [66]. *Flags and Bunting (c.* 1935) [67] owes something to both Klee and Delaunay and has a landscape analogue in *St Monan's* (*c.* 1934) [ni]. Both works test whether an extreme, figurative, abstraction, similar to that of the watercolour *In Arniston* (1934) [60], might be achieved in oil through a gestural, more impastoed style not found in Delaunay or Klee.

Gillies said he found a freedom in knowing a subject so well that he could take liberties with it, hence the harbours, funnels and flags. We see this also in a set of works that push towards an extreme abstraction of a place he knew well. In *Rocks, Morar* (*c.* 1933–4) [70], photographic detail [69] is reduced, the palette is restricted and tonal contrast again exploited to achieve a quasi-surreal combination of light and form. After a preparatory drawing [71] for *Rocks and Sea* (*c.* 1935) [72], the same rocks are then painted with a similar palette and tones but now with wavy forms accented by dashes and stripes. These marks continue into a blue area at the top that is contextually indeterminate. It could equally represent horizon and sky, or water lapping the sand amid projecting rocks, or clouds reflected in broken water.

These, I think, are the rocks that also figure in Soden and Keller's (1998, 120–1) ground-breaking demonstration of Gillies' way of working. He simplifies his subject in preparatory drawings and eventually removes all traces of the human (and canine) [73 and 74]. *Rocks and Water, Morar* (*c.* 1932–4) [75] then moves the rocks and setting to the most extreme figurative abstraction he reached in his oil landscapes.

He went almost as far in the watercolours too, but, in a sense, allowed the snowstorm to come to him – a diffuse, particulate, entity (or event?) at once solid, liquid and gaseous, like the world itself – assailing the retina, provoking hand and eye to search for form and recognition. Klee thought painting akin to the event of creation itself. Gillies' handling of this medium is analogous. The coastal watercolours of the 1930s rest on his ability to coax form, light and relationship out of the diffuse suspension of colour in water as it moves across paper and is absorbed. This 're-cognition' of form, in and from formlessness, is evident in the abstract element in these works and helps explain the freshness of vision in all he later did.

Thus, the forms in *Highland Landscape [with] Suilven* (1936) [76] have little mimetic reference. They emerge from a primordial, formless unity into solid, liquid and gas as though close to the point of creation, still being shaped into recognition by Klee's cosmological time, wordlessly 'expressed' (brought forth and forward) by palette and gesture. *West Coast Sunset* (nd, *c.* 1936) [77] is more determinate. At first sight, *Threatening Storm* (1936) [78] is more determinate still, the forms more clearly defined. But their impact is

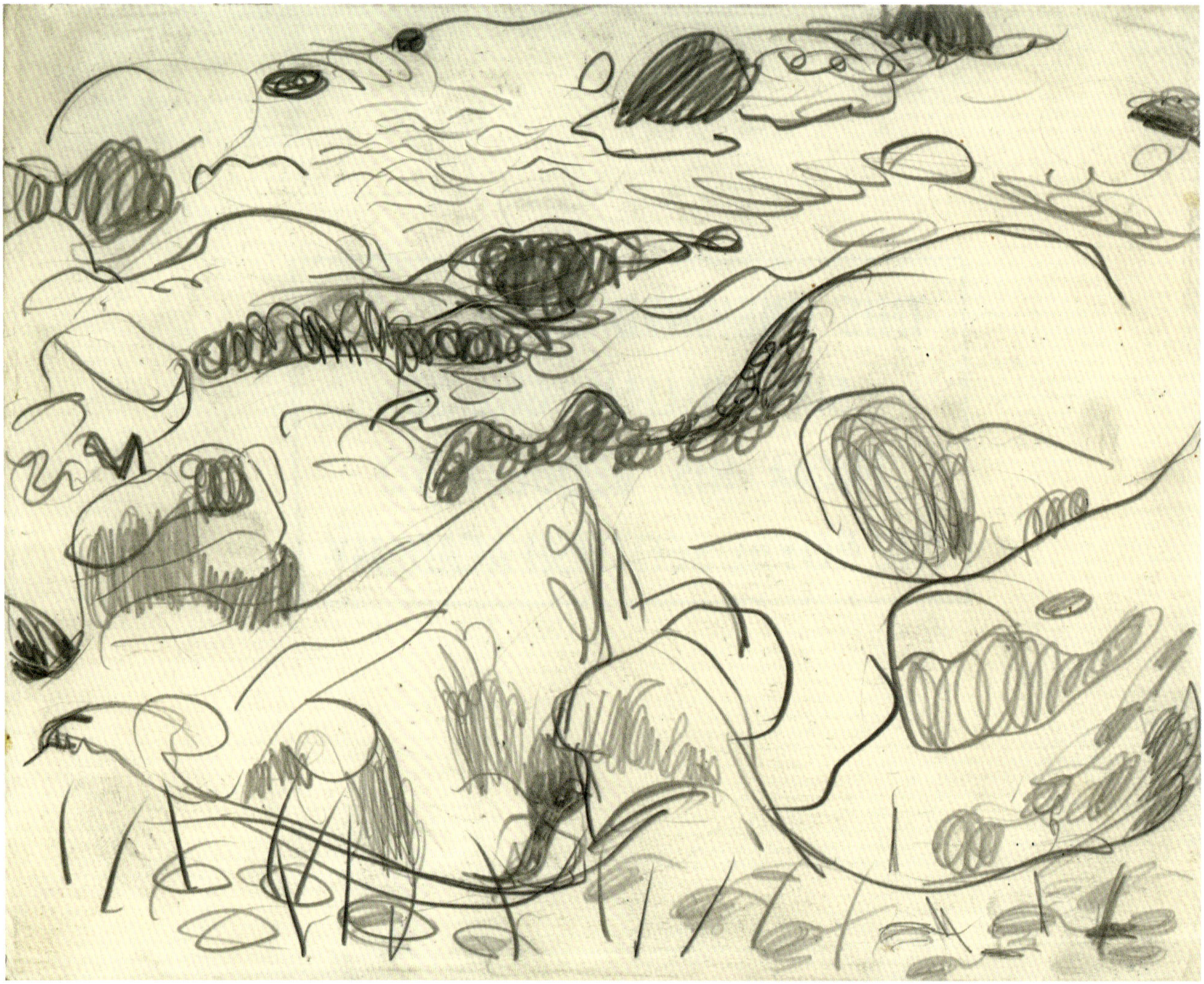

71 Drawing for *Rocks and Sea* (*c.* 1935) [72 below]. Pencil, 18.1 cm by 23.8 cm

more than mimetic. Sky and beach are painted with similar punctuations of black on off-white and there is a pervasive gestural unity.

In *Resipol* (1938, 1936?) [79] the communalities of colour and gesture are even clearer. They convey a sense of formless primordial contingencies (revolving gravitational gas) becoming the concrete (actually rocky) realities of our planet. The blues and browns of the foreshore carry this idea into the sky and make it as architectural as the rocks. Clouds are formed from shapes found in *In Arniston* (1935) [60] – triangle and zig-zag – and from an ascending rectilinear line that represents nothing in experience but releases the idea of

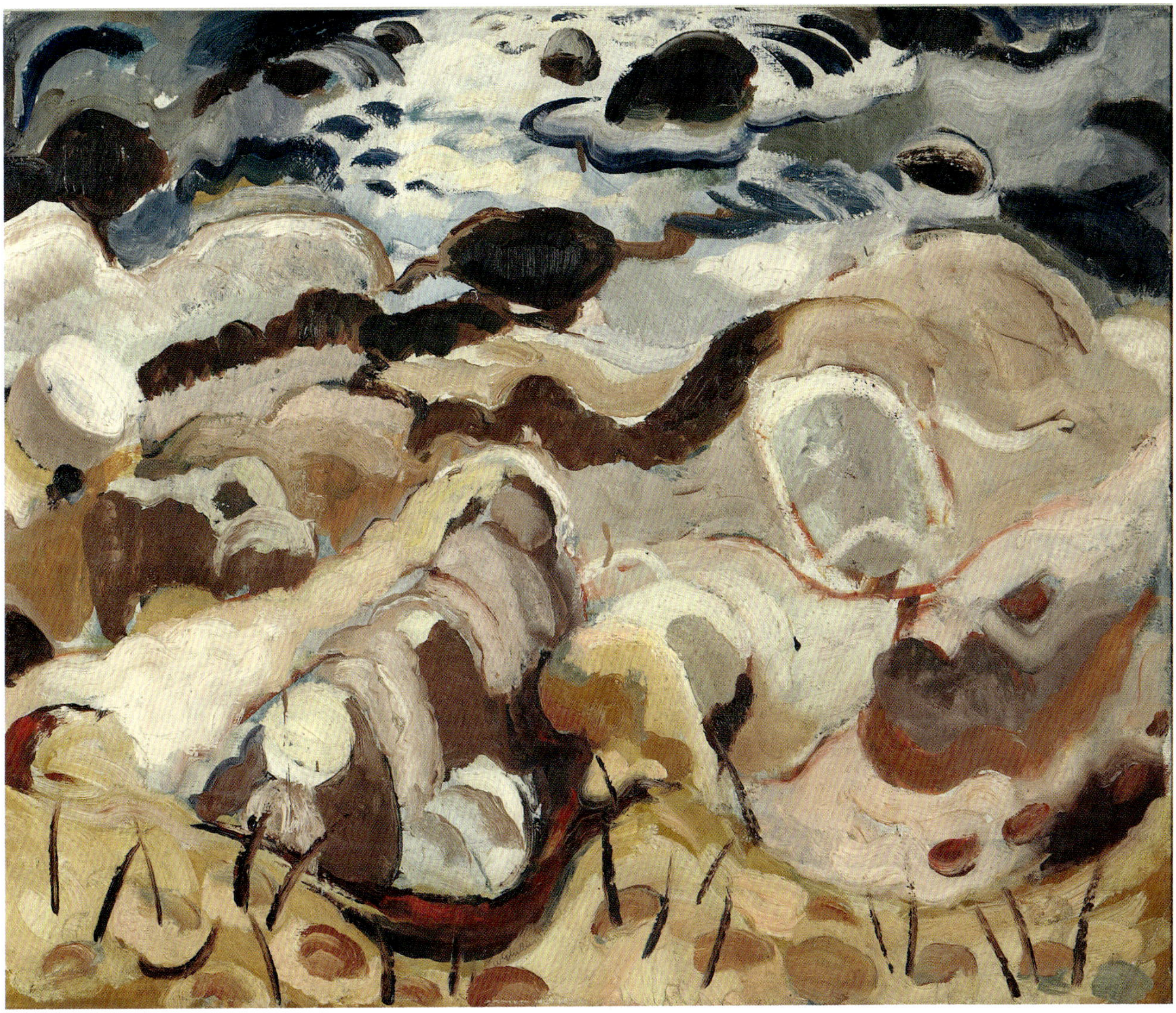

72 *Rocks and Sea* (*c.* 1935). Oil, 64 cm by 76.5 cm

form just as Klee's quadrilaterals do when placed over the amorphous solids, liquids and gases of *Drohender Schneesturm* [63].

By the same token, we can invert or rotate many of these coastal works (or ourselves) to find an orientation that transforms them into non-figurative abstracts, where nothing needs rearranging internally for them to achieve their effect. This is possible only because there are few or no persons or animals there, or trees, or rectilinear artefacts (crofts, pitched roofs), nothing determinate, nothing that would trigger intrusive conceptual processing of retinal experience, nothing that would, in the 'right-way-up'

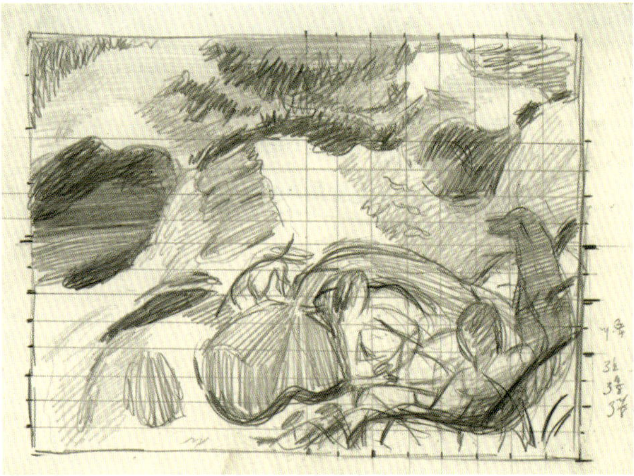

73 *Picnic on the Beach, Morar I* (*c.* 1932). Pencil, 17.9 cm by 22.8 cm

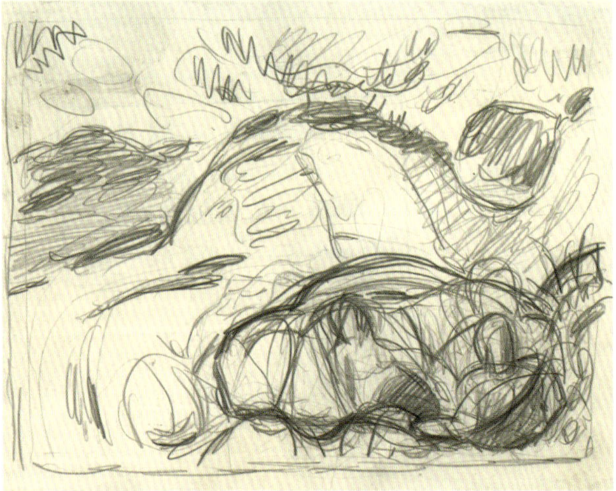

74 *Picnic on the Beach, Morar II* (*c.* 1932). Pencil, 17.9 cm by 22.8 cm

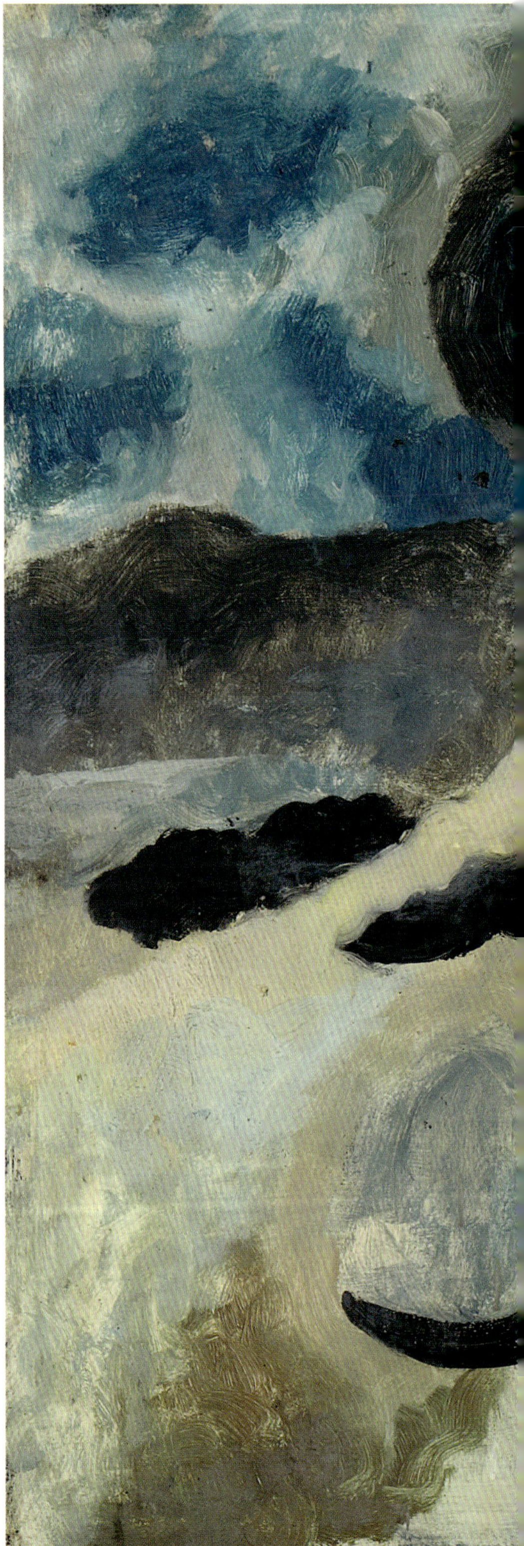

75 *Rocks and Water, Morar* (*c.* 1932–4). Oil, 74.8 cm by 110.8 cm

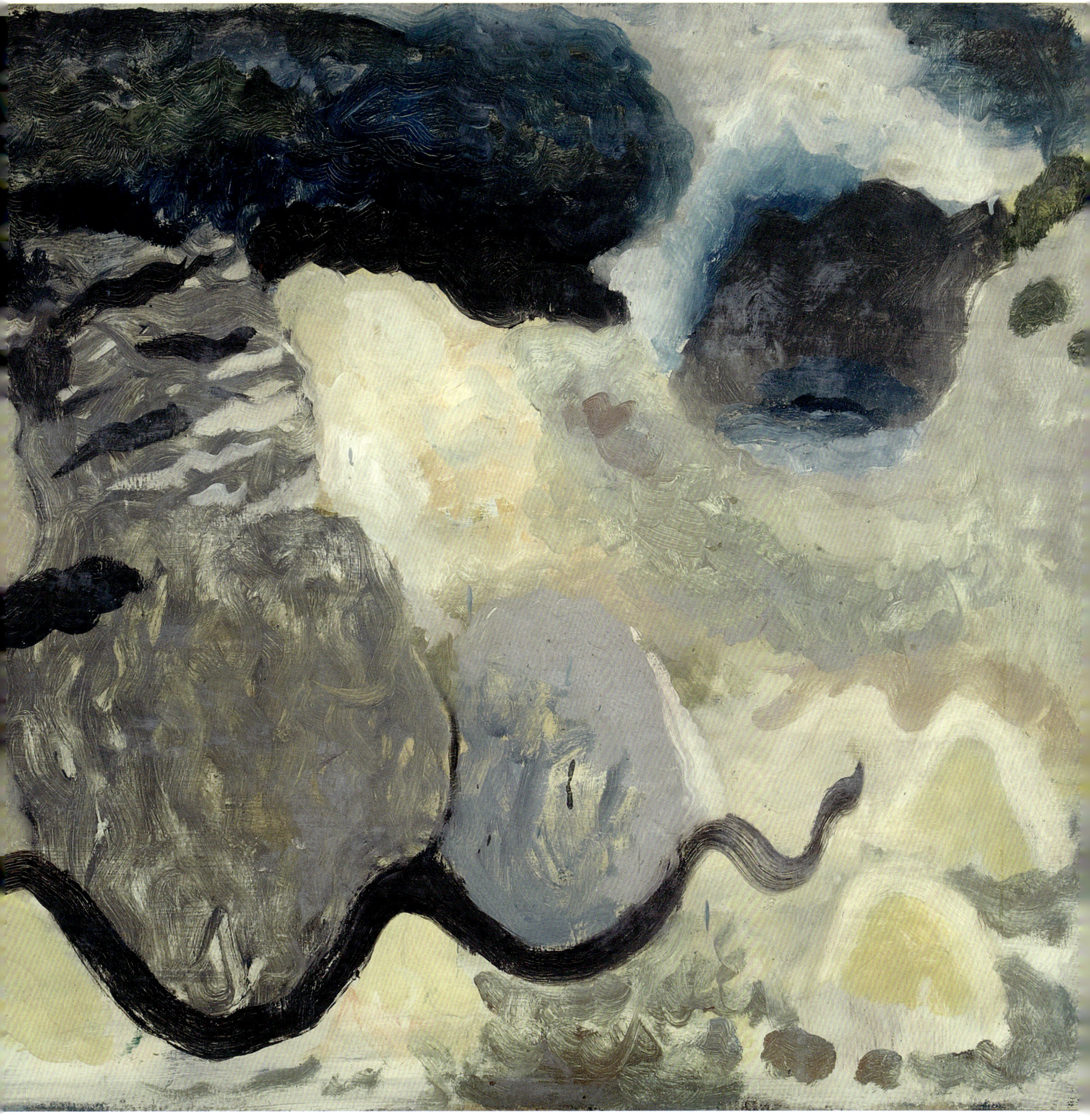

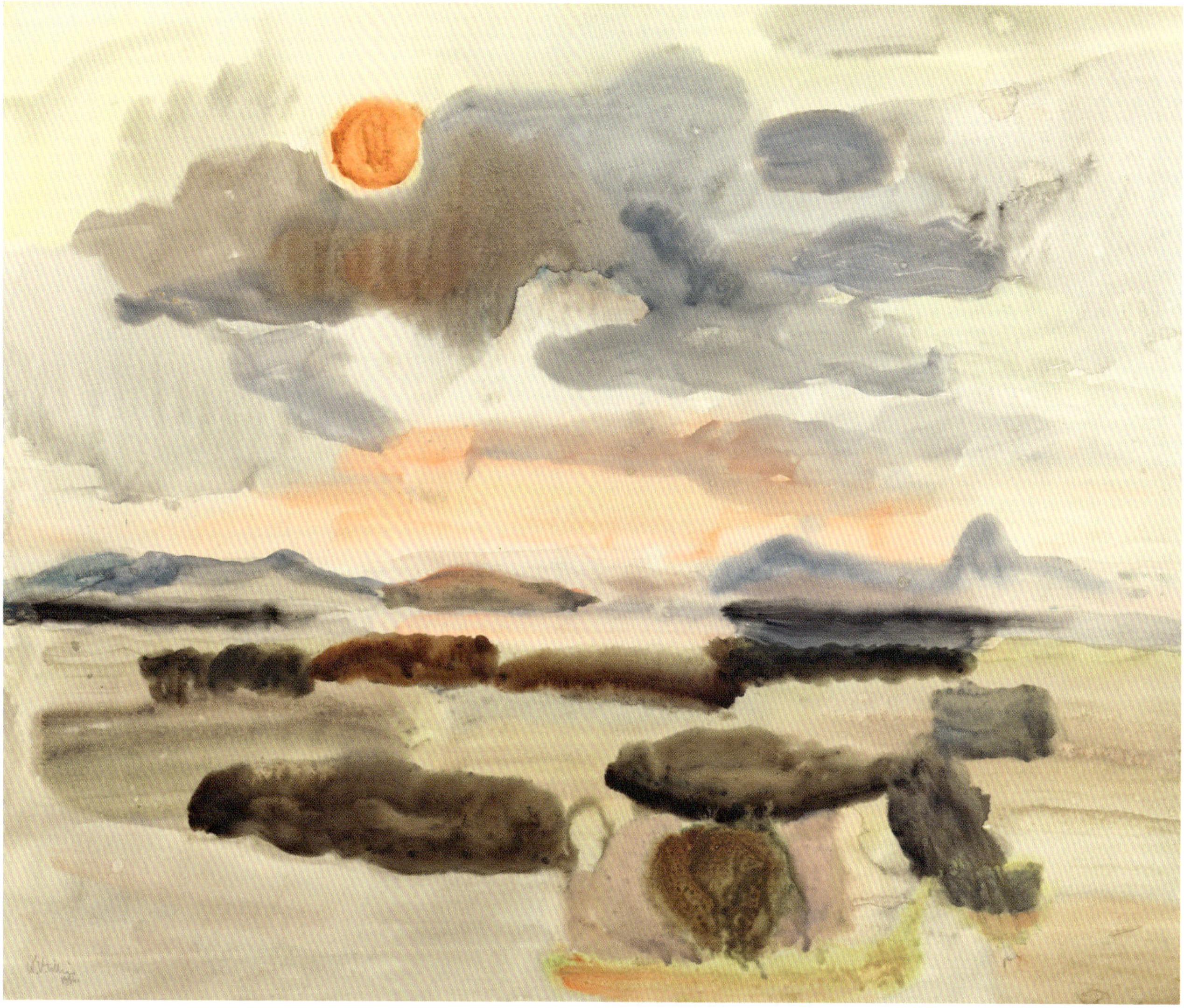

76 *Highland Landscape [with] Suilven* (1936). Watercolour, 51 cm by 63 cm

orientation, restrict the eye otherwise open to plural possibilities. This is something he wanted from abstraction.

Wester Ross (*c.* 1934, *c.* 1937?) [80] exploits the sparing use of ink line and accents within large areas of undifferentiated wash. Occasional delineations are based on striations in the rock and on communalities of form that emerge over millennia in the eroded beach-scatter of boulder and pebble. We instinctively interpolate, within and across the wash voids, and between striated rock and the forms that emerge from the action of the elements on the rock, elements that first reveal form but ultimately return it to the sensuously

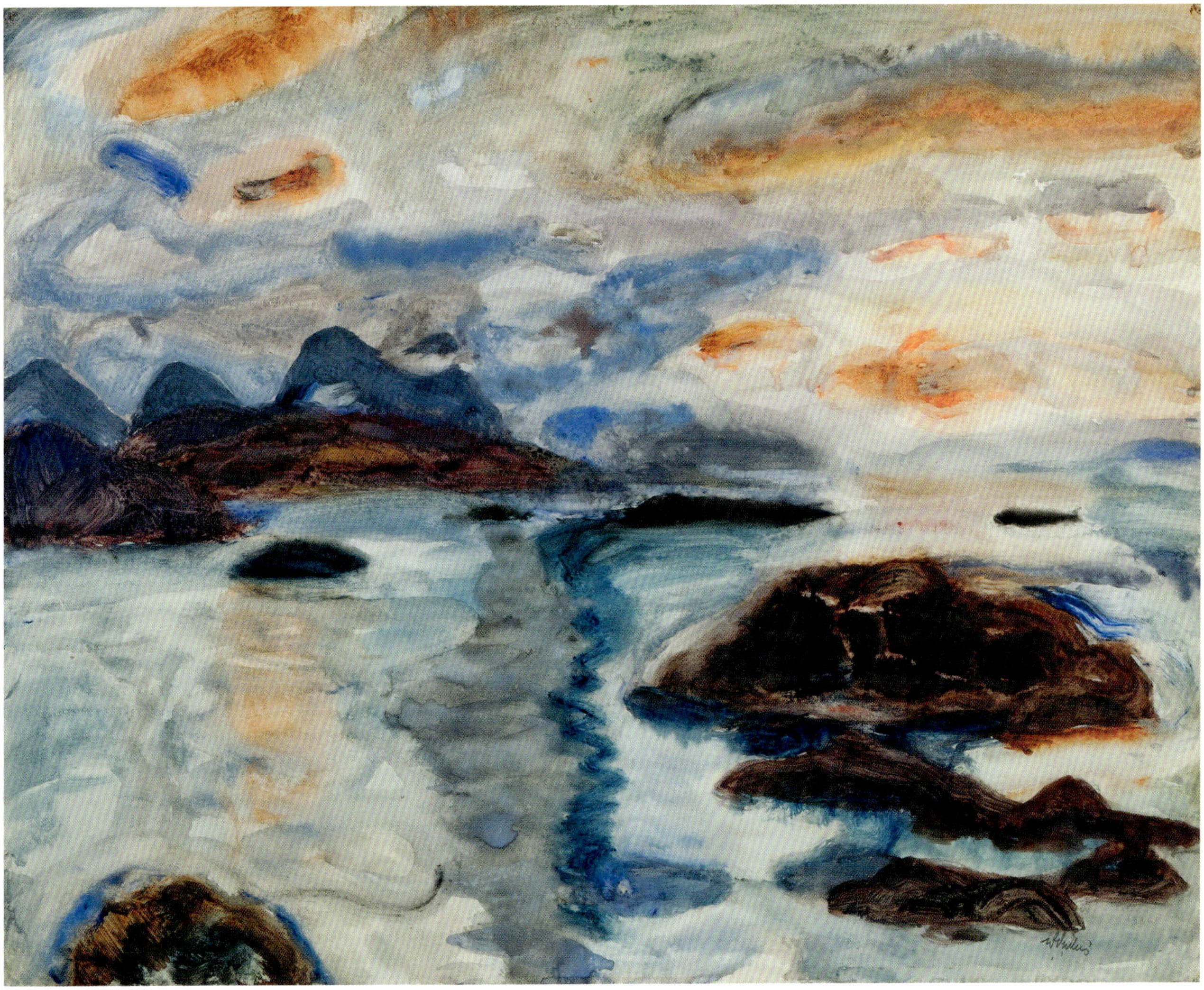

77 *West Coast Sunset* (nd, *c.* 1936). Watercolour, 50.4 cm by 63.3 cm

formless, shape-shifting or intangible (dust, liquid, vapour, gas). This interpolation opens us to the wider idea. In finishing Gillies' sentence, we join him in a timeline where apprehension (sense of the world) itself is revealed as finite, and therefore all the more mysterious, whether in the span of the self, the species or the cosmos. This is something he wanted from a mimesis repurposed through abstraction and reconfiguration.

One senses feelings of awe in these works, some painted shortly after cremation had returned his sister Emma to the primordial states of matter, and when Gillies' awareness of finitude was surely acute. He spoke of the 'fine threat' of *In Ardnamurchan* (1936) [81] and the 'honest, rather pathetic' note struck by the 'elderly people' among the rocks. Mrs Gillies, in black mourning, walks towards the storm from which he cannot protect.

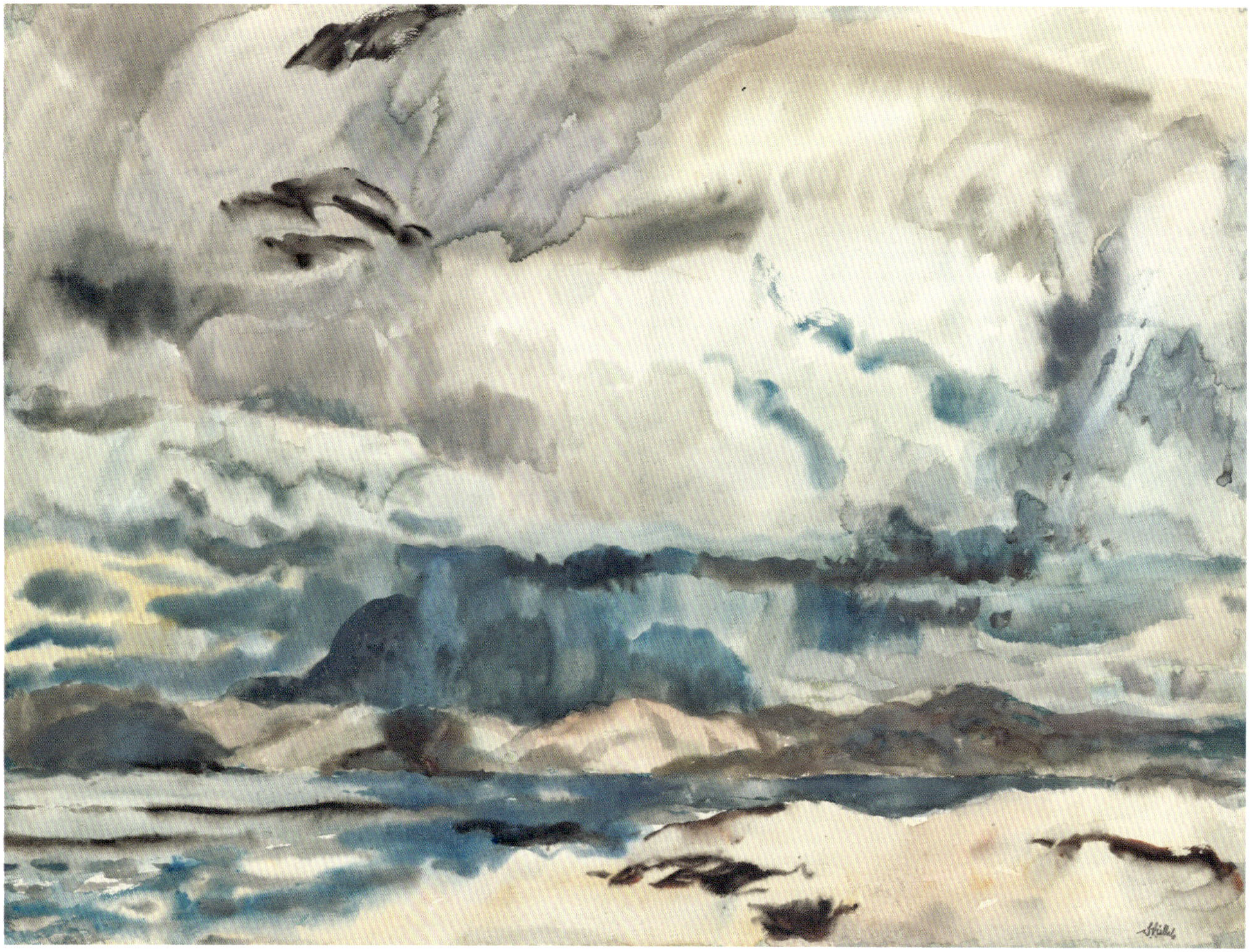

78 *Threatening Storm* (1936). Watercolour, 56.5 cm by 77 cm

Pathetic and empathetic. It was the only time he put his family into a landscape, but the triangles, zig-zags, quadrilaterals and gestures would remain features of his landscape idiom.

Klee's use of naive, primitive, even Mesolithic, imagery may also have struck a chord with Gillies. Herbert Read and others in Edinburgh subscribed to the then popular belief that the entire history of art, of how humans came to see and represent the world, was re-enacted in the art of the developing child. In this now discredited view, opening one's eyes to cosmology, to the mystery of human apprehension, was also to look inward to oneself, back into one's developing sensibility, and further back still into pre-history. As Soden and Keller (1998, 104) have suggested, it may be no coincidence, too, that Gillies had earlier painted in the port of Tréboul at the same time as Frances Hodgkins and Cedric Morris. The simplicity of their paintings anticipates the primitivism that

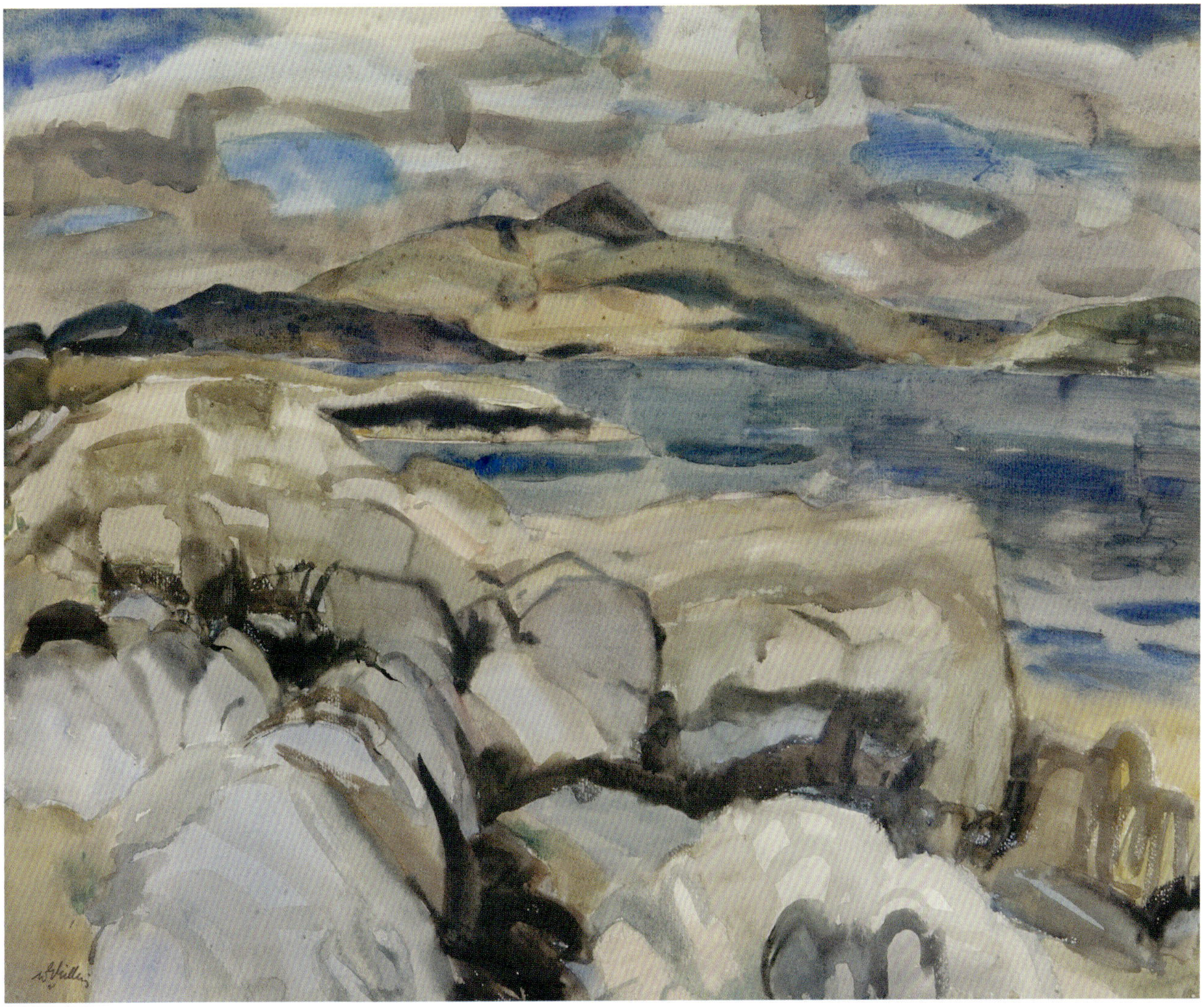

79 *Resipol* (1938, 1936?). Watercolour, 51 cm by 64 cm

attracted Christopher Wood to the area and, along with Ben Nicholson, to the naive work of the Cornish fisherman Alfred Wallis.

A thread of naivety also entered Gillies' work at this time (*Tréboul* (a) (1927) [137], *Mallaig* (1928) [138]). It extended through the 1930s, both in urban settings (*Piershill* (nd, *c.* 1933) [141], *View from 162 Willowbrae Road, Edinburgh* (1932) [142], *Landscape with House and Two Heads* (*c.* 1930) [143]) and also elsewhere (*Clachan of Laide* (*c.* 1930, *c.* 1937) [ni], *Kyleakin* (*c.* 1936) [ni], *Kyleakin* (1938) [149], *Acharacle* (*c.* 1938) (two versions) [ni] and *Highland Hamlet* (nd, late 1930s) [ni]). In works like *Achgarve* (*c.* 1937) [82], token buildings create a fruitful disjunction between the abstracted, vertically tilted landscape and the naively

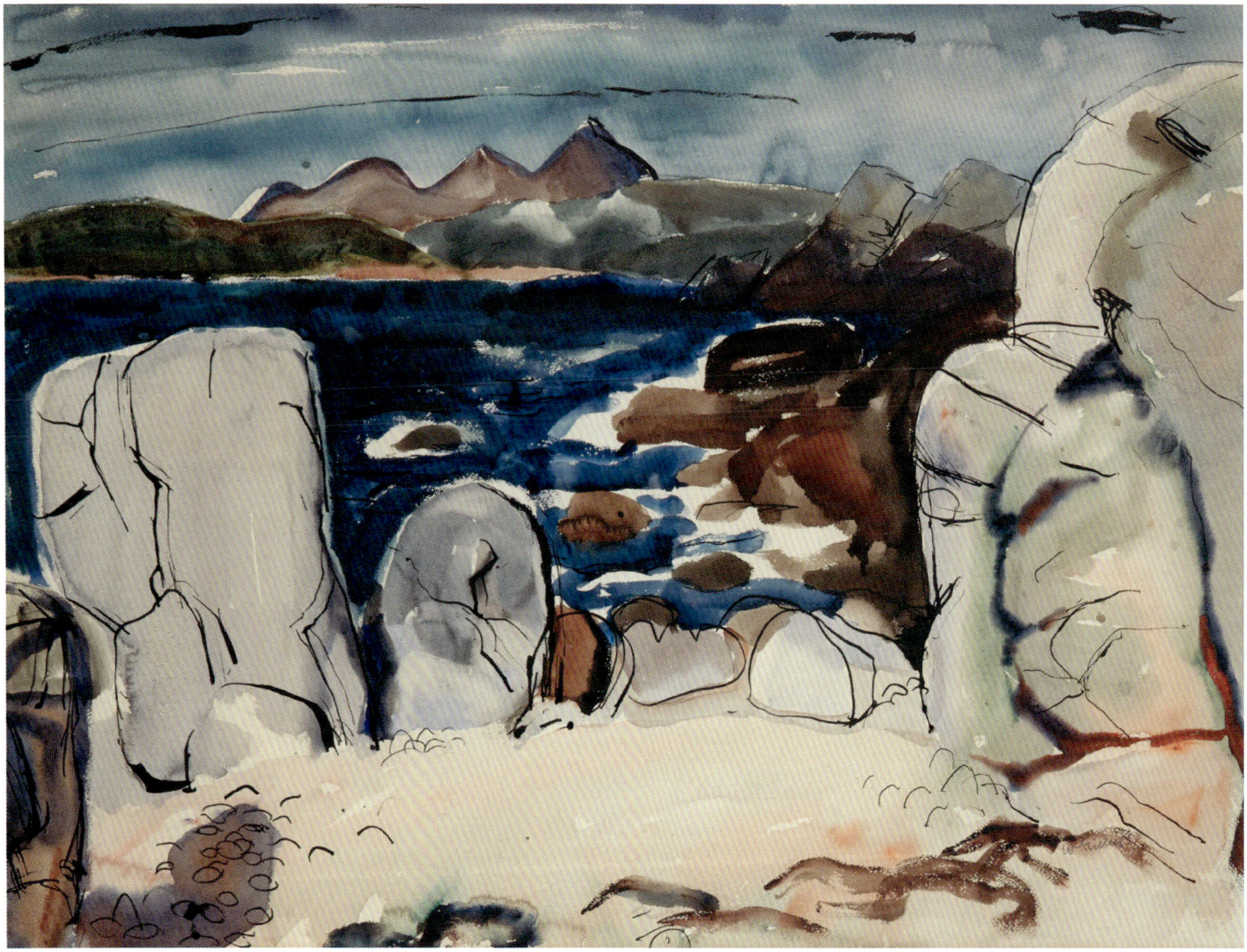

80 *Wester Ross* (*c.* 1934, *c.* 1937?). Watercolour, 55 cm by 75 cm

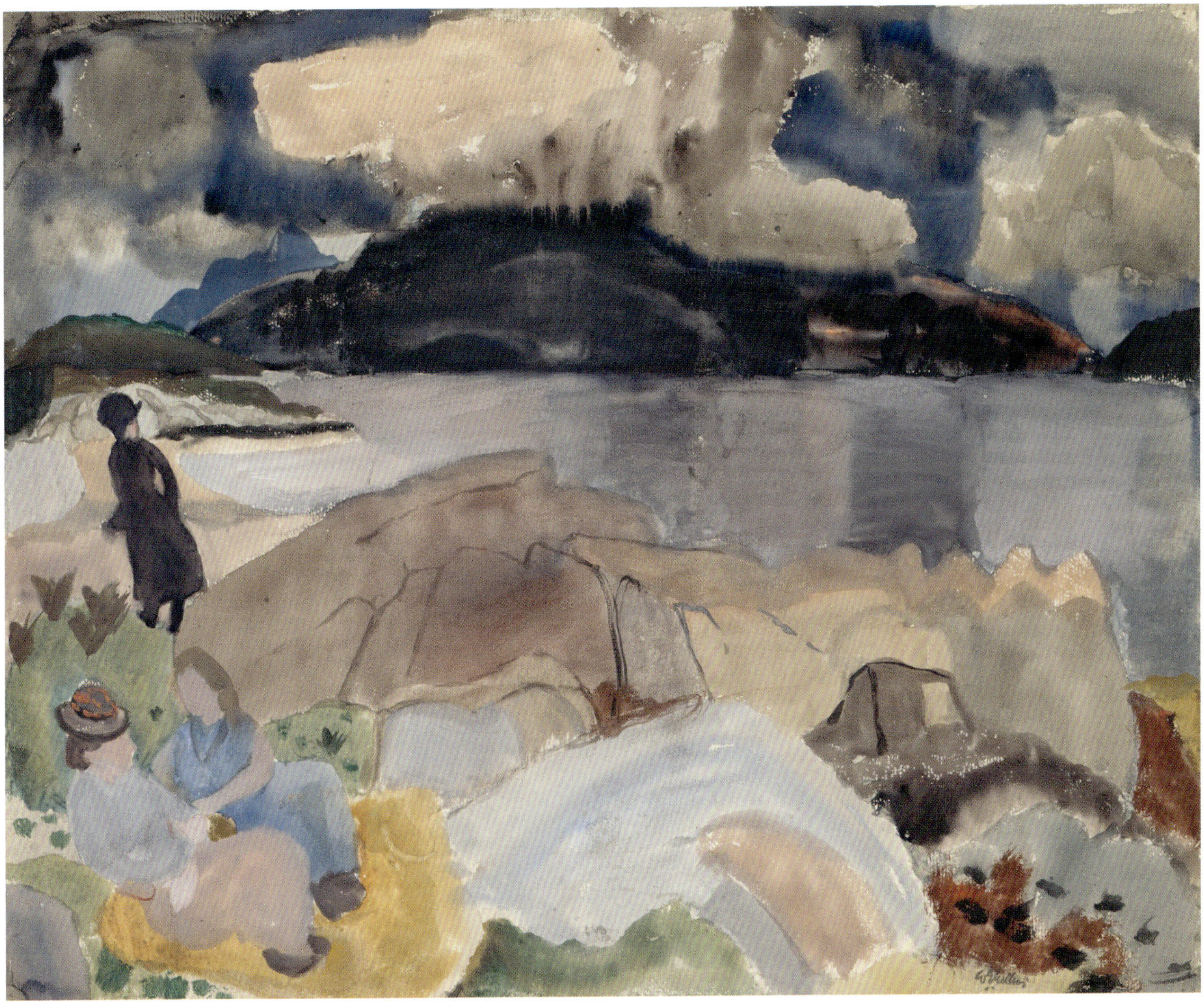

81 *In Ardnamurchan* (1936). Watercolour, 50.6 cm by 63 cm

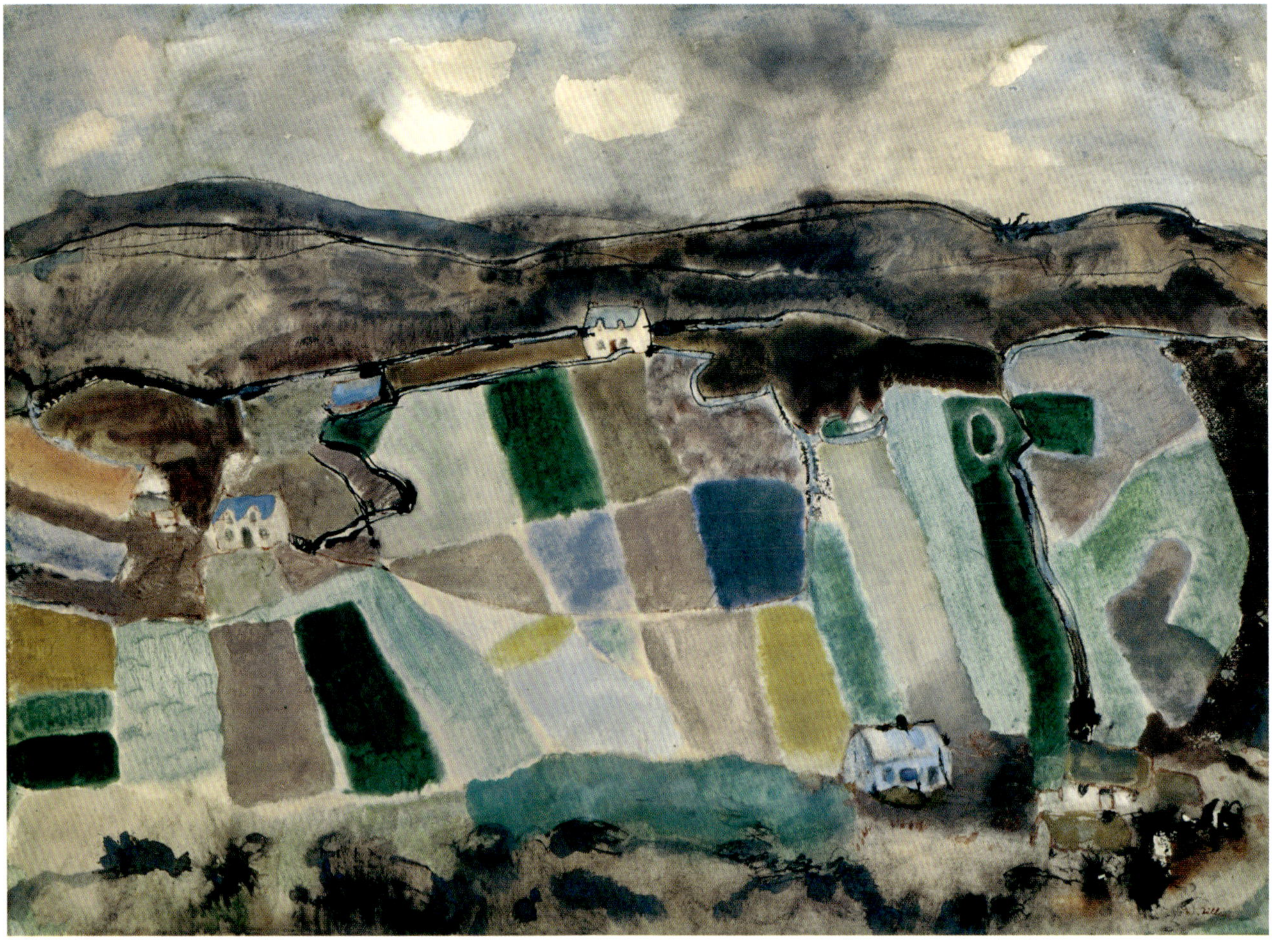

82 *Achgarve* (*c.* 1937). Ink and watercolour, 56 cm by 77 cm

realistic crofts that somehow inhabit it. We find ourselves in plural realities where the mundane exists also as a world of forms that extends beyond the boundaries of human presence and understanding. What, we ask, is humankind doing in such a place? Hereafter, numerous 'empty' oils and watercolours would ask this question in their apparent naivety and astonish with their resultant freshness.

The potential for such effects was a further reason to retain some element of figuration in his abstraction. It is also why Gillies rejected the example of the Surrealists, the other main option open to modernists at this time. For Gillies, their work was too mimetic, had too many 'finicky perfections' to accommodate indeterminacy and the truly surreal wonder of the extraordinary in the mundane.

Nicholson's imperative of pure, non-figurative abstraction destabilised the membership of the 7 & 5. After two years of painting in this way, the English artist John Piper explained his return to

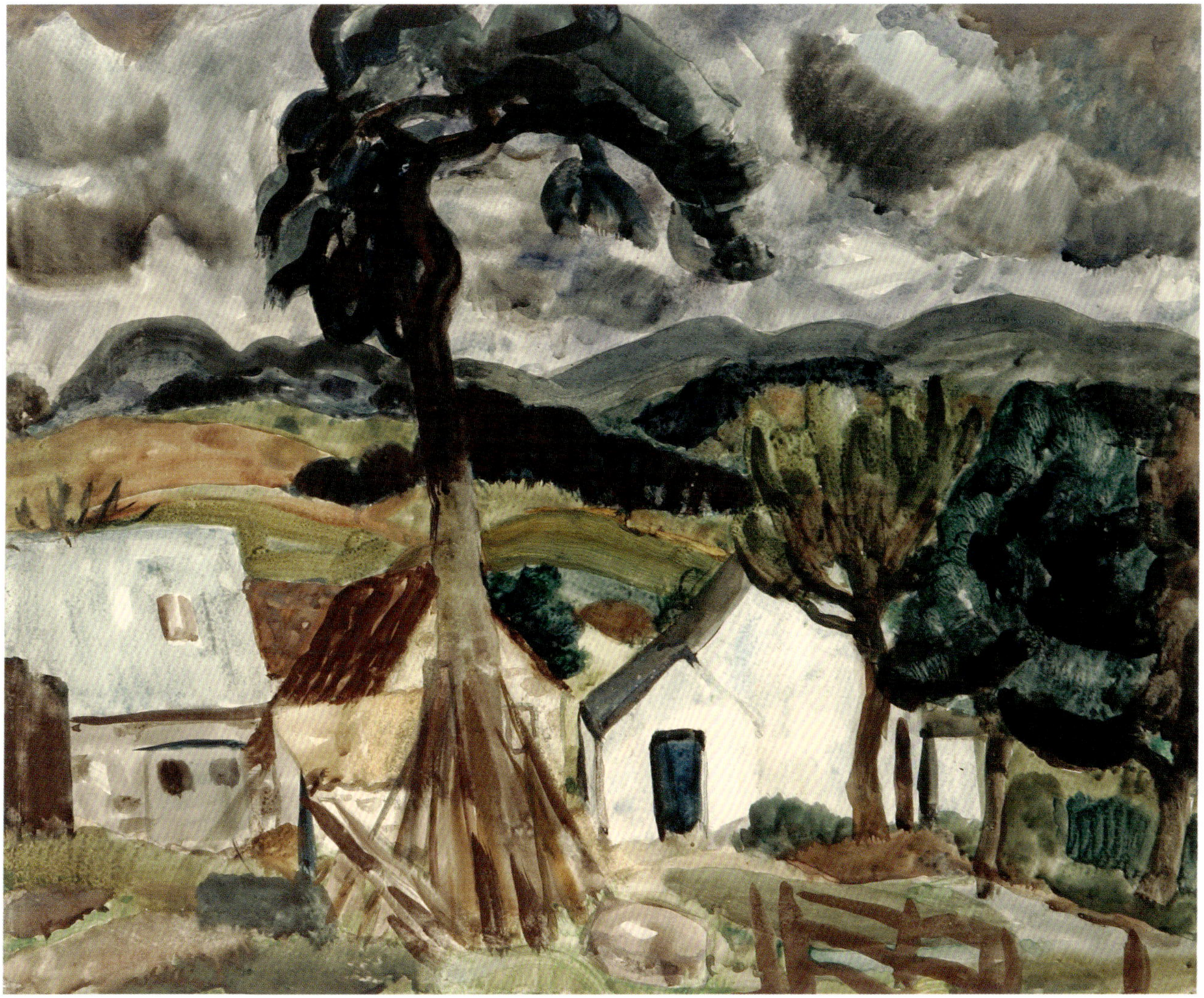

83 *Untitled view of the Cleish Hills* (nd, *c.* 1932). Watercolour, 51 cm by 63 cm

figuration by saying in 1937, 'It will be a good thing to get back to the tree in the field'. This was his metaphor for the observed world (tree) in context (field). 'Field' referred to environment, the form of a tree (for example, stunted by wind) being a testament to its life. And he extended its meaning to the culture that gives the tree meaning (Spalding 2011, 119–22). Thus, the metaphor can embrace the time spans of cosmology and consciousness, including the span of humankind's seeing and imaging.

An occasional but recurrent feature of Gillies' landscapes from around 1932 is a single tree placed centrally, like the tree in Untitled View of the Cleish Hills (nd, *c.* 1932) [83]. Often it disrupts the composition, much as his own position disrupts

Interior (1938) [42]. Here [83], it is shaken along with land and sky (in contrast to a staid version painted alongside him by his friend Alan Ronald with the title *The Cleish Hills near Dunfermline* (1932) (ni)).

It is not known whether Gillies already knew by then of Klee's metaphor of the artist as a tree. But, in *Autumn Moon* (1934, *c.* 1934–7) [84], we see a central, though less intrusive, tree used again. Gillies valued this work. It hangs behind Mrs Gillies in *Interior,* where he articulates his position as artist, and it indicates his own take on Piper's position. He showed it in London in 1942 and in the 1970 film. By that time, he could not remember whether he had painted it in 1934 or 1937. But the date of its first exhibition (January 1938) adds to the evidence for his dialogue with modernist contemporaries.

The central tree here is painted as an ideogram or cipher and is set against a field (ground) of yellow and lime. Above it is Arthur's Seat, site of Edinburgh's Neolithic hill-forts and of one of the origins of modern, cosmological geology. The colour of the gibbous moon links it to the tree in its field. The form of composition is now that of strata: sky, land and, at the foot of the painting, an indeterminate plane that may be horizontal or vertical to the viewer. It could have been prompted by reflecting water, or by a vertical geological cut. Or it could simply be an inducement to the eye to by-pass expectations of foreground and go straight to the tree. Colour and tone offer no help. There is no tonal ('aerial') recession, and colours are improbably shared between the strata. Signifiers of night and day are confounded: moon but colour; colour therefore light; light but no shadow or tonal recession; no tonal recession but some spatial (proportionate) recession; the degree of spatial recession itself dependent on whether the lowest stratum is mimetically read and its plane horizontal or vertical.

The artist by now could only be Gillies, rehearsing modernist uncertainties by scrambling elements of mimesis. He simultaneously describes the world and throws it in doubt, draws the viewer in by offering alternative ways of seeing, and links introspection to observation of the phenomenal world.

The work is not topographical or realist in any secure way. Despite what may be tacit references to Piper and Paul Nash (contextualised tree, hill-fort), neither is it neo-Romantic. There is no *genius loci* here. Meanings are layered but interacting. On the one hand, they are elements of a mimetic landscape. On the other, they are part of some other, ordered, way of seeing that treats these elements ironically. Here the work of ironic quotation is done, not by the cubist trope of a window or stage-set, nor by the Surrealists' trope that juxtaposes disparate objects removed from their mimetic context or 'field'. It is done, rather, through the dual status that cipher and symbol have as both signifier and signified. The effect can nevertheless be termed surreal in the sense of coeval, conflicting, interacting, multivalent responses to retinal reception. This is achieved through the use of indeterminacy and the contradictions (of colour, light and recession) released by the moon's presence. *The Scotsman* lampooned *Autumn Moon* but Norman Reid thought it good enough to buy for his personal collection.

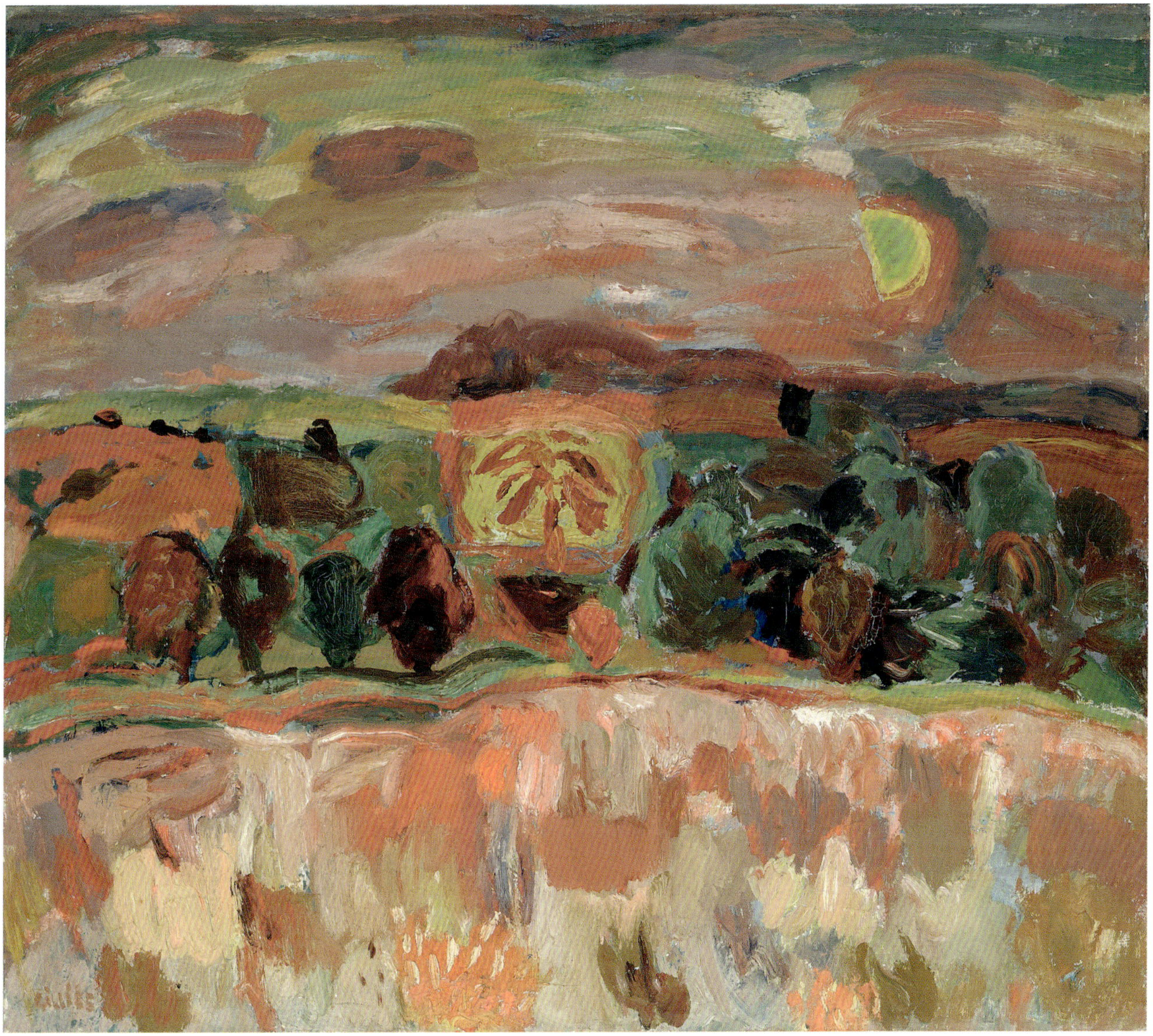

84 *Autumn Moon* (1934, *c.* 1934–7). Oil, 71 cm by 82 cm

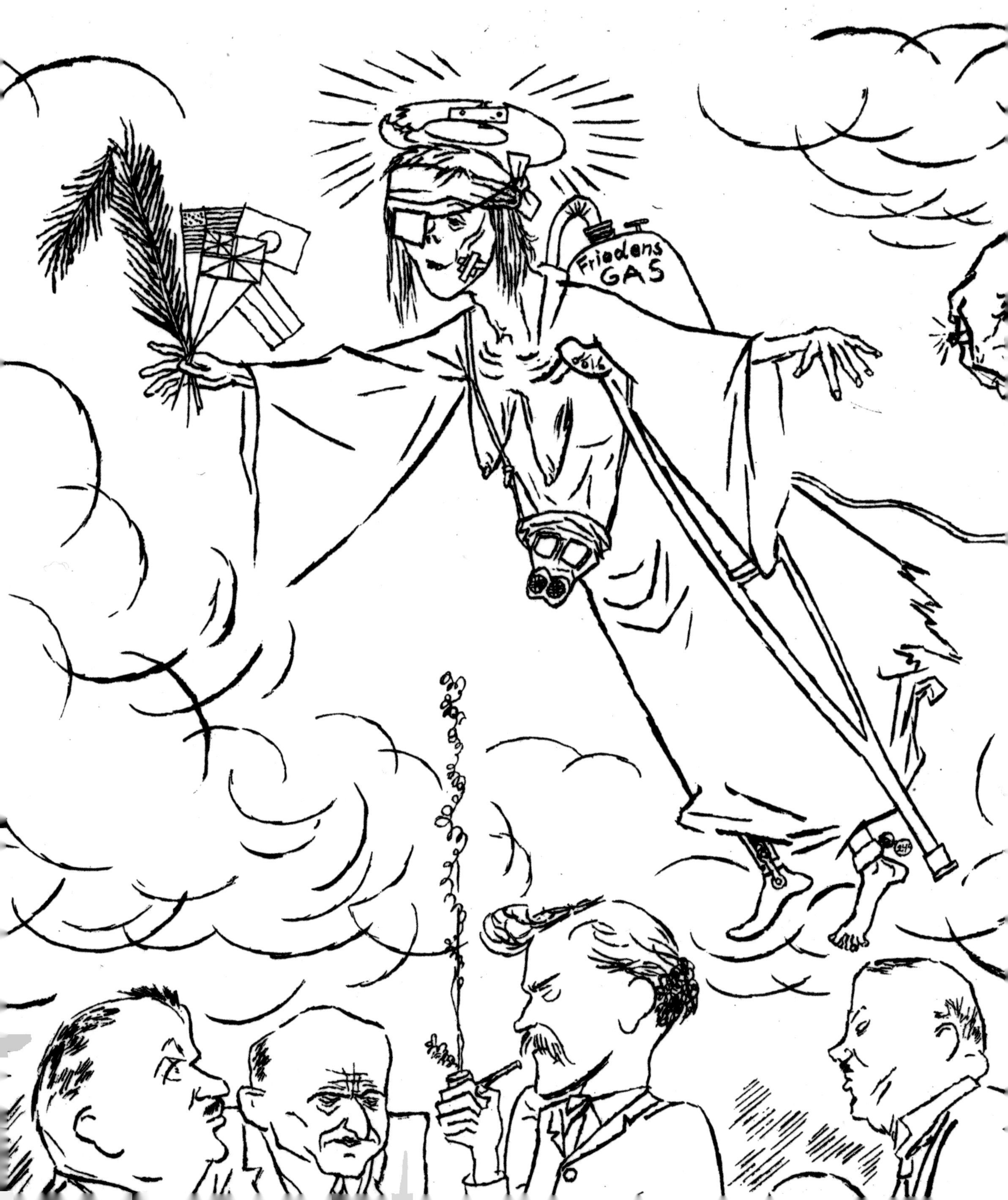
Friedens
GAS

Nie Wieder Krieg: Wartime Landscapes

On 23 August 1939, Gillies was planning to send laundry home from his camp in Aberdeenshire so he could stay on there and paint. War was declared eleven days later. Six days after that he paid an inflated price in cash for a property in Temple that was not to become his permanent home for another ten years.

Their move was so rushed, the Gillies family had to live for some weeks with one of the vendors, George Scott-Moncrieff, before George joined his wife Ann at her sister's in a move to save money. Gillies told George he feared for the safety of his own family when Edinburgh was bombed, and not unreasonably. A Zeppelin in 1916 had virtually tracked Gillies' friends and relatives across the city, bombing in Leith, near the ECA, near Crozier's Marchmont home close to the lodgings Gillies was shortly to occupy, and in Merchiston, near an aunt. The Temple property was substandard, the worst the asthmatic Janet had ever occupied and her mother for forty years past; and there was no prospect of renovation. The Gillies' Edinburgh home was two miles from the target of Leith Docks, itself on the flight path for the key strategic target of the Forth Rail Bridge. But, like the Geisslers, who lived nearer the docks and also left town, they hoped to return once danger was past.

The move to Temple features in the countryman narrative as the return of the native to the land that had raised him. But no evidence supports the assumptions behind 'return' or 'raised', or the contention that Gillies disliked Edinburgh. It had everything to offer, the cinemas he loved, sociability and access by car to varied countryside. It was a secure base for his mother and Janet during his long summer escapes, and there were relatives close by from both sides of the family. Temple was already one of the many places in and around Edinburgh where he painted. Had he wanted to move, there had been ample opportunity in the three years after Emma's death. His account in 1970 of the move is typically disingenuous: 'I needed to live in the landscape I was painting'. Indeed he did. Fuel would be scarce during the war, but the Borders train into Edinburgh stopped at Gorebridge station, under three miles from Temple, and there was open landscape in and around the village.

The fears that prompted *Nie Wieder Krieg* (loosely, *No More War*) (*Seifenblasen* 1930 [85]) and, more specifically, the fear of death from the air, stalked Gillies in the 1930s. In Paris in 1937 he saw the impact of bombing in Picasso's *Guernica* (1937) [ni]. He also knew *Reisende in Friedensartikeln* (loosely, *Peace Delegates*) (1930) [86], a George Grosz satire on the prospects for peace. Smoke from Ramsay MacDonald's pipe mixes with gas spread by a crippled and captive angel of peace, the soul of a body dismembered by 'the new ruling class' satirised by Grosz. She grasps an olive branch, broken into a quasi-ogive form that will recur in the flower-stems of Gillies' still lifes following the Second World War.

Temple was a temporary bolt-hole, and Elder Dickson's contention, that the new environment soon moved Gillies' painting towards the tonal values and austere simplicities of the Border hills, is an error that has passed unremarked. The wartime still lifes were neither austere nor simple, and innovation in the landscapes was a decade away. The subjects change, of course, to those of the immediate vicinity ([87], [88],

Opposite:
Detail from *Reisende in Friedensourtikeln* ([86] – see p. 114)

[89]). In dealing with these, however, Gillies goes back into his repertoire, even, in *Temple Village* (early 1940s) [ni], to the never-to-be-repeated Neo-Impressionism of some of his student work. Paintings like *Temple, Midlothian* (nd, mid-1940s) [88] revert to his early response to Derain and Munch. *Dusk at Letterfearn* (*c.* 1947) [90] shows that this continued after the war, when he could travel again and headed north-west. Klee's naivety is evident in *Landscape, Temple* (nd, *c.* 1942) [ni] and *Midlothian Village* (*c.* 1944, *c.* 1942–4) [ni]. And there is nothing austere or tonally subdued about the Fauvist colour of *Temple, Midlothian* (1942) [ni], *Temple* (mid-1940s) [ni], *Temple Village* (*c.* 1969, *c.* 1940s) [92] or *Early Morning Temple* (*c.* 1942) [91].

One thing, however, does appear to change. The number of drawings probably increases, particularly drawings in ink [89] and often with added watercolour wash [87]. Gillies had been knocked off course by Emma's death and had struggled to produce enough landscapes in oil for the Society of Eight exhibition of 1937. But he painted watercolour assiduously in the late 1930s and turned

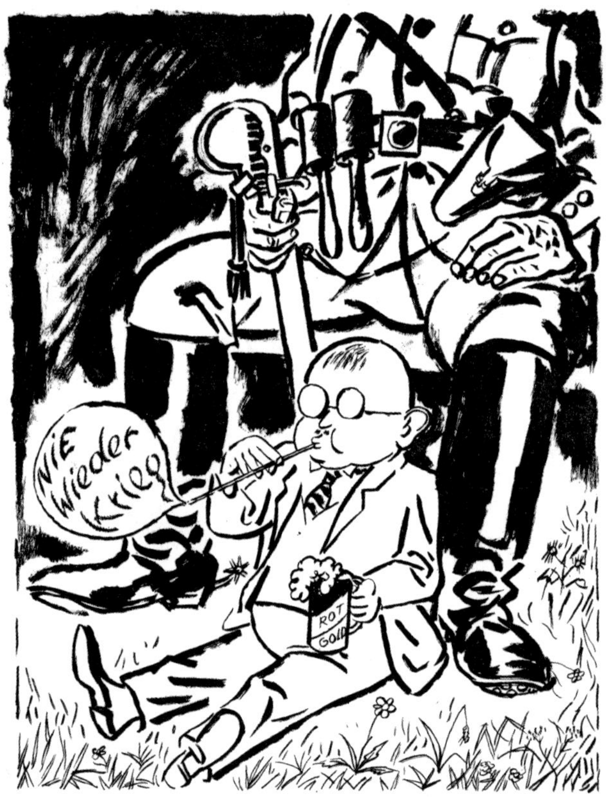

85 *Seifenblasen* [Soap Bubbles] (1930), by George Grosz. From an image owned by Gillies

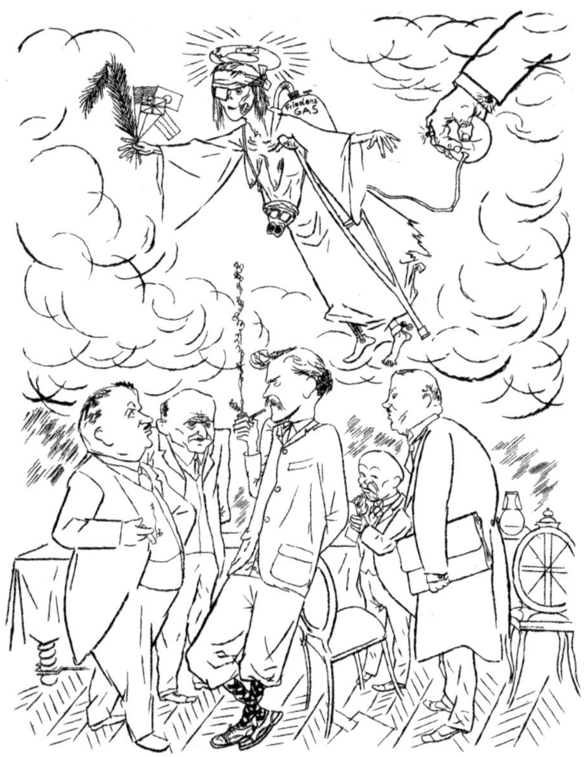

86 *Reisende in Friedensourtikeln* [loosely, Peace Emissaries] (1930), by George Grosz. From an image owned by Gillies'

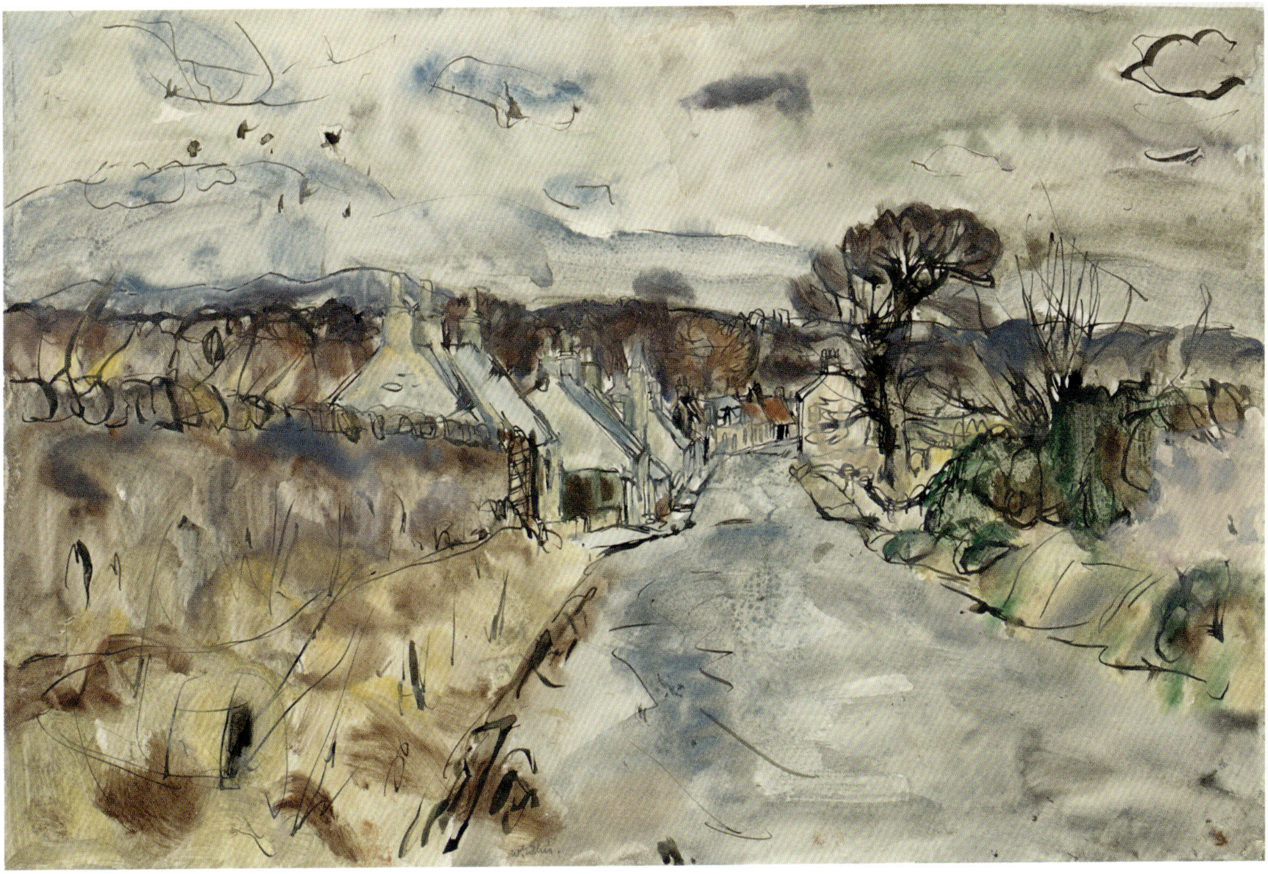

87 *Winter Afternoon, Temple* (*c.* 1942). Watercolour, gouache, pen and ink, 34.2 cm by 51.1 cm

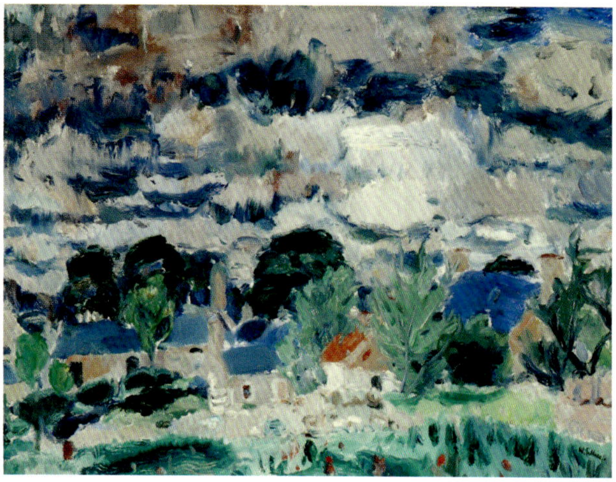

88 *Temple, Midlothian* (nd, mid-1940s). Oil, 44.7 cm by 60 cm

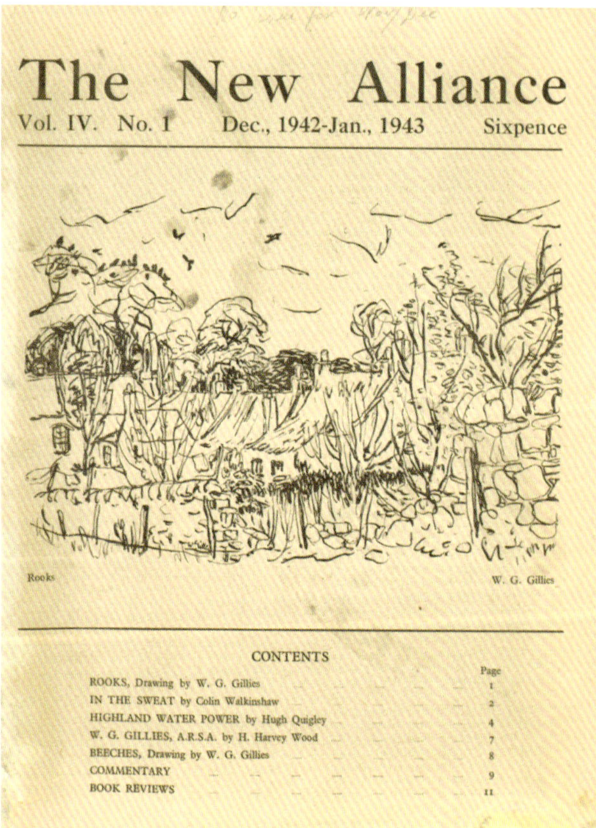

The New Alliance

Vol. IV. No. 1 Dec., 1942-Jan., 1943 Sixpence

Rooks W. G. Gillies

CONTENTS

89 *Rooks* (nd, *c.* 1942). Pen and ink, from *The New Alliance* (December 1942)

more often than before to ink with wash. He had been impressed by this when he saw the work of the French artist Raoul Dufy at the SSA in 1936 and again at the Paris Exposition of 1937. So had Maxwell. Unlike Maxwell, however, Gillies rarely drew over wet watercolour. By 1940 he almost always applied the wash once the ink was dry.

It was a technique well suited to wartime conditions. As an air raid warden, his nightly patrols left him less time to paint in oil and he gave priority in this medium to his still lifes. He had lost his exhibiting outlet with the Society of Eight and had yet to establish one with the Scottish Gallery (Aitken Dott) (the full name of Scotland's principal commercial gallery). The number of works he was allowed to show and sell at the RSA and the SSA had been reduced. But landscape drawings were small, cheap and relatively quick, could be strengthened by ink, and further enhanced by watercolour wash. Colour, said Harvey Wood, was 'just what the times demand'. Though Gillies began to find influential customers for his oil landscapes at the Scottish Gallery in 1942, it was the washed drawings that sold best. He always drew anyway, drew sublimely, and could wash many at a time. These relatively safe works were also among the first of his bought by his future patron, Robert A. Lillie.

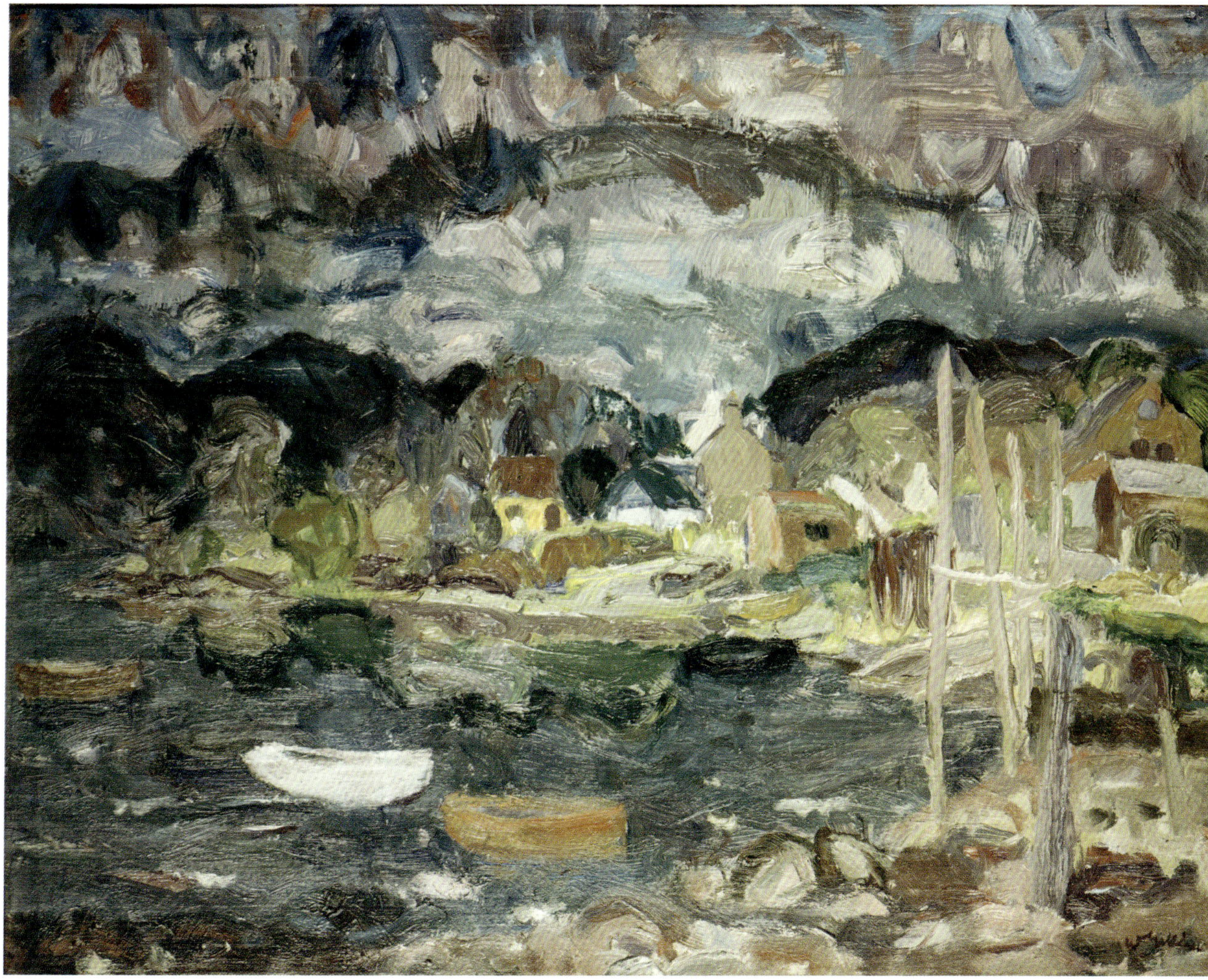

90 *Dusk at Letterfearn* (*c.* 1947). Oil, 49 cm by 61.2 cm

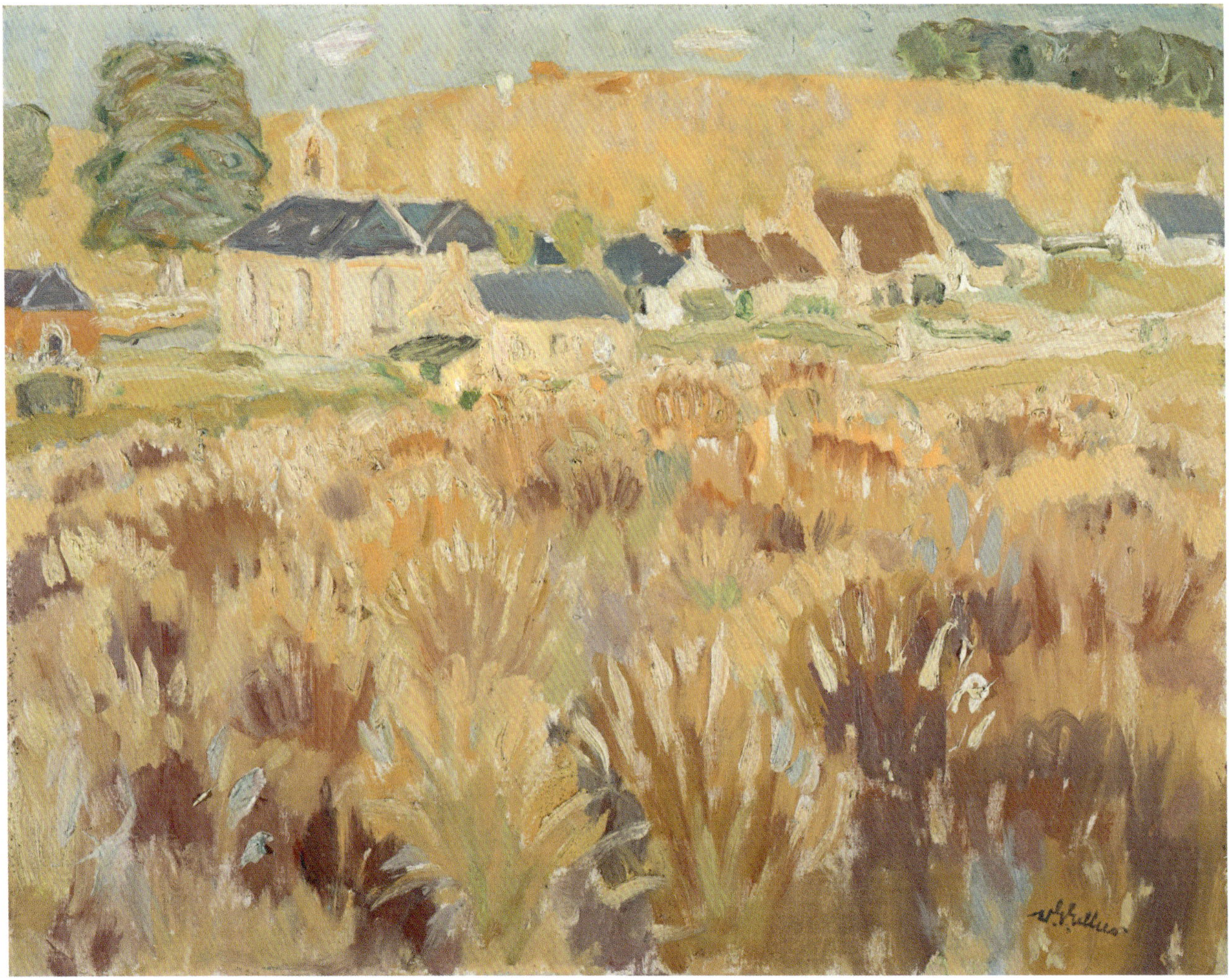

91 *Early Morning, Temple* (*c.* 1942). Oil, 54 cm by 69 cm

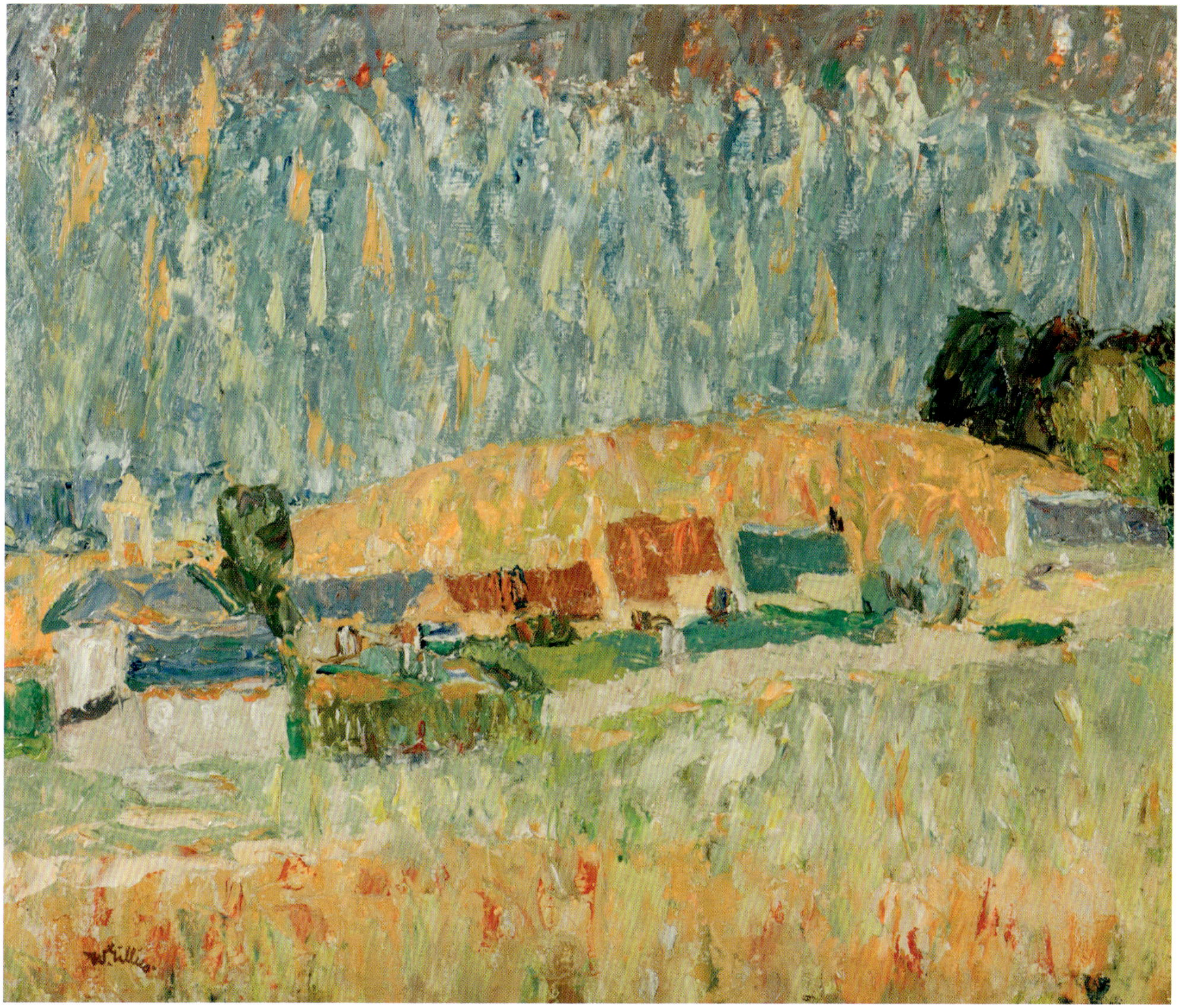

92 *Temple Village* (*c.* 1969, *c.* 1940s). Oil, 50 cm by 60 cm

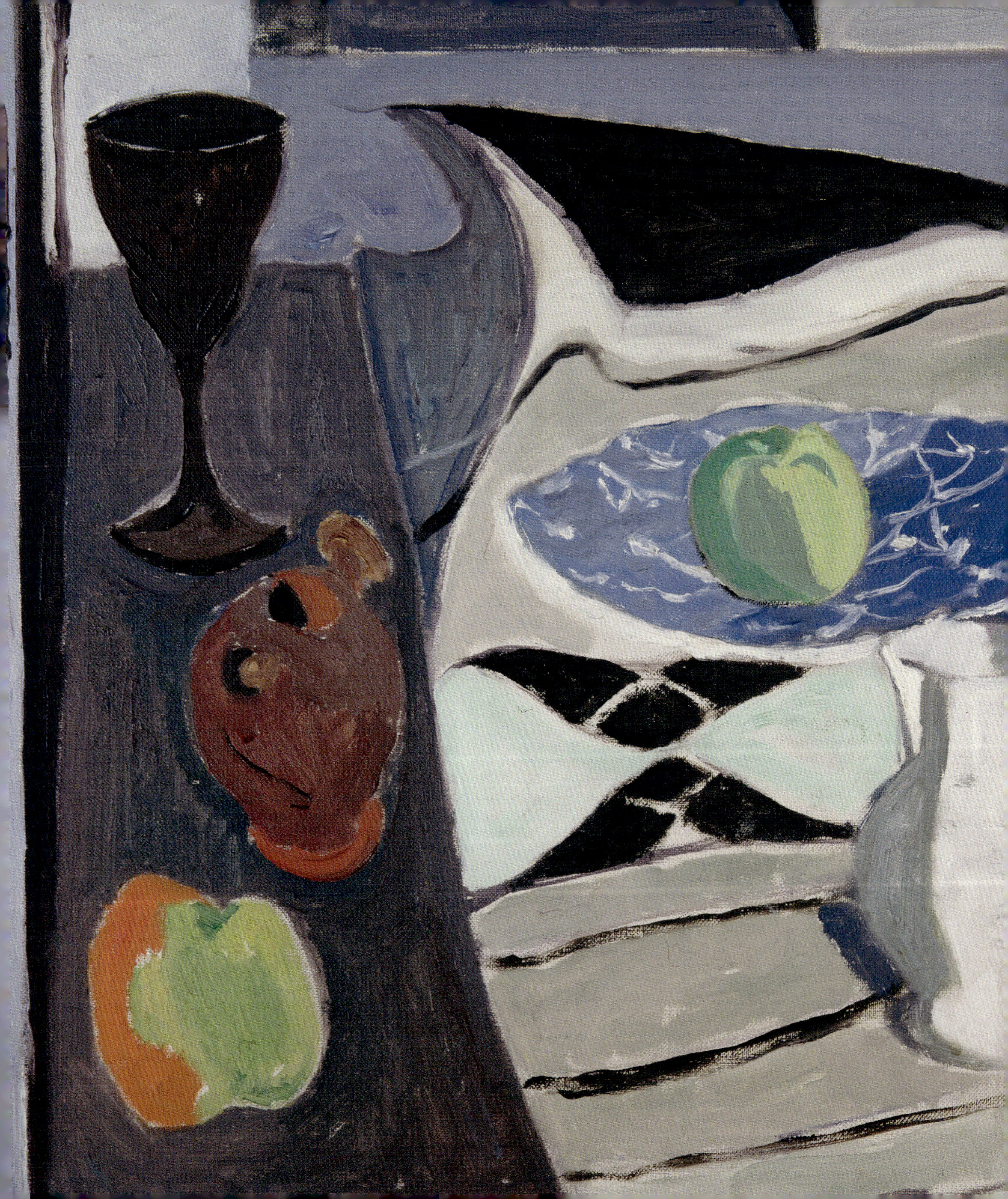

Still Lifes 1939–60

Until the mid-1950s, still life was in the mainstream of British modernism. The artist-critic Patrick Heron wrote in 1949, 'One paints the portrait of a jug if human beings elude one's vision'. Gillies painted possibly as many as 400 still lifes after 1924, at an average of one every six weeks. Almost all were in oil. This was not a trivial undertaking. Something is known about some 300 of them (308 for the purposes of analysis) and around 200 of these (205) are also known visually, as either the original work or as an image thereof.

The element of memorialisation in the still lifes constituted by the presence of Emma's ceramics has rightly been noted, but on insecure grounds. There were plenty of her ceramics lying around, and others too. Gillies could have picked them up at random or chosen them solely for their visual contribution and not as signifiers. A stronger case for memorialisation is needed. The black vase, too, has been noted, but only as 'ubiquitous' and not for its possible allusions. The signification of poppies has passed unnoticed, and so too has the migration into the still lifes of the existential issues explored in the portraits of the 1930s. Hence the default 'countryman' view that the still lifes are about the domestic felicity of 'a very still life' (Smith's 1991 subtitle).

Two further explanations for the still lifes have also been offered. One is that they were a test-bed for ideas then to be applied to landscape, his first priority. I claim that landscape was its own test-bed between the wars, and still life an equal, and at times greater, priority in the fifteen years after 1939. Again, it does not help that Elder Dickson has subverted a statement Gillies made around 1960 on the greater meaning he had achieved in still life relative to his work in landscape (see the next section). Erroneously, he turns it into Gillies' alleged recognition that still life could never satisfy his countryman instinct.

It has also been mooted that still lifes were something to paint during long winter evenings when a Gillies who was tied to his mother's apron strings compensated for a personal emotional deficit by trying too hard to be modern. Similarities to Braque's still lifes are cited here, but mistakenly. There is nothing of Braque in Gillies' still lifes of any period that he would not already have met during his visits to Paris in the 1920s. Braque showed in Edinburgh in 1935 and in 1956. Yet Gillies at both times was moving away from anything that might be called derivative. Nothing remotely comparable accompanies the exploration of cubist space in *Still Life with Black Jug* (1933) [11] apart from *Two Pots, Saucer and Fruit* (1933, *c.* 1933?) [ni]. Had he wanted to pastiche Braque, he would have done a different and better job, and did so on one occasion when he showed *Still Life with Black Fishes* (1965) [168] at the Royal Academy in London to mark the artist's death and his own election. Critics found Braque in the Gillies still lifes of the late 1940s because Braque was all they knew. They could not know, or did not allow, that these works were but an intermediate stage of a journey that had started in a different place in the 1930s with the early and sometimes pedantic symbolic remembrances, and would end in a different place in the mid-1950s with the coexistence of life and death, joy and suffering, held in a single vision that could not be mistaken for Braque's. Gillies mastered the scales of modernism in his twenties but composed his own themes, at times of his own choosing.

Opposite:
Detail from *Still Life* ([101] – see p. 135)

Some numbers supply a first support for the argument. The annual totals of known still lifes (making up the 308) vary over the years between 1925, when Gillies became a professional artist, and his death in 1973. Numbers alone can tell us little about the 1920s because of gaps in the evidence and the paucity of images. But this problem largely disappears with his election to the Society of Eight. His period of greatest sustained activity, which coincided with a darkening in the mood of these works, was in the seven years 1948–54, when the annual average of known still lifes was at its highest, at fifteen a year. This compares with an annual average of around five both for the eight years 1932–9 and for the last eighteen completed years of his life. These are large differences that are unlikely to have occurred by chance, and there are further, more period-specific, fluctuations within them. Rising numbers in the 1930s were stalled and reversed in the three years after Emma's death before the rise resumed to reach an initial high point of eighteen in 1942. From there the annual numbers fell away successively to just a single work in 1946, before returning to double figures in 1947 and the sustained period of high volumes that followed. This period in turn ended in the mid-1950s but with a sharper drop, to annual levels mostly back around five or less, where they stayed until a final modest burst of higher activity immediately following his retirement.

Half of the works known visually (103 of the 205) show at least one of the symbolic objects – the poppy, the black vase, a brown jug and Emma's ceramics. The black vase, for example, appears twenty-eight times but is not ubiquitous. There is no sign of it until 1933, not long after Crozier's death. It then appears in eight out of the twelve works from 1933 to 1935 for which images survive. A similar initial eruption followed with the poppy flower. One was painted before 1936, the year of Emma's death, but at least eight of the remaining ten have dates between 1936 and 1942 inclusive. Possible anemones are excluded from all counts. I also include as a symbolic object the brown jug, decorated with poppies, that Gillies introduced in 1950 and used a further nine times, mostly in combination with other symbolic objects. It is probably not one of Emma's. None of Emma's ceramics can confidently be identified in the paintings before her death in 1936. Thereafter, they, too, are more common at some times than at others. I use rigorous criteria for counts of these ceramics: they must conform to known ceramics or decorative motifs of hers and also be clear in the paintings.

Two former colleagues who have an expertise in statistical modelling that I lack generously gave much time and thought to the best way to distinguish real (that is, non-random) changes from random (statistically, chance) fluctuations across the years 1925 to 1972. Regression analyses were done separately for the 305 still lifes (testing changes in the overall number of still lifes each year) and, using what is known as a logit transformation, for the 205 (testing changes in the proportion of still lifes each year that show at least one memorial object). Uncertainty over the precise date of paintings was taken into account through the use of weights related to the estimated precision of dating. These methods allow for testing hypotheses, such as that of a step-change in volumes of paintings over a given period of years, while taking account of the modelled relationship to year of painting over the whole period (Ecob and Burnhill 2023). Also, locally weighted fitting procedures ('LOWESS') were run to facilitate understanding of such shorter-term variations in numbers and proportions (NIST/SEMATECH 2022, 4.1.1.4).

One of these shorter-term variations proved of particular interest when tested by regression analysis. I had hoped that the more prolific the year, the higher would be proportion of still lifes from that year that showed memorial objects. From this one could have inferred, without too many additional caveats, that an intensity of engagement (proxied by the number of still lifes) was driven by an urge to memorialise (proxied by the proportion with memorial objects). But the relationship between the two measures proved no stronger than chance when tested across the forty-eight years 1925–72.

There were two possibilities. First, and self-evidently, the annual numbers of still lifes may be proxies, not only for an urge to memorialise, but also for constraints and opportunities, only some of which are known. These could affect annual volumes in diverse ways and swamp any effects of motivation. Second, it is possible that Gillies was indifferent to the memorial objects themselves. There is, however, some statistical support for thinking this improbable. In the five years 1949–53, regression analysis showed that the proportion of works showing memorial objects was indeed significantly higher than before and after. These were the years of Gillies' darkest and most sustained attempt to resolve his existential dilemma through his still-life idiom, and the five-year phase falls within the seven years of his most extended period of high-volume production, 1948–54.

As indicators of Gillies' engagement in still life, these comparisons are imperfect approximations. They suffer from the lack of a comparable series for his landscapes. Also, correlations are not causes, causes are often multiple and agency is shaped both by opportunities, such as his election to the Society of Eight, and by constraints, like his time as Principal of the ECA or an illness at the end of 1960s. Other constraints, however, may have had mixed effects. The war, which reduced time available for painting, also ended landscape holidays and may thereby have contributed to a jump in the number of still lifes in the early 1940s. Conversely, his most sustained period of heightened activity was between roughly 1947 and 1954. This coincided with a renewed freedom to travel but also with the return of ex-service personnel and his appointment to Head of School of Drawing and Painting at the ECA in 1946. As mentioned, nearly all the still lifes were in oil so, for these years at least, it is easier to argue that the high level of still-life activity resulted from a renewed urgency – from decisions to paint a still life rather than an oil landscape when time allowed. And that case is strengthened when we consider the development of the works themselves, as we now do.

The Red Squirrel (1941) [93] originates in Gillies' first response to Emma's death and to the further disruption that came with war. Emma is here, her red squirrel scarcely more visible than it was in *Interior* (1938) [42] (where it is half obscured by Mrs Gillies). But the attempt at happiness is even more determined in the wartime still lifes. Indeed, the vase is painted white here rather than black for the only time in all its appearances. (Neither the vase in this instance, nor its possible poppy, is included in the counts of signifiers.) Torn from their family home, the Gillies are now bereft of Emma, with no electricity and little heat. Robert Lillie would eventually buy a new grate

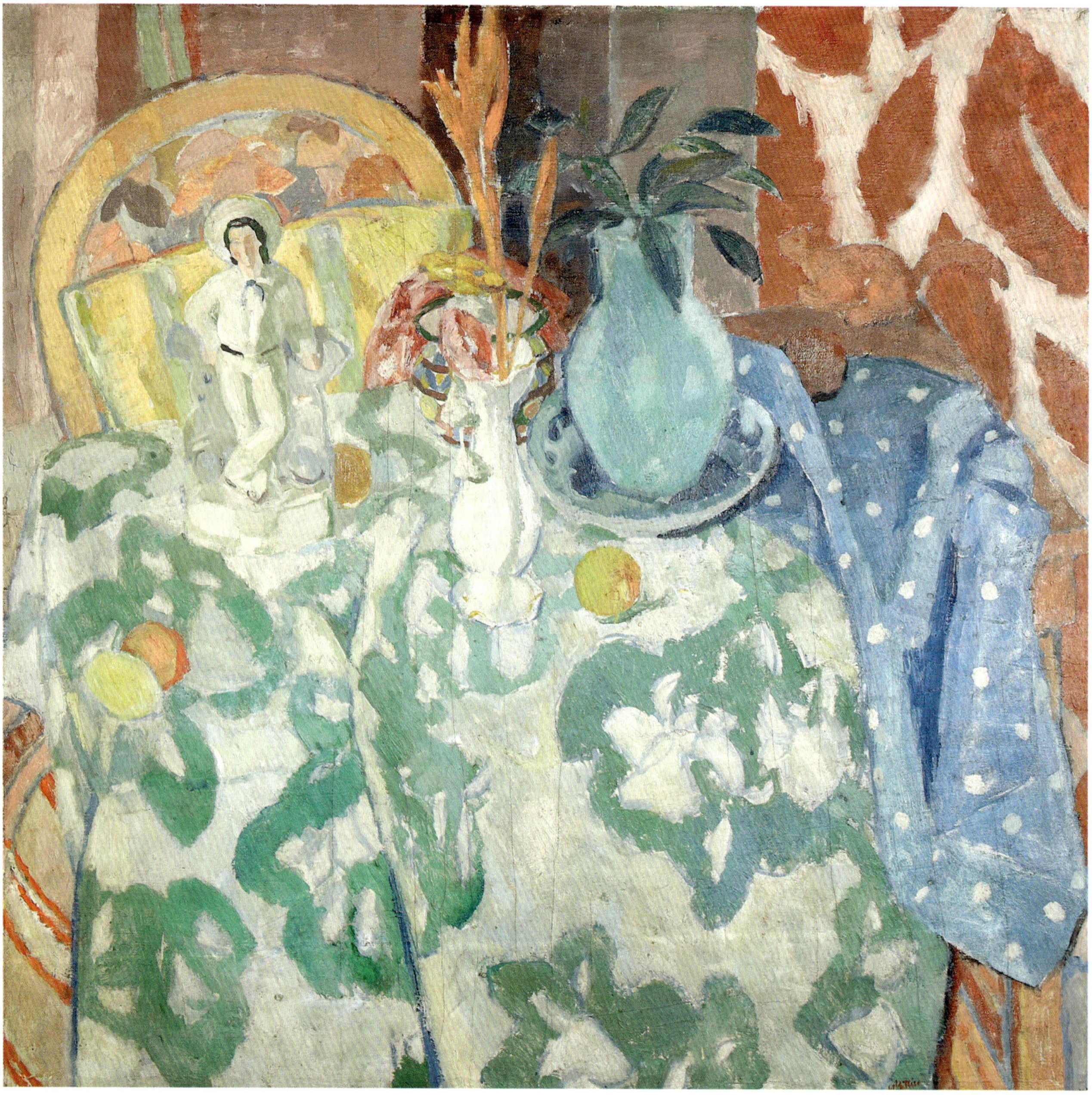

93 *The Red Squirrel* (1941). Oil, 111.8 cm by 114.9 cm

for Gillies' studio and the logs to burn. Meantime, Gillies warms himself with the glow of Matisse.

Almost all the wartime still lifes, both the large table-top arrangements, like *Flowers on a Sideboard* (nd, *c.* 1941) [153], and many of the flower-pieces, like *Still Life with Roses* (*c.* 1943) [ni], have this keyed-up colour; 'Just what the times demand', but also a kind of hunkering down in the effort to survive. Most of the large table-top arrangements take fabric and colour across the whole canvas, and exclude natural light and the world beyond the blackout curtain. This suggests that memorialisation was put on hold, became a more distant priority, sometime around 1942. There is evidence of only twenty-one works from the four years 1943–6 and only four of the ten known images of these show memorial objects, all before 1945. Possible explanations for the extension of this pause into the immediate post-war period are his resumption of communal landscape forays to Fife and the north-west coast; encroachments on his time with the deaths in Dundee in 1945 and 1946 of two of his mother's siblings; the visit to Paris in the summer of 1946 that he organised for his students; and his new responsibilities that year as acting head of painting during the military demobilisation and negotiation of new national salary scales. Only one still life from 1946 is known, and that a pen and ink drawing, *Flowers in a Pot* (1946) [ni].

But then, around 1947 or 1948, there begins the extended period of change, mentioned earlier, when Gillies' use of memorial objects and the overall numbers of still lifes are both at a peak. We now see a gradual decluttering of composition, a darkening of tonality, an increased use of black, but a continuing use of symbol (in raw numbers, fifty-eight per cent of the seventy-six images known to me between 1948 and 1954 inclusive). There is also the first use of sharpened and shard-like forms with the potential to function analogously but universally in a way that private signifiers cannot. The implied space changes too, no longer wall-to-wall colour and indulgent design, but something simpler and plainer.

These changes allow the threat of the outside world into the domestic interior and were disliked by Robert Lillie and some critics for what struck them as their puritanical severity. This was not the Gillies they thought they knew or wanted to know. In the eight years from 1947 to 1954, two-thirds of the oils Gillies showed at the RSA and SSA were still lifes. So was the exhibit he sent by invitation to the main art competition of the Festival of Britain in 1951. This was a purpose renewed and it soon found a staunch advocate in the person of Eric Newton, a prominent English critic of the 1950s.

Still Life with Shells and Flowers (nd, *c.* 1947) [94] is a douce, early example. Untitled Still Life (nd, *c.* 1950) [95] is more sinister. In both works, the black vase is back and the fir-tree pot is Emma's. Everything now is angular and pointed, even the feminine lace, seen also in the 'savagely zestful' *Still Life, Doyley* (*c.* 1948) [96]. The cubistic painting of its draped cloths sharpens the sense of menace. Shadows on the newly exposed wall add to it.

Gillies used shadow for some six years during the transition. He knew a version of *La Condition Humaine* (1935) [ni] by the Belgian Surrealist René Magritte. It expresses the limited capacity of humanity to understand our place in the cosmos from appearances alone and it refers obliquely to Plato's metaphor of the shadows cast by humans gathered in a cave with a fire, a source of light.

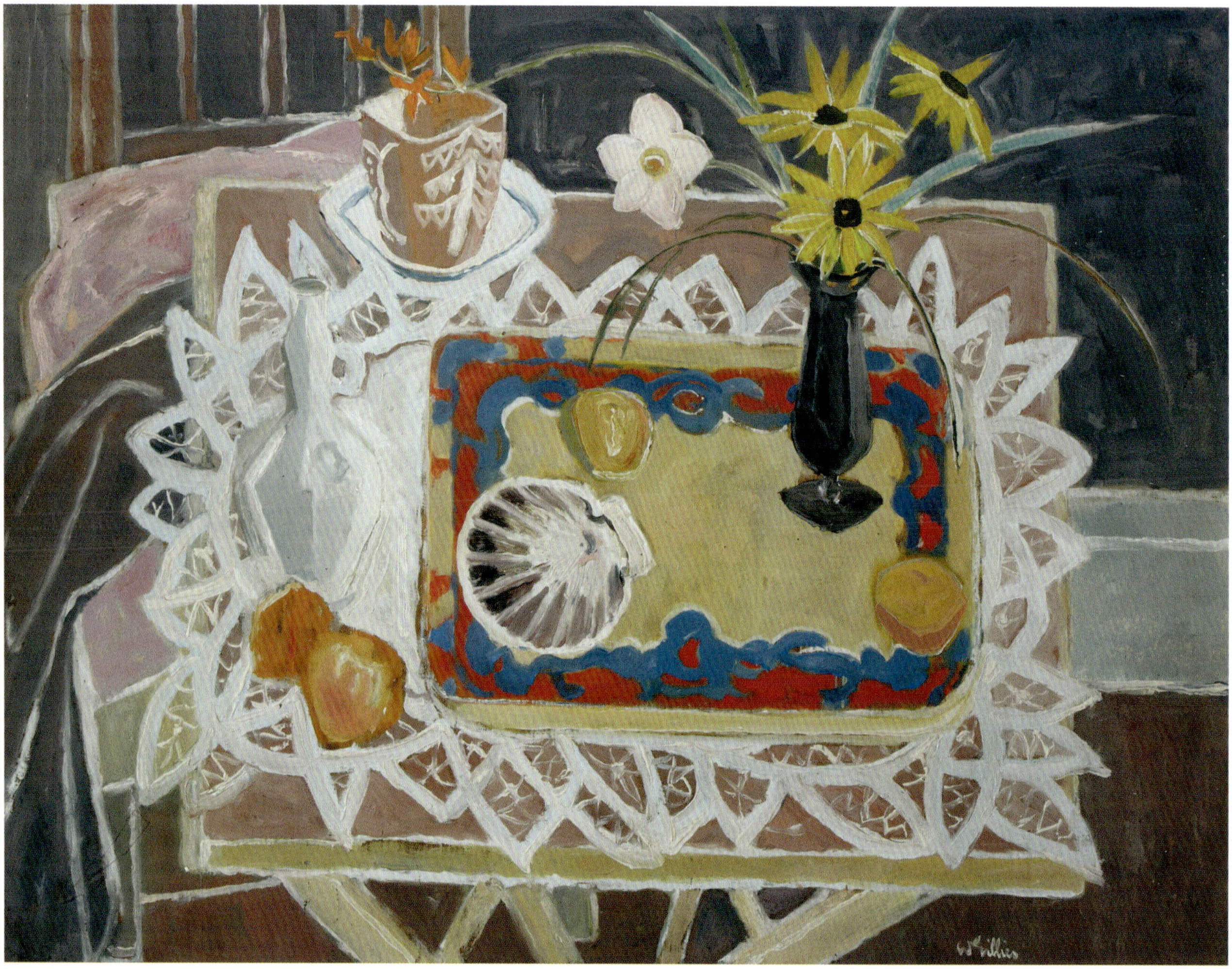

94 *Still Life with Shells and Flowers (Studio Window Still Life)* (nd, *c.* 1947). Oil, 86.6 cm by 114.6 cm

Gillies attributed his own shadows to a Tilley oil lamp, his only source of light at night. Again, this is typically disingenuous, but no one asked him why shadows do not feature in the wartime works made under this light.

Shadow contributes to *Melon on Platter* (1950) [99]. A promise of plenty after years of austerity, the melon is fecund and feminine. Pale flesh surrounds the labial crescents and the seed within. It is framed by darker angularities and by crescents multiplied by shadow. It lies on a domestic table where the folds of a draped cloth are formed by further triangles and crescents. These forms also figure, both here and in other works, in monochromatic areas of fruit and the shadowed interiors of shallow bowls and dishes.

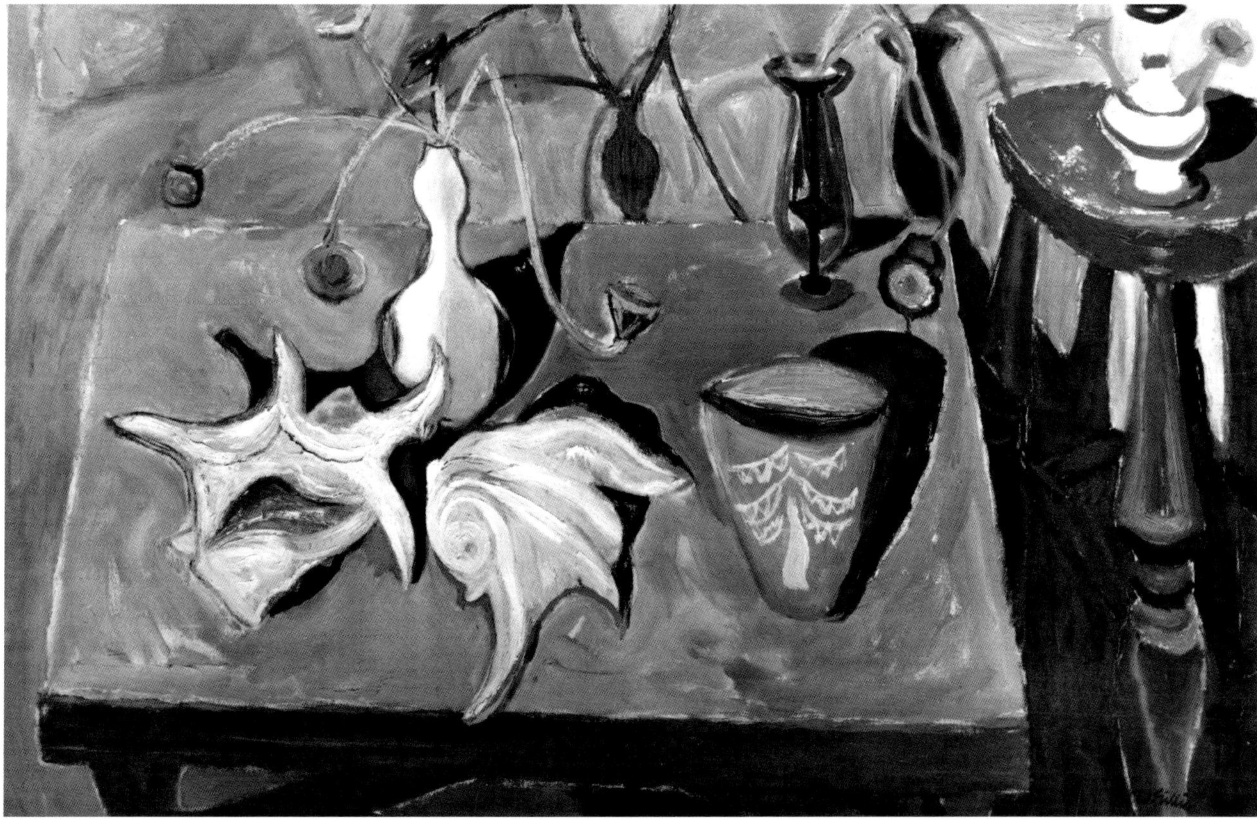

95 Untitled still life (nd, *c.* 1950). Oil, dimensions unknown. From a photograph of the untraced work

The symbolic carriers of remembrance, with their limited visual potential, are now being superseded by a more powerful combination of form (angularities), colour (yellow and white for good and light) and tonality (dark for death, but dark that enhances colour with its embrace). Here and hereafter, darkness and black – deprivation of light – function as a transcription into the visual of the, hitherto purely cognitive, logic of the *memento mori*: life is enhanced by the embrace of death.

The melon is framed by the sides of the tables. Emma's ceramic at the top is displaced. Its visual contribution is minimal. We still have her presence symbolically, and also the contrast between the withered flower heads and the seed of the freshly exposed melon. In other works, however, flowers also contribute through form, specifically the quasi-ogive formed when an erect stem is bent sharply down. Such ogives add to the angularities in Untitled Still Life (nd, *c.* 1950) [95], *Still Life* (nd, *c.* 1950) [97] and *Still Life, Lamplight* (*c.* 1953) [98]. Typically, they are contrived from dead stems, spider grass, and living but etiolated stems. In *Sunflower* (nd, *c.* 1954) [25] this etiolation, by virtue of the implicit contrast with the well-known sunflowers of Van Gogh, speaks of

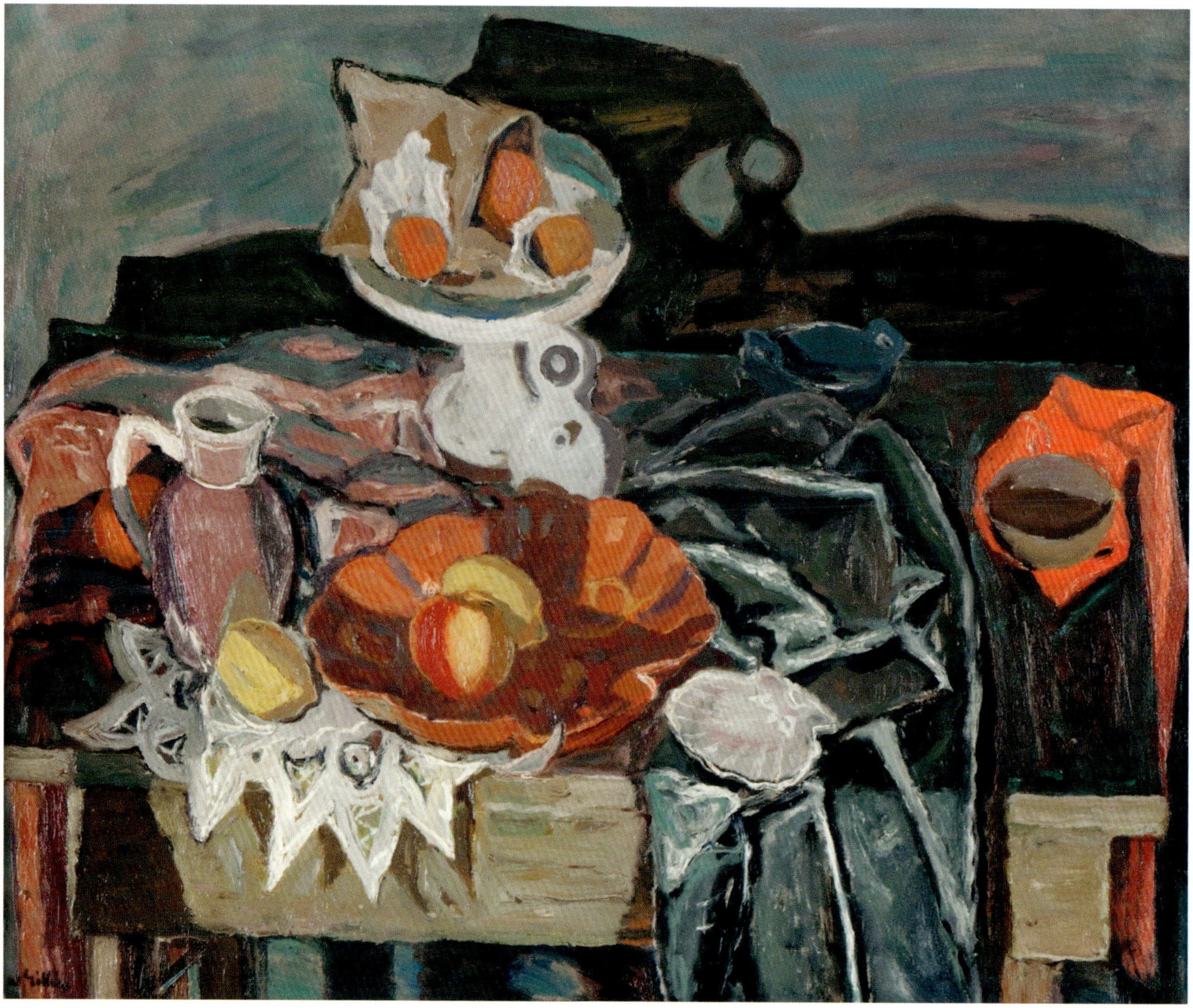

96 *Still Life, Doyley* (*c.* 1948). Oil, 83 cm by 102.8 cm

the struggles of life towards light, struggles that are recorded in distortions of other organic forms, such as trees.

The table is decluttered in works like *Still Life* (nd, *c.* 1950) [97], *Two Jugs, Flowers and Conch Shell* (*c.* 1952) [100] and *Still Life with Yellow Flowers* (nd) (*c.* 1953) [161]. This creates space for the forms, colours and tones of fecundity/life, and of menace/death, to establish their own, purely visual, relations with each other in works of greater abstraction. As things are abstracted (removed) and simplified, forms become clearer, spaces between them become forms as well, and areas of colour can interact both with them and

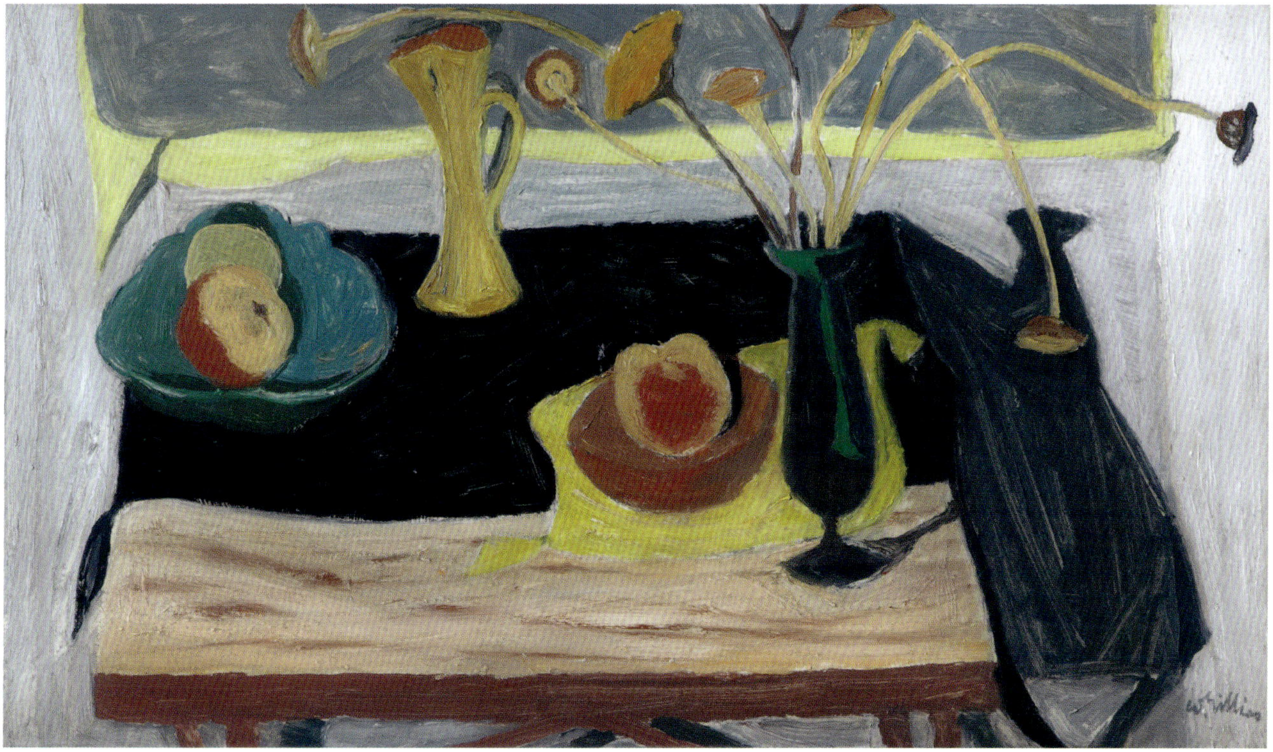

97 *Still Life* (nd, *c.* 1950), oil, 41 cm by 73.1 cm

with each other. Dark and light, angularity and curve, comprise a deeper counterpoint in which overt symbolism is potentially redundant or an irritating, cognitive, intrusion on a 'negative capability' to respond. *Still Life Blue and Brown* (1952) [ni] and *Still Life* (nd, *c.* 1954) [101] extend this move and, together with his Diploma work for the RSA ([102], discussed below), mark the culmination of this transition both qualitatively and quantitatively.

Late in his life, Gillies described the effect of early (analytic) cubist works by Picasso and Braque as a 'bomb blast' (that war again) when he had first seen images of them as a student in Edinburgh. The imagery of destruction ran deep among artists of his generation, an affinity they sensed between the shards of conflict and the broken sections of reality that pre-1914 Cubism had revealed to the world. Its angular forms found their way through Vorticism and Futurism into images of the war itself and thence into the sensibilities of a post-war generation; into the etchings and verses of Paul Nash (his *Places,* 1922) and later into the cognate imagery of Graham Sutherland. Sutherland's *Thorn Tree* (*c.* 1945) [ni], *Crucifixion* (*c.* 1946) [ni] and *Deposition* (*c.* 1946) [ni] shocked some who saw them at the SSA exhibition of 1948, a time when the Holocaust and Hiroshima were reminding a post-war generation of the inhumanity in mankind and the means of global destruction we now possess.

With its echoes of the shattered world of Cubism's early years, the sequence of still lifes that Gillies began around 1948 returned to existential issues he had tried to suppress immediately after the First World War and had put on hold during the Second World War: the coexistence of consciousness, love, life and joy with the vulnerability of the human condition and the arbitrariness of fate. The images tell how he had met these inevitabilities in his own life – through the shards of war, the unscripted deaths of the young and the withering of youth by a winter no spring could restore. Even the woman's realm is vulnerable, the domestic space sanctified for his mother and Janet by religion and the Kailyard. He knows that, even in times of peace, their beliefs cannot shelter them from arbitrary threat, and that neither can he.

Emma's ceramics released an accumulating body of images (meanings and visual realisations) among the paintings in which they were enshrined, elements of an emergent and self-referencing vocabulary of forms, colours, gestures and feelings: 'often now I merely start off with a notion, a symbol, of one or two of these objects. They seem to group themselves in my mind automatically and my picture is really an extension of this notion' (Films of Scotland and Scottish Arts Council 1970). This is also, I think, the sense in which he spoke of his move into 'almost pure abstraction' with these works.

When this began to happen, as I think it did in the late 1940s, explicit symbolic reference became redundant and still life became intuitive (in its 'second-nature' or 'learned' sense). We no longer have to wonder whether he saw, in the ogive, the broken olive branch of peace [86] or reached for Emma in a vase when she eluded his vision [38], for this intuition, founded in his long exploration of how pictures work, had led him towards a reflexive accommodation of imagination with perception, and a more universal language of feeling and sign.

When elected a full Academician of the RSA, it is customary for the artist to donate a signature painting (their 'Diploma' work) to the Academy. Gillies was elected in 1947 but waited eight years before giving the Academy, not the landscape many expected from the countryman they thought they knew, but *Still Life, Yellow Jug and Striped Cloth* (*c.* 1955) [102]. Two of its features, rare in his work, are also found in *Poppies in a Yellow Vase* (1934, *c.* 1936?) [46], his first attempt in still life to address the prison of mimesis: in both works, much of the meaning hangs on a painting within the painting, and on a diagonal of receding rectangles. On several counts, therefore, the Diploma work [102] asks to be read as one of his occasional, set-piece assessments of endeavour, painted mindful of that early statement [46] and of the conjunction of figuration with signifier at which he had now arrived. Perhaps also he was readying himself for a new departure in which the genres of still life and landscape would themselves be similarly conjoined.

Still Life, Yellow Jug and Striped Cloth (*c.* 1955) [102] configures three elements: the external world (objects), retinal experience (light, dark and colour), and ways of imaging this experience. Imaging occurs principally in five rectangular spaces, the painting itself and four of the five grey rectangles. The pictorial space defined by these rectangles becomes less mimetic as we move across the painting from the left and up

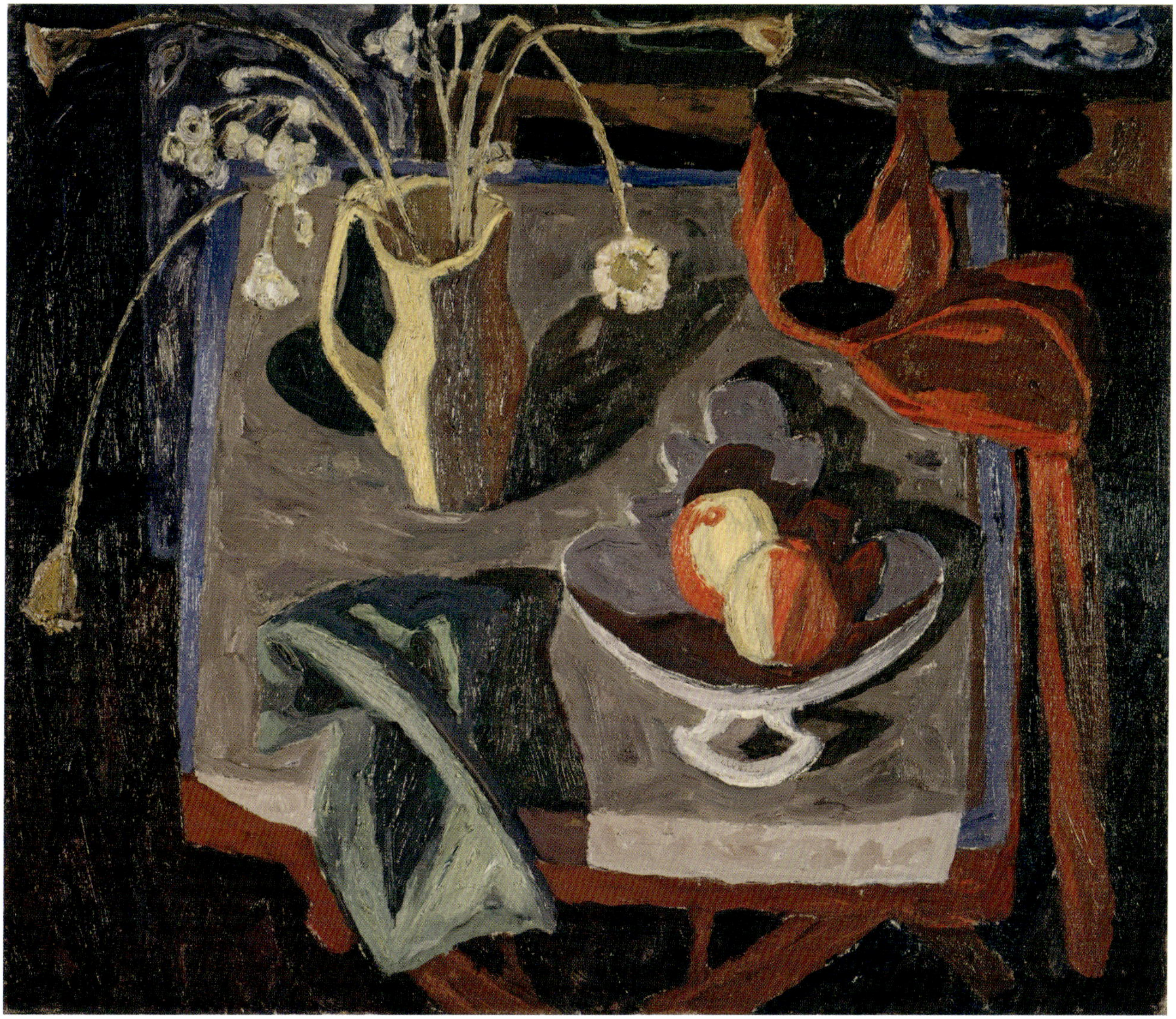

98 *Still Life, Lamplight* (*c.* 1953). Oil, 61.5 cm by 73.5 cm

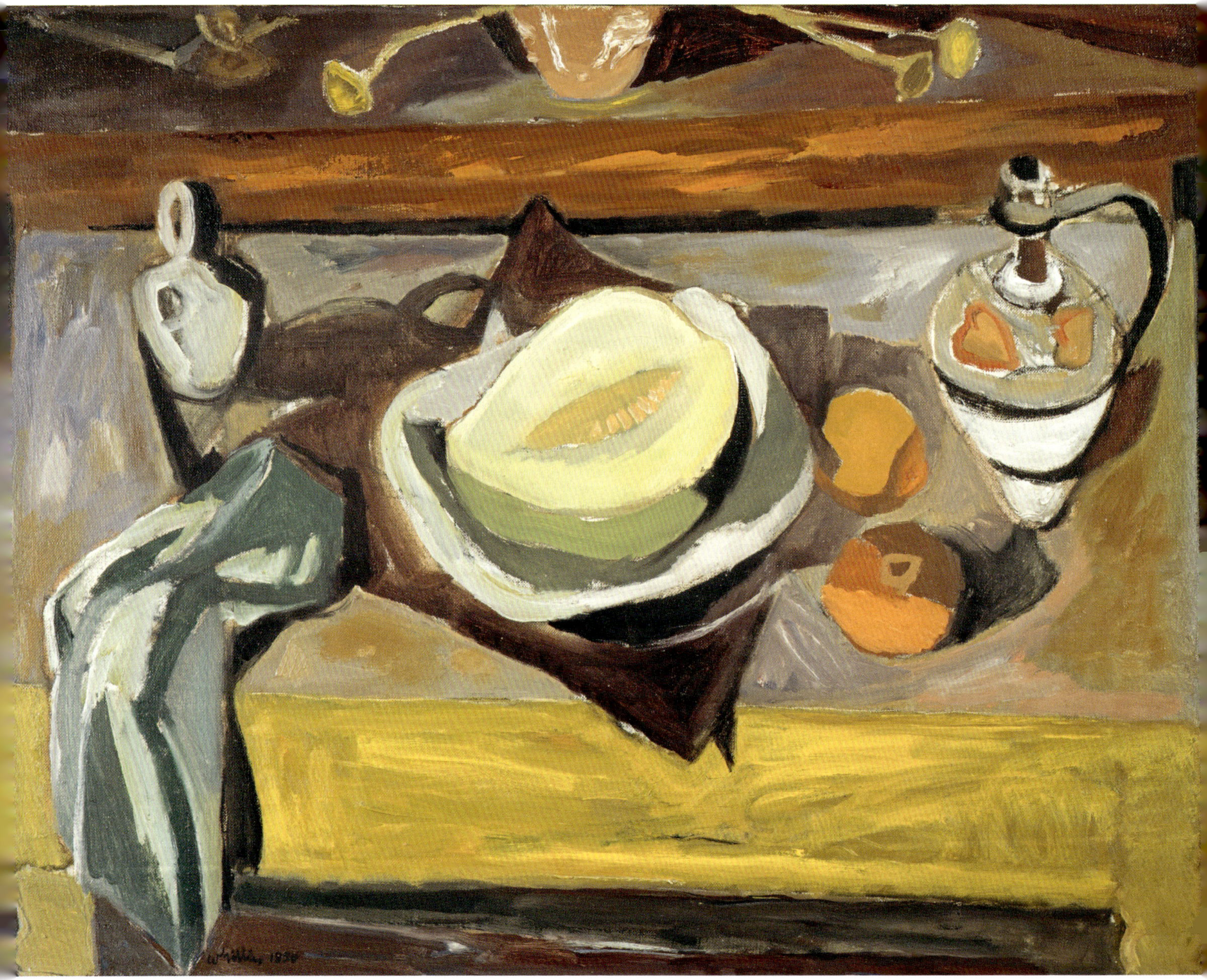

99 *Melon on Platter* (1950). Oil, 67.7 cm by 93 cm

the diagonal of rectangles to the window and garden, top right. Thus, the drawing of the external world, the harbour, is mimetic both in its content (proportionate recession) and its apparent placement. It is upright, virtually flat against the red wall and parallel (isometric) with the canvas of the painting – a mimetic vertical that in turn implies a mimetic Temple interior. The plane of the adjacent card table, however, is indeterminate, neither horizontal nor vertical, though it does support Emma's two (possibly three) ceramics and the dried flowers.

Moving up the diagonal, the third grey rectangle further scrambles mimetic convention. The vertical of the easel and canvas of the occluded internal painting are isometric to that of the main painting and, in this respect, obey the mimetic convention of the picture of the harbour. But the grey plane supporting this second still-life arrangement is again indeterminate and the two leafy stems in one of Emma's vases extend 'impossibly' (in mimetic terms) beyond its outer edge. This is the space in which Gillies places himself (the artist as easel), the place where, in his terms, he 'felt able to go into almost pure abstraction'. Thus, the pictorial space within the cottage is now simultaneously mimetic (simulated quasi-Euclidean) and non-mimetic, and the canvas of the occluded still life is simultaneously vertical and horizontal, with the potential to evoke plural meanings from the objects and juxtapositions it houses, and to transmit this potential to the main painting itself.

If we hold fast to mimetic expectation, the maker of this painting [102] appears to be the open book that the critics of the last century thought they could read, a realist artist who allowed his pleasure in simple things to fill his house, his life and his work. In this reading, the non-mimetic vector, signalled by the pervasive ambiguity of space and the diagonal of grey rectangles, must remain the mistake of an artist who was trying too hard to be modern. For Gillies, however, this vector is where he reaches towards an extended human apprehension, where mimetic convention is but one, incomplete, way of imaging a world in which retinal experience and idea both have their say in perceptual imaging and in the making of artefactual images.

Overall, the space of the painting is indeterminate but has the quality of reflexivity, of exchanges within the painting that reflect (or are analogous to) the influence of parameters of human perception on experience of the world and representations of it. Thus, the contents of each rectangle influence the reading of the others. The grey of the rectangles is also important. It is not so much a colour as a meeting of dark with light. For Klee, this is the point, the 'grey point' (Klee 1969, 1–4, 475) where imaging begins. Light becomes tones, is refracted into spectral colour, becomes forms and spaces that are then re-imaged in artworks. The world, in other words, dawns on one, as it did literally for Gillies when the Stand To Arms sounded.

The diagonal of artefacts does not reveal the private meanings that Gillies invested in Emma's pots, or his attempts to move these towards a more universal visual language. But the dried and colourless stems on the card table themselves speak of life and the passage of time. They also contrast with the living blooms in the garden and the live analogues in the imaginations of the easel painting. There is a real-life analogue too, shown in the fir tree that Emma applied to the terracotta pot, a cipher in this signature painting

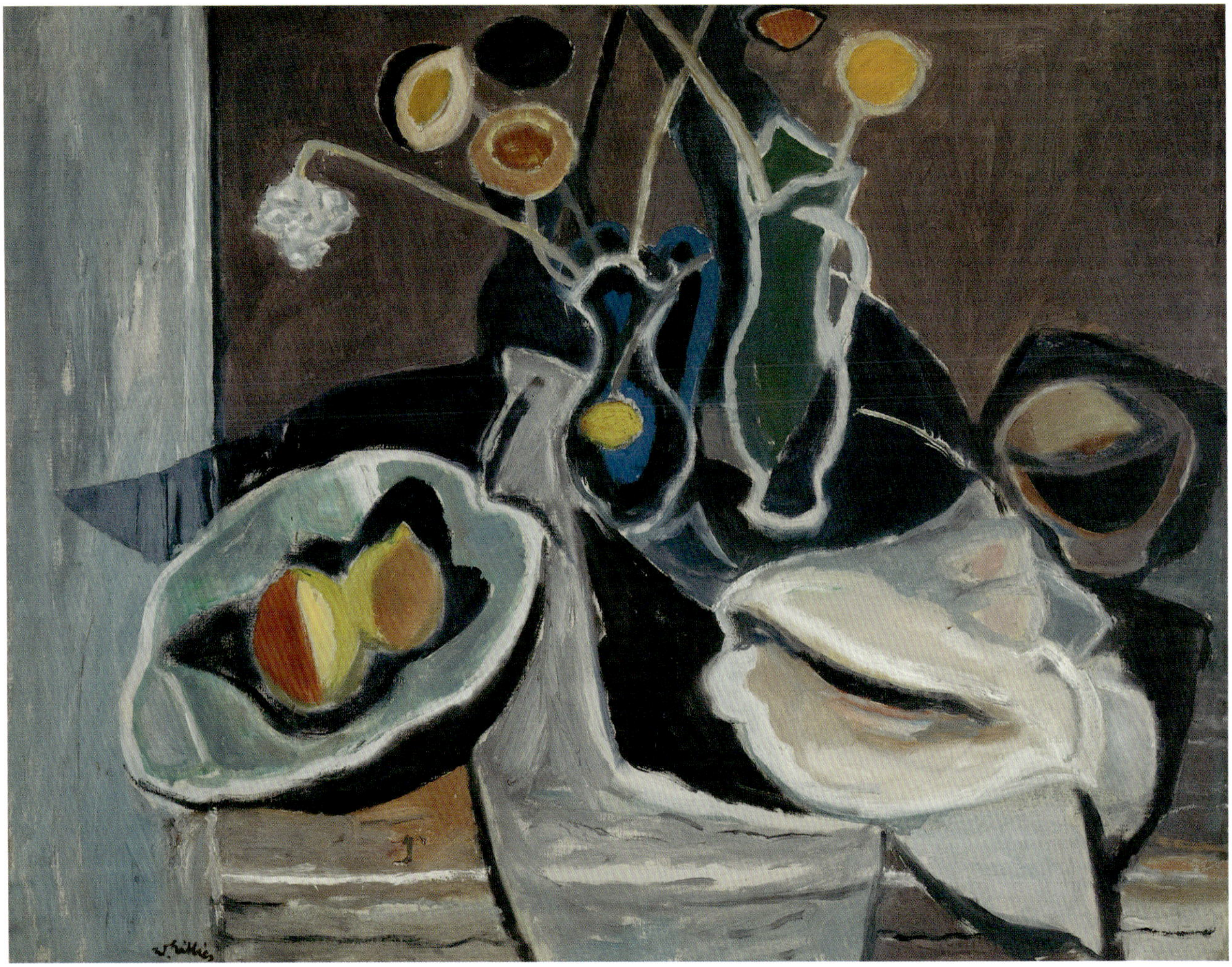

100 *Two Jugs, Flowers and Conch Shell* (*c.* 1952). Oil, 66.7 cm by 88.9 cm

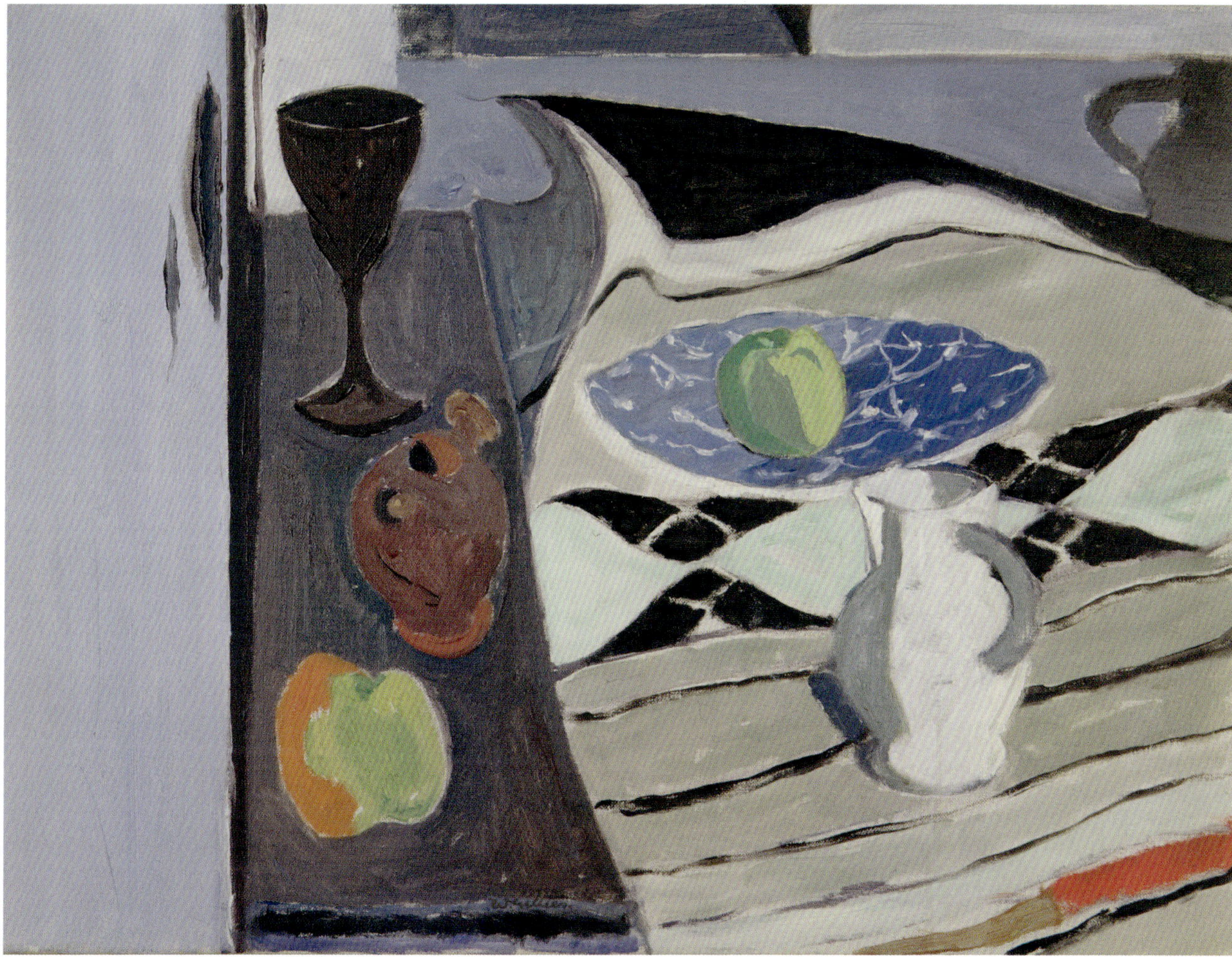

101 *Still Life* (nd, *c.* 1954). Oil, 58.4 cm by 78.7 cm

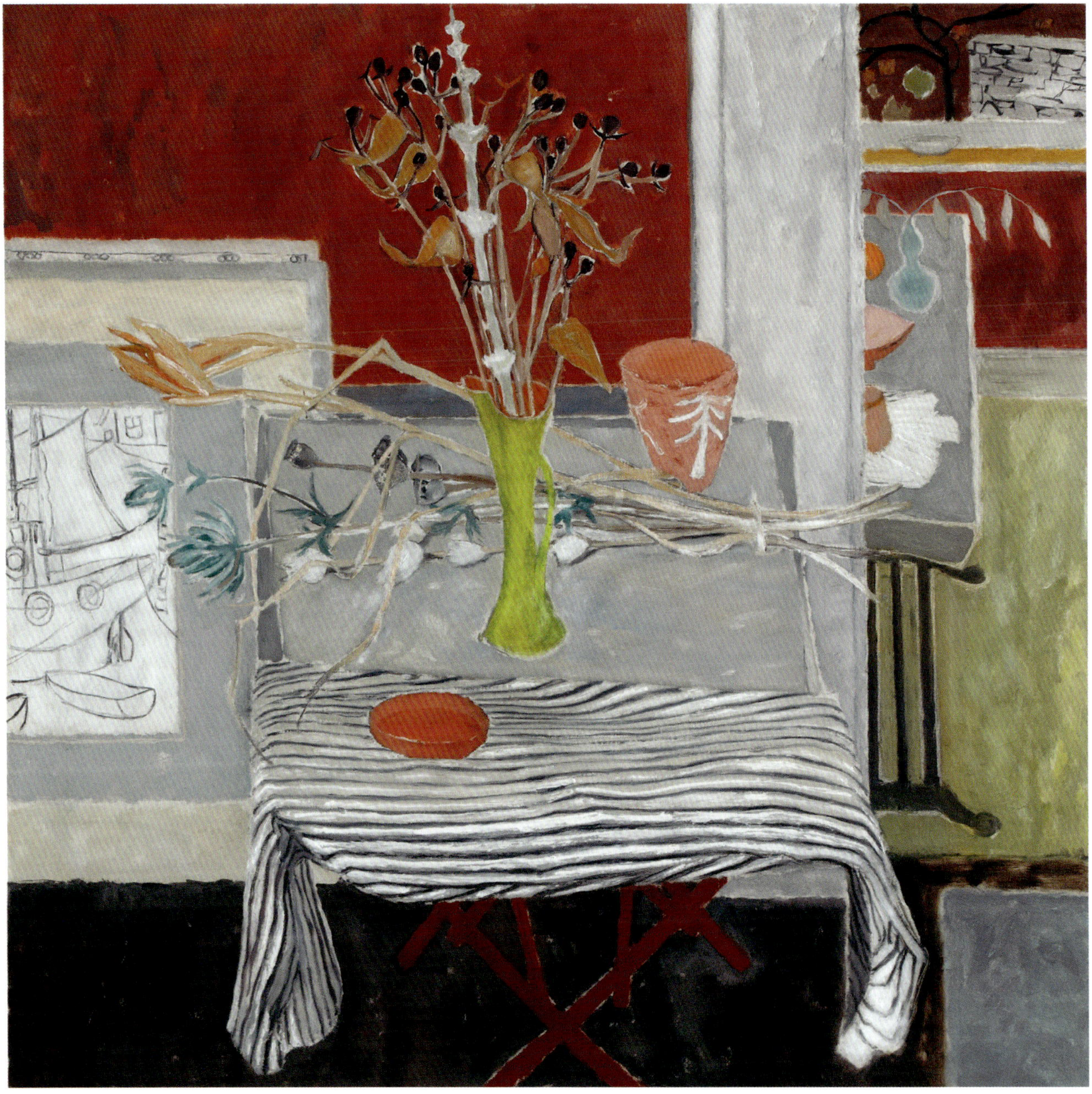

102 *Still Life, Yellow Jug and Striped Cloth* (*c.* 1955). Oil, 112 cm by 114.7 cm that was one of Emma's own potter's signatures. Paintings and ceramics alike – surviving artefacts, but also personalised as 'Paints' and 'Pots', Gillies' and Emma's affectionate names for each other – these elevate memory to a temporising defiance, arresting time, asserting life, owning the self to the other. The diagonal no longer excludes the agency of painter or potter, nor darkens in the prison of mimesis [46].

This gives the overall space its qualities, Gillies qualities one might say, that extend to his landscapes too. It is open, honest, based on repeated observation, fructive, multiple and reflexive. Like *Poppies in a Yellow Vase* [46] and *Interior* (1938) [42], it is open both to the world (objects in themselves, learned through practice) and to the artist. It does not pretend to be the world, only an image of the world, observant, but also receptive and suggestive. It carries associations (direct memories and visual analogues for these, intended or not) personal to the artist. This also opens it to associations that are potentially more universal or more widely shared, whether or not fully understood; associations of feeling with colour and form, the passage of time, memory, growth, knowing and doing, decay and death – in short, opens a space for being and becoming.

Hence, the external world framed beyond the window now studiously avoids the mimesis of the first grey rectangle. Its flowers are token, its tone and colour close to those of the studio itself. And the fourth grey rectangle it contains, a wall (as I eventually realised), is even more token, little more than a sketch, a first idea of the outside world, banked for later use outwith the cottage, awaiting its own 'extension' in paint. Finally, the fifth grey rectangle, bottom right, is completely blank. Is this merely a mat? Or a canvas awaiting its transformation like that in *Interior* (1938) [42]? Or both at the same time, the place where Gillies takes his stand, '(re-)cognising' himself in conversation with the world?

Much later, *Still Life, Study in Grey* (1968) [118] would likewise converse. The studio, his 'space where imaging begins', is set to the immanent spectrum of *Schneesturm* [63] and the rectangles of *Striped Cloth* [102]. The objects are his 'notion or symbol', grouped, as he said, 'automatically', and painted as such, formed in memory but some, in places, transparent or retinally incomplete, yet to be fully 'extended'. If this is an attempt to paint the impossible, to show the purely cognitive component of perception, maybe Heron's aphorism can help us again. Were the men whom life eluded in 1918 on Gillies' mind when, exactly fifty years later, he painted his mundane objects and jugs in owning to others the elusive survivor's self he at last owned as himself?

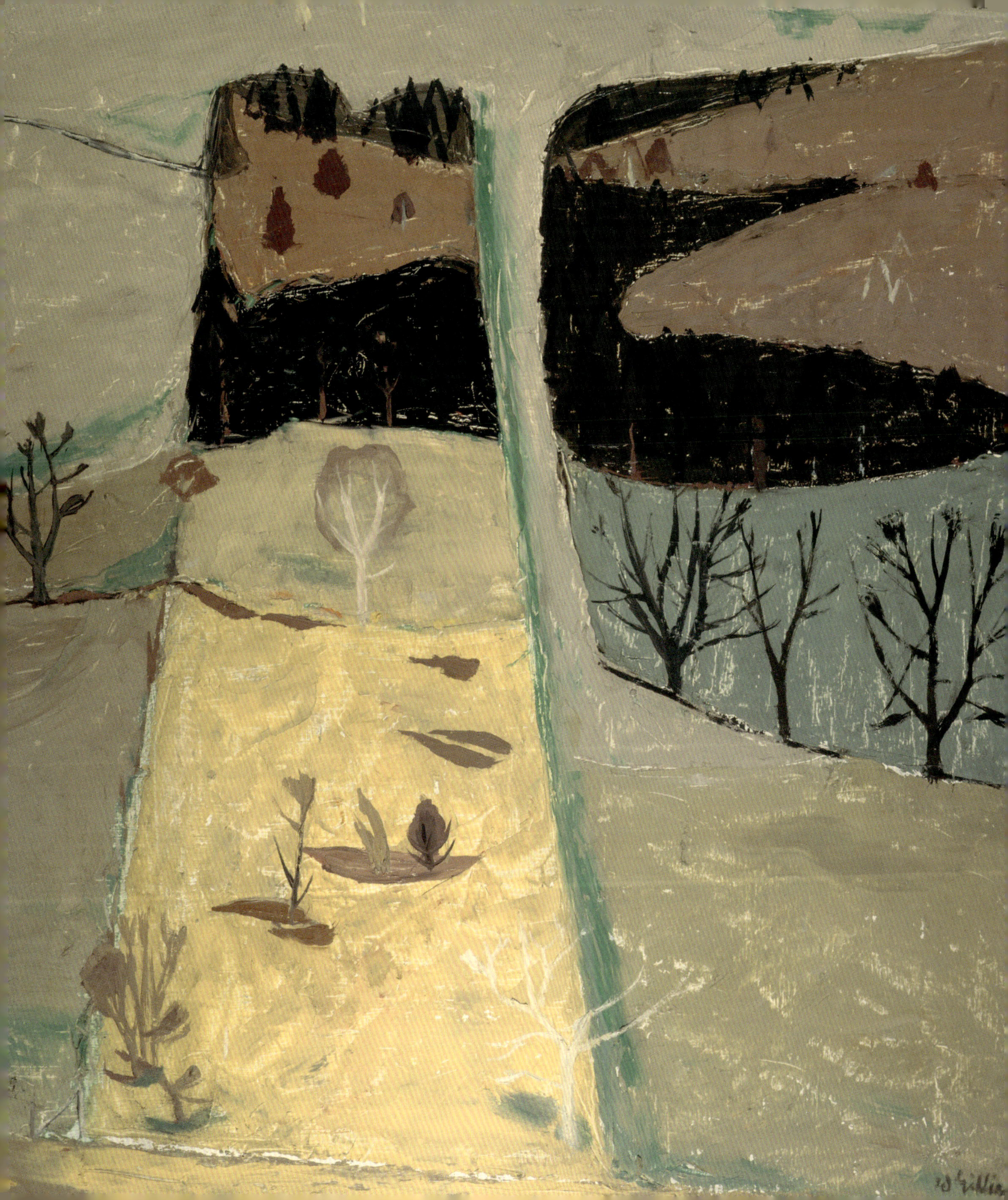

Oil Landscapes 1945–60

What Gillies said around 1960 in the statement Elder Dickson subverted in his 1974 monograph was this: 'In Still-Life I have felt able to go into almost pure abstraction – in landscape, there seemed always a limit beyond which the content became empty and meaningless. I believe that gap is now closing.' It was closing because, around 1948–9, in what was the first new departure in Gillies' landscape oils for more than twenty years, the angular forms of his current sequence of still lifes began to appear in his oil landscapes as well. (The landscapes on paper are a different story, to which I shall come.)

'I did not feel that my imagination was in conflict with the real, but that reality was a dispersed and disintegrated form of imagination.' This was Graham Sutherland's (1942) description of his relationship with an area of North Wales that became a special place for him. It equally serves to describe Gillies' relationship to the Borders countryside south of Temple. But the oils of neither artist were about the *genius loci*. Gillies' watercolours and drawings continued. He took immense pleasure, he said, in 'recording swiftly in line and watercolour the fugitive, the subtle and the grand in nature'. But they were not his main project: 'A landscape has to be digested. Working *from nature*, one is distracted by the perpetual change – I get led astray from the original conception. I seek the permanent in nature' (Gillies in Smith 1961 and 1965; original emphasis). And he looked for it in his oils.

When Elder Dickson changed Gillies' 'line and watercolour' (above) to 'line and colour' in his 1974 monograph, he subverted a distinction that was important to Gillies but difficult to reconcile with Elder Dickson's view that the watercolours were nearer to the heart of things than the oils. Nor does the evidence of the paintings support his monograph's case that Gillies' wartime oils (both still life and landscape) were an atavistic response to the Border hills. The still lifes clearly were not, but nor were the landscapes. Between 1940 and the end of 1948, Gillies exhibited over 100 landscapes in all media but only eight of these had Borders subjects, and there is only one before 1946. What is more, key paintings in his new style showed views from locations that lie within an hour's walk of Temple and were accessible even in wartime (if they were not, he could hardly be said to be within their sphere of influence). Two oils from the early 1950s and a related watercolour, *Near Howgate* (1951) [103], are illustrative.

To use Graham Sutherland's language, the angular forms of Gillies' imagination are dispersed across the watercolour *Near Howgate* but latently rendered, less pronounced, and interrupted by the detail of fine drawing. In the two *Mount Lothian* oils (*c.* 1948, *c.* 1953; nd, *c.* 1953) [104, 105], both the season and the time of day (or night) are uncertain. The place itself has become more indeterminate too. He has stripped out of the oils ancillary information – dwellings, posts, details of trees and cattle – that would diminish our response to form and tone. This makes space for discrete touches of colour, some bordering on recognition, others mere marks that offer new possibilities in return for our willing suspension of mimetic expectation. We are taken beyond any topographically specific sense of place, time, season or weather, towards something more universal.

We see this again in the contrast between the oil *Mauve Landscape* (*c.* 1956, *c.* 1952) [107] and

Opposite:
Detail from *Wooded Hillside* ([109] – see p. 147)

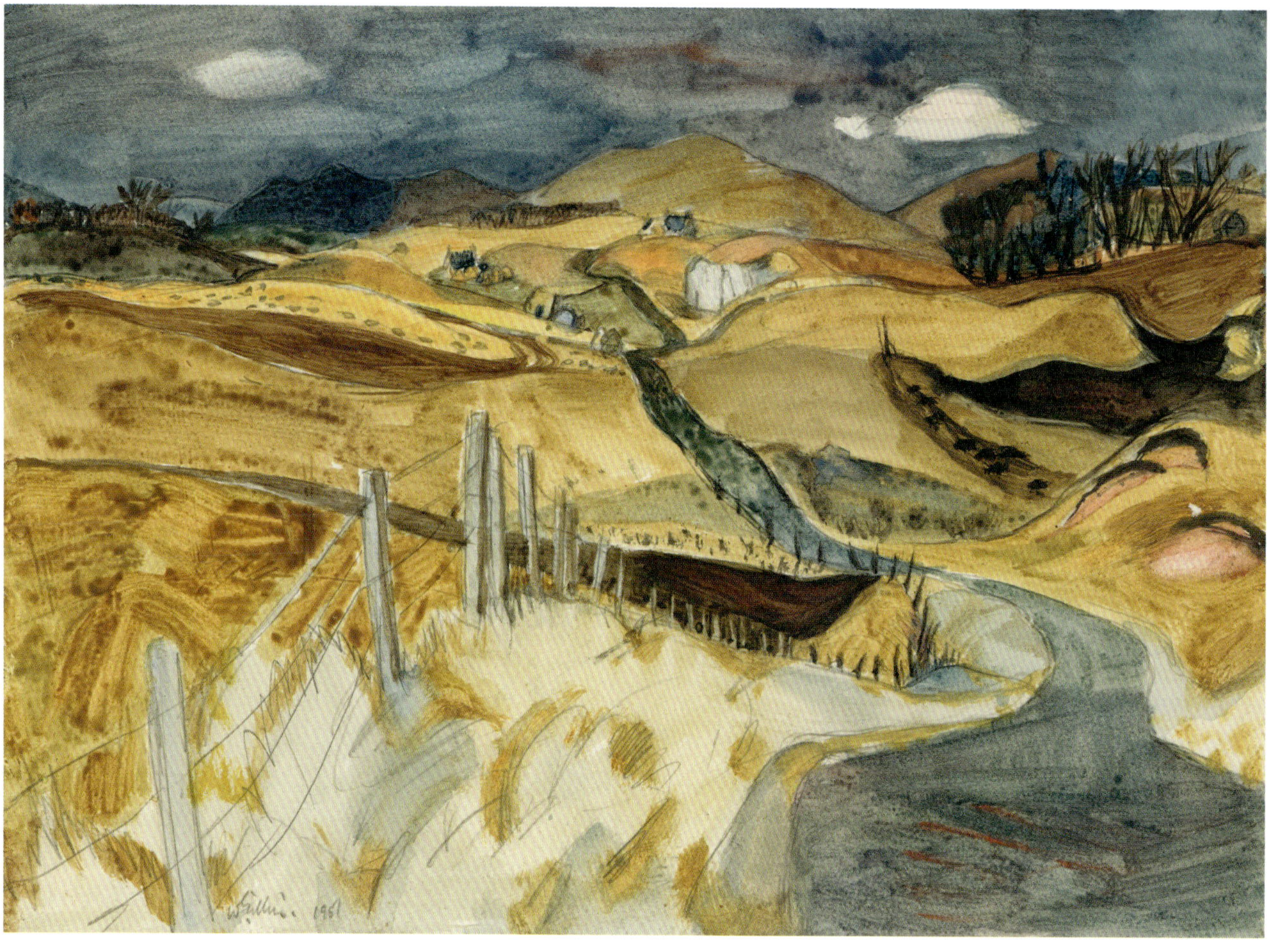

103 *Near Howgate* (1951). Watercolour and pencil, 25.2 cm by 35.4 cm

Empty Fields and Willows (1952) [106], one of several related watercolours. In the oil, a hillside has been moved left and detail removed. The colour reflects Gillies' ironic epigram that nature always gets the colour wrong. Aerial (tonal) recession has diminished. Below the horizon, the planes of the landscape-forms are indeterminate, somewhere between the near horizontal and the plane of the canvas itself, vertical to the viewer. The squarer proportions of the oil compress and intensify the image, and the tree accordingly, making it spikier. The branches now have the whitened, etiolated quality of *Sunflower* (nd, *c.* 1954) [25]. The effect is heightened by the darkened tonality of a background that is broken into shards by the inverted ogives of the branches, and broken further by the formalisation of its own shapes into Gillies' angularities. A fictitious bield (stand of trees) broods darkly and the distant hills, darkened and sharpened into triangles, lend their colour and pointed tendency to the stream at the foot of the tree. The absence of a trunk in the oil again adds an uncertainty to the location of our viewpoint and judgement of recession.

Mauve Landscape [107] is an instance of Gillies' continuing dialogue with contemporary London and of the whispers he lays from time to time in all genres of his work. Gillies is, again, the central, disruptive, tree and we are, again, seeing through his eyes. At the base of the tree in the oil he has added a fallen branch. It arguably relates to what Garlake describes as two 'key images which reveal the fundamental themes and motivations of neo-Romanticism'. One was by Michael Ayrton and the other by John Minton. Both men were much influenced by Graham Sutherland, and also by Samuel Palmer (1805–81), in whose landscapes they found metaphors for paradise and loss. 'Conspicuous in the foreground of both [the key images]', Garlake writes, 'is a tortuously twisted fallen branch, lying across a path leading to distant open hills'. In one of them, 'brightly lit hills' promise both the 'earthly paradise' of Samuel Palmer's vision of Eden and 'the release of war's end', while the path meantime is both 'route and refuge' (Garlake 1998, 88, 91, my bracketed insertion). When Gillies' work was painted, Paul Nash was dead and other neo-Romantics, younger than Nash and with no experience of the Great War, were moving on from their pre-occupation with the wartime incursions on personal freedoms. But Gillies' path was still blocked by the twisted branch, and there was no refuge yet in hills that were conical and dark.

The topography of the Borders hills presents its own tilted planes, its own elimination of fore-ground or middle distance as one looks across a steep-sided valley, even its own elimination of sky where the line of vision is low and the valley narrow. Unless a form breaks the horizon, its boundaries, planes and angularities can appear indeterminate or variable according to the viewpoint. Equally, the seasons and husbandry of the Borders hills create their own scattered palimpsests of colour, their own vagaries of track and line.

Gillies responds to these features in his post-war oils but they were not, as the country-man position argues, features he learned there. There are occluded skies and tilted planes in his pre-war landscapes. Klee taught him that a line could wander, that formless colour and discrete line could animate each other even though spatially separate, that indeterminacy could encourage active engagement and interpolation by the viewer. Likewise, the uncluttered Borders hills can indeed be 'austere'. But Gillies already knew from his still lifes the gains that came with simplification. The shape of things, and of the spaces between them, became clearer. Space itself became form, facilitated rhythm and counter-point, allowed areas of formless colour, secondary and tertiary, to work their effects beyond their own boundaries.

In *Fields and River* (late 1950s) [108], form (abstract), palette (restricted), tonality (uniform) and space itself are taken towards extremes. The artist has nowhere to hide here, and nothing to hide. Remove the line of trees with the building, exclude the grey strip at the top (so there is no sky 'on-top-of') and we have an abstraction as great as that of *In Arniston* (1935) [60]. But that is not what Gillies wants. In even the most abstract of works, there is now some human presence, often barely discernible, as here, or some token sky, to remind us that this compelling alternative is available to us in the here-and-now. We can, if we wish, interpret the marks that transect the

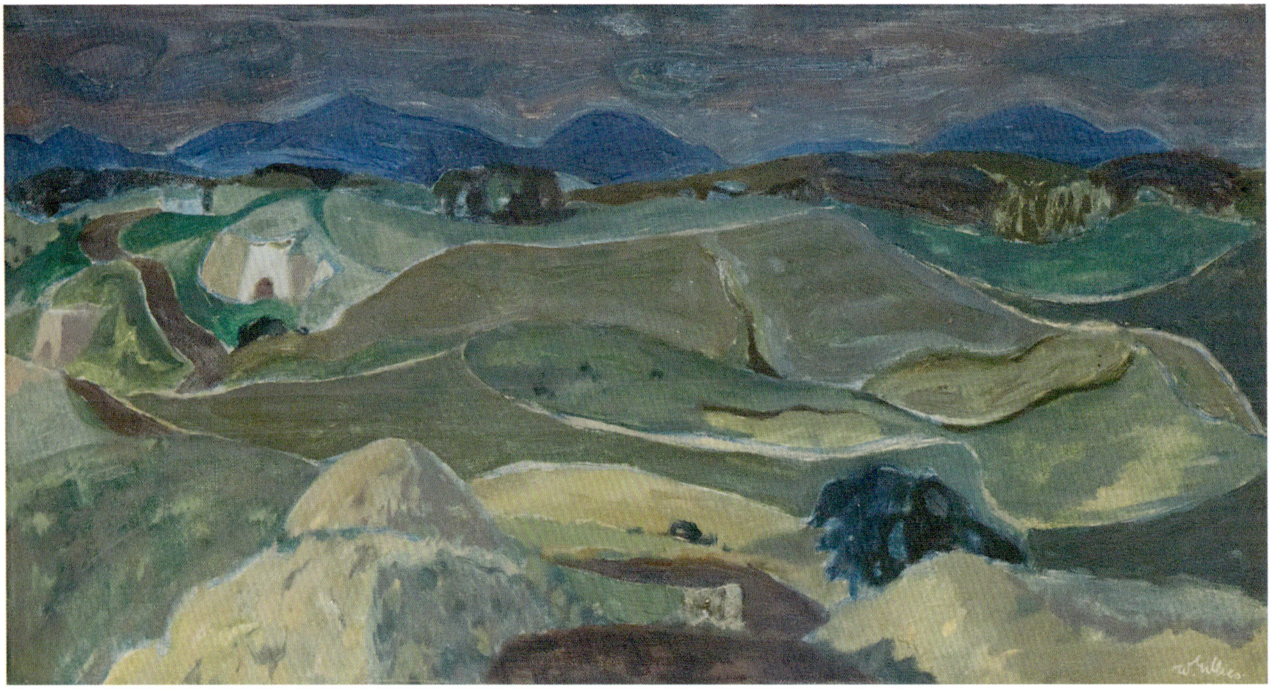

104 *The Pentlands, Mount Lothian* (*c.* 1948, *c.* 1953). Oil, 42 cm by 79 cm

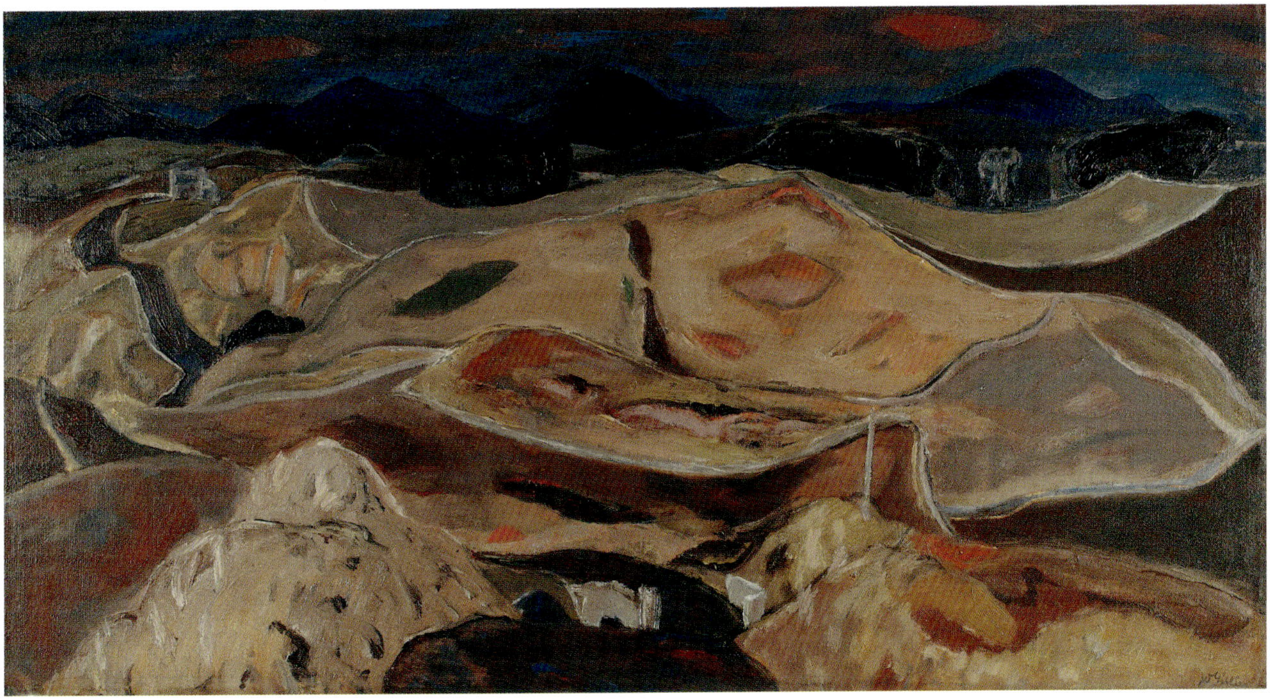

105 *Mount Lothian* (nd, *c.* 1953). Oil, 61 cm by 113 cm

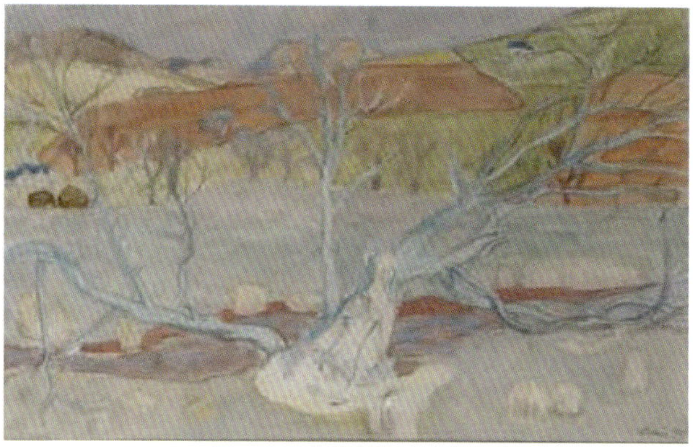

106 *Empty Fields and Willows* (1952). Watercolour and pencil, dimensions unknown

wall on the upper hills as made by sheep moving to an area of winter feed, but the forms in the lower half approach pure form, and are mimetically interpretable only because we know the title of the work and which way is up. A sense of place? Or a sense of space-time, and the wonder of human apprehension catching us unawares?

A further clue to the impetus behind the oil landscapes of the 1950s is that they lighten in the same way and at the same time as the still lifes, and that then, around 1960, an attempt is made to merge the two genres using the communalities they share. *Mauve Landscape* [107] is itself an early example of this search for an accommodation between menace and joy, for Gillies painted a second version of the work. Untitled Landscape (nd, *c.* 1952) [ni] retains the essential forms but replaces the predominating mauve with a range of ochres and blue studded in the foreground with discrete and formless dabs of red. What was sinister is made vibrant. *Wooded Hillside* (1957) [109] retains angular forms but again uses ochres and lightens the tone. *Shadowed Hill* (1958) [166] goes further, gentling the forms and allowing greater play to abstract colour in tones even lighter.

By the time of *Dusk* (1959) [110], the post-war sequence of still lifes and the 1950s sequence of extensive oil landscapes were both ending, if only because Gillies could no longer continue. In 1957, he remade his will (for reasons unknown). In 1960, he was made a very reluctant Principal of the ECA. A 'caretaker government' it was called by the new Principal who liked to be mistaken for the caretaker. For the next seven years, he had little time to paint. An undisclosed illness required time in hospital. Janet died in November 1960 and his mother in February 1963. John Maxwell's untimely death in 1962 was another grievous loss. Two large oil landscapes from these years that Gillies particularly valued can be treated as summations.

Winter Thaw (1962) [111] lays bare the transience of form and human apprehension. It looks across Gladhouse Reservoir to the Moorfoot hills and the habitable land below. Gillies sandwiches this land, humanity's space, between three strata. Scoops of white suggest residual snow in the gullies of hills left largely to our imagination. In reality, forms emerging from the elements like this can take away what breath a climb has left one. It is no different here in the painting. Below, the black–white contrast of the snow along the stane dykes demarcates humanity's small domain. We see immediately that it is the elements that determine artefacts and occupation. The walls follow contours that have been sculpted by water and ice. Humanity's space is confined, our generative fields wrestled from shards. Below, the band of thawing ice anchors this cosmology, visually and conceptually. The renewal of spring is temporary, forms temporary too, human powers

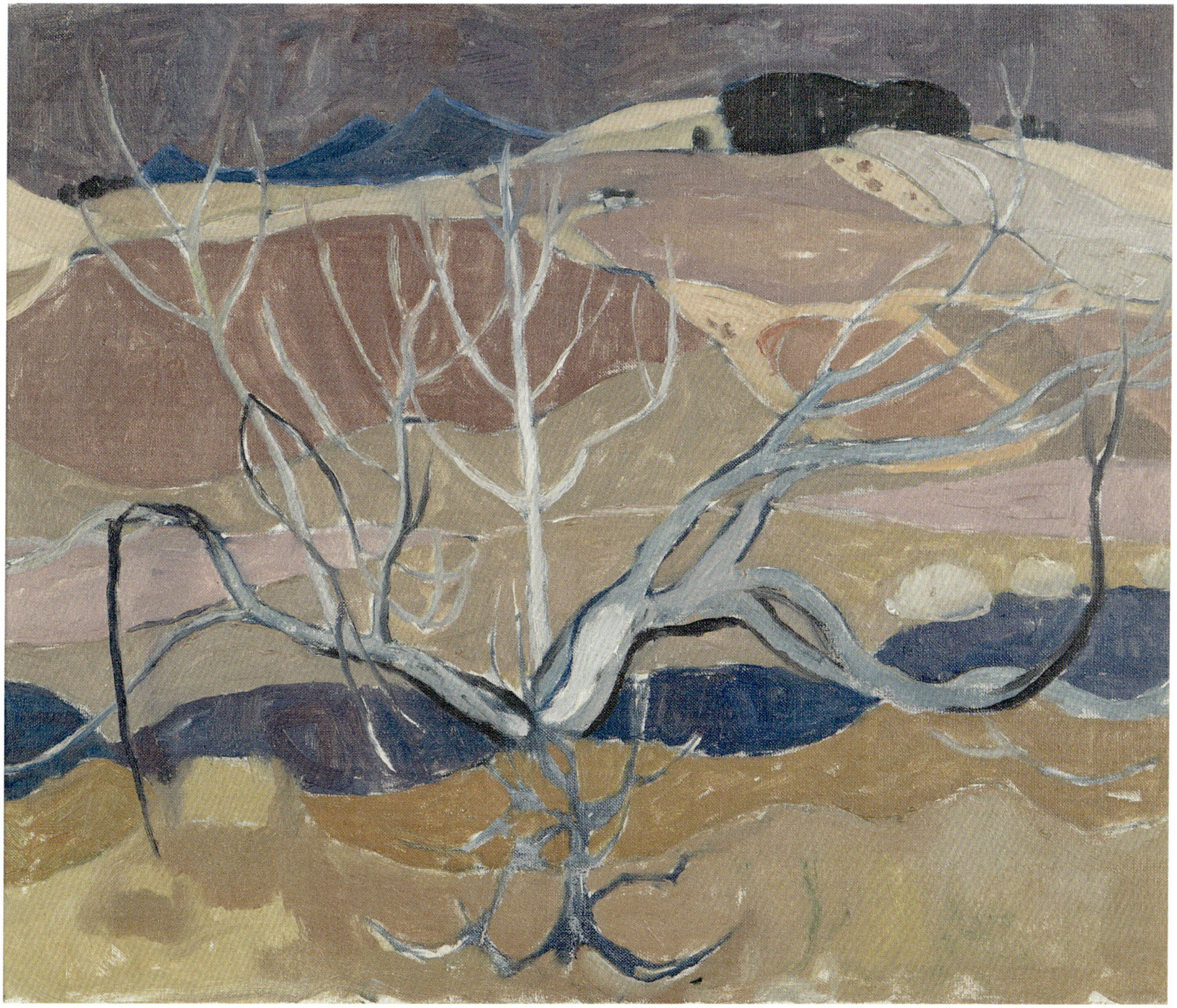

107 *Mauve Landscape* (*c.* 1956, *c.* 1952). Oil, 61.5 cm by 74 cm

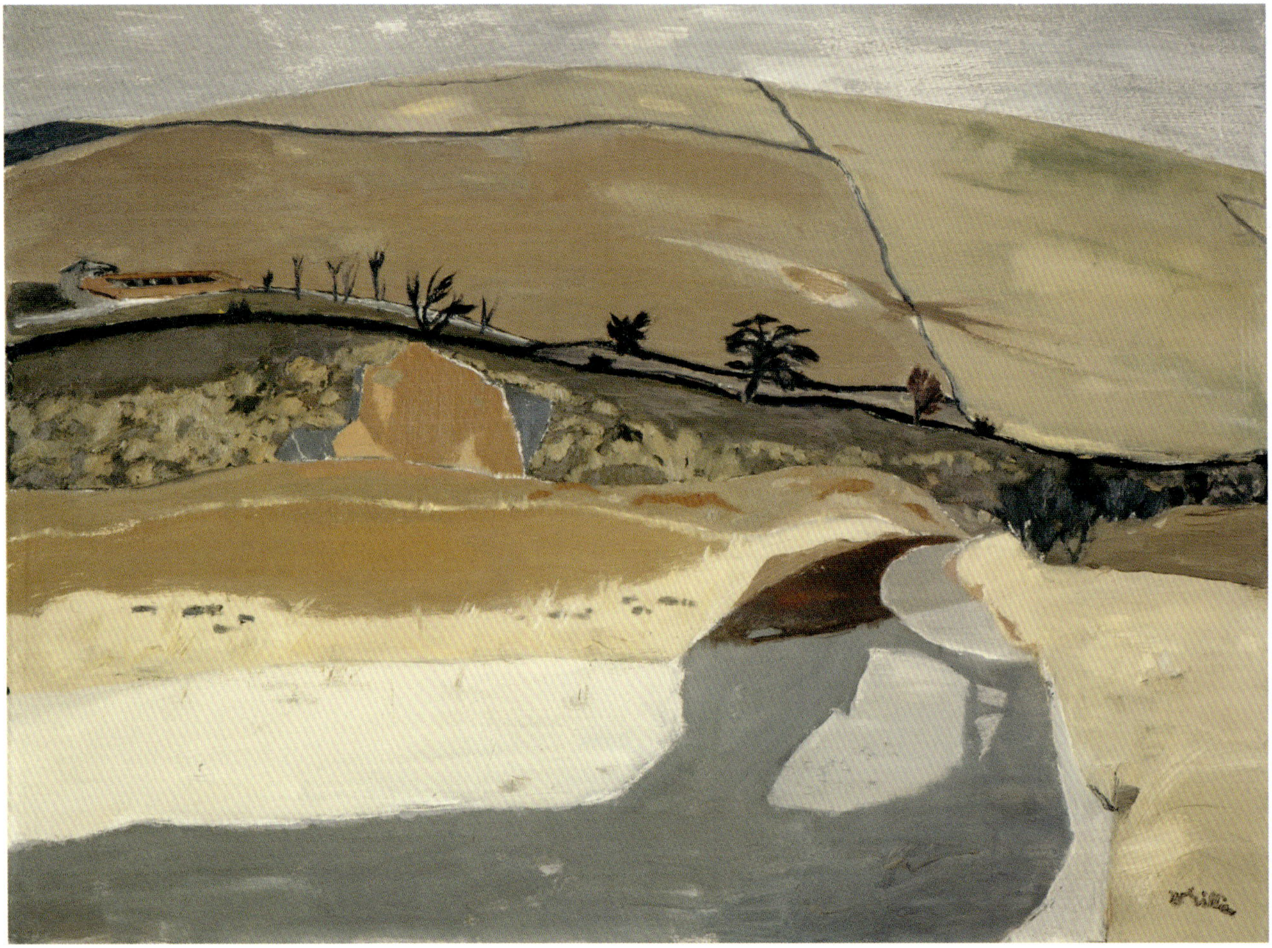

108 *Fields and River* (late 1950s). Oil, 64 cm by 87 cm

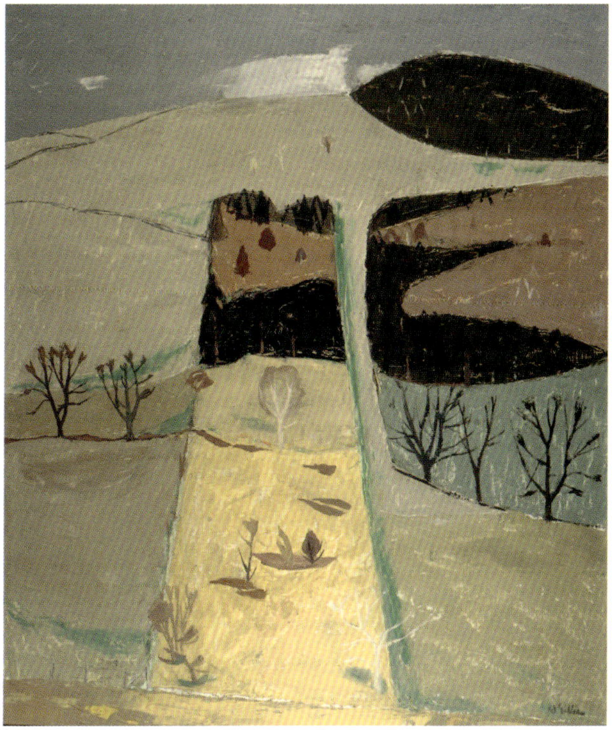

109 *Wooded Hillside* (1957). Oil, 95.7 cm by 80.5 cm

fractured and finite, cosmological time an infinity interrupted somehow by consciousness. A photo shows Gillies painting *Winter Thaw* in his College studio, overlooked by the erupted and eroding Castle Rock with its own memorial, itself only temporary, to lives transcended and transected. On the studio sill are ceramics, probably Emma's. In studio, too, the artist has nowhere to hide.

There is somewhere to hide in the central stratum of *Hill Pool* (1960) [112]. But is this stratum aligned vertically, like the wall of a trench obscuring the middle distance, or does it slope towards the uplands? Another uncertainty is the replicated sky in the water at its base, ceding nothing to the sky on top, asking us to look in two directions at once, increasing our unease. Which way is up?

There may never be an agreed reading of *Hill Pool*. If, however, I had to choose just one work that evokes the emergence of the infantryman-artist from his earthy *patria* into a landscape changed beyond recognition by war, into a world that could be reconnoitred only through contact with the immediate, that could be made habitable again only by a sustained engagement with the threats and promise of the human condition, then this work – with its visceral geology and tactile impasto, painted around the time of *Ferniehirst* [23] and *Aldermaston Hadeans* [22] – would be it. The yellow, 'brightly lit' uplands would then become Palmer's 'earthly paradise' and the 'release of war's end' in a resolution that is permanent to the extent that an honest acknowledgement of the truths of the human condition has produced a vision of the world, call it beauty if one will, that lies beyond the corruptions of sentimentality.

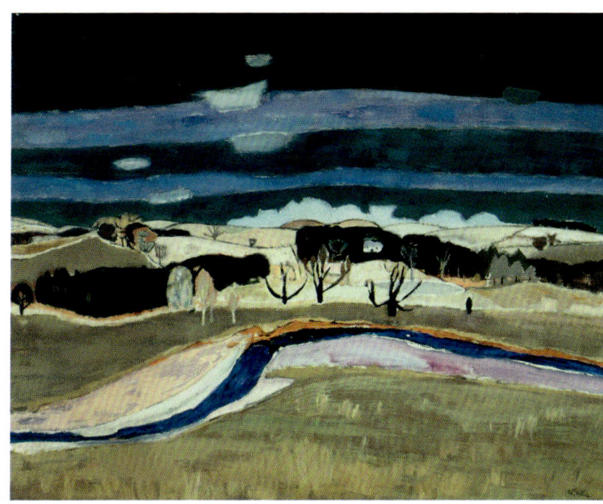

110 *Dusk* (1959). Oil, 74 cm by 94.4 cm

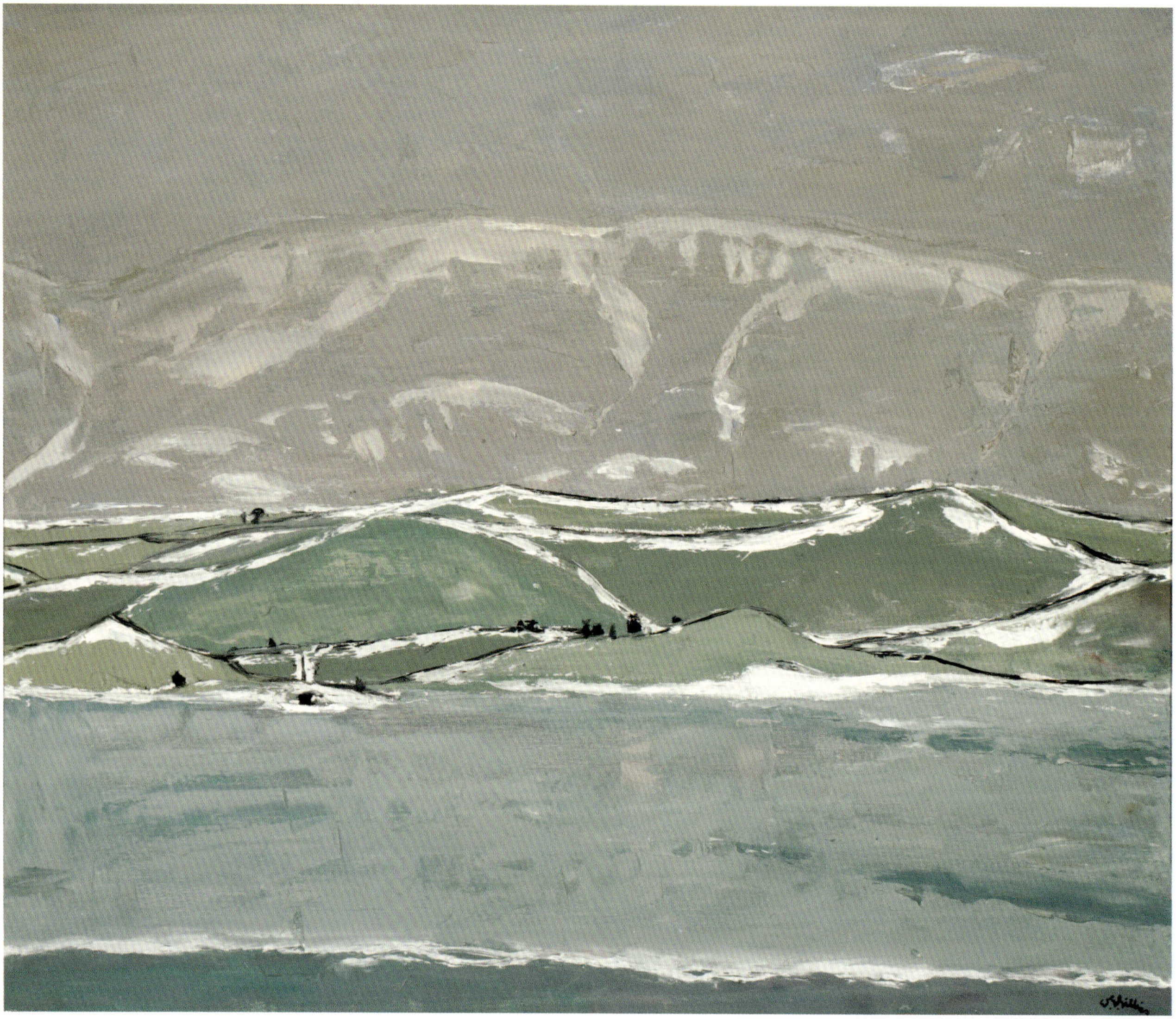

111 *Winter Thaw* (1962). Oil, 74 cm by 91.5 cm

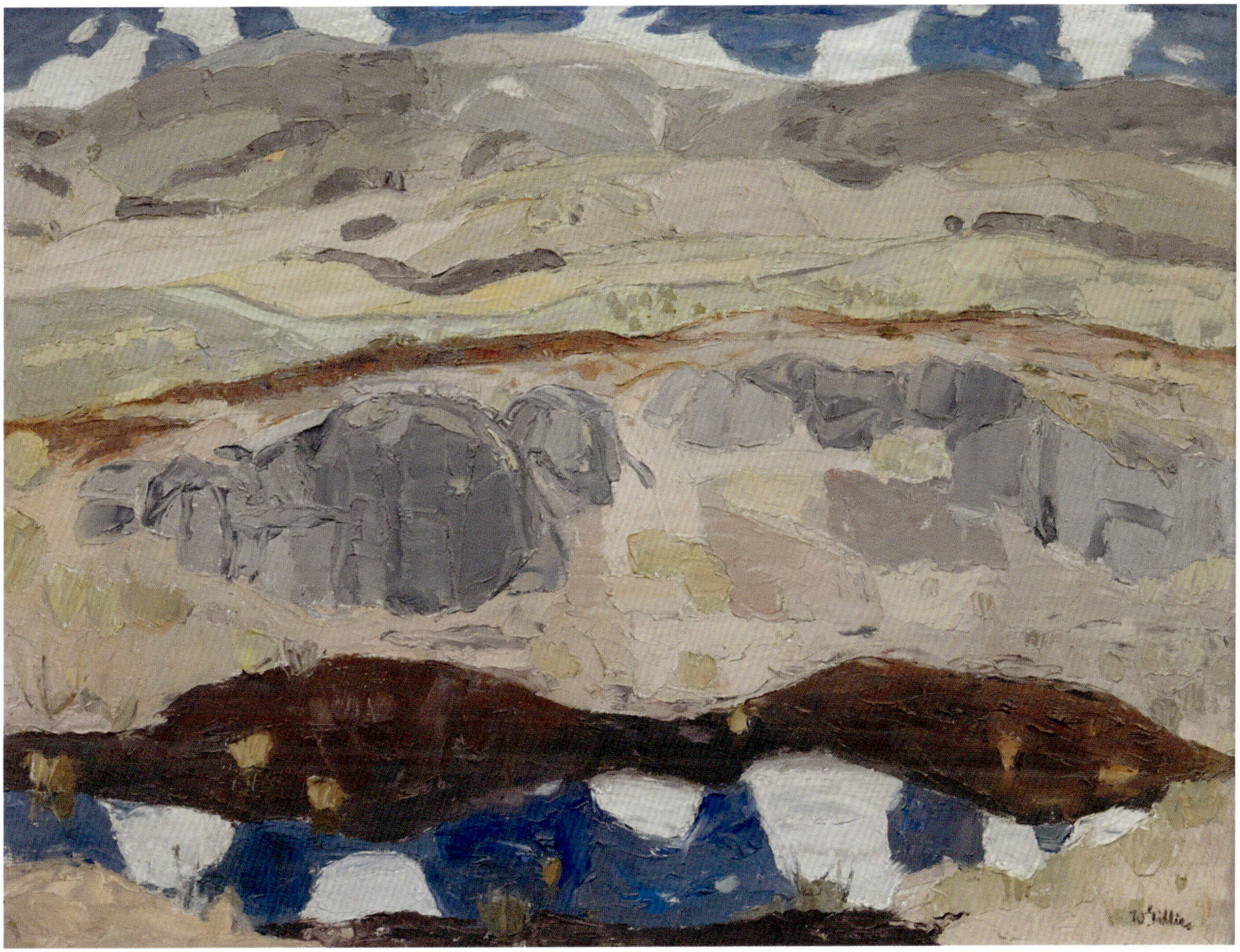

112 *Hill Pool* (1960). Oil, 76 cm by 101 cm

Last Years

When his duties as Principal brought the 1950s phase of Gillies' oils to an end, we lose a potential source of insight into why it began and continued as it did. Various considerations must be weighed. When the Edinburgh house was sold in 1948, prospects were good. Capital was now available to upgrade the cottage and his transport. As the new head of painting at the ECA, he had, for the first time, a full-time, permanent contract on an incremental salary scale. It doubled the pay that had been offered to him in 1945 in what at the time was an annual renewal of one-year contracts. He could travel abroad again and around Scotland. In 1947, the RSA elected him a full Academician. Yet this was also when the still lifes entered their darkest period.

Part of the explanation may be the pressure of unaccustomed responsibility exacerbated by the numbers of demobbed students. With the demise of the Society of Eight, he had yet to find an outlet where he could show more than a handful of oils each year. Fewer friends were available to accompany him on the extended landscape excursions of the inter-war period, though Henderson Blyth was a willing arrival at the ECA. Margery Porter's untimely death in 1948 recharged a grimly familiar theme at the very time that Graham Sutherland was articulating the angst of the New Apocalypse. An Iron Curtain now divided a nuclear Europe. Any or all of these could have contributed. But I also suggest that, having survived a second war, he could now return to issues that the exigencies of wartime had displaced.

By 1952, however, the bulge of ex-service personnel had passed through the College. He could be fairly sure he would now escape or at least survive exophthalmos, and opportunities to exhibit were improving. Indeed, a sufficient explanation for the lifting of mood may simply be recognition, for this meant he was connecting, was finding a voice that was heard. The Arts Council in London had asked him to contribute to several London exhibitions. He was one of the seventy artists Herbert Read included in his 1951 book on contemporary British art. Eric Newton could write that '[n]o one in England could paint a big still-life with … [Gillies'] combination of dash and discipline'. In 1953, an Edinburgh exhibition of his landscapes on paper was an outstanding success and the ACGB offered him a two-man exhibition with John Maxwell in London for 1954.

This was a reputational apogee of sorts, but brief. Gillies wanted a large say in the choice of exhibits and objected to the high-handed approach to selection adopted by the ACGB. Its Scottish sub-committee then intervened to support him. In the event, and in keeping with his priorities at the time, Gillies showed more still lifes than landscape oils. But the Council's foreword to the catalogue mentioned only the landscapes, and the catalogue essay did likewise. The latter was written by Peter Westwater, Gillies' former colleague and later art critic for *The Scotsman*. Among almost 1,000 words on Gillies, Westwater gave only four to his still lifes. He presented Gillies as 'essentially a painter of the Scottish scene' inspired by 'the unforced intuitive love possible only to the country-bred native', and the tone of his essay was abrasively dismissive of the 'ingenuous' English ("'We'll keep oor ain fish guts for oor ain seamaws'"). Critics were bemused and their praise was faint. This reaction may help explain why the volume of still lifes was already falling in the later

Opposite:
Detail from *Nairn Beach* ([121] – see p. 165)

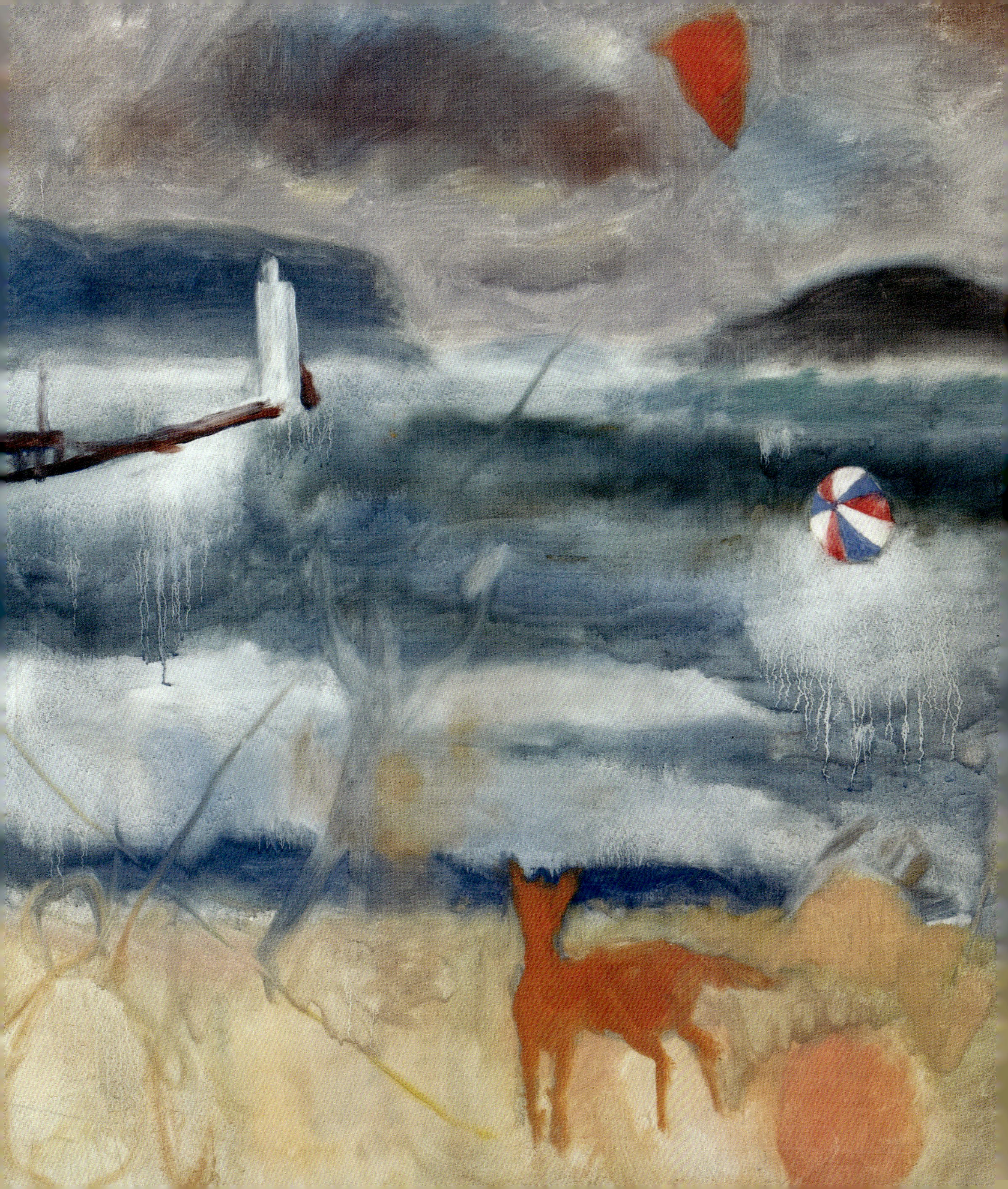

1950s, before he was made Principal. (There may have been health issues too, associated with the remaking of his will, but I do not know whether the number of oil landscapes, and thus his overall level of activity in oil, was also falling.) With the arrival of American Abstract Expressionism in the mid- to late 1950s, the further move towards a non-figurative abstraction by artists like Patrick Heron may also have given him pause. And Janet and his mother were failing.

When they died, however, Temple Cottage could become an extension of the landscape of his mind that he was free to remodel in both fact and imagination. He built a wider studio window looking over the garden, bringing landscape closer to the life within. In this setting and solitude, nature and the artefactual were more easily apprehended as a single world of phenomenal experience, attenuating the boundaries between the interior and exterior of the cottage, between still life and landscape, and between perception and imagination.

Though I have been unable to view it directly, I think this attenuation to be already apparent in the large *Garden, Winter Sunshine* (1960) [113]. Its signature forms are still the quasi-ogive and triangle or shard. Some are formed by the branches of the black tree that appears to press hard against the window. Others are interpretable, just, as gable-ends and eaves. Yet others, entirely black, cannot be read in mimetic terms. Astragals and their shadows form a grid of some dozen areas with contents that range from the virtually empty to the wholly abstract or the solely mimetic. Low winter light throws the shadow of a tree across the internal sill, creating the impression that the garden is invading the house. The continuation of the shadow across the uncertain orientation of the

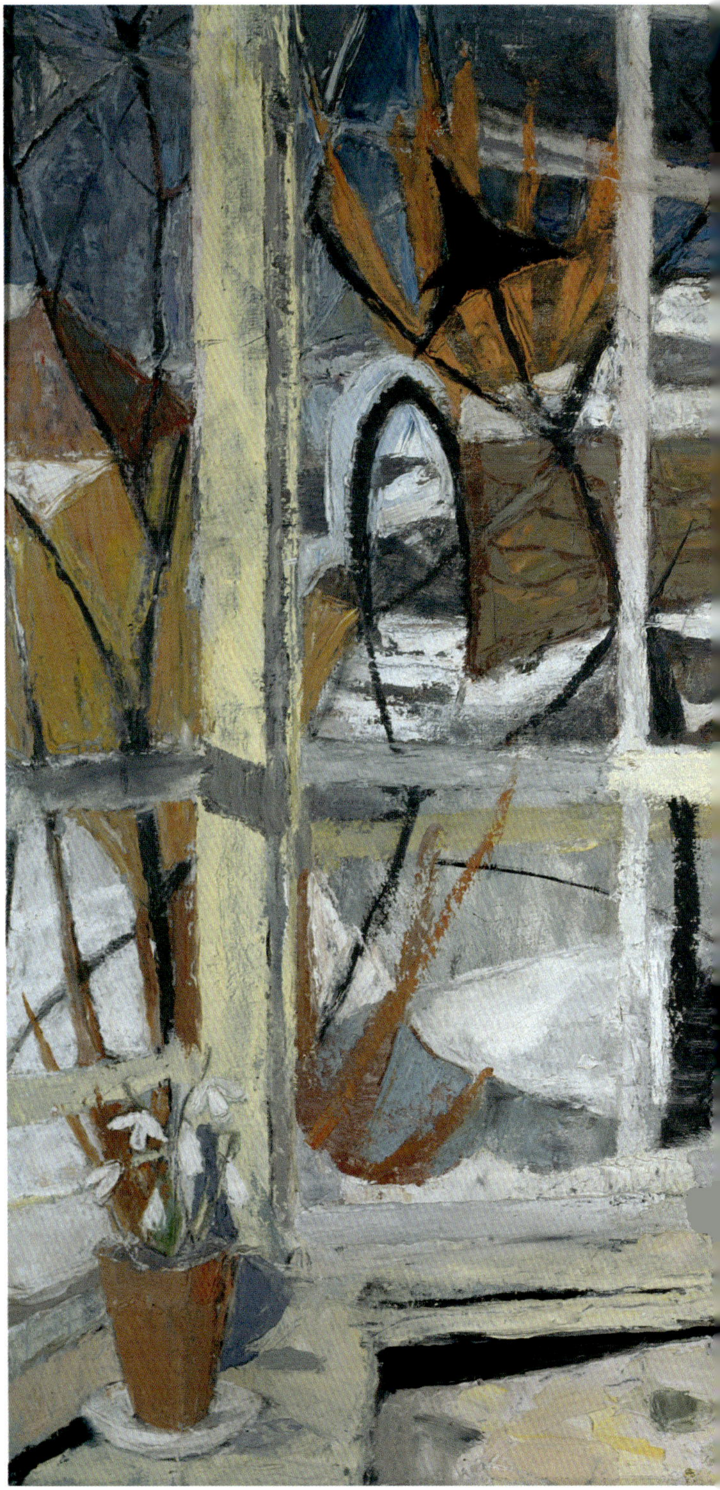

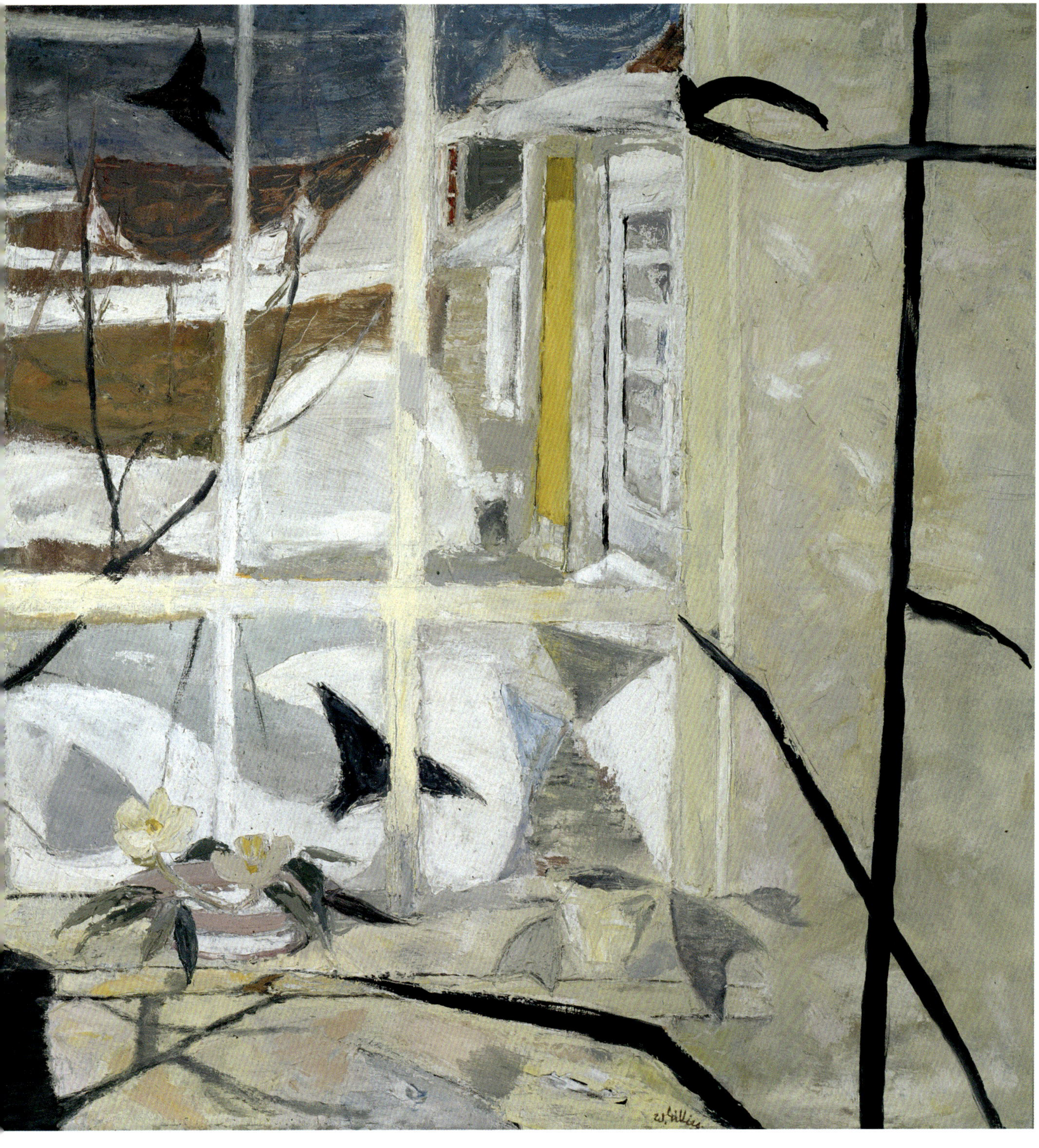

113 *Garden, Winter Sunshine* (1960). Oil, 102 cm by 152 cm

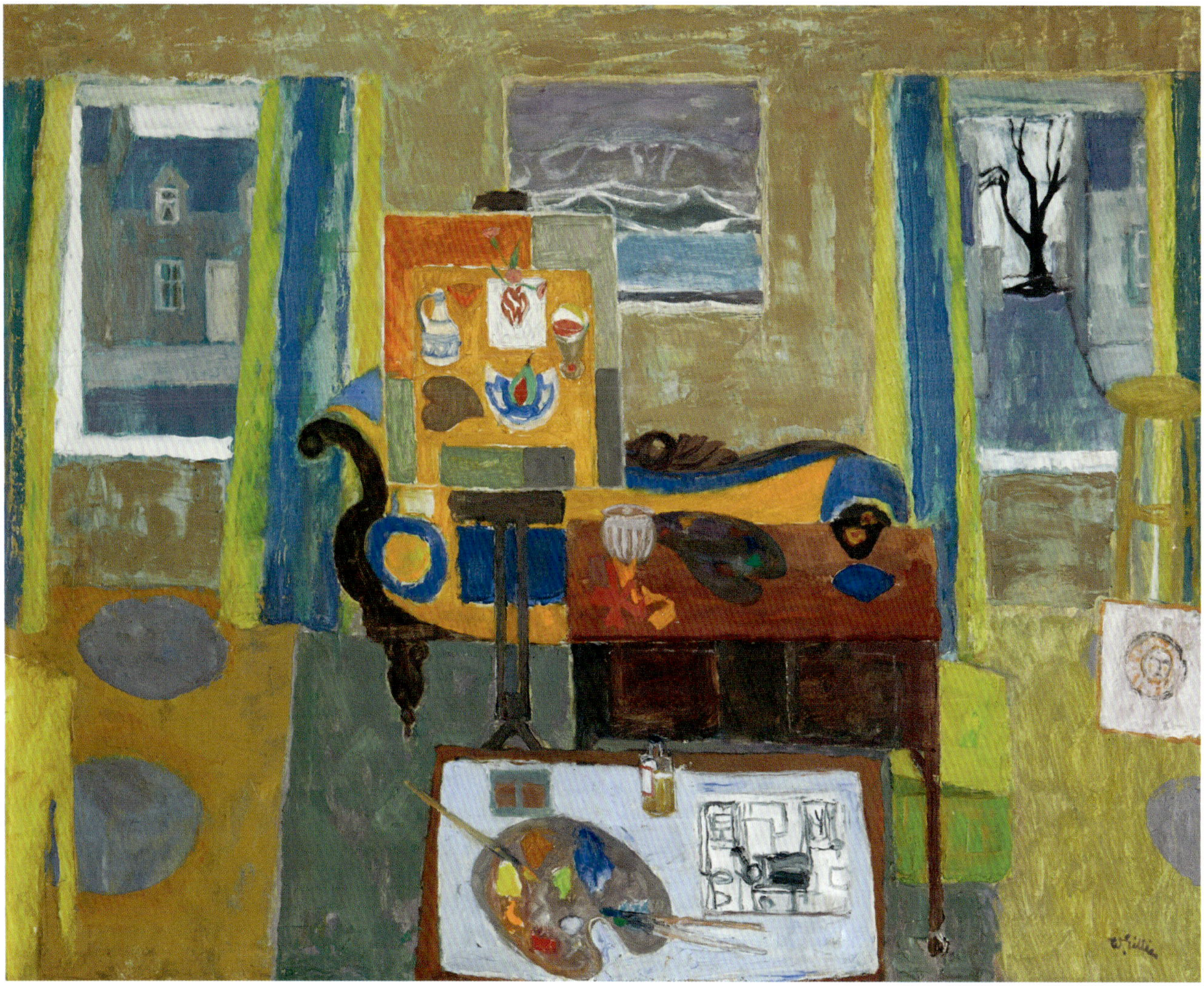

114 *Interior of Studio, Temple* (*c.* 1965). Oil, 97 cm by 122 cm planes at the base of the work suggests even that the tree is rooted in the house and has escaped to the garden from Gillies' imagination, as though to re-join the tree in its setting outside, perhaps even becoming Gillies again, as tree again in Piper's field, or walking a line with Klee.

Other large oils, all set at dusk, use the window trope, placing on the inside more still-life objects in more prominent positions. Instances are *Winter Dusk* (1961–3) [115], *Lit Window, Early Dusk* (nd, *c.* 1966) [ni] and *Large Still Life* (nd, *c.* 1966) [ni]. But this was as far as it went. Indeed, a feature of the still lifes of these last years is his casting around and back for new beginnings, experimenting with merger and reflexivity, returning to familiar memorial symbols, looking at new artists and new possibilities for still life in watercolour. There was, however, a continuing concern with light and its fading, prefigured in these works and in *Dusk* (1959) [110]. Gillies painted this at the time that a rapid loss of sight was ending the long exhibiting career of his friend and colleague, the print-maker, glassmaker and watercolourist William Wilson. The friendship was close enough for Gillies to have wanted him as an executor of his new will.

Still life remained a priority when his election in 1965 to Associate of the Royal Academy in London gave him a new exhibition outlet and his retiral in 1966 restored his time to paint. In his seven annual showings at the Royal Academy, two-thirds of the thirty-three works he sent were still lifes. So too were twelve of the fifteen oils shown in his 1970 retrospective from the years of his retirement. In six of these late works, a glowing point of interest is set on a dark ground and, in several, is made the focus for a reworking of familiar themes. In *Still Life with Spider Plant* (1966) [116], the crystalline star of a single ashtray comprises four shards. (Gillies gave this painting to the Royal Academy in 1971 as his Diploma work – a smoker's mischief, perhaps.) He also picks up familiar memorial objects again. The burning orange arrangement at the centre of *Interior Winter* (nd, *c.* 1966) [ni] reprises a work like *Still Life in Lamplight* (1949) [ni] but with the addition of the black vase. In *Still Life on a Cupboard* (*c.* 1966) [ni], the central motif of a single fruit on a lucent pink and white artefact is enhanced by the black dish on which the latter sits. This in turn is embraced by a drape, so dark as to render almost invisible the presence, again, of the black vase. If only for a time, the light that shines against the dark comes close to negating the *memento mori* that tracks him through life.

In many of these late studio works one can sense the presence of the artist, and in none more than *Interior of Studio, Temple* (*c.* 1965) [114]. It can be read as a considered summation of his existential journey. The palette and brushes indicate his presence in the work. The outline sketch signals that it is premeditated. (A contemporaneous watercolour, *Studio Interior, Dusk* (1964) [ni], shows, by contrast, a tonally subdued, cluttered studio dominated by the blues of dusk.) Yellow had helped to convey his growing optimism in the early 1950s, but never like this, spilling everywhere, garish even. At some point, we notice the head in the cartoon propped against Gillies' black stool, here painted yellow. It is possibly an image of Mithras, the sun god. It dawns on us that the bath of yellow is sunshine. The leafless tree then tells us it is winter sunshine.

Like *Garden, Winter Sunshine* (1960) [113], this interior, again with its black tree, visits the place where internal and external worlds meet,

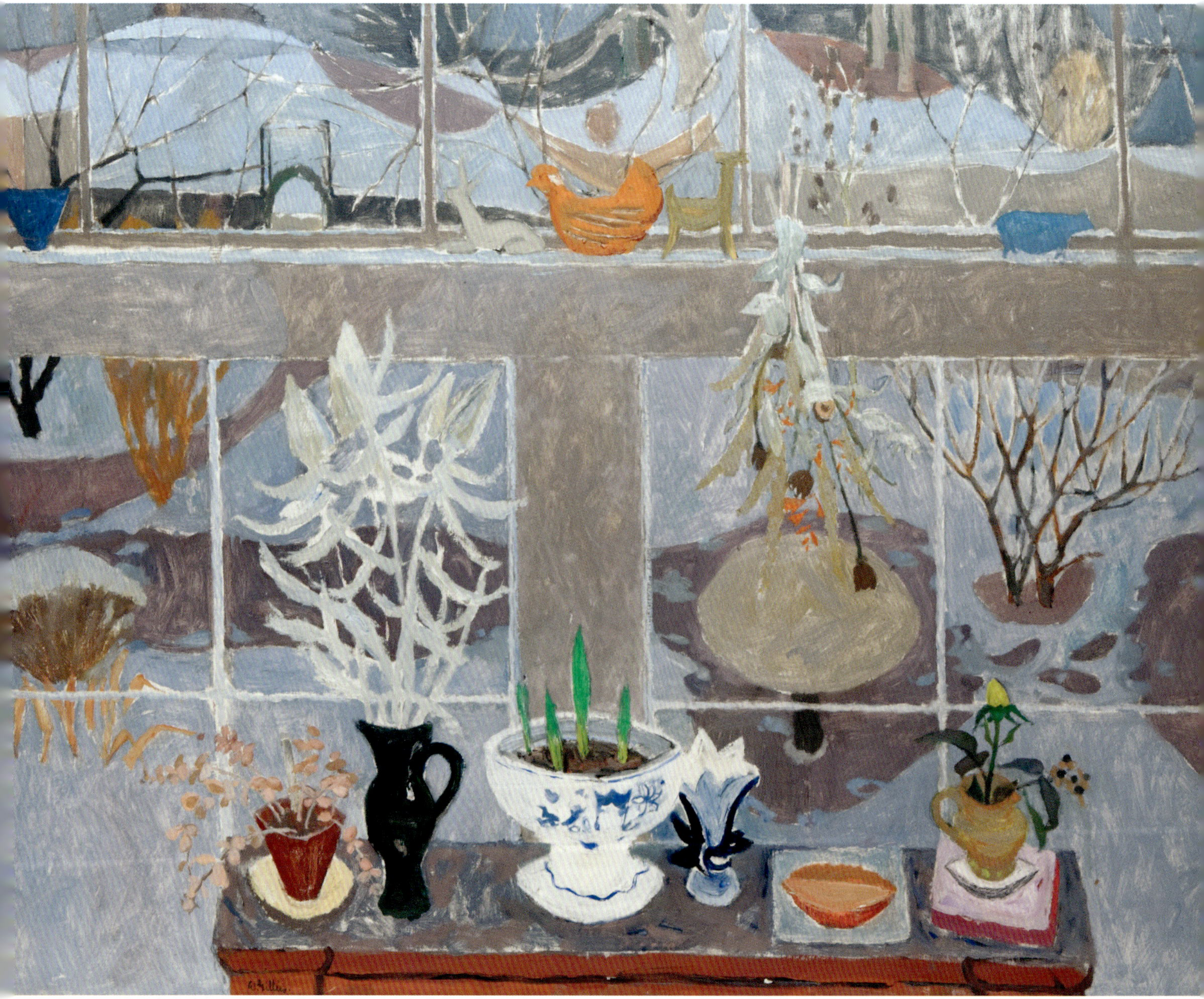

115 *Winter Dusk* (1961–3). Oil, 114.3 cm by 152.4 cm

retinal reception with idea and memory. Again, windows help to convey the meaning. Here there are two. Both are painted with curtains drawn apart, a cubist trope for realism as staged fiction. Their surrounds too act as frames for the image within. The external world thereby becomes two pictures of the external world that have the same status as the real pictures within the studio. The cottage across the street, which looks uncommonly like his own, can now represent his own if he chooses. Similarly, the tree that indeed stood opposite can once again function as metaphor, for the shaping of nature by time, for a tradition of landscape painting that has this idea at its heart, and for the artist himself, shaped and enabled by the past. Klee's artist-as-tree was sustained through unseen roots by the seasonal recycling of organic life and by nutrients laid deep in the past, minerals from cosmological time. Emma, now returned to this time and form, gave years of her life to this tree and is annually renewed in the astonishing transformation of its summer showings, a reincarnation of sorts. But in winter the tree waits patiently outside, for Gillies and as Gillies, stark, black and not to be denied.

Between these two images of interior and exterior, of domicile and landscape, of life and death in conjunction, sits *Winter Thaw* (1962) [111], his summation of humanity's place in time's landscape. There are also, I think, evocations here of two earlier domestic interiors. The palettes and preliminary sketch recall his abortive attempt, in the preparatory sketch [ni] for *Interior, Temple Cottage* (1951) [159], to find a place for himself in the painting. The suggestion of a triptych recalls the *Interior* of 1938 [42] (follow the lines of the curtains and green carpet down, and look at the structuring in the sketch). Gillies never did produce an harmonious image of himself with his family that he was happy to show. But now, of course, these spaces are emptied of his mother and Janet, and his own central space is expanded to become the whole work. There is no longer any point in a mirror-image of his external self because his subject is the existential reality within or beyond the mirror's reflection of surface.

In attempting this, he reuses the flattened, rectangular structures of his RSA Diploma work, *Still Life, Yellow Jug and Striped Cloth* (*c.* 1955) [102]. There and here they convey the reflexive relationship between retinal reception of the world and the realities which consciousness makes of this. Here, in the light of the sun, they converse with each other in an exchange of sensory experience with idea, of perception with imagination and memory. The real still life on the easel in *Interior of Studio, Temple* [114] (possibly *Bright Little Objects* (*c.* 1965) [ni]) becomes a place where an actual palette on a brown chest can show itself as a metaphysical heart (a metaphor for self-disclosure from the Elizabethan poet John Donne that was, I argue, shared between Harvey Wood and Herbert Grierson, and probably Herbert Read as well). The rectangles recede towards the external world like those in his Diploma work [102], and those in *Poppies in a Yellow Vase* (1934, *c.* 1936?) [46]. In the pre-war work, the attempt of mimesis to mirror the external world was bound by the laws of physics to destroy light. But now the sun that brings the thaw turns the dark of the winter tree into the light and life of the work on wall and easel, the work in itself, for itself, of himself and for himself.

It is unlikely that external constraints were the only reason for the ending of the sequence of still lifes that began in 1948 or thereby. Towards the

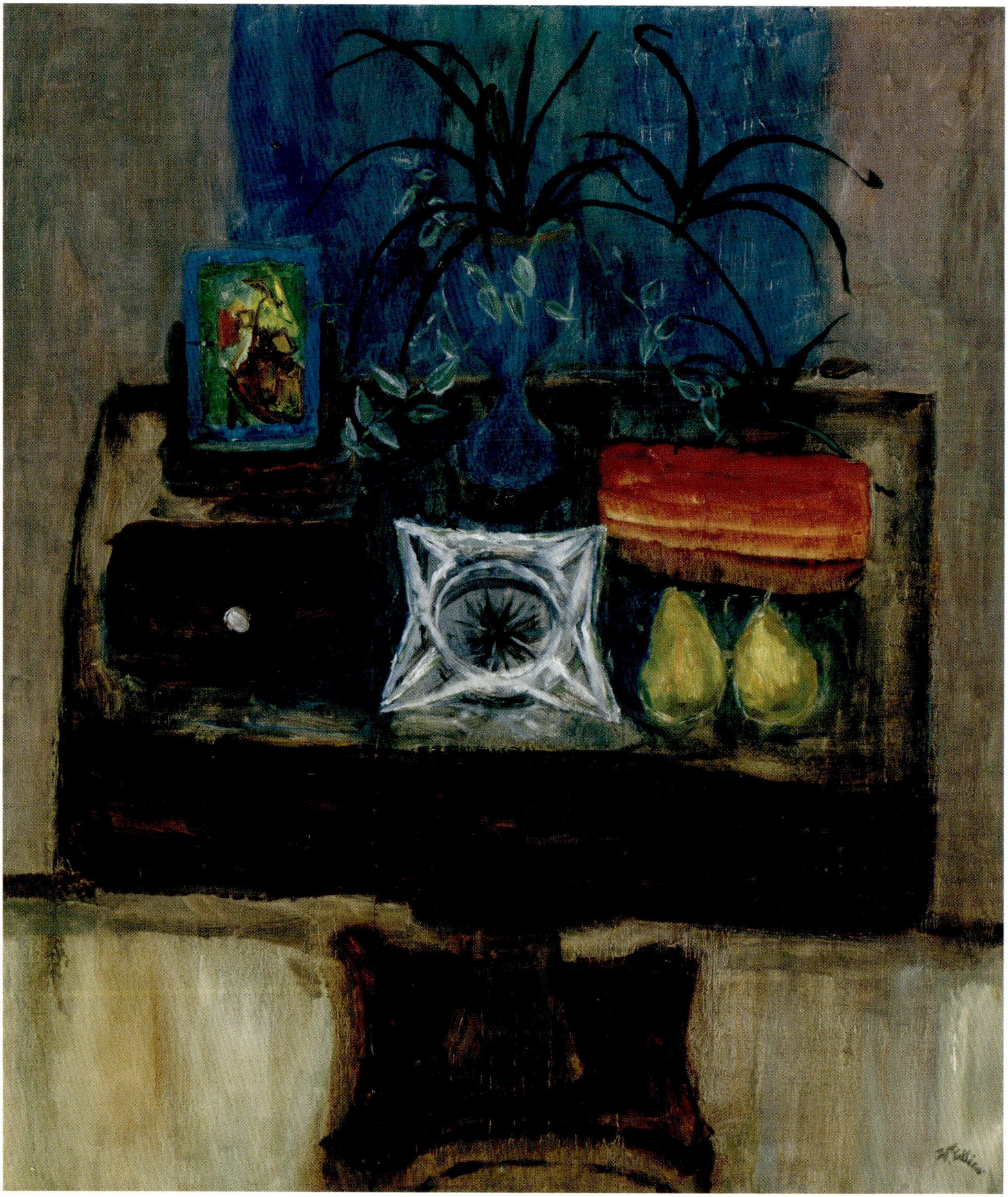

116 *Still Life with Spider Plant* (1966). Oil, 103.8 cm by 91.6 cm

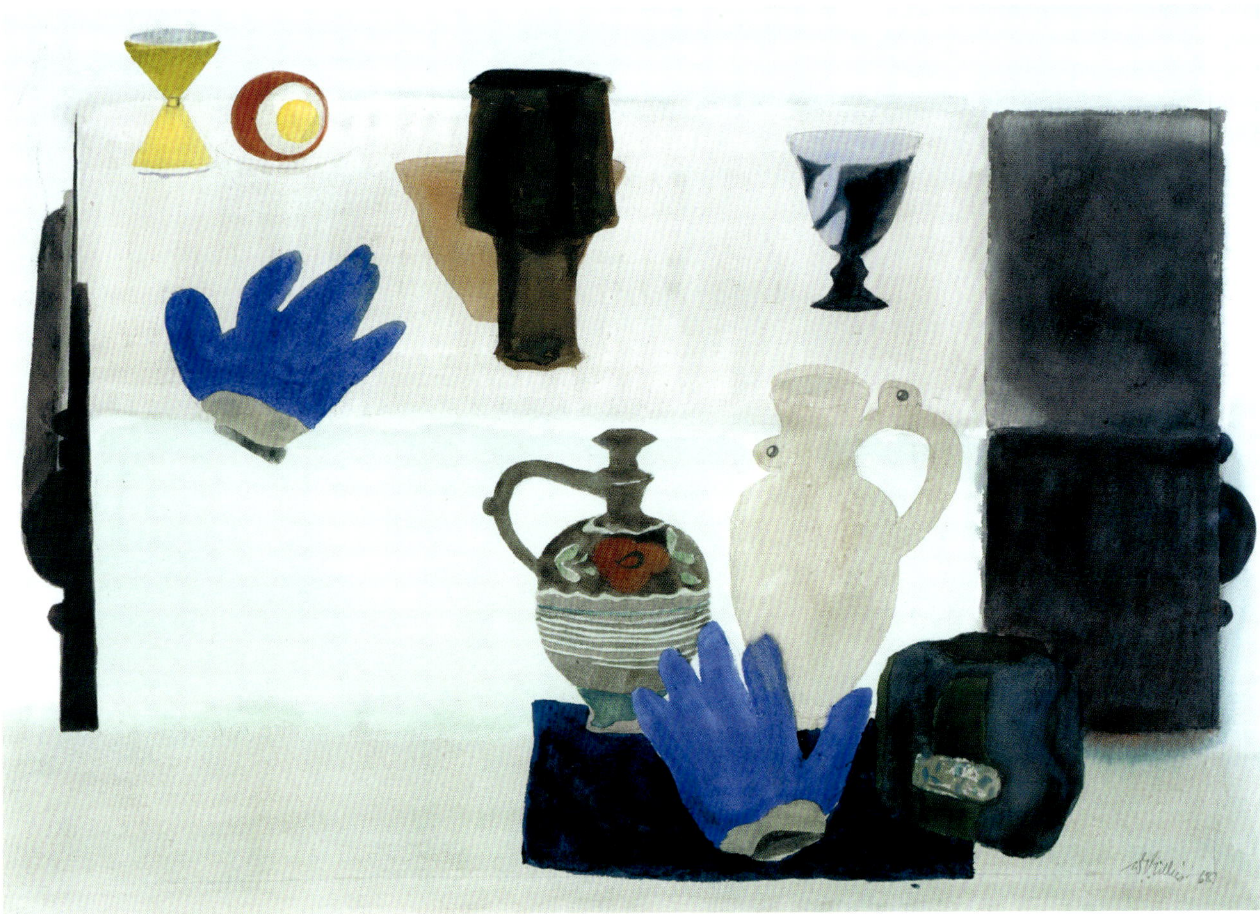

117 *Still Life with Blue Gloves* (1968). Watercolour, 65.4 cm by 91.4 cm

end of the 1950s, light and its fading become a central theme of the oil landscapes too, with a focus on the brief witness of consciousness itself. Drawings and watercolours of Borders subjects continue but there are very few extensive oil landscapes now of the Borders hills. Instead, we have works based, with a few late exceptions, on Temple Cottage. The majority of these are gloaming or moon-lit works. They begin early with the oil and watercolour versions of *The Garden, Temple, Winter Moon* in and around 1961 [ni] and continue with the mixed-genre work and *Temple, Dusk* (1968) [ni]. Many of the non-gloaming minority are, nevertheless, delicately lit. Only one, *Early Spring* (nd, mid-1960s?) [ni] has a Temple subject. *Between Raeshaw and Carcant on Heriot Water* (*c.* 1968) [119] and *Trees Rosebery* (*c.* 1970) [ni] are meditations on light and colour based on simple subjects. None is concerned with form or rages against the dying of the light. Rather, the constituents of light itself are exploited for the vitalities that consciousness finds there.

Two of these last landscapes can also be read as summations. *Kitchen Garden in Winter* (1968–9) [120] was painted around the time of *Still Life, Study in Grey* (1968) [118] and the fiftieth anniversary of the German Spring Offensive. It revisits these years with a reference to Paul Nash, whose paintings of war he acknowledged as 'a strong private influence'. Gillies paints a stand of trees behind Temple Cottage as one of Nash's cherished Wittenham Clumps and places over it the gibbous moon of *Autumn Moon* (1934, *c.* 1934–7) [84]. The garden is a featureless expanse of brown, a virtual wasteland, that throws into relief its one strange and lucent growth. It is a typical, centrally placed, intrusion, not a tree in this case but a stalk of kail in an emptied kailyard. The whole is framed by an assemblage of structures that are oddly aligned with each other, as though accumulated discretely over the generations in makeshift fashion, closer to the piecemeal alignments of allotments or crofts.

This is Gillies' mundane world of finite endeavour and understanding. But he lights the walls, eerily, both from the moon to his front and from the unseen house from which he looks, and he paints them in 1920s cubist fashion to suggest theatrical flats. Our attention is thereby funnelled back, along the symbolic vector that links the sole survivor of the Kailyard of his kin – a survivor, too, of the wasted landscape of war – through the clump of trees that embody a lifetime's history, to the moon and sky. Here the clouds repeat the icy gullies of *Winter Thaw* (1960) [111] with its emergent hill forms and cosmological reference. No such hills could be seen from Temple Cottage, of course. But now, in this small and finite holding on this physical place, we sense another holding too, a holding on an idea illuminated, hologrammatically one might say, at the convergence of light from his inner and outer worlds. And so, he paints a wall across the base to mark the point where strict mimesis ends and a greater truth is found, beyond the wall's proscenium, on the stage the flats define. It is, again, an answer of sorts to the question posed by *Trees and Coppice* (1928, *c.* 1928) [29], a different, metaphysical, sensing of place. Martin Baillie pronounced it a 'gaunt, desolate painting different … from anything that has gone before' and, as such, a work that confirmed Gillies' continuing development as an artist of international stature.

Nairn Beach (*c.* 1970) [121] is a similar transformation of the memorialising impulse that runs through Gillies' life. The memories go

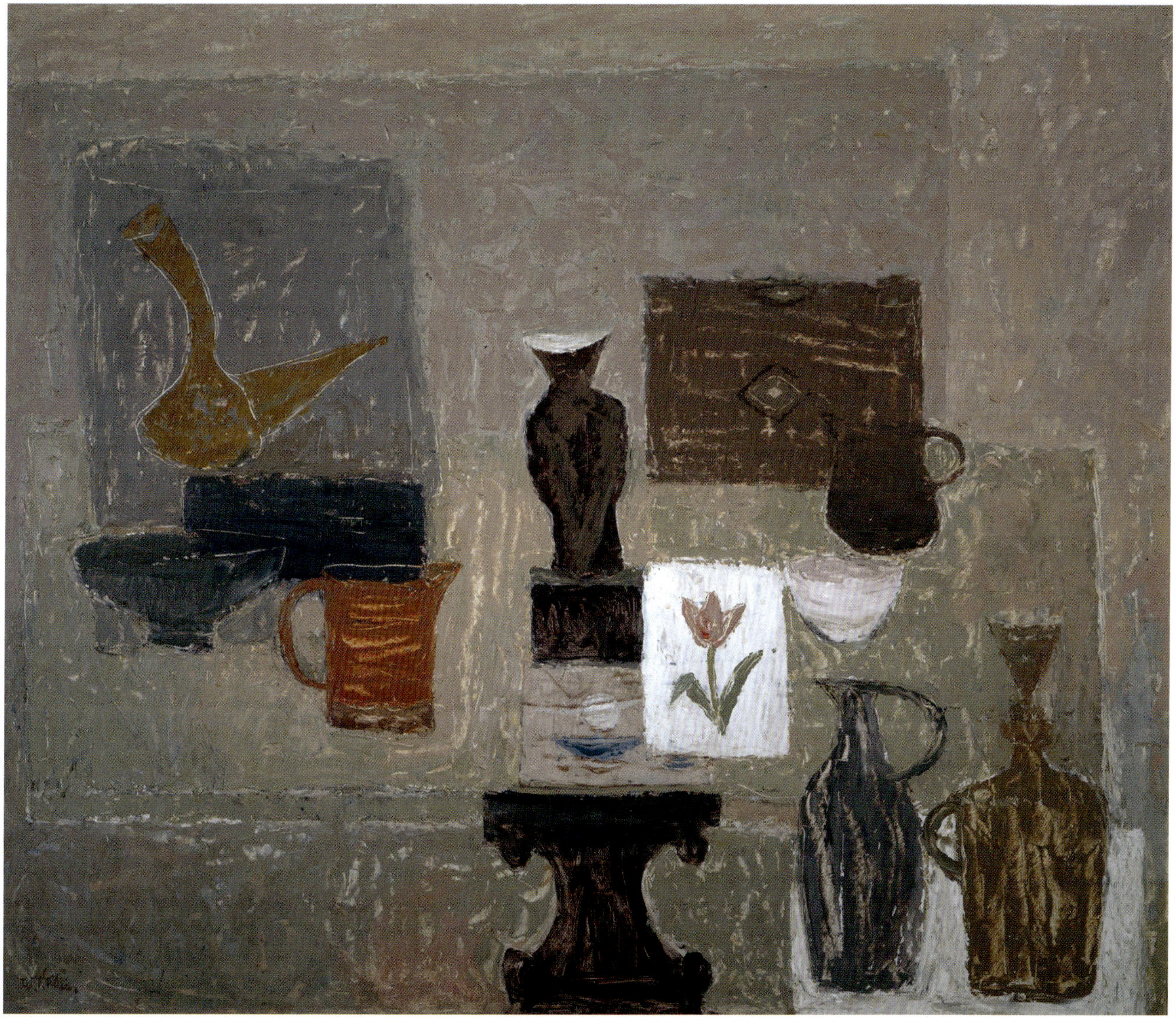

118 *Still Life, Study in Grey* (1968). Oil, 81 cm by 98 cm

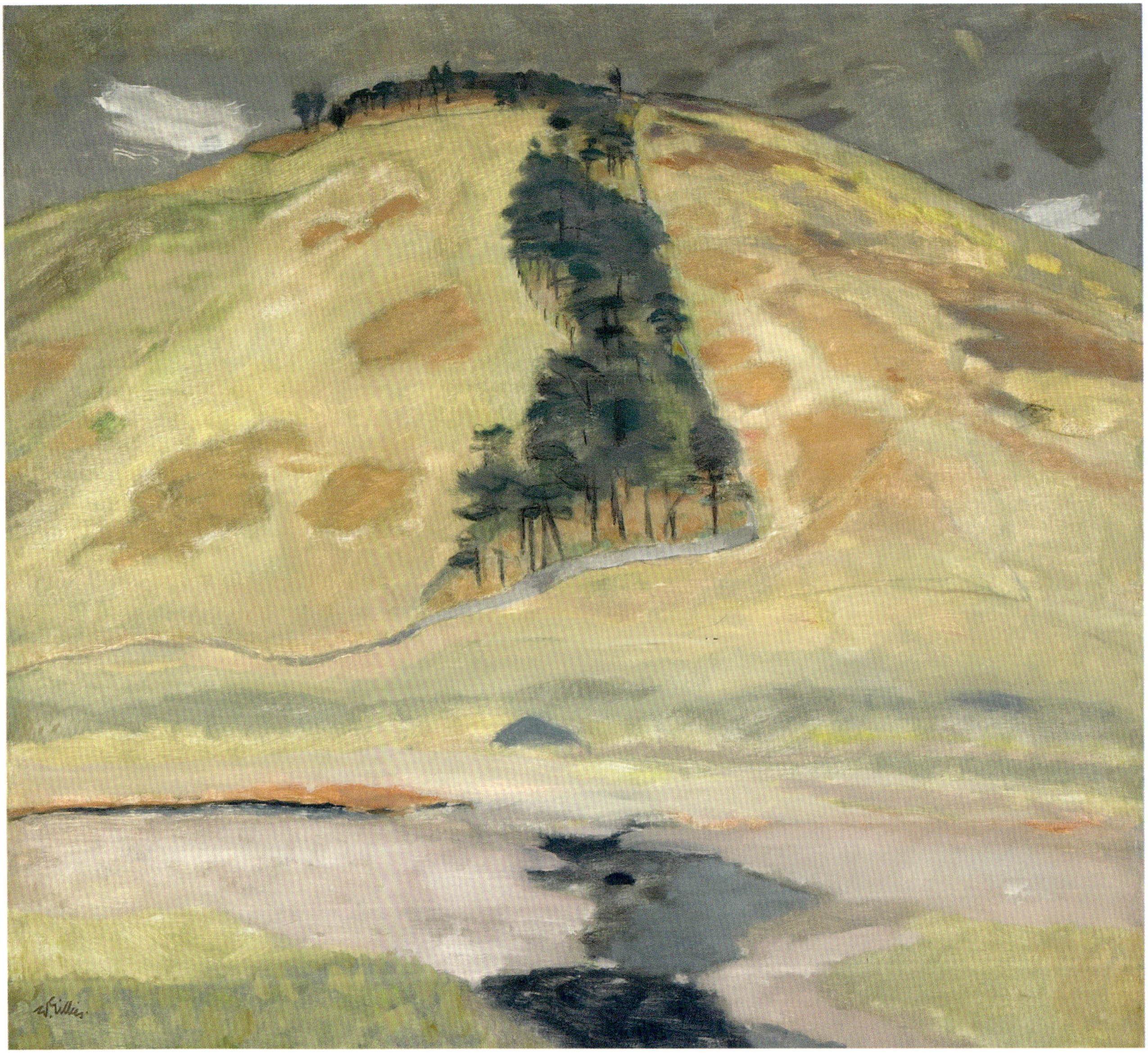

119 *Between Raeshaw and Carcant on Heriot Water* (*c.* 1968). Oil, 83.3 cm by 96.6 cm

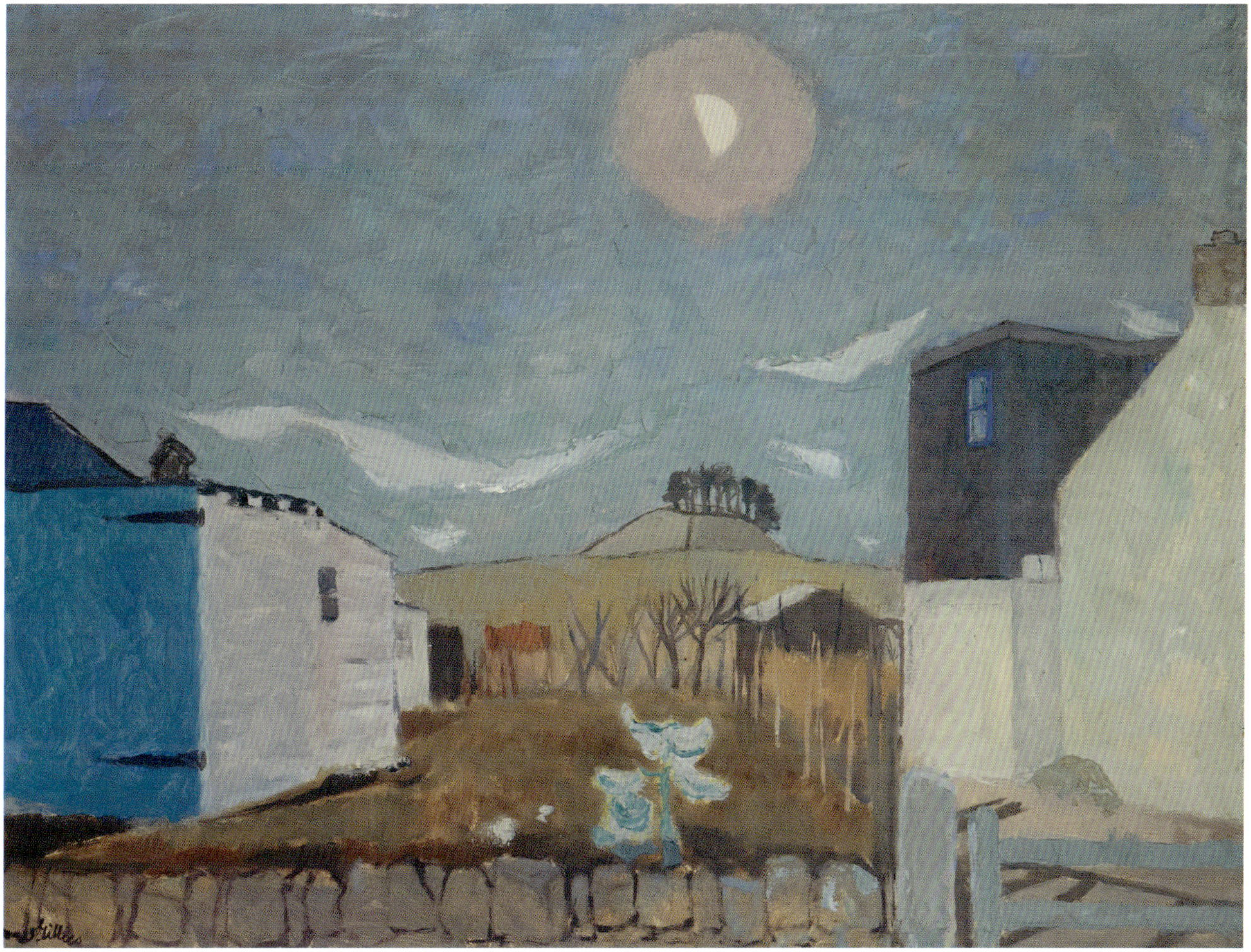

120 *Kitchen Garden in Winter* (1968–9). Oil, 79 cm by 107 cm back to a Gauguin dog that first prompted his sense of colour, and to William McTaggart's (1835–1910) wraiths on the beach (that Gillies probably saw as a young man in the company of the older artist's grandson, William MacTaggart). We are reminded, too, of his own beach watercolours of the 1930s, of his time with his family in Ardnamurchan in the summer after Emma's death [81], and of John Maxwell's *Harbour with Warning Light* [ni], about which Gillies spoke so movingly in his funeral oration for Maxwell. Inevitably, too, we think of the final journey here of Ann Scott-Moncrieff.

The painting works both as an image in its own right and because of associations prompted by an understanding of his life. This ever-modest man – this ironic, surviving, stalk of kail in his wasted landscape – wanted to conjure a joy from the human condition that did not deny the realities of human folly, vulnerability and cruelty. In doing this, he gave his life to his art and, against his initial inclinations, struggled with some success to open his art to his life.

Across the darkened forms that emerge from sea and sky, three artefacts are suspended as though by Klee – a kite in the form of a shard; a beach ball formed from crescents truncated to triangles in the colours of the flag Gillies saluted at school; and a mole with lighthouse signifying danger, shelter and a source of light itself. The figures that play on the strand harness and challenge the elements but are, in their fragility, subject to them as well, made from them and, ultimately, returned to them. Their brief lives, too, are suspended, in the span of his memory and the abstracted forms of his idiom; and the whole, himself included, is set against the emergent forms of cosmological time we saw in *Highland Landscape [with] Suilven* (1936) [76] and other inter-war paintings from the beach.

He has found a place where extremes meet, darkness with light, death with life, absence with presence, isolation with conviviality, danger with play. If words are laboured here, perhaps what they attempt is not. On *Nairn Beach*, the play's the thing. Extremes are only whispered and are freed to sport with each other, flying metaphorical kites, sparking meanings with their collisions and associations. Out of this an art emerges, an art of plural realities, of human fragility turned to creative advantage. Two caravans supply quotation marks for the fictions of mimesis and a refuge for those who will rest in the place they have found.

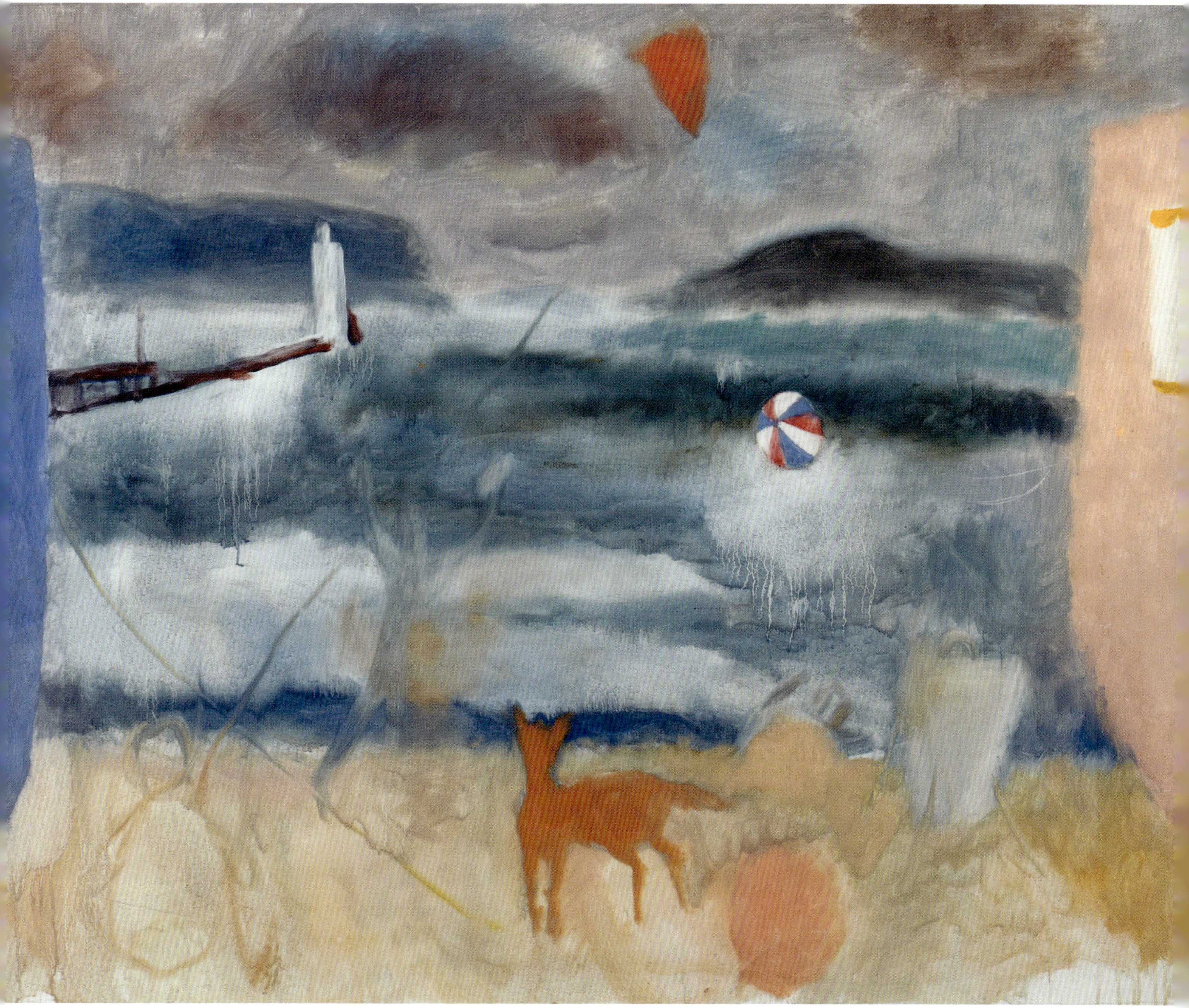

121 *Nairn Beach* (*c.* 1970). Oil, 88.2 cm by 114.8 cm

Politics, Patronage and Later Landscapes on Paper

Patronage is not just about money. It is also about the position that money can buy and the power that position confers, power even to set the criteria that define quality and thereby license plutocratic claims to meritocratic entitlement. During the Second World War, Kenneth Clark used his position in government, and wealth he inherited from the textile industry in Scotland, to support his preferred artists and to elaborate war aims they were then well placed to fulfil. He and John Piper spun a Neo-Romantic narrative of an island nation washed by an aqueous light that gave Britain its romantic sensibility, poetry and art. It was an art, Clark claimed, of individual inspiration that was resistant to totalitarian control. But it was not beyond the control of Clark or Keynes in the 1930s and 1940s, as their undergraduate network moved into the making and governance of the arts.

Little of this patronage trickled down to Scotland during the war. Both men resisted demands led, among others, by Stanley Cursiter, Director of the National Galleries of Scotland. He wanted a gallery of modern art for Scotland that was integrated into the craft, industry and life of the country, along lines similar to those advocated earlier by Herbert Read. Cursiter disputed criticisms of Scottish painting voiced by Talbot Rice, Read's successor in the Edinburgh chair of fine art, and refused to cooperate with some of the exhibitions sent up from London by the predecessor body to the Arts Council of Great Britain. He wanted more Scottish control and outreach, whereas Clark and Keynes opposed decentralisation and any form of support that smacked of art as social service or adult education. They saw culture as a hierarchy topped off by God, genius or refinement.

The inception of the Edinburgh International Festival in 1947 was a mixed blessing for artists working or exhibiting in Scotland. The greater part of its budget was controlled from London by the ACGB and visual art was not part of the official programme. Makeshift arrangements to fill this void in the early years occupied space in the Academy otherwise used for the exhibition of work by living Scottish artists, while the exclusion of visual art meant that the world would be coming to Edinburgh each year but would see no contemporary Scottish painting as part of the official Festival. The implications for the exhibition of Scottish art, whether in Scotland or England, were ominous. As early as August 1947, the ACGB pulled out of an arrangement with its Scottish sub-committee for a joint exhibition of contemporary British painting that treated Scots artists coevally with artists elsewhere in Britain.

This was the point at which Gillies became a pawn in the argument. There was already a large 'fringe' exhibition of Scottish art at the inaugural Festival, organised in protest by the artist Anne Redpath. Now Robert Lillie decided to use his growing collection of Gillies' works, as he said, to 'put Mister Gillies on the map'. In 1948, he showed fifty-six of them in exhibitions he organised at the French Institute in Edinburgh and the City Art Gallery in Aberdeen. It was the start of a thirty-year promotional effort of his, but also an element in a wider campaign that saw the French Institute used for a series of exhibitions of contemporary Scottish work, and several initiatives by Elder Dickson as President of the SSA. Cursiter had asked him to promote his cause,

Opposite:
Detail from Book launch of *Scottish Country* ([123] – see p. 170)

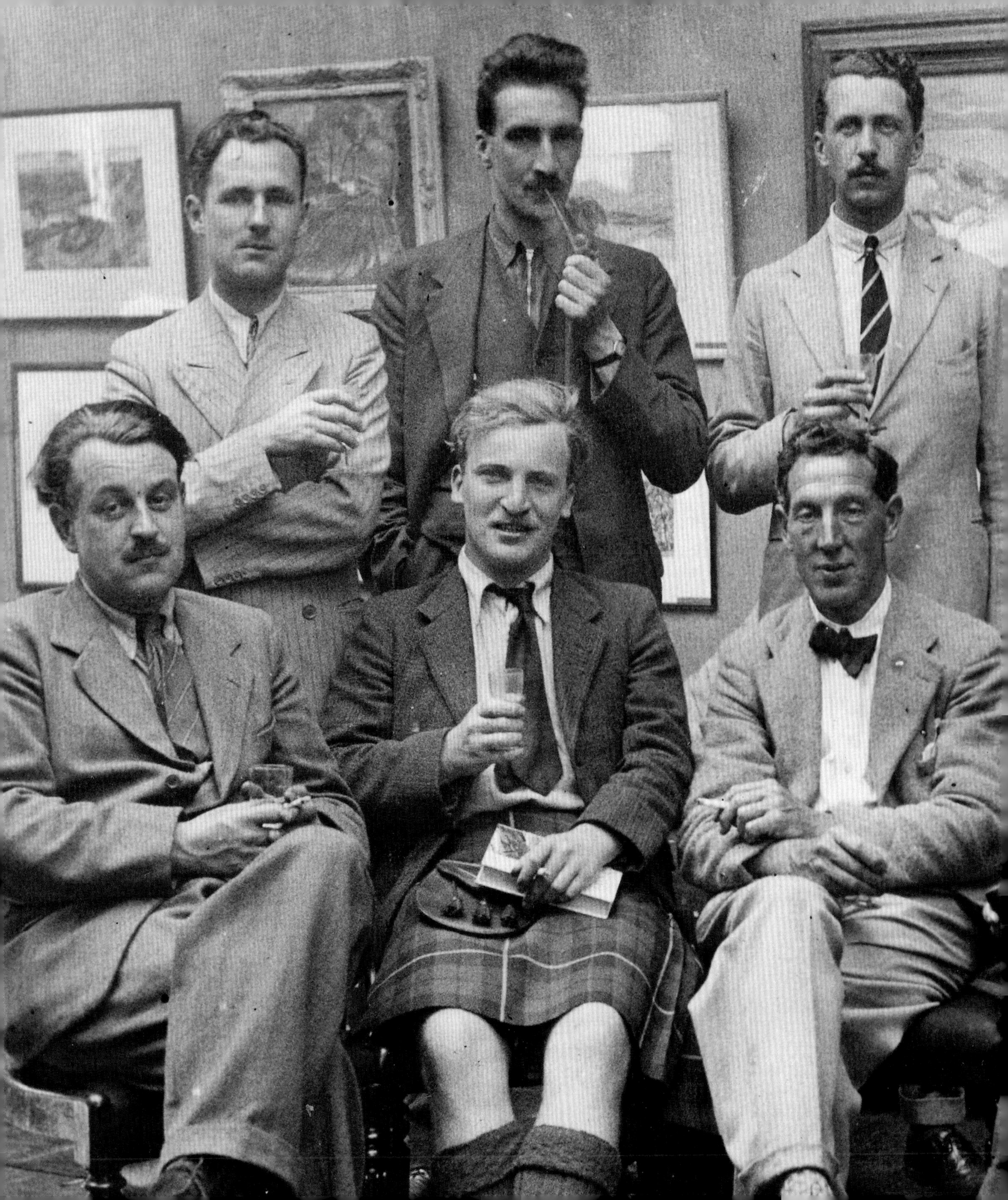

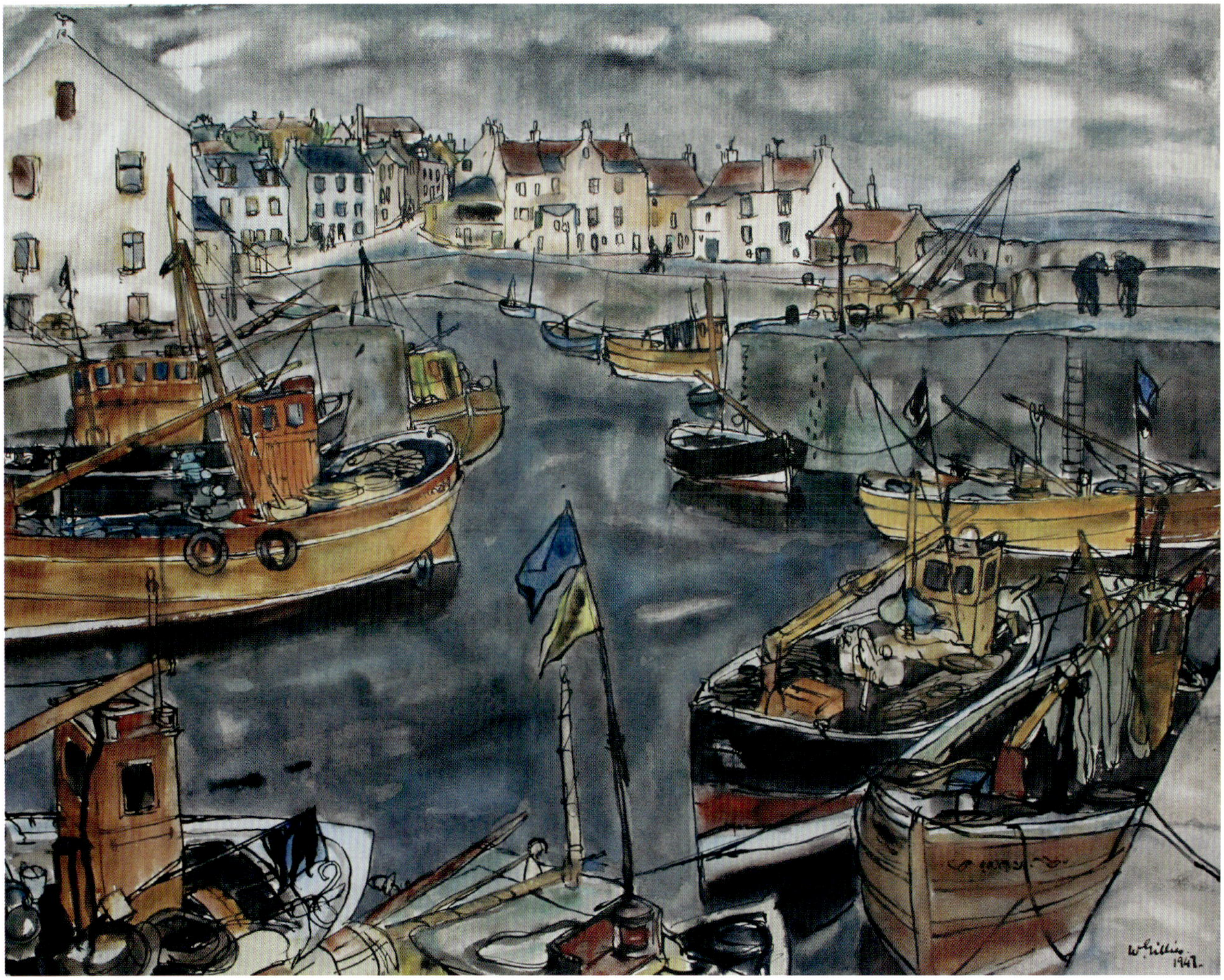

122 *Pittenweem* (1947). Watercolour, pen and ink, 51 cm by 61 cm

being unable, as a civil servant, to do so himself in public. Elder Dickson brought a major exhibition of contemporary French painting to Edinburgh in 1945, took the annual exhibition of the SSA to London in 1947 and Glasgow in 1948, and endorsed Cursiter's cause in the press without mentioning his name.

Lillie's first two exhibitions were a critical success in Scotland and fuelled demand for works on paper like *Winter Afternoon, Temple* (*c.* 1942) [87] and *Pittenweem* (1947) [122]. He typically preferred the type of landscape with drawing to which Gillies had turned during the war. These works are more realistic and less ambitious than the pre-war watercolours or the post-war landscapes in oil. The type of abstraction found in the oils after 1948 is rare. Only watercolours like *Near Howgate* (1951) [103] and *Moorfoot Hills* (1956) [2] begin to approach it, and, if less obviously, *March, Moorfoot* (1951) [124]. Quality varies. Many, like *St Monance* (1949) [125], have the courage of simplicity. The drawing can be breath-taking, as in *Balquhidder* (nd, 1950s) [126] and *Arniston Pond* (nd, *c.* 1960) [127]. At times, it is spare and suggestive, liberating the colour with staccato accents and arabesques. At other times, however, the drawing constrains the managed serendipity of watercolour and this special quality of the medium, and Gillies' mastery of it, does not emerge. To my eye, *Shiplaw Farm* (1950) [ni] comes close to painting by numbers and is not alone. Others disagree.

The success of Lillie's two exhibitions was a mixed blessing for Gillies. Lillie had bought mostly from society exhibitions or direct from the artist. There had been little profit for the Scottish Gallery (Aitken Dott), which was Gillies' best potential outlet for his oils during the Festival. The gallery, however, could not afford to alienate Lillie, a good customer for its other artists, but it could and did take profits from further exhibitions of Gillies' works on paper. It was not until 1952 that it gave him a show during the Festival in which he could exhibit his oils (and then only a joint show with other artists). Thereafter, in exhibitions Lillie did not control, Gillies' exhibitions moved towards his preferred mix of roughly equal numbers of still lifes, oil landscapes and landscapes on paper.

Between 1947 and 1954, the average number of Gillies' works shown in some venue each year was over eighty. The vast majority of these were landscapes on paper. What his growing audience knew, therefore, were mostly works made since 1945 in his more realistic mode depicting smaller inland communities or coastal habitations. It saw little of his pre-war work and few still lifes, particularly ones that Lillie considered severe or abstract and accordingly disliked. These were the years in which the National Covenant campaign, and latterly the Coronation of 1953, returned the issue of Home Rule to the fore. They were also the years in which the countryman narrative emerged, with its claim of synergies between Gillies' watercolour landscapes and his intuitive sense of a collective national consciousness.

George Scott-Moncrieff [123] had backing from the very top for the exhibition of Gillies' landscapes on paper that he organised in 1953. He was a founding member of the National Trust for Scotland and of the Saltire Society, formed in 1936 for the promotion of Scotland's culture. Like the Church of Scotland, education and the law, these were entities through which a nation that had lost its Parliament in 1707 conducted unresolved aspects of the business of civil society. Their two memberships were diverse, influential and overlapping, cultural-national in tendency, and home to the various strands of romantic, communitarian and liberal thought evident in the several forms that political nationalism took in its early years.

Members of two dynastic families were of particular importance. John Patrick Crichton-Stuart, the Third Marquess of Bute (1847–1900), was a wealthy coal-owner, conservationist, scholar, patron of the arts and Catholic convert. His extensive philanthropic legacy was intended in part to revive the intellectual and spiritual life of pre-Reformation Scotland on both the mainland and the Hebridean islands with Catholic populations. During the war, Scott-Moncrieff worked closely with John Patrick's son John Crichton-Stuart, the Fourth Marquess (1881–1947). He was the main philanthropic ally of the National Trust for Scotland in its first fifteen years and led much of its work. Among his gifts was the

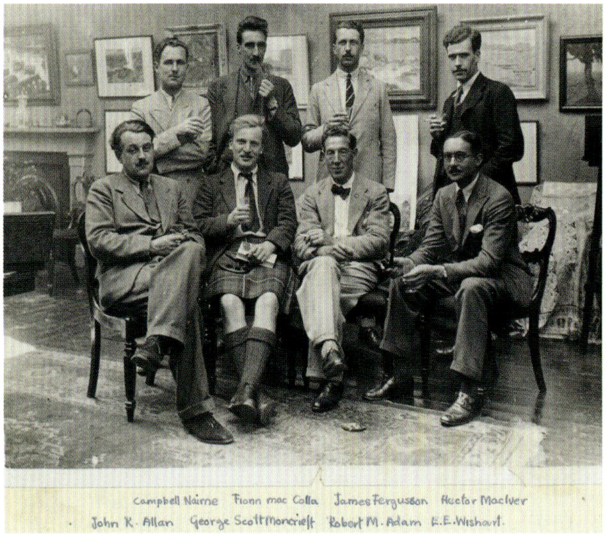

123 Book launch of *Scottish Country* (1935), edited by George Scott-Moncrieff (kilt), Garret Studio; others, clockwise, Campbell Nairne, Fionn MacColla (pipe), James Fergusson, Hector McIver, E. E. Wishart, Robert Moyes Adam, John R. Alan. Ink annotation by David Cleghorn Thomson

Georgian townhouse in Edinburgh where Gillies' watercolour landscapes were shown in 1953.

The other family was that of David Lindsay (1900–75), an undergraduate friend of Clark, Rothenstein and Talbot Rice and by now the 28th Earl of Crawford and 11th Earl of Balcarres. Lindsay was a considerable figure, a Unionist politician who had married into the Cavendish family, itself one of the great Conservative political dynasties. He was Episcopalian, a sometime government minister and, for over thirty years, a 'uniquely influential' presence in the governance of galleries and other cultural institutions in England and Scotland. He was also a close family friend, political ally and erstwhile academic collaborator of Kenneth Clark, whose television lectures were to define civilisation for the Christian cultures of the Anglophone world. The Lindsay family fortune, depleted by death duties, came from coal and steel, not long since nationalised by the first post-war Labour government.

Lindsay used the opening of the National Trust for Scotland exhibition in 1953 to attack planners, housing schemes and abstract art. He told his audience of 500 that Gillies stood for the opposite of these, a reminder of what was at risk. Gillies 'understood Scotland' and found it, 'not with the unadulterated gloom which taints so many painters … for we are a good and happy and not a morbid and bilious people'. In the great tradition of Western art, Lindsay said, Gillies had not abandoned representation but had married it to abstraction. In other words, evolution, not revolution, was the story of the nation that its art should promote.

Behind Lindsay's remarks lay his anathemas of modern art, non-figurative abstraction, political nationalism and communism, as personified by Picasso and MacDiarmid. The latter had become the figurehead for the contrarian, and allegedly communist-sympathising, People's Festival that ran annually in Edinburgh from 1951 to 1953–4 to celebrate indigenous popular culture. The 'bilious people', I think, were those like MacDiarmid who challenged the equation of culture with that of the official Festival, did not defer to 'men o' established reputation', but who thought with him that '[t]he condition o' Scotland today ca's for a' the bitterness we can possibly distil'.

Lindsay did not name MacDiarmid, but he made no secret of his hostility to Picasso and to non-figurative abstraction. Picasso was no such painter, of course. But his name was synonymous with modernism, and his membership of the Communist Party appeared to vindicate a common contemporary equation of modern

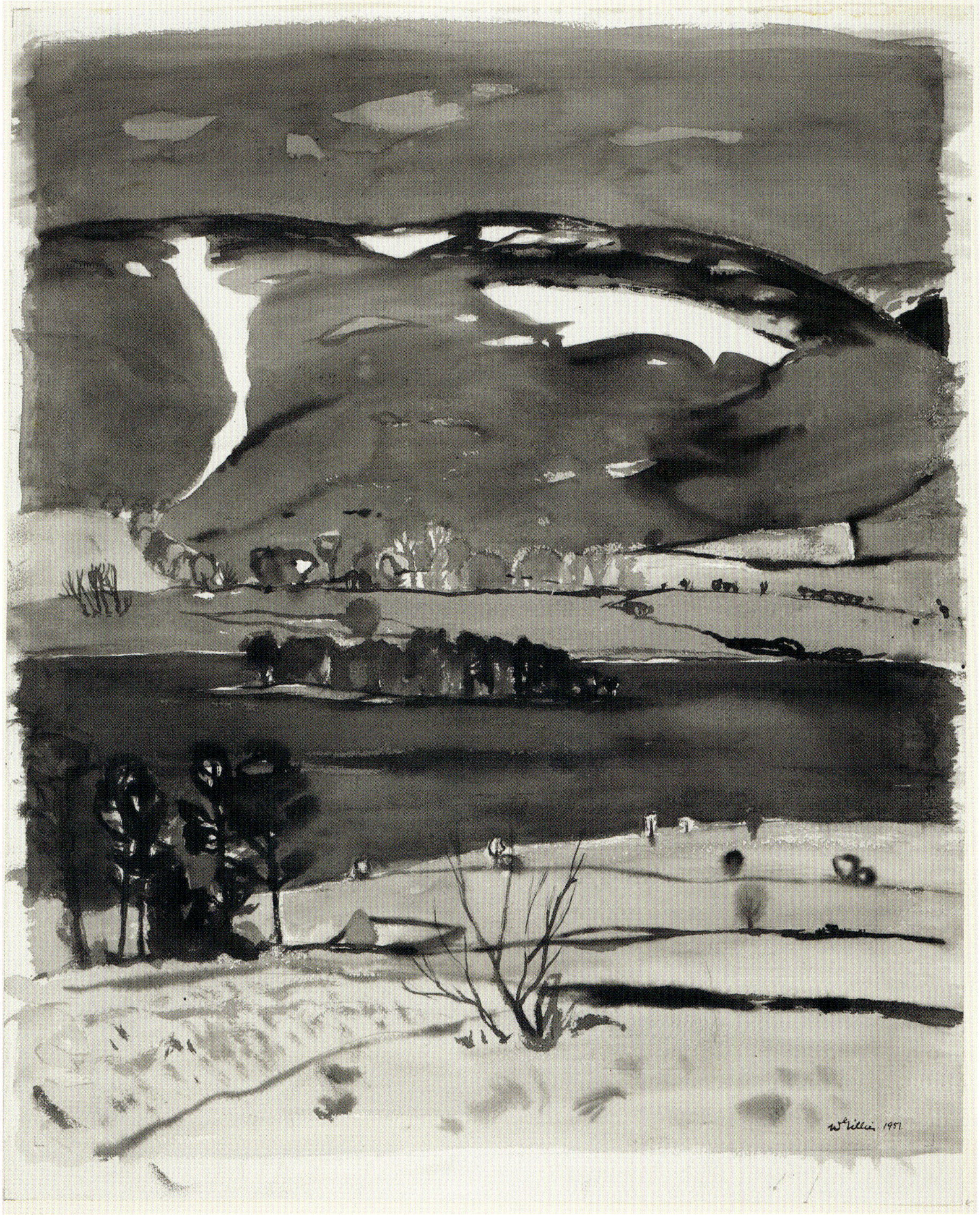

124 *March, Moorfoot* (1951). Watercolour and pencil, 66.3 cm by 55 cm

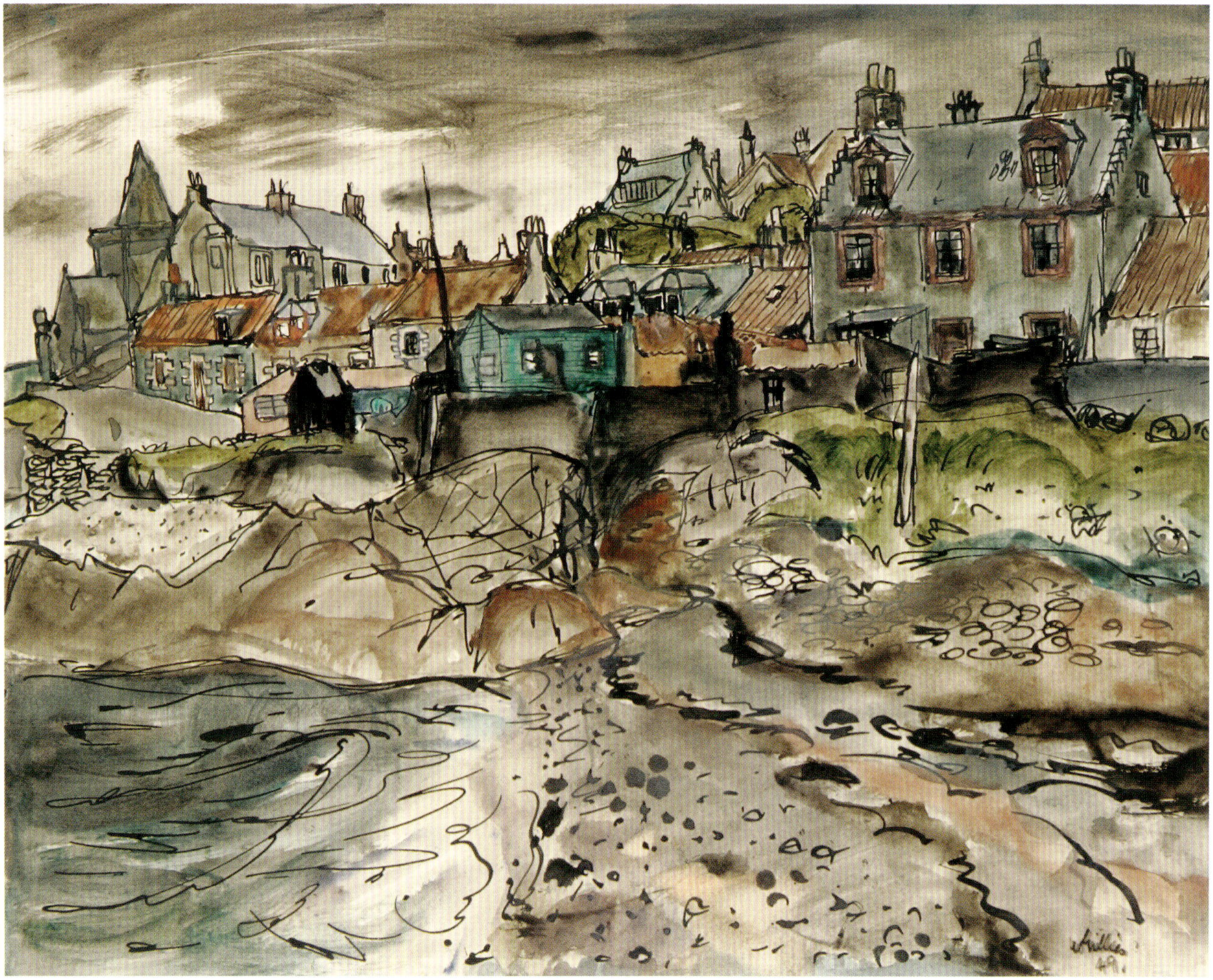

125 *St Monance* (1949). Watercolour, pen and ink, 24 cm by 31 cm

art with violence and the communist creed. Lindsay's gloss on Gillies' watercolours was that it was possible to be Scottish but deferential, contemporary but gradualist, respecting tradition and celebrating heritage. Gillies was an artist who knew his place, in both senses of the term. The contrast between Gillies' apparent asexual domesticity and the Dionysiac imaginings of Picasso and MacDiarmid was left unspoken.

This was a message someone wanted the world to hear. The National Trust for Scotland exhibition of 1953 was the only time an incorporated body gave Gillies a one-man show during the Festival. It was seen by 6,300 visitors in three weeks and a detailed account of Lindsay's remarks was circulated to the 5,000 members of the Trust. There followed the 1954 ACGB exhibition for Gillies and Maxwell in London and

John Rothenstein's journey to Edinburgh in 1955 to call for the renewal of 'a common stock of imagery, which unites the artist and layman once again'. Rothenstein purchased works by Gillies for the Tate, and Gillies was made Companion of the British Empire in 1957. Around this time also, he painted at Cartmel near Lancaster, where the family seat of Lindsay's Cavendish wife was situated. It all adds up.

George and Ann Scott-Moncrieff had bought Temple Cottage in 1936 with an inheritance of Ann's. They loved it as the first home they could call their own, and for its beeches. The cover of an issue of *The New Alliance* three months after Ann's death was illustrated with a single beech tree drawn by Gillies. When George and Ann sold to Gillies in 1939, the network of nationalist intellectuals, journalists and broadcasters that was served by *The New Alliance* [89] lost its Temple meeting place. But it was restored after the war when Hector McIver [123], a former student of Grierson's, moved in next-door to Gillies. He and his wife Mary, herself a teacher of art, hosted there the poets and critics who were to interpret Gillies to the post-war world.

George himself eventually settled permanently in Haddington, having spent much of the previous five years on the island of Eigg raising his three children. He brought to the countryman narrative a strand of Vatican social philosophy advanced in Britain by G. K. Chesterton and Hilaire Belloc, two contacts whom he had originally 'inherited', along with T. S. Eliot, from his uncle Charles Scott Moncrieff. Charles, like Eliot, encouraged his nephew's nationalism. George's solution to the problems of modernity had an affinity with the Kailyard – simple country living based on family, reverence for nature, and life and work as a unified witness to God. He held that these virtues were Catholic, had survived from pre-Reformation Scotland, and were most evident in areas, both Protestant and Catholic, least affected by industrialisation. But they could now be preserved and extended only through political action founded in individual spiritual renewal under a higher authority. He saw Gillies' family, 'profession' and move to Temple as instantiations of a Catholic ideal. But he did not mention what he knew of the fears that drove Gillies from Edinburgh in 1939. When Gillies battered at the door of Temple Cottage in September that year, and this is a truth stranger than fiction, Scott-Moncrieff had already prepared a kailyard setting for the very room that was to become Gillies' studio. It was from there in 1936 that the BBC broadcast an entertainment he had scripted for Hogmanay. In it, real and fictional villagers, including the local minister, celebrated the passing of the year with music, song and frequent affirmations that the moral fabric of former Temple life could yet be restored.

Elder Dickson supplied the countryman narrative with a psychoanalytic perspective on Gillies, virtue and the countryside. He attributed the acclaim in Scotland for Gillies' watercolours to the artist's intuitive ability to tap into a 'collective unconscious' common to all mankind. As described by Carl Gustav Jung, this concept comprises universal 'archetypes' of experience, laid down in the individual psyche in the early millennia of humanity, but historically and culturally diverse in their actual manifestations, and most accessible to individuals of extreme sensibility, such as shamans, artists and poets.

These features gave Elder Dickson the latitude to explain Gillies by adding a further, Thrumsian, thread to the Neo-Romantic narrative spun by Piper and Clark. If wartime Britain could have a distinctive cultural sensibility based on 'aqueous light', so, too, could Scotland, throughout its history, with a light that was yet more aqueous. He thought it self-evident that the medium of water was key: Gillies' watercolours evoked a way of seeing a primordial land, today called Scotland, that was distinctive, shared among 'Jung's "silent folk of the land"', and woven into the history and character of the nation.

So, Elder Dickson, who knew little of Gillies' family circumstances, gives us a Gillies who was 'nurtured in the Scottish democratic tradition' by a mother who possessed 'all the typical virtues of her Scottish ancestry'. An iconic trope for this tradition is the 'lad o' pairts', an able pupil or student from a less advantaged family background who progresses through education to higher things (Elder Dickson himself was one such). The trope was celebrated in the fiction 'Domsie' by Ian Maclaren (1895), a contemporary of J. M. Barrie. Maclaren's scholar-hero dies in his father's tenanted farm with fellow students from Edinburgh University at his bedside and sheep bleating outside.

For Gillies' sister Janet, his appointment as Principal of the Edinburgh College of Art affirmed the democratic tradition. Later, Smith (1991) based his embellishment of the Elder Dickson monograph for a new generation on Maclaren's kailyard trope. By then, however, the idea of Scottish Democracy had been reinvigorated and intellectually transformed with the publication of *The Democratic Intellect* by the philosopher George Davie (1961). A neo-Kantian like Lillie and the Edinburgh Professors, Norman Kemp Smith and Norman Porteous (himself a lifelong friend of Gillies from their schooldays together), Davie, too, was part of the Scott-Moncrieff network and, in the words of Duncan Macmillan (2007, 33), 'gave us back our intellectual heritage as Scots'.

The campaign of fifty or more years for a national gallery in Scotland that would show the work of living Scottish artists was only partially realised on the day in 1960 that Kenneth Clark opened the Scottish National Gallery of Modern Art (SNGMA). Lindsay wanted a gallery in Scotland of modern art and not a gallery of modern Scottish art. It is little surprise that Talbot Rice was made a trustee. Douglas Hall, the first Keeper of the SNGMA, had few resources of space, staff or budget to support a compromise with the cultural-national position, and little inclination either. He had, at best, only a qualified regard for the Edinburgh school (both artists and the ECA). It was, he thought, part cause, part symptom, of a paradoxical malaise in twentieth-century Scottish art having, he said, the strengths to remain aloof from international development but only because of a narrowness of vision that was depleting these strengths. Buying and showing the work of artists living in Scotland was a lesser priority.

Neither Hall nor Lindsay thought Gillies a modernist. What Hall knew of the activities of Gillies or the SSA in the inter-war period is not known to me. But it was nothing he thought worthy of mention in his accounts of the period. And MacTaggart complained bitterly that Hall had shown no interest in the fight for modernism in the 1930s by members of the SSA when he interviewed MacTaggart in 1968. Nor did Hall attempt, even in the years when Gillies was Principal, to have any close discussion with Gillies about any aspect of painting of any period. Hall knew by then that the SNGMA would eventually have to decide which, if any, of Gillies' works it

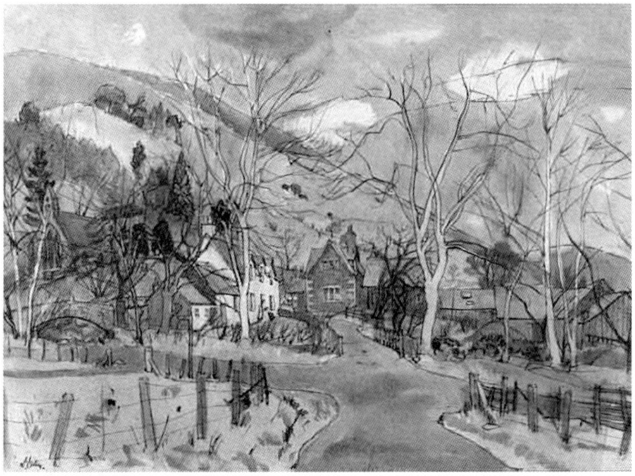

126 *Balquhidder* (nd, 1950s?). Pen, ink and grisaille, 55 cm by 77 cm

would accept from the bequest that Lillie planned to make (along with many works by other, more coveted, artists). And Gillies, it goes almost without saying, never approached Hall. So, the scholarship on Gillies was left largely to Lillie, to Scott-Moncrieff and associates, and to Elder Dickson, who then took the fight to Hall.

In 1963, Elder Dickson and Eric Newton organised an exhibition of works by fourteen contemporary Scottish artists at the gallery of the Commonwealth Institute in London. Hall reviewed the exhibition and named nine of the contributors but avoided all mention of Gillies and the ten works he sent. Among them were *Hill Pool* (1960) [112] and *Winter Thaw* (1962) [111]. Elder Dickson and Hall then traded letters in the national press. Despite attempts at mediation by the artist the second Earl Haig, relations worsened in the mid-1960s when Hall gave his backing to the 'Open 100' exhibition, a bold initiative by the ECA graduate and cultural entrepreneur Ricky Demarco. They deteriorated further when Demarco mounted the exhibition 'Strategy Get Arts' (a palindrome) during the Festival of 1970. Elder Dickson thought it negatively iconoclastic, objected to its presence in the ECA and again confronted Hall in the press.

Elder Dickson's 1974 monograph on Gillies was gestating in the early 1960s, when two student artists swayed by MacDiarmid's example, John Bellany and Alexander (Sandy) Moffat, challenged the authority of the ECA and RSA. It was written in the early 1970s, when two postgraduate students, one of them Gordon Brown, the future British Prime Minister, had successively and legitimately (as Rectors elected by students) occupied the chair of the managing authority of the University of Edinburgh, which had joint authority with the College over the degree in fine art. Elder Dickson's sub-text is his opposition to an alleged subversion of aesthetic standards; to the aleatory (randomising) art admitted by Norman Reid to the Tate; to Hall's critique of the Edinburgh school of artists; to Hall's conduct of the SNGMA; and to his promotion of the art of William Johnstone, an associate of Demarco and MacDiarmid, who had returned to Scotland in 1960. The remedy it proposed was the Gillies of Westwater's country-bred intuitive, thirled to his nation by a Scottish appropriation of Clark's Neo-Romantic narrative, his watercolours redolent of his country's 'aqueous light' and 'far nearer to the heart of things' than his oils and still lifes.

There is no evidence, however, that Gillies subscribed to any of this and much evidence that he did not. But myths are mythogenic and the countryman myth nurtures offspring: that Gillies was anti-intellectual, that he was not politically aware or interested in books, that he was opposed to non-figurative abstraction and that he was a lifetime beneficiary of a lasting ECA prejudice

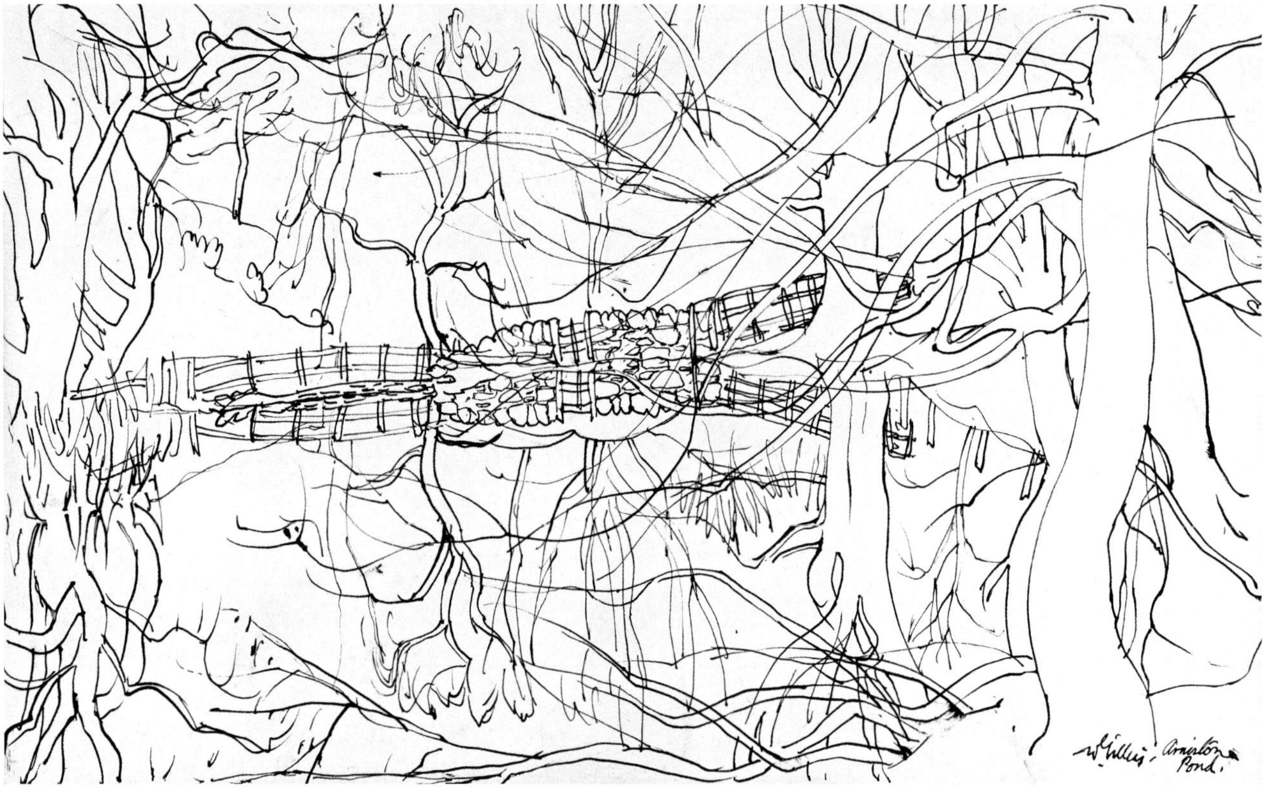

127 *Arniston Pond* (nd, *c.* 1960). Pen and ink, 21 cm by 35 cm

against Johnstone from as early as Gillies' post-graduate year.

Not so. As Gillies slips further into history, and from history, such claims should not pass unquestioned. (A recent history of Scottish art, welcomed as 'definitive', does not mention Gillies or 1930s Edinburgh at all.) All these claims are questionable. Some are demonstrably ill-founded, and some mistake the mantle of Principal for the conduct of its bearer. This was a post Gillies never wanted, that others had refused, and that he tried initially and unsuccessfully to finesse by continuing to teach. It took six years from his painting life, years he would doubtless add to those he had lost to war. Even at the time of his earlier promotion to head of painting, he was troubled by the prospect of exercising authority over friends. Nor was he comfortable with the size of the studio that went with that post. He told Maxwell it was so big 'you feel nothing less than a Lord Provost or the Chairman of the Board should be painted there'.

Conclusion

One of his closest friends in later years, the artist Robin Philipson, described Gillies as a man of 'massive intelligence' that he made a deliberate effort to hide. This effort explains much of the condescension that he also attracted in the course of his life, and still attracts as the alleged leader of an alleged B team of stay-at-homes. Gillies valued the distinctive idiom above all else. 'A fine, personal painting' was said to be the highest compliment he could pay. In the context of his times, his own contribution was neither isolating nor isolated. It was part of that diversity among his generation of artists who, looking to each other, questioned all authority and all prescription ungrounded in experience. To position himself at the sharp end was not an anti-intellectual act. It was a corollary to the heroic scepticism of the infantry private – of a David Jones in his earthy *patria* – and a visual analogue of Private Ball, through whom Jones eventually found the voice of *In Parenthesis* (1937), his epic attempt at a poetic voice to make sense of the First World War.

Gillies, too, was one of history's privates, one of the unsung infantry. His imagery was solely visual, however, unlike that of Jones. He did not follow Jones into the Catholic faith nor attempt, like Jones, to resolve his existential dilemma within a reasserted tradition of sign and belief. But his search for signification was likewise an attempt to end the silence of Benjamin's survivor – unable to share experience through existing narratives, contradicted in vital aspects of his being by the dysfunctions of modernity.

The nature of his search is, I think, apparent in a remark that is as revealing as it is unpretentious. When answering Elder Dickson's questions, around 1960, he volunteered, unprompted, that his works reflected a lifetime of convivial practice, the cumulative outcome of which he had initially neither wished nor anticipated: 'I seem to have left out the important influence of J. Maxwell, W. MacTaggart, R. H. Morton, Henderson Blyth, all intimate friends … with whom I have worked, shared studios, gone holidays, and who have all helped me, unconsciously, to find myself'.

Exactly so; world and self mutually realised in conviviality. That this could develop, 'unconsciously' as he said, into a coherent response to his existential isolation was owing to the acuity of his engagement with fellow moderns, his empathy with the struggles of intimates, and the eventual opening of his art to the conflict in his life between feeling and belief. Ever mindful of the living and the dead, and of the meeting of extremes in the transience of being, he was an artist of the eye and not of the word, a modernist whose modesty obscures.

But we have only to listen to the few things he did say, and to understand the origins of this modesty in universals of the human condition, to see the truth of the matter in the works themselves. These constitute another meeting of extremes. His art both augments and moderates unrealised aspects of the world and its beings. By confronting the dilemmas of alienation and doubt, his art touched potentials in life that could be apprehended only through a reciprocal recognition of the modesty of human capacities when set against this return. Whatever its worldly origins in his life or worldly consequences for his reputation, his legendary personal modesty can therefore be seen as both facilitator and outcome of this endeavour, as a self-correcting and generative aspect of a virtuous circle of profession.

His modernism was founded in a scepticism that extended to the tropes of modernism itself and was based on the primacy of an individual's search for signification in a world of boundless meanings whose very instability was a mixed creative blessing, full of possibilities but of pitfalls too, and with no certain outcome that could be served up as dogma. That it shares these origins with those of post-modern critique, and is prefigured in Ruskin's analysis of the fate of the sceptical artist or poet in an epoch of faithless modernity, are further reasons to consider existing narratives of modernism in the light of Gillies' example and across this wider span of years.

Towards the very end, he was still searching for simplicity, still looking forward as well as back. When his own time came, it chanced that he was alone and that, mercifully but fittingly, it arrived out of the blue. On 15 April 1973, he was found at the table, spoon in hand, slumped over his lunchtime soup. Among images on his studio wall were reproductions of two works by Joan Miró, an artist much admired by Klee, and two of his own oils showing Emma's ceramics. On his easel was *Still Life on a Dark Ground* (*c.* 1971) [169]. Lucent objects are set on black with shades of grey and immanent blue. The white jug at the centre is one of Emma's. It holds stalks of spider grass bent back on themselves, like the broken olive branch of peace, like time itself.

Opposite:
Detail from *Still Life on a Dark Ground* ([169] – see p. 214)

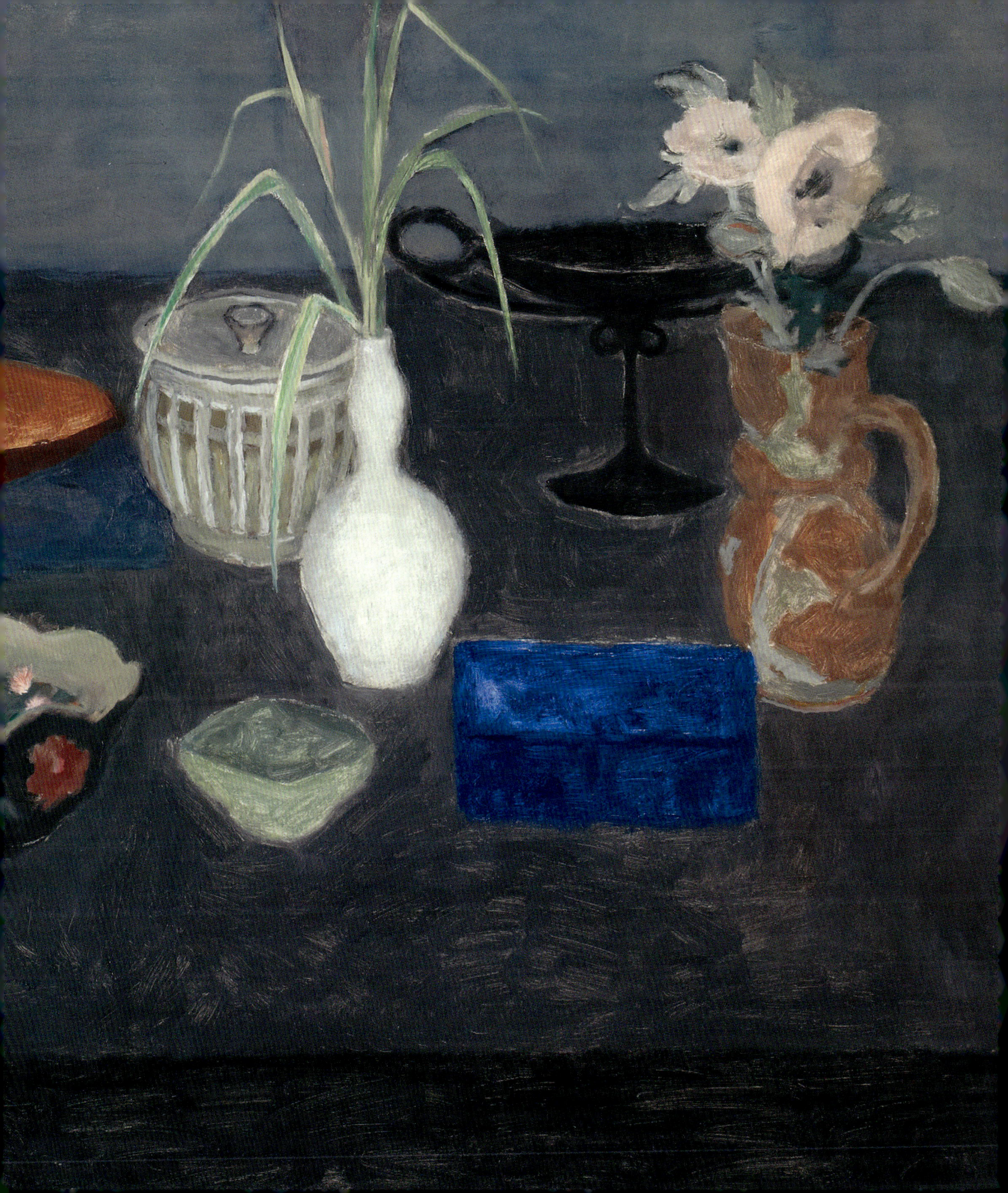

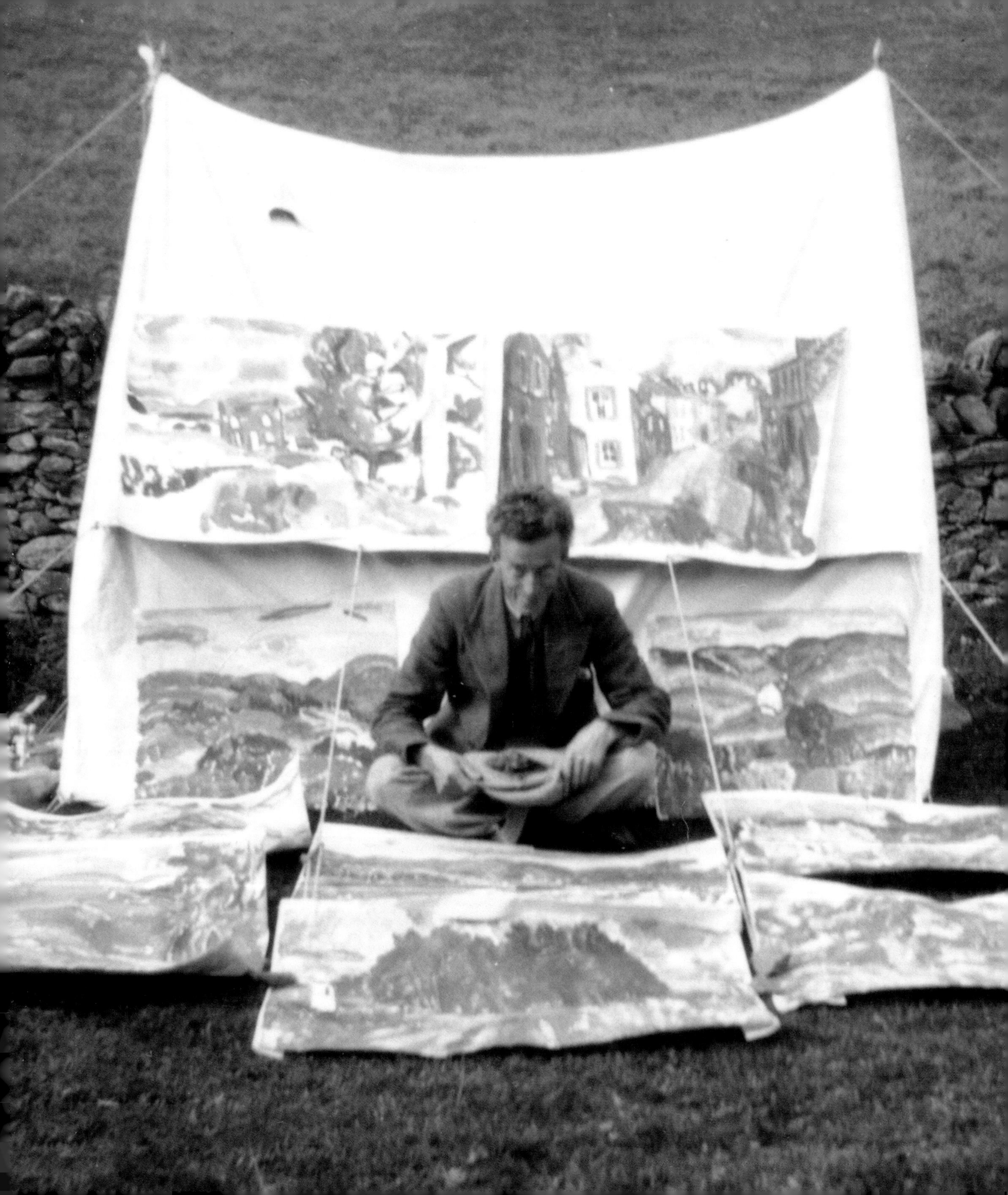

Further Illustrations 1916–71

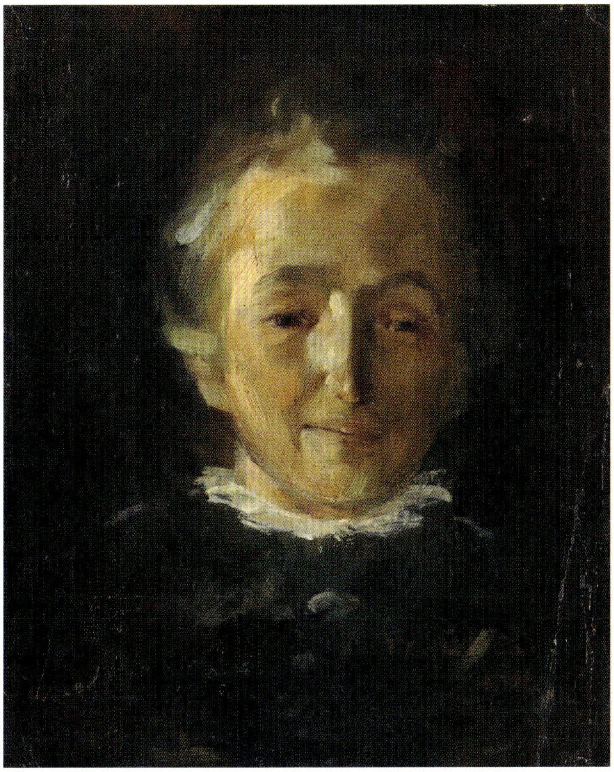

128 *My Mother* (1916). Oil, 34.1 cm by 29.2 cm

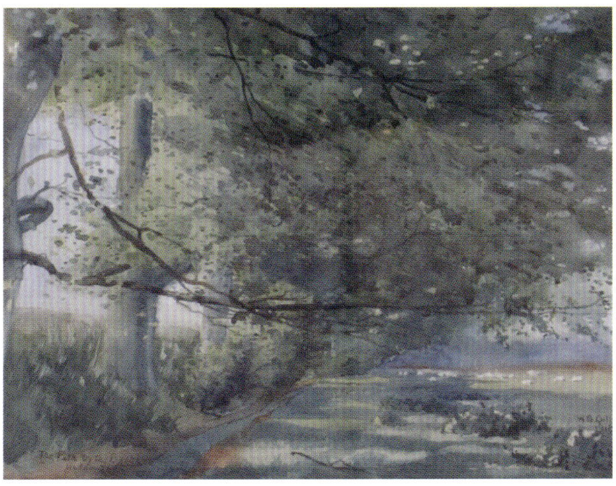

129 *The Path by the Beeches, Haddington* (1916). Watercolour, 22 cm by 25 cm

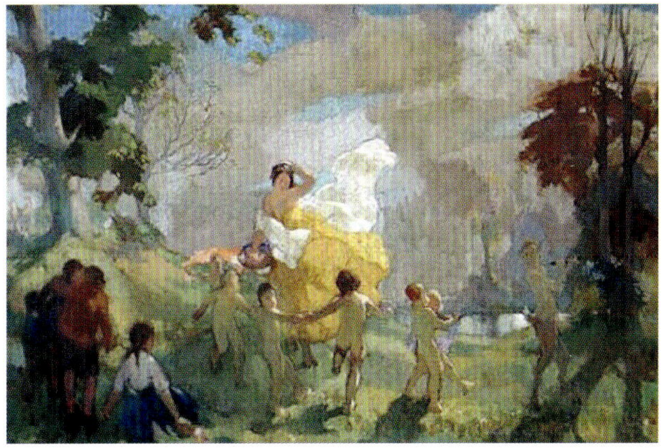

130 *Spring* (nd, *c.* 1921). Oil, dimensions unknown

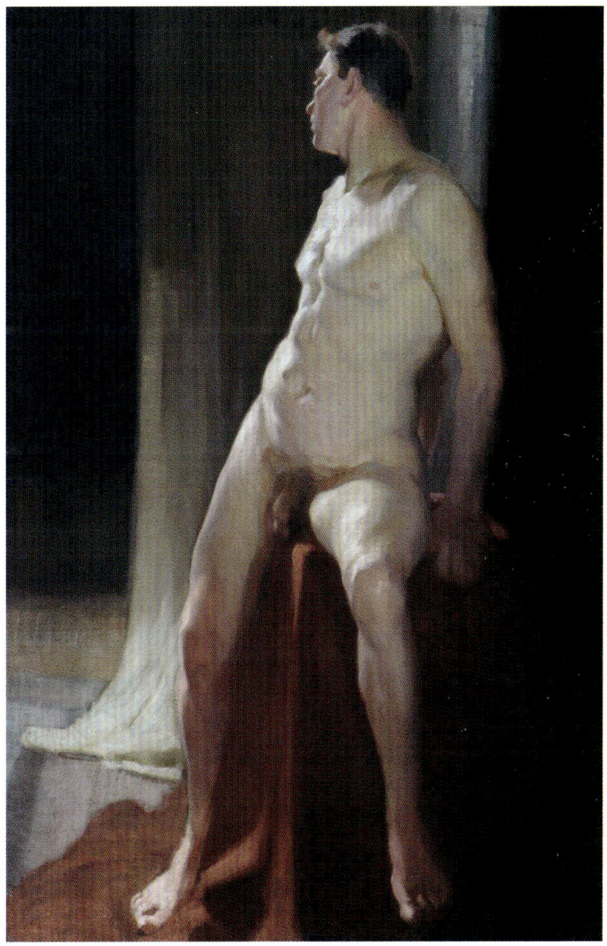

131 *Life Study* (1922). Oil, 91.5 cm by 61.2 cm

Opposite:
Detail from Gillies at his Calidon show ([177] – see p. 221)

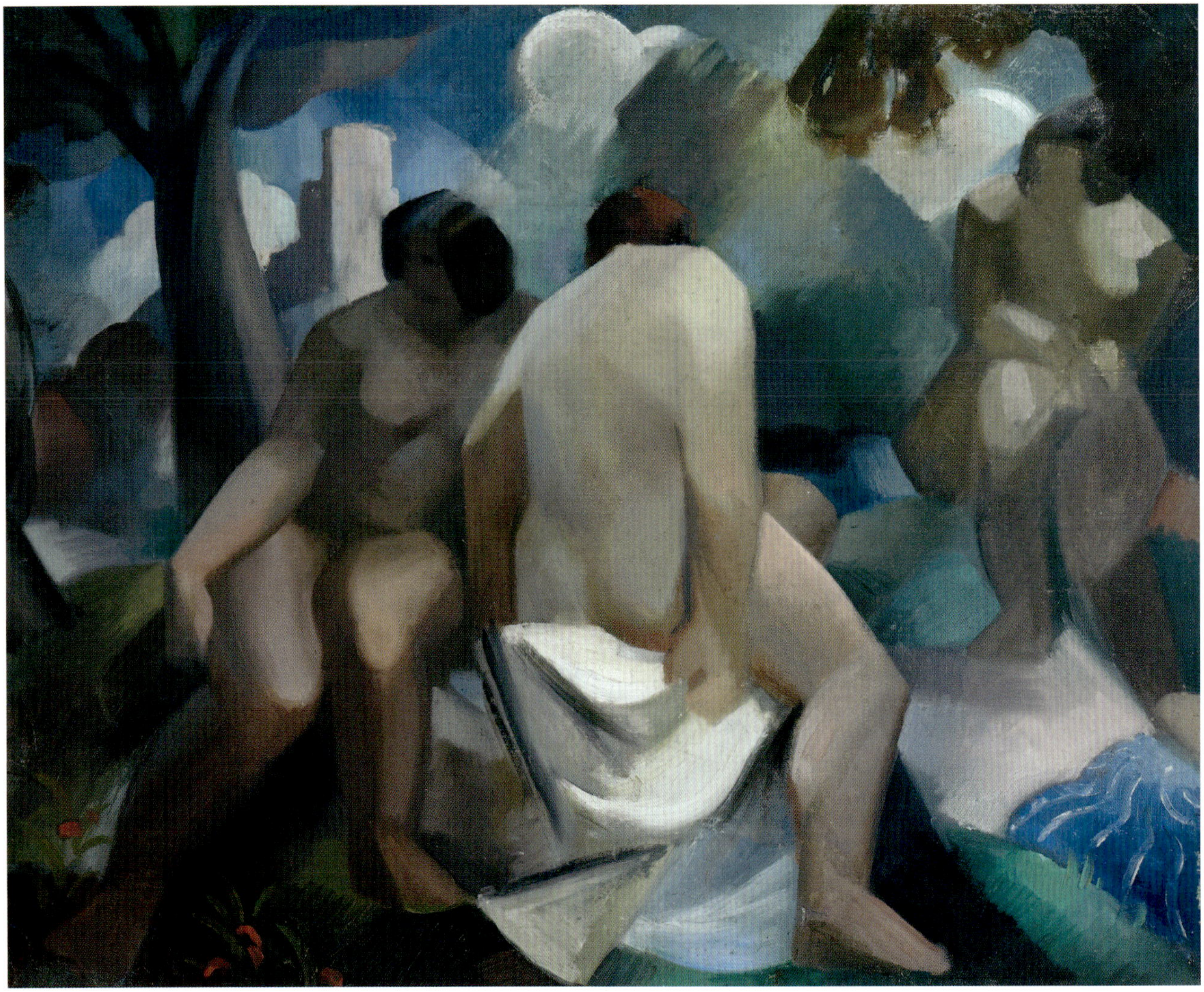

132 *Bathers* (*c.* 1924). Oil, 58.7 cm by 73.8 cm

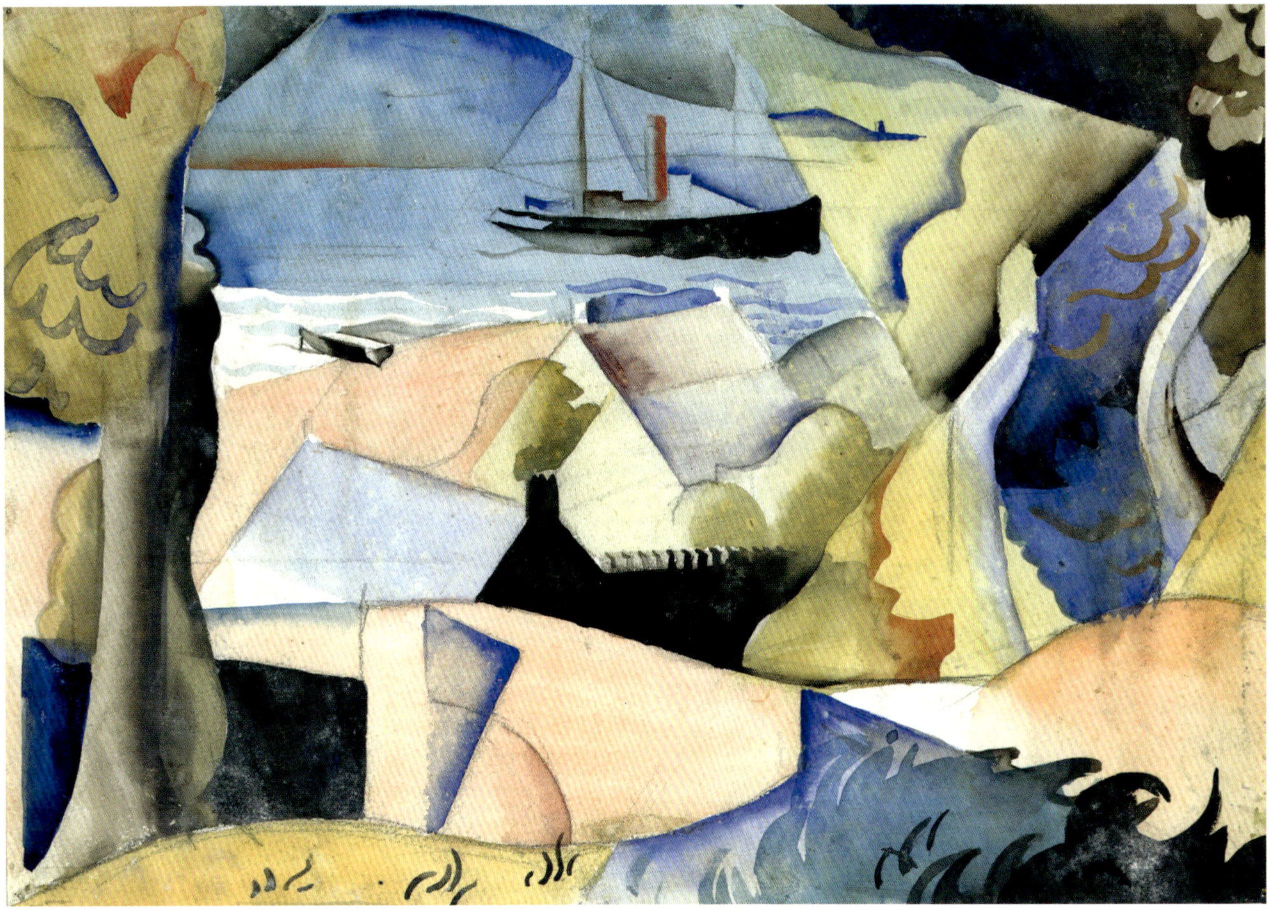

133 *Inverness* (1925). Pencil and watercolour, 25.4 cm by 35.6 cm

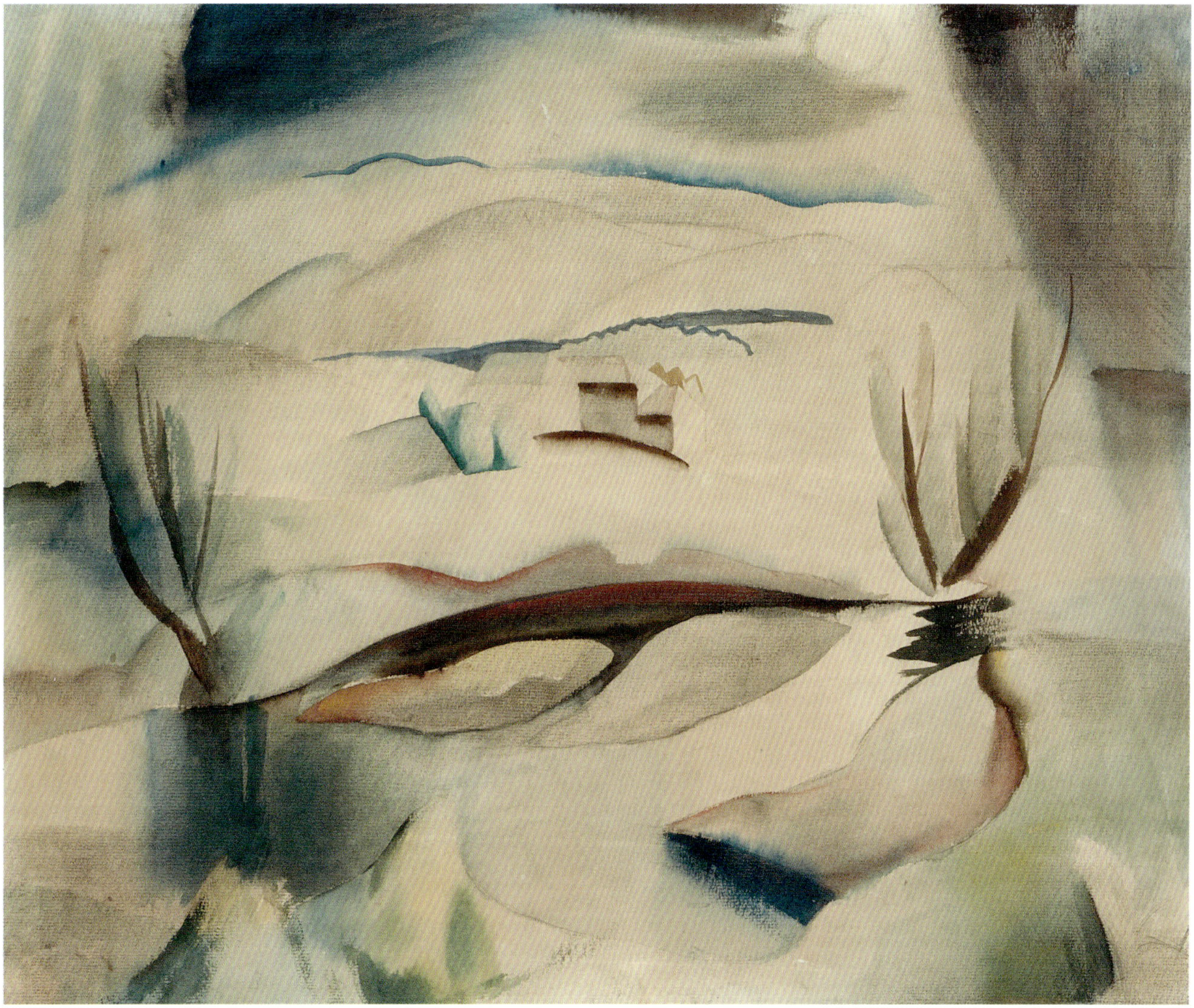

134 *A Highland Farm* (nd, *c.* 1925). Watercolour, 43 cm by 53 cm

136 *Trees on the Tyne, Haddington* (*c.*1924). Oil, 55.8 cm by 64.8 cm (*right*)

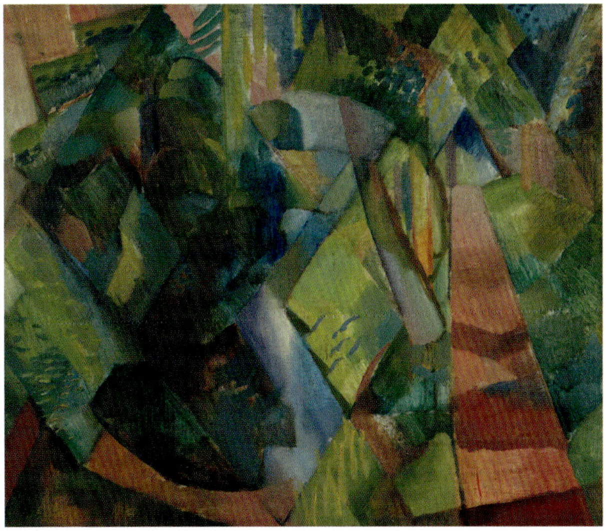

135 *Autumnal Wooded Landscape* (1925). Pencil and watercolour, 25.5 cm by 36 cm (*below*)

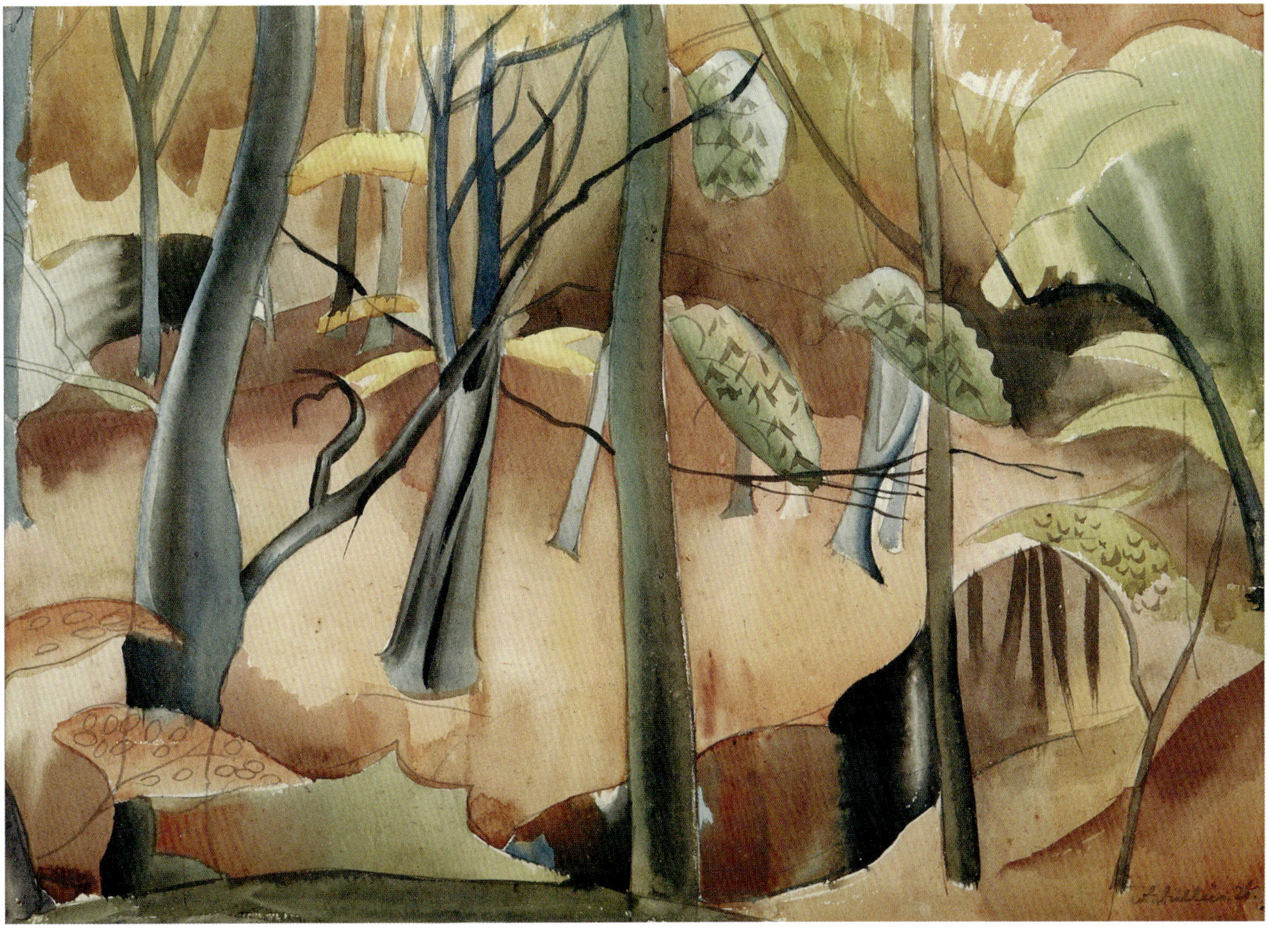

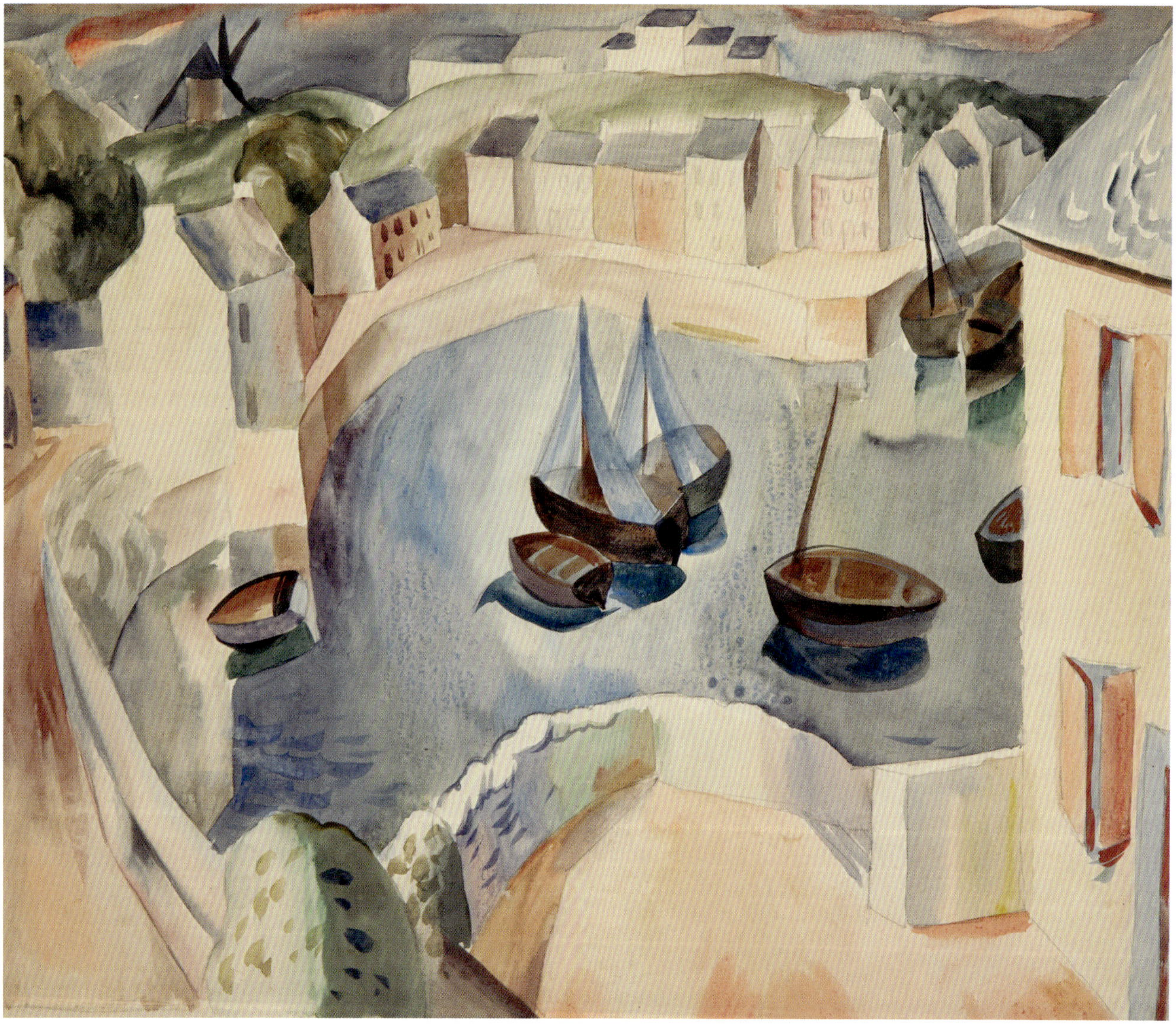

137 *Tréboul* (a) (1927). Pencil and watercolour, 46.1 cm by 54.5 cm

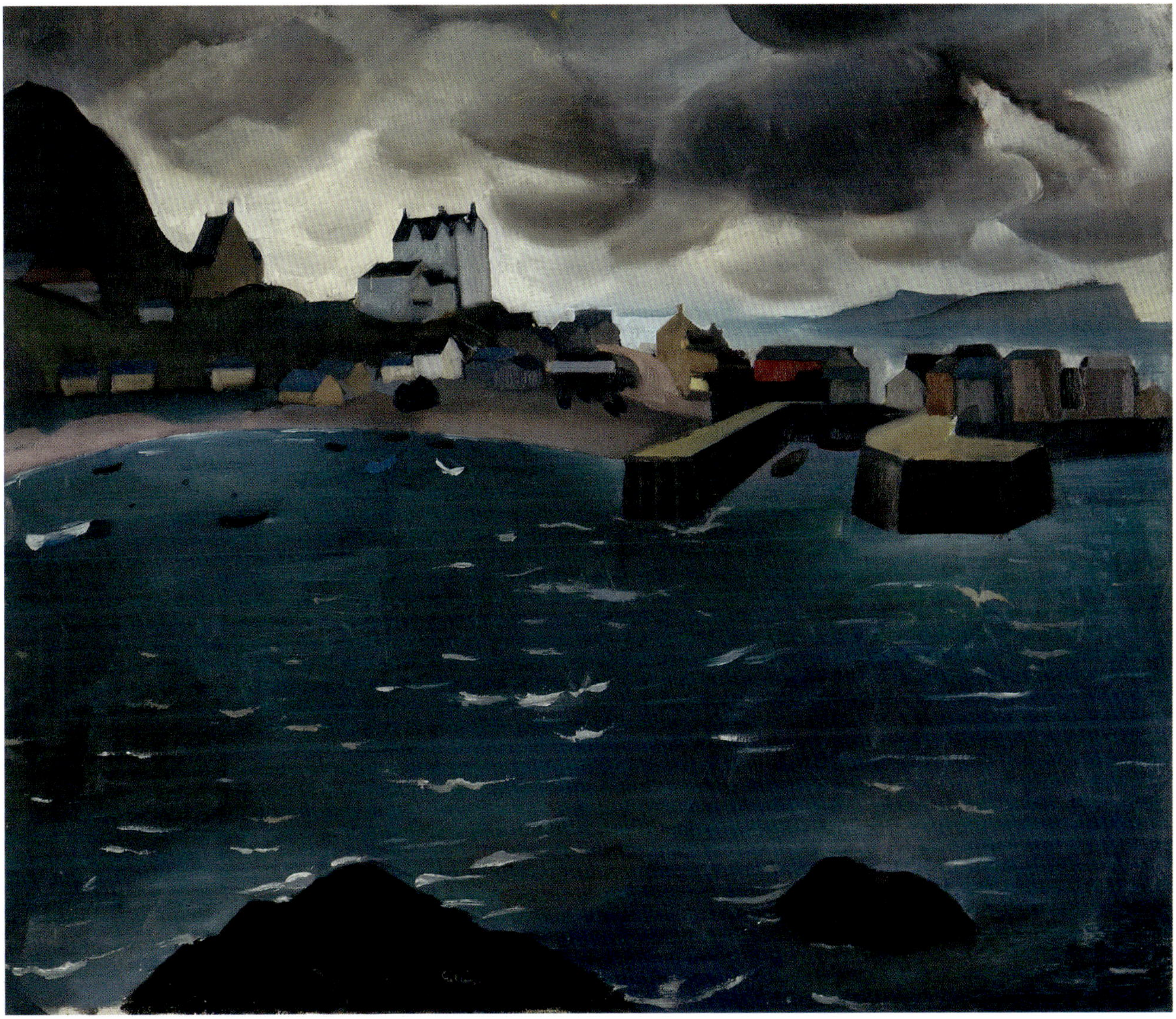

138 *Mallaig* (1928). Oil, 55.9 cm by 65.7 cm

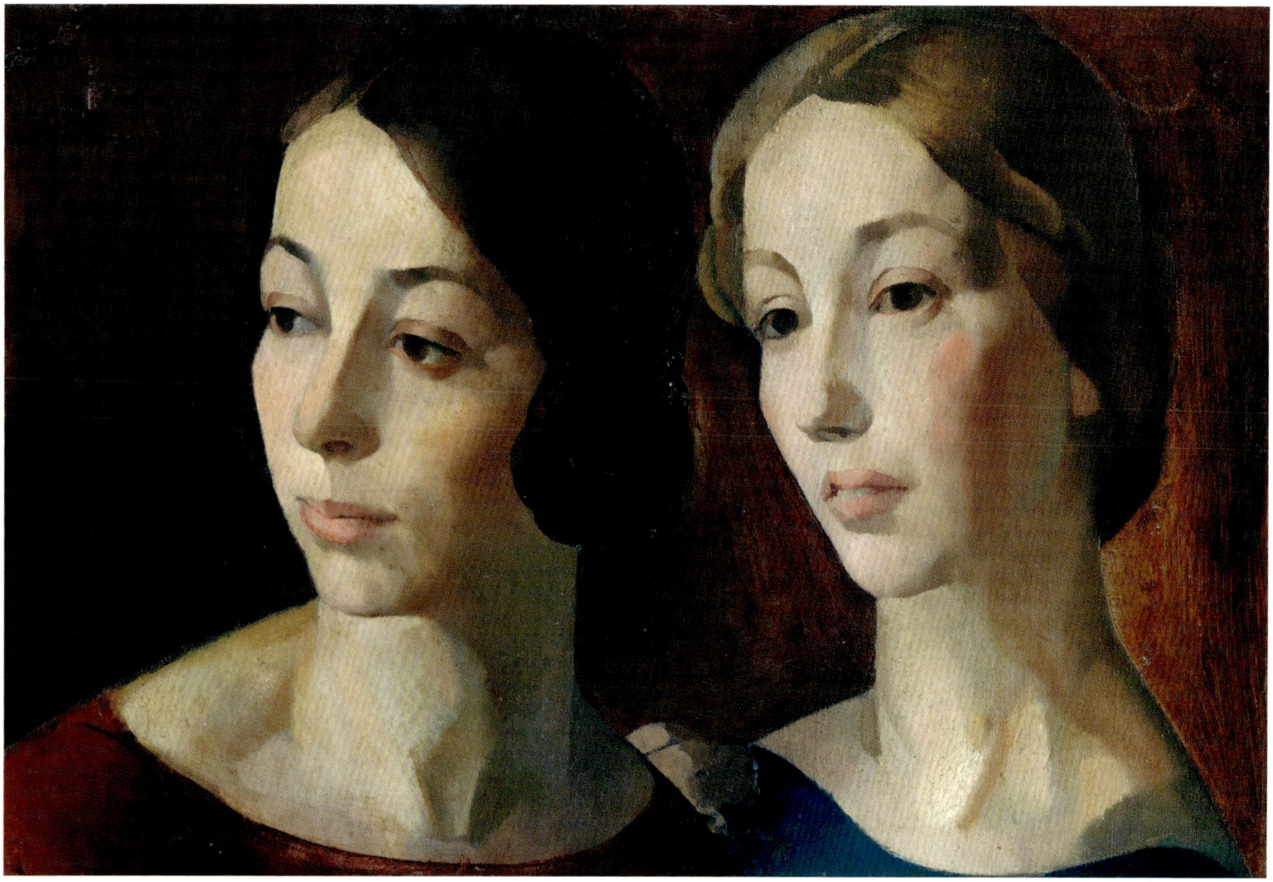

139 *Emma and Janet* (*c.* 1925). Oil, 33.4 cm by 50.4 cm

Opposite:
140 *Emma* (nd, *c.* 1931). Oil, 60.5 cm by 52.5 cm

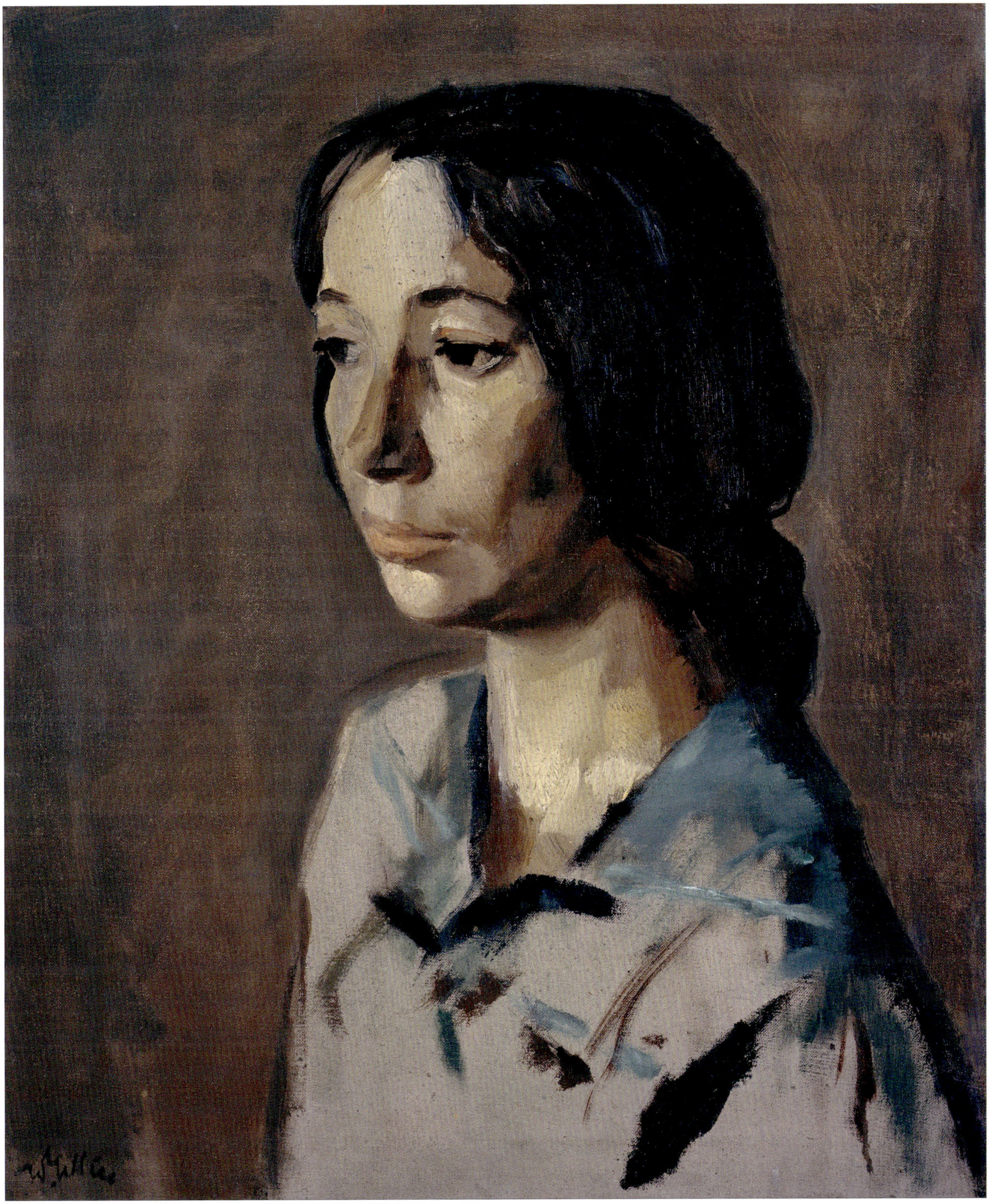

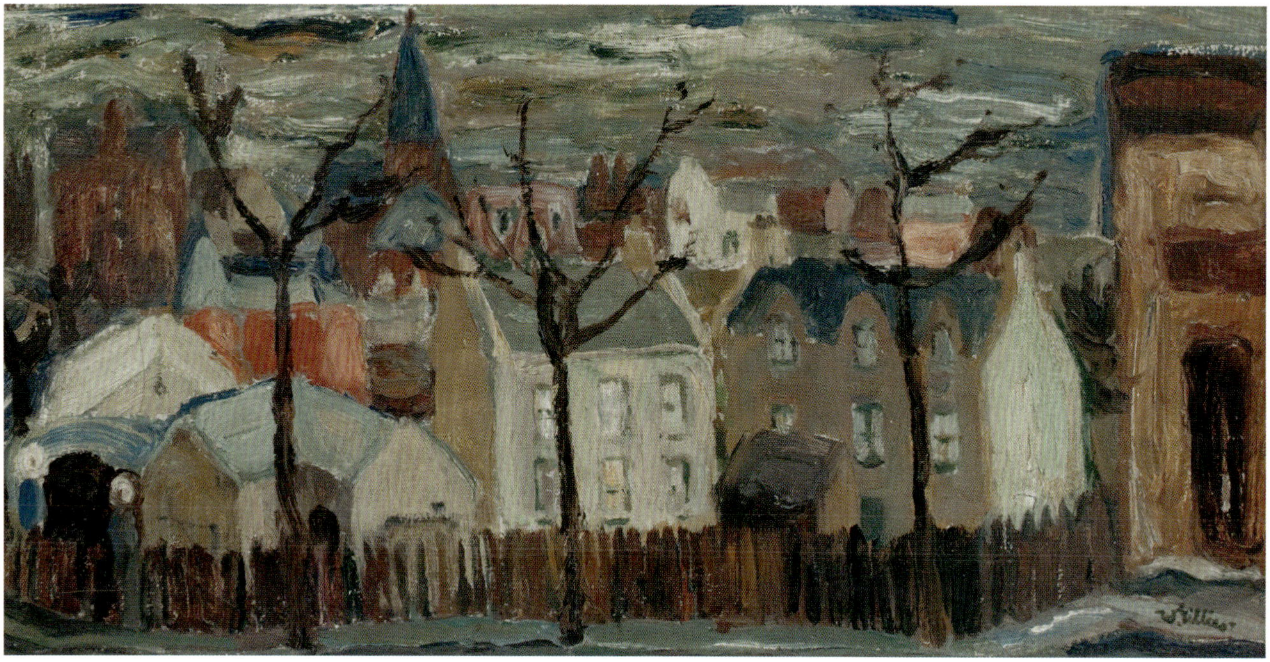

141 *Piershill* (nd, *c.* 1933). Oil, 33 cm by 67 cm

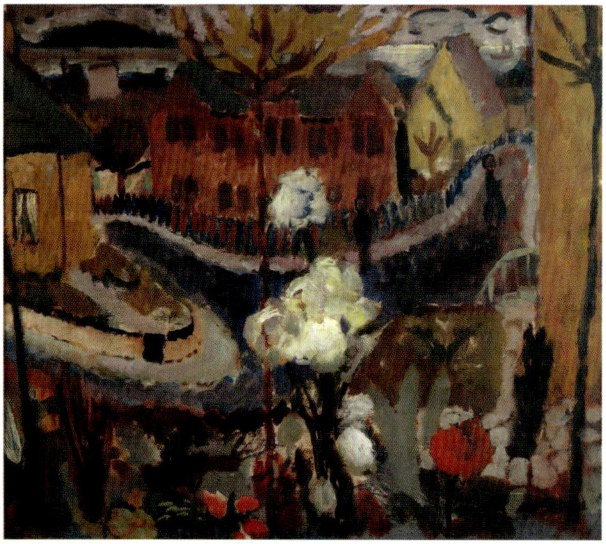

142 *View from 162 Willowbrae Road, Edinburgh* (1932). Oil, 65.6 cm by 76.1 cm

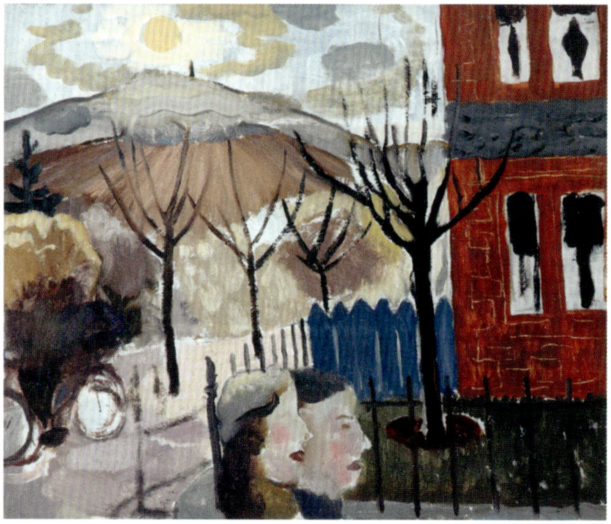

143 *Landscape with House and Two Heads* (*c.* 1930). Oil, 63.8 cm by 76.8 cm

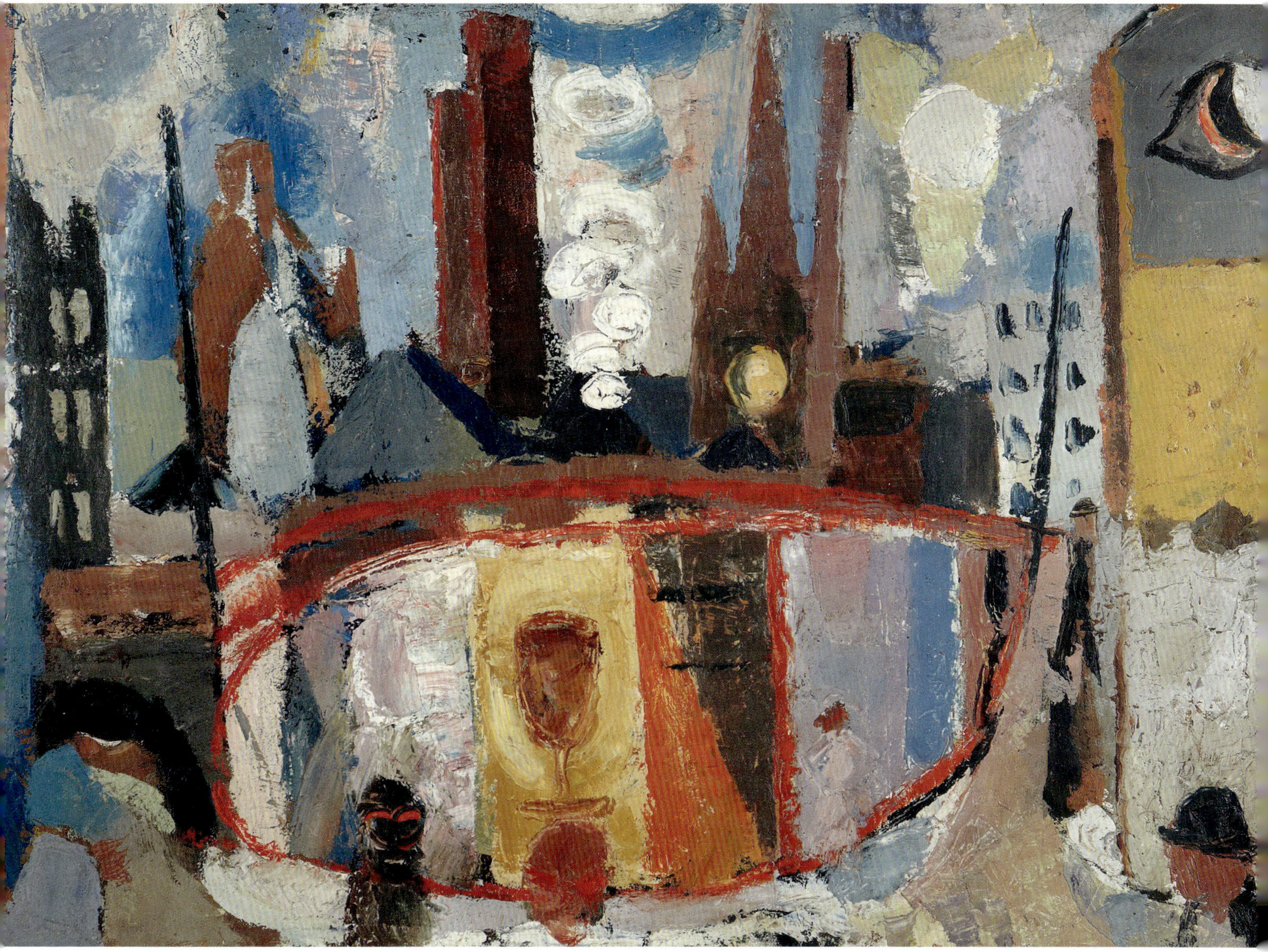

144 *Edinburgh Abstract* (*c.* 1935–6). Oil, 75.3 cm by 112 cm

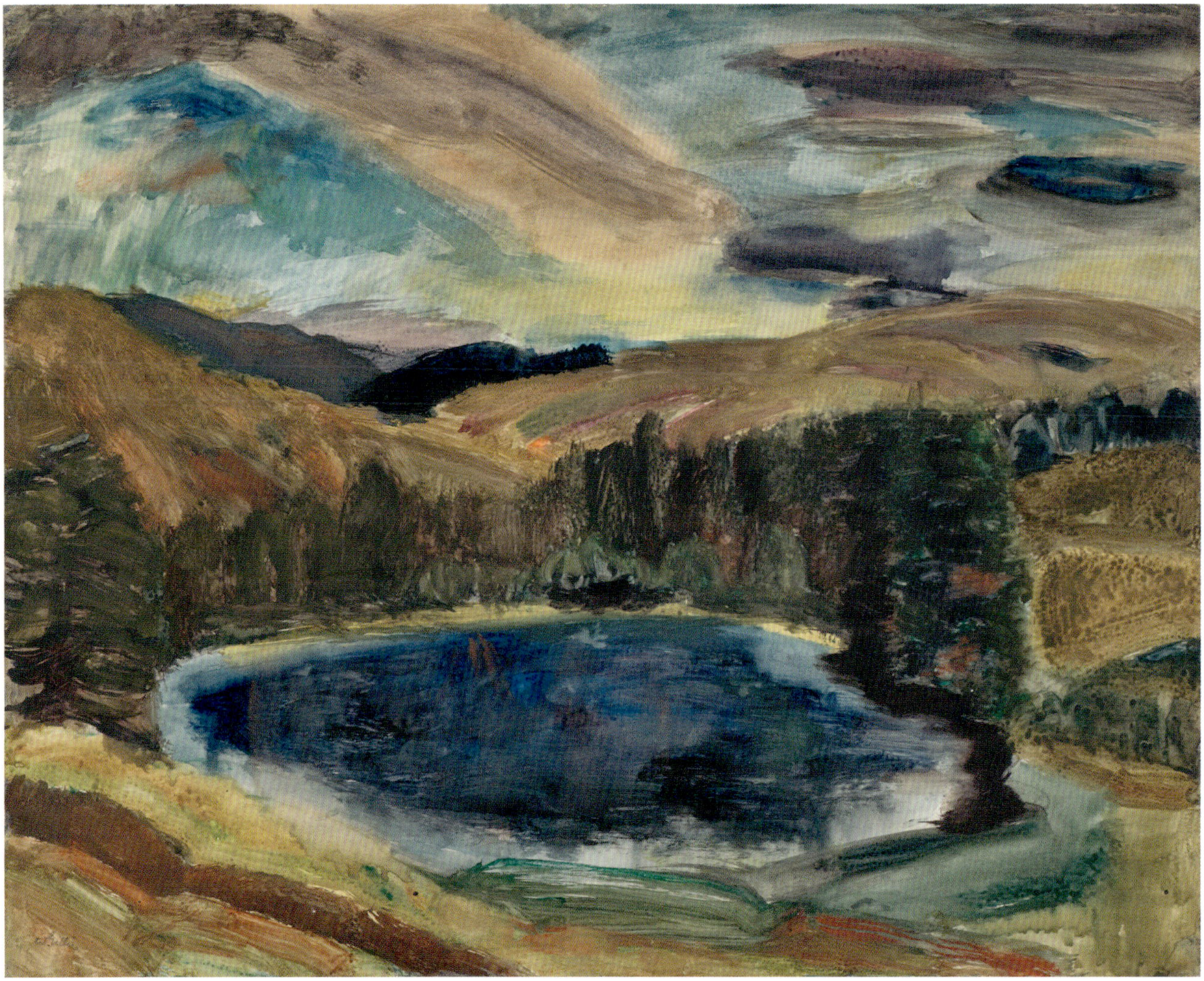

145 *The Dark Pond* (*c.* 1934). Watercolour, 50.4 cm by 63.6 cm

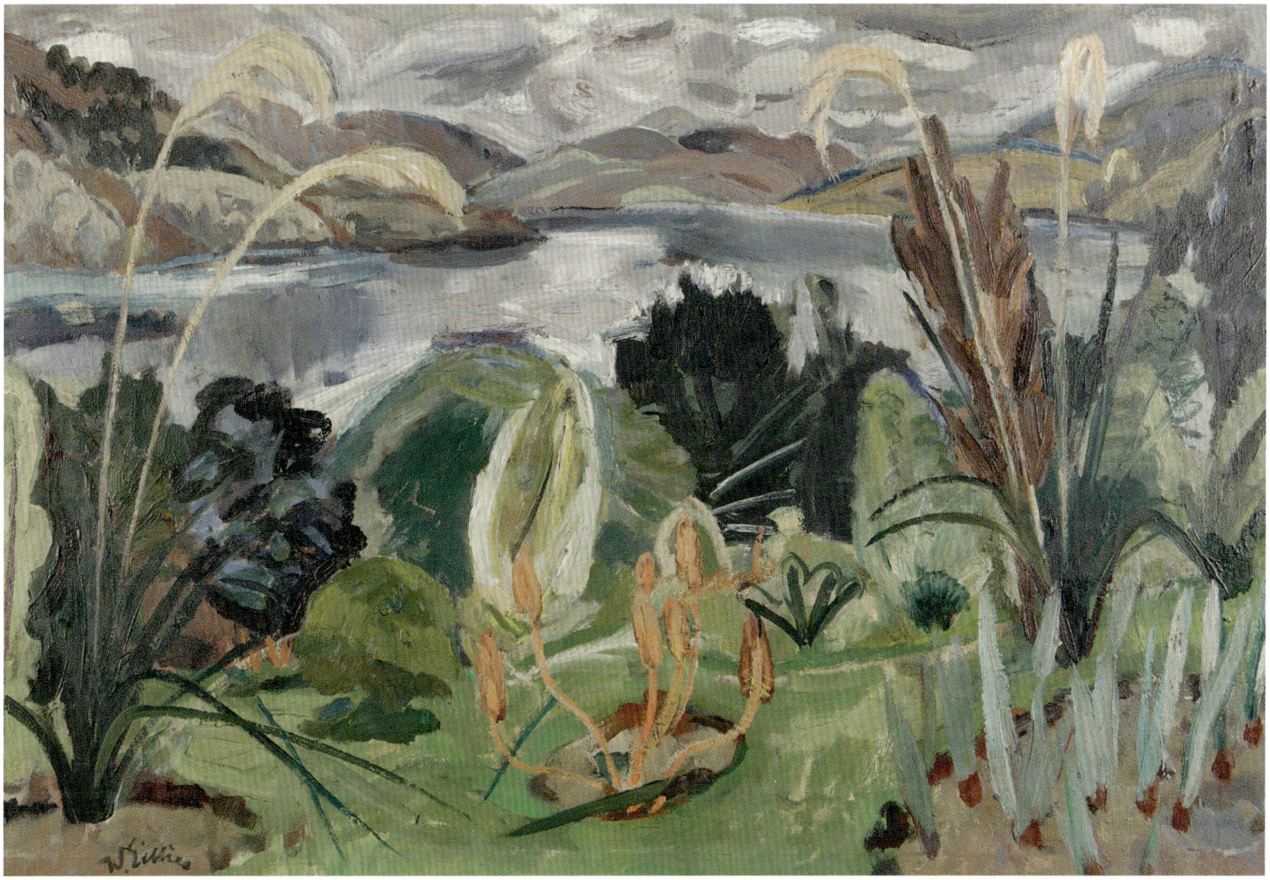

146 *Pampas Grassies, Fearnan, Loch Tay* (nd, *c.* 1935). Oil, 69 cm by 103.5 cm

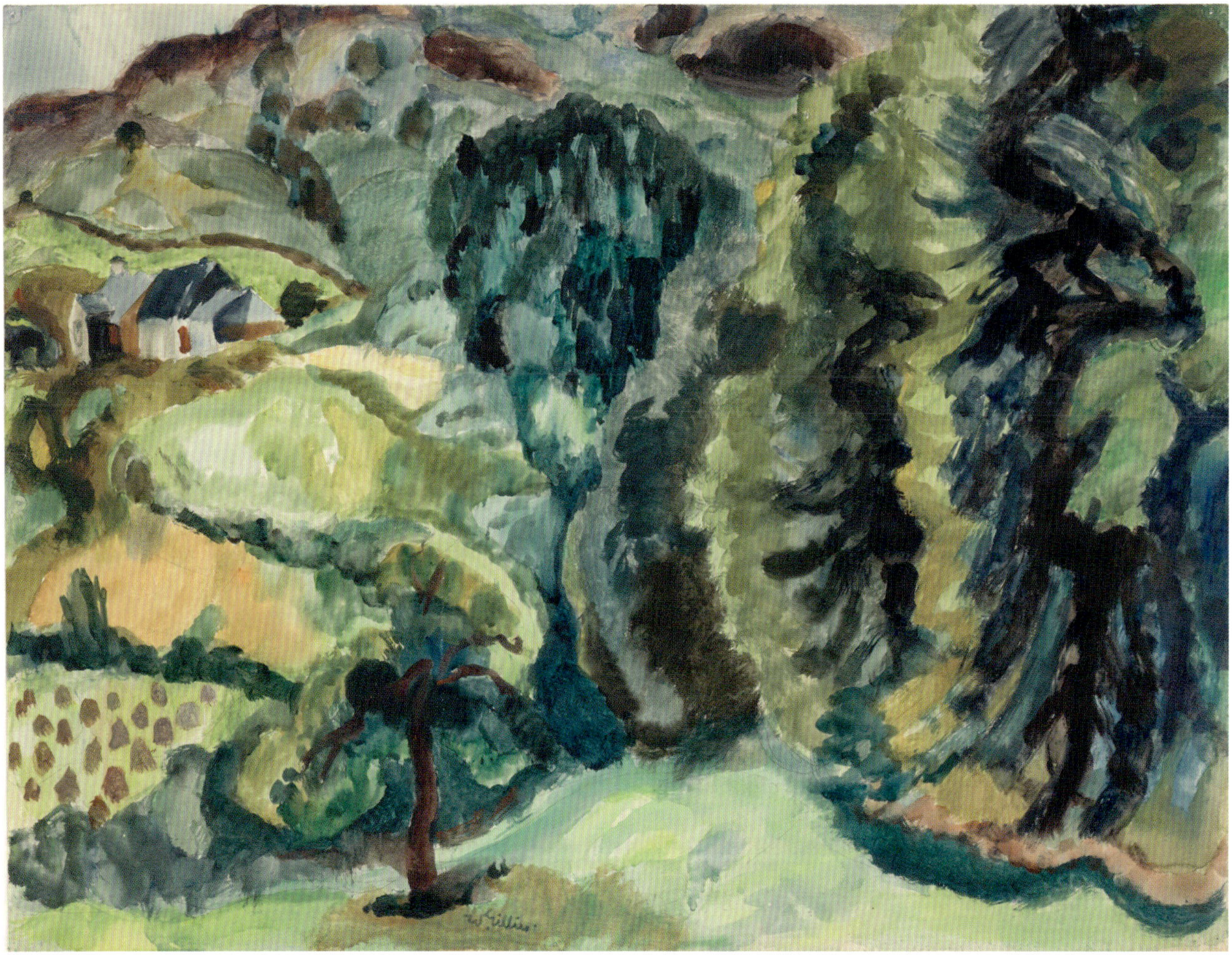

147 *Head of the Glen* (nd, mid- to late 1930s). Watercolour, 55.5 cm by 73.5 cm

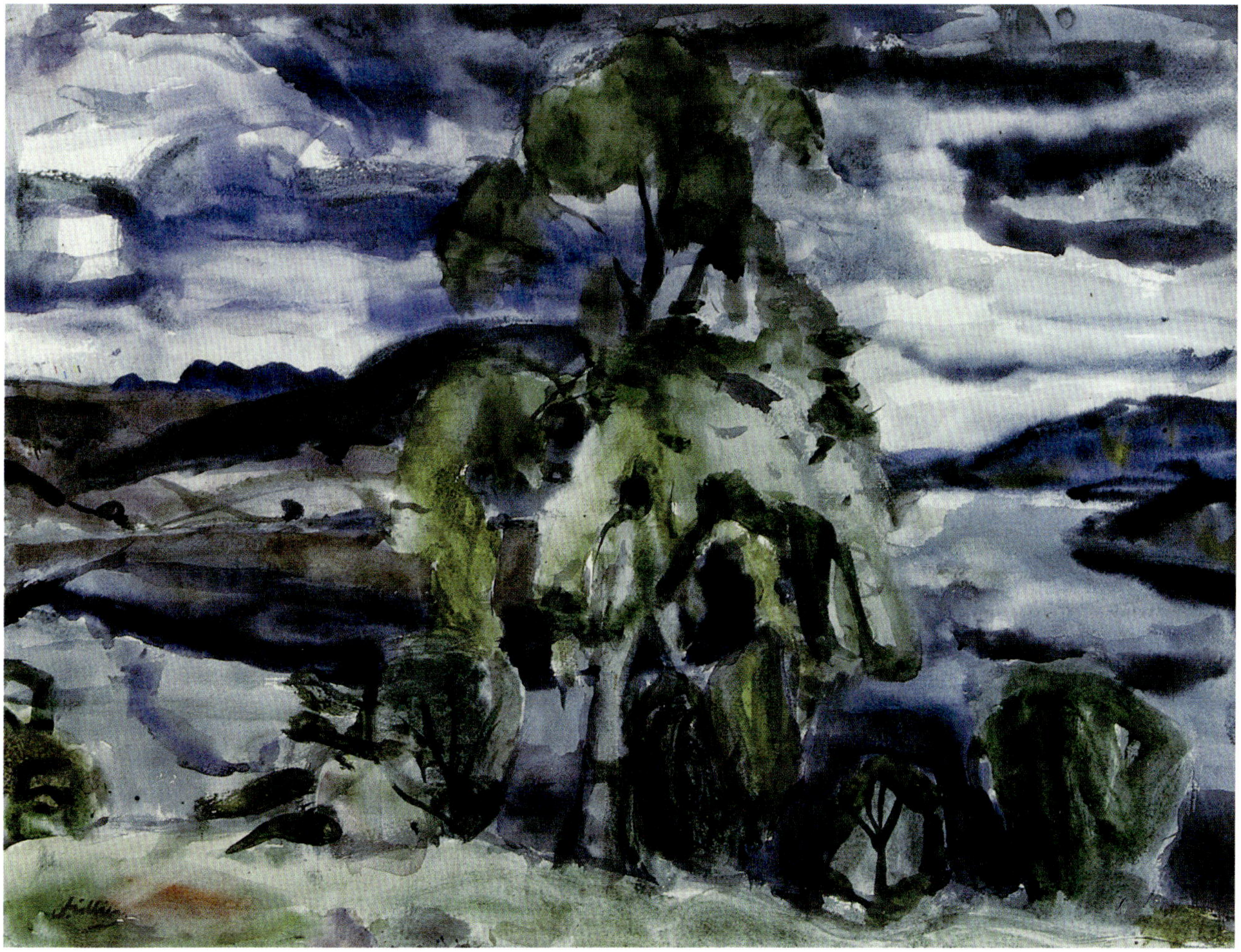

148 *The Highland Loch* (nd, *c.* 1932–50). Watercolour, 41 cm by 56 cm

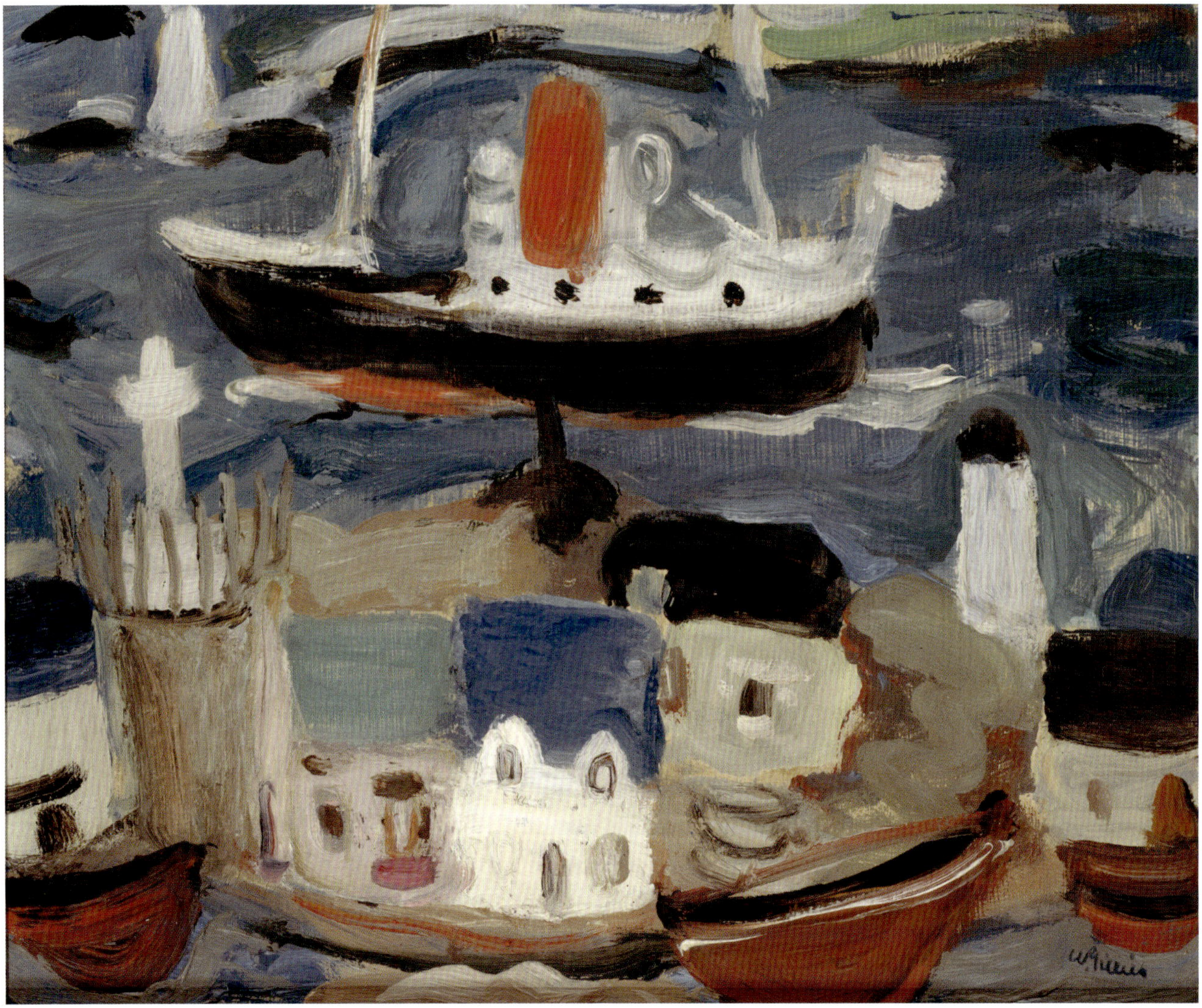

149 *Kyleakin* (1938). Oil, 18 cm by 26 cm

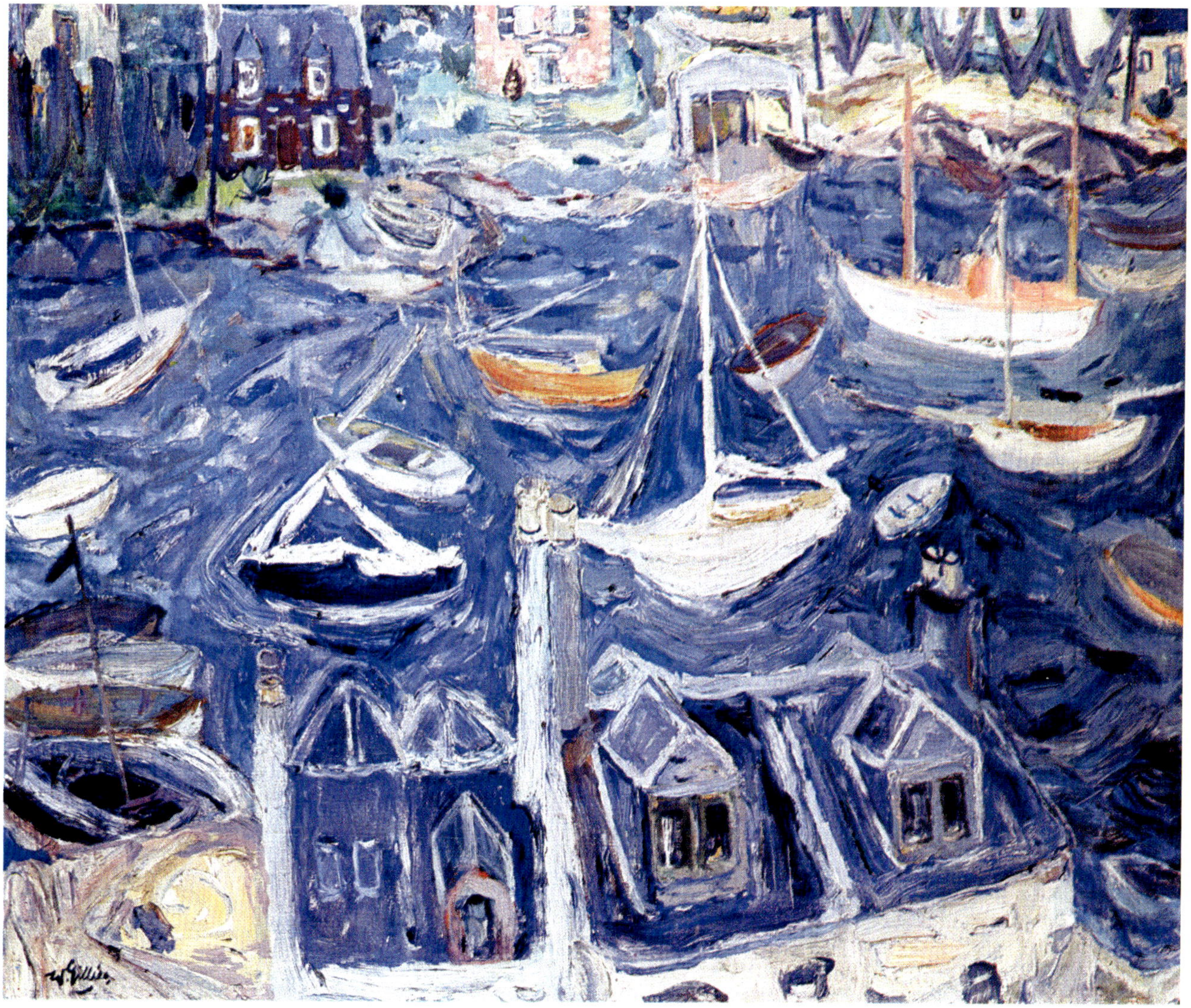

150 *Summer Harbour* (1938). Oil, 86 cm by 101 cm

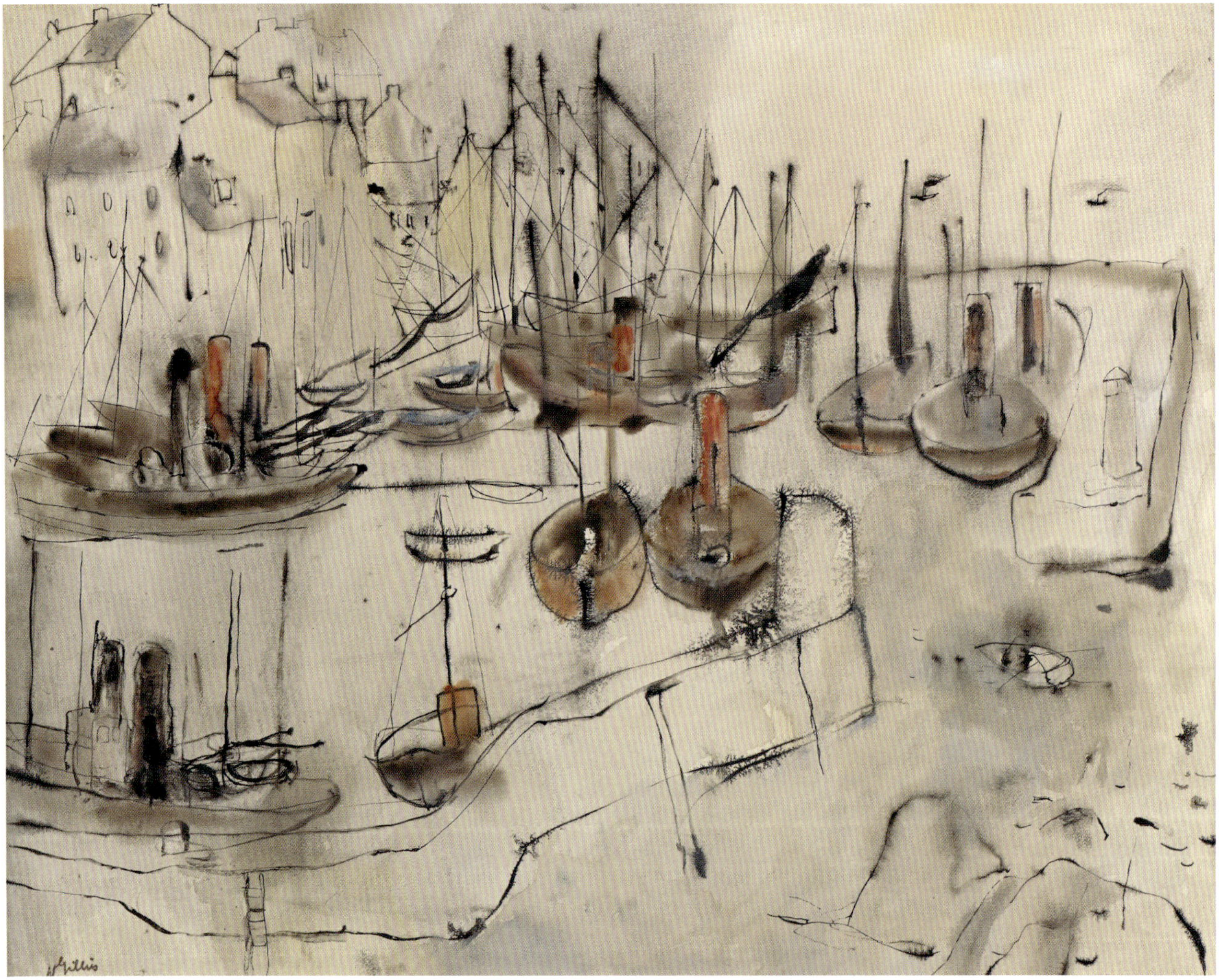

151 *Harbour, Anstruther* (1937–8). Watercolour, 54 cm by 69 cm

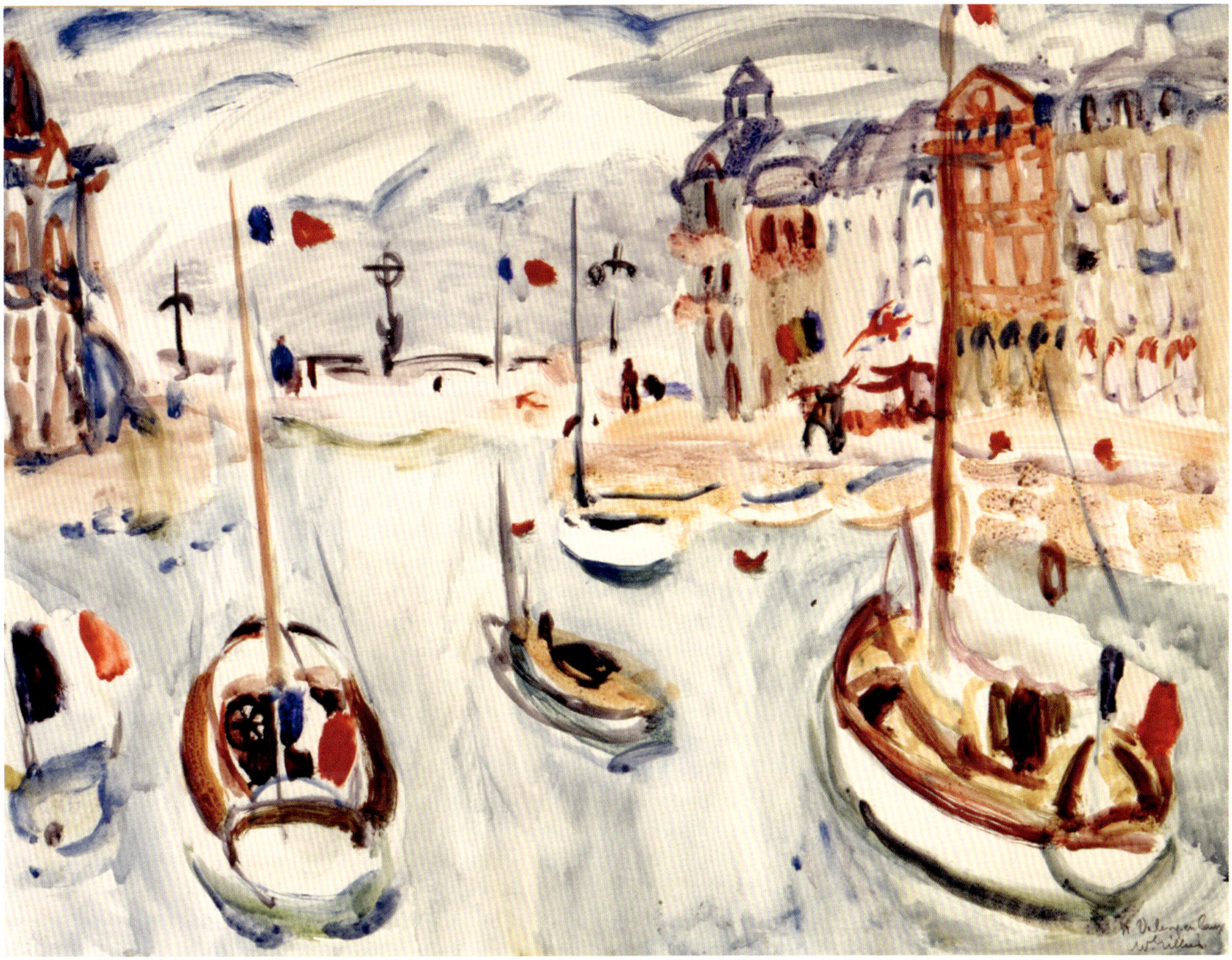

152 *Boats at St Valéry en Caux* (1938). Watercolour, 47 cm by 63 cm

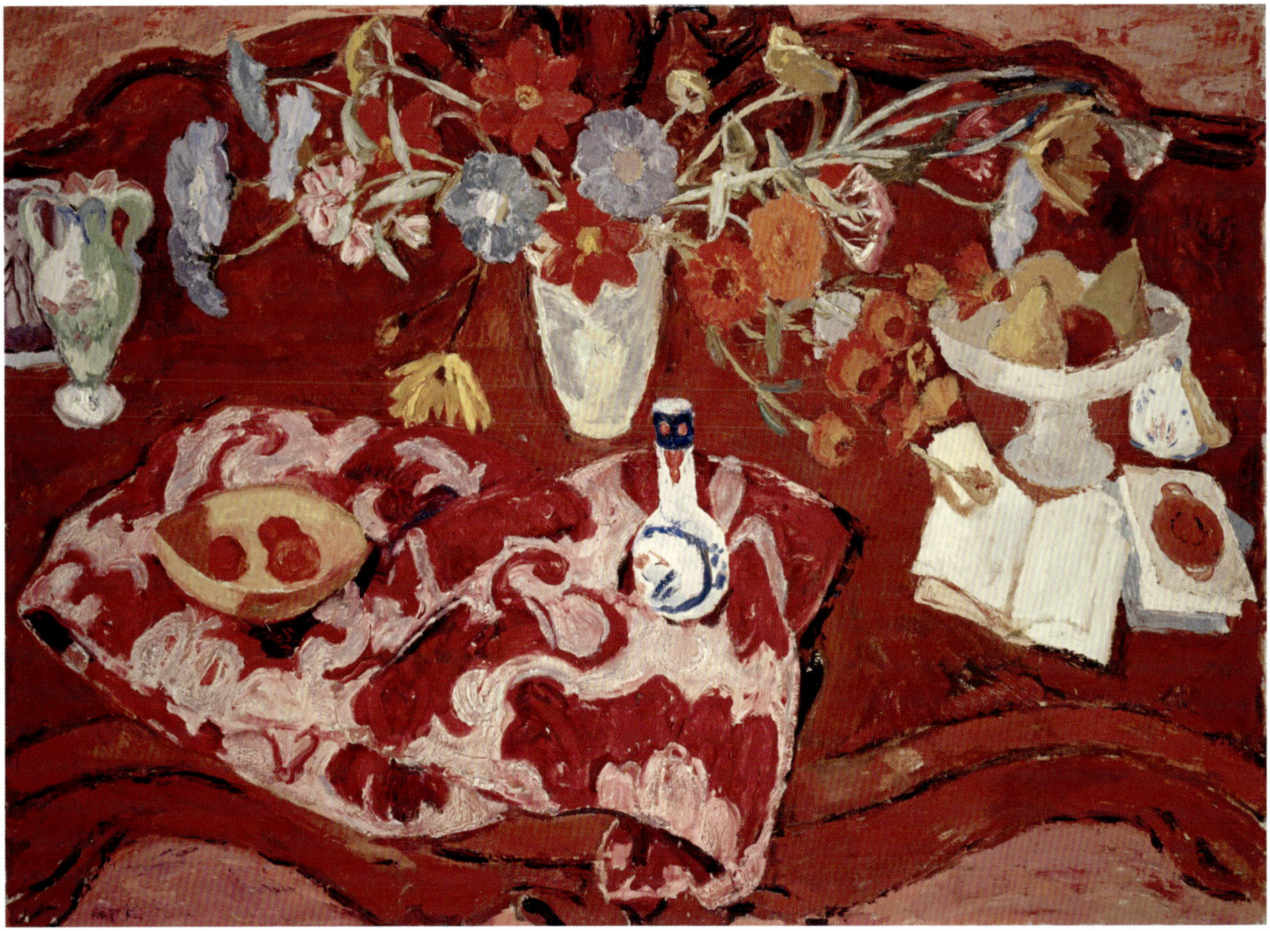

153 *Flowers on a Sideboard* (nd, *c.* 1941). Oil, 88 cm by 124 cm

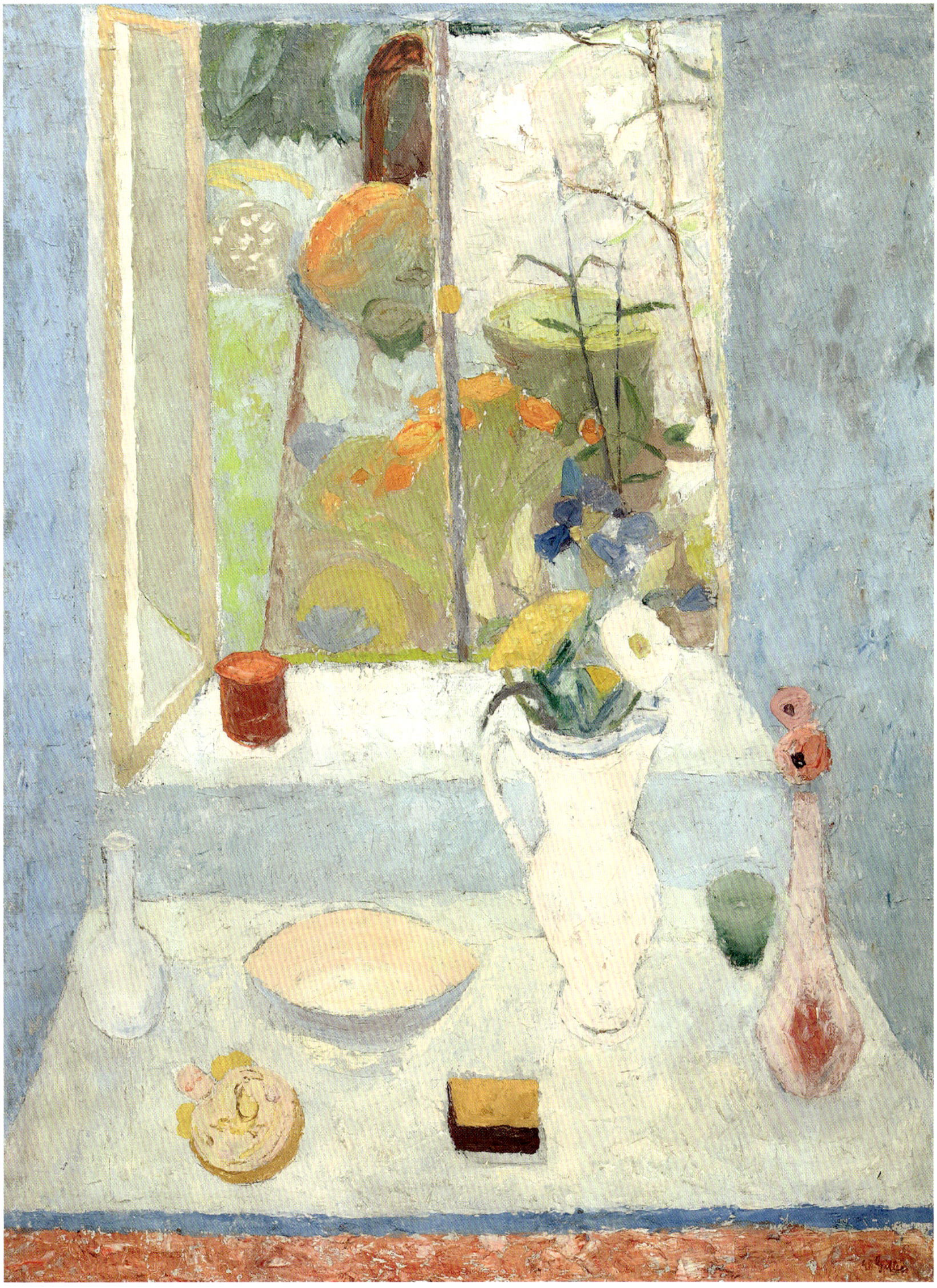

154 *The Blue Window* (*c.* 1940). Oil, 122.1 cm by 91.3 cm

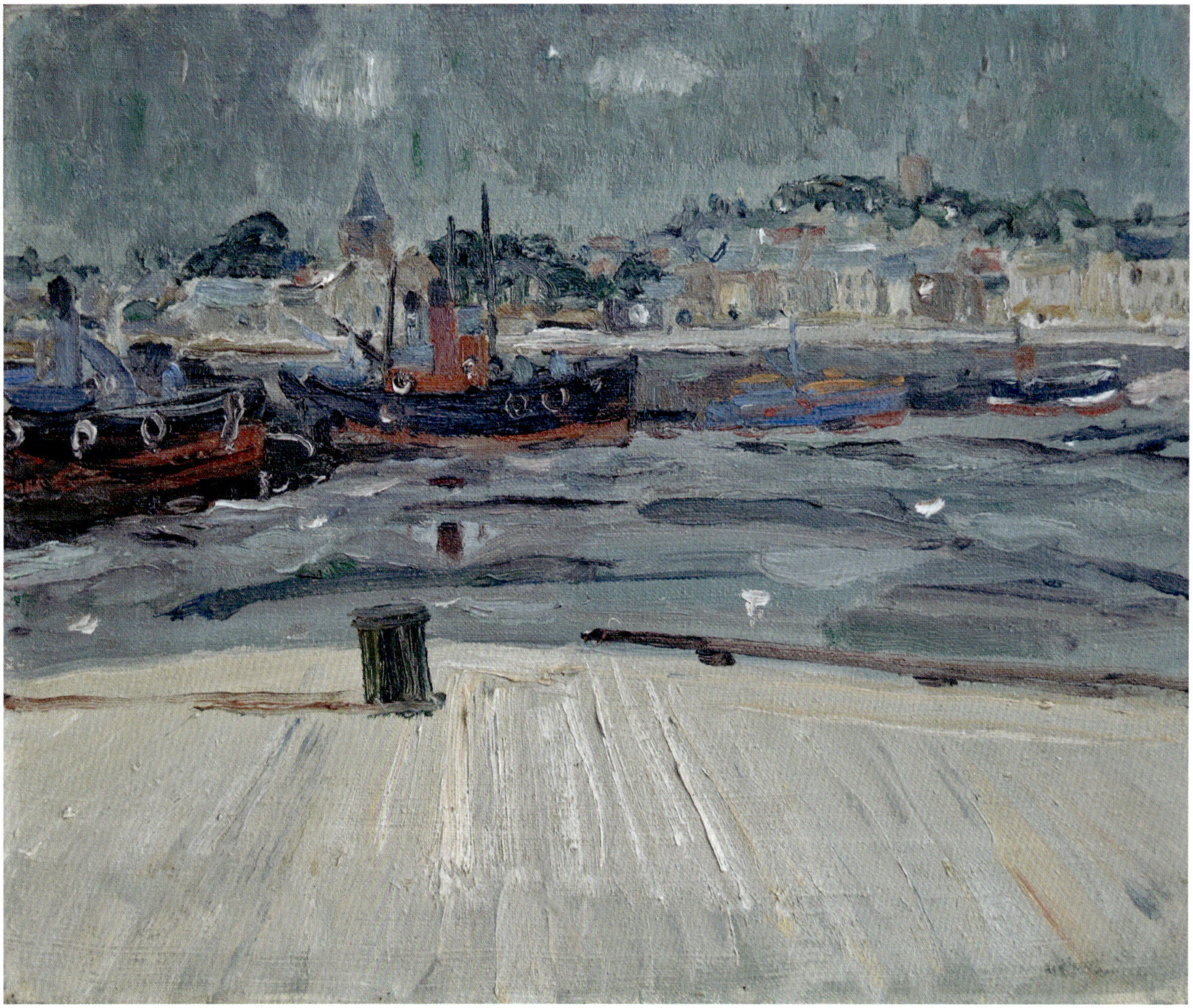

155 *Anstruther from the Harbour* (1946). Oil, 46 cm by 56 cm

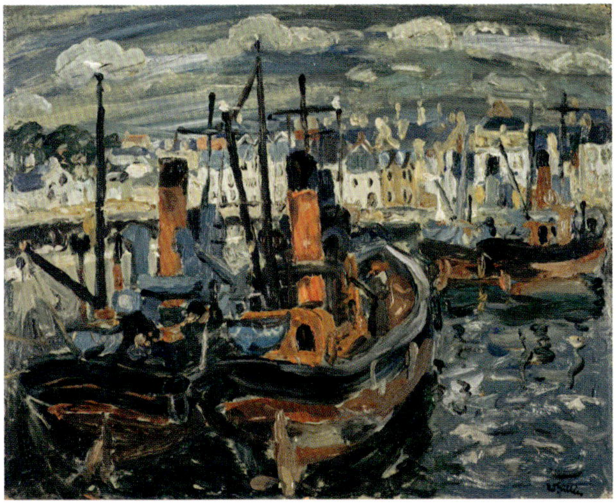

156 *Fishing Boats, Anstruther Harbour* (*c.* 1945). Oil, 48 cm by 60.5 cm

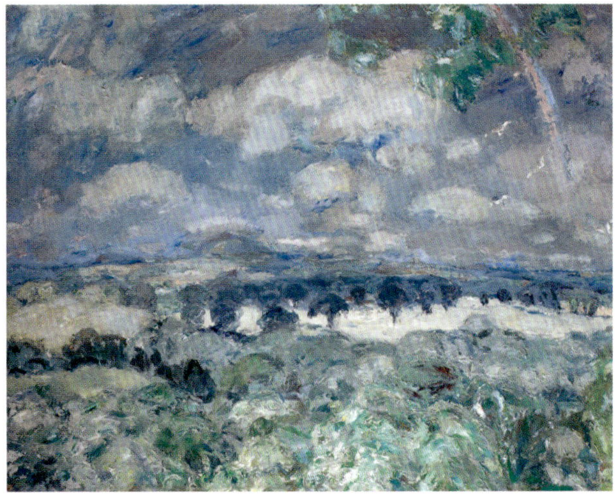

157 *Arniston Woods, Midlothian* (nd, *c.* 1944). Oil, 62.5 cm by 76 cm

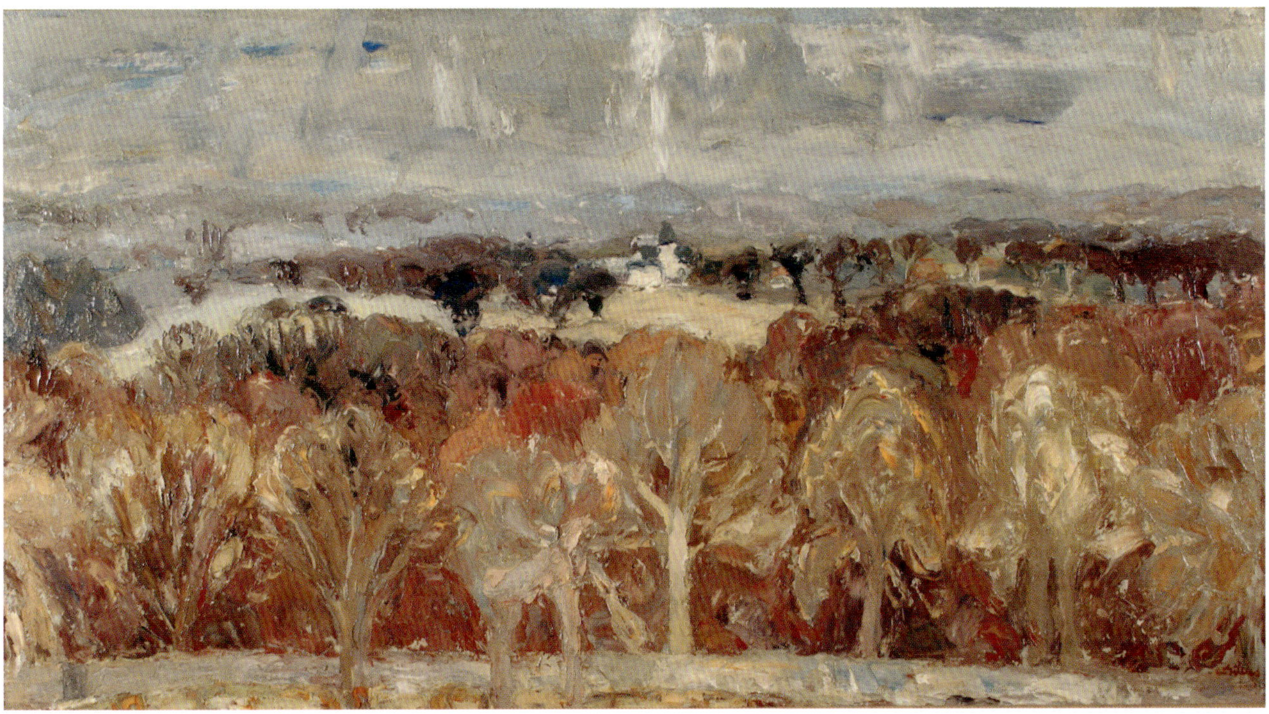

158 *Sunlit Wood* (nd, *c.* 1944). Oil, 44.7 cm by 85 cm

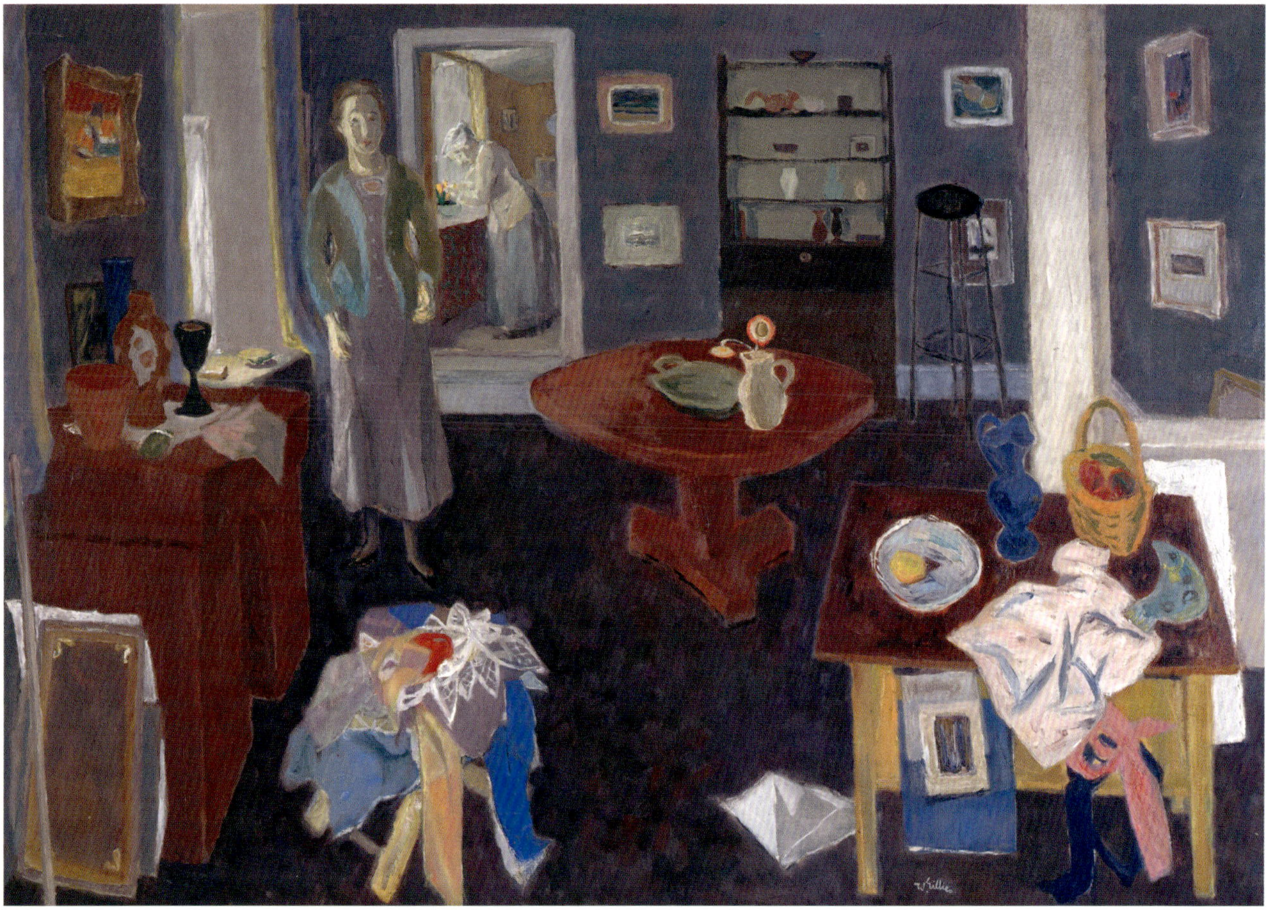

159 *Interior, Temple Cottage* (1951). Oil, 117 cm by 168 cm

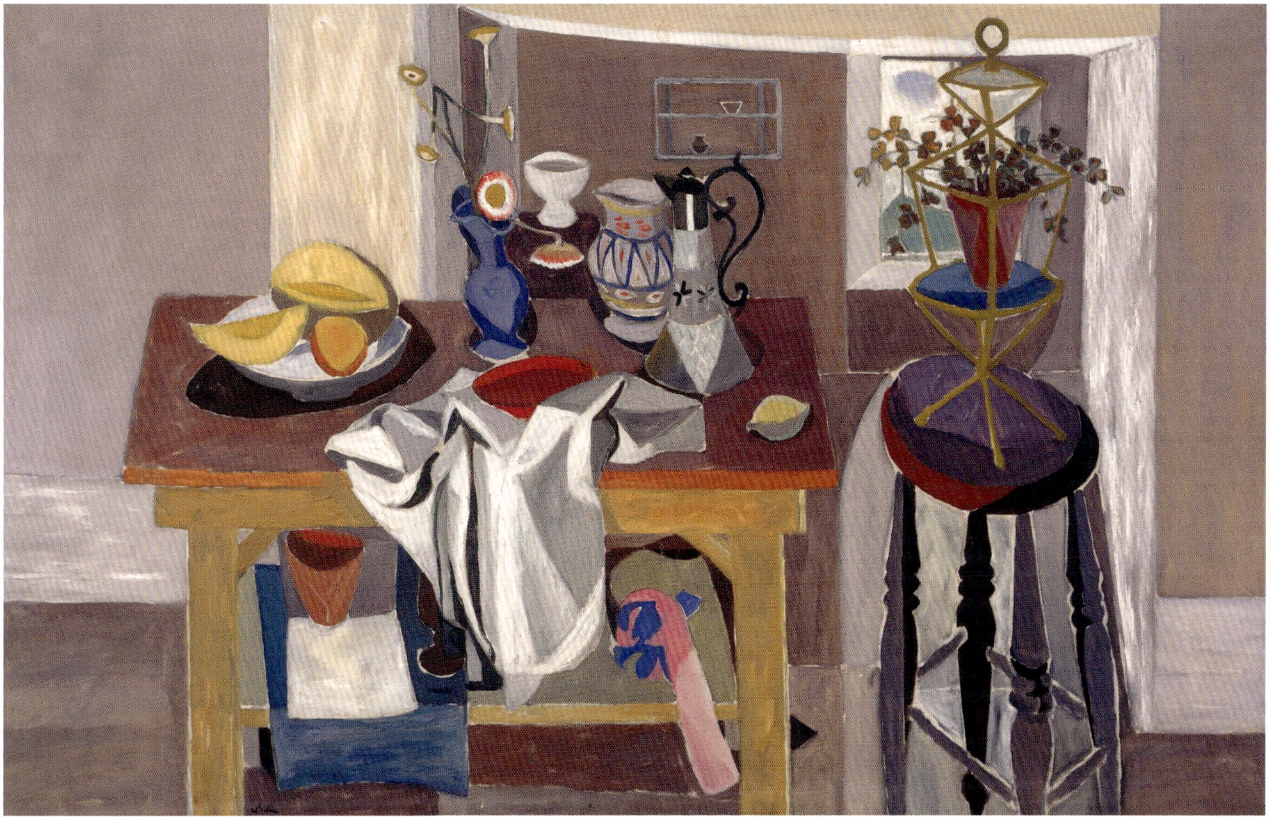

160 *Studio Table* (1951). Oil, 118 cm by 187 cm

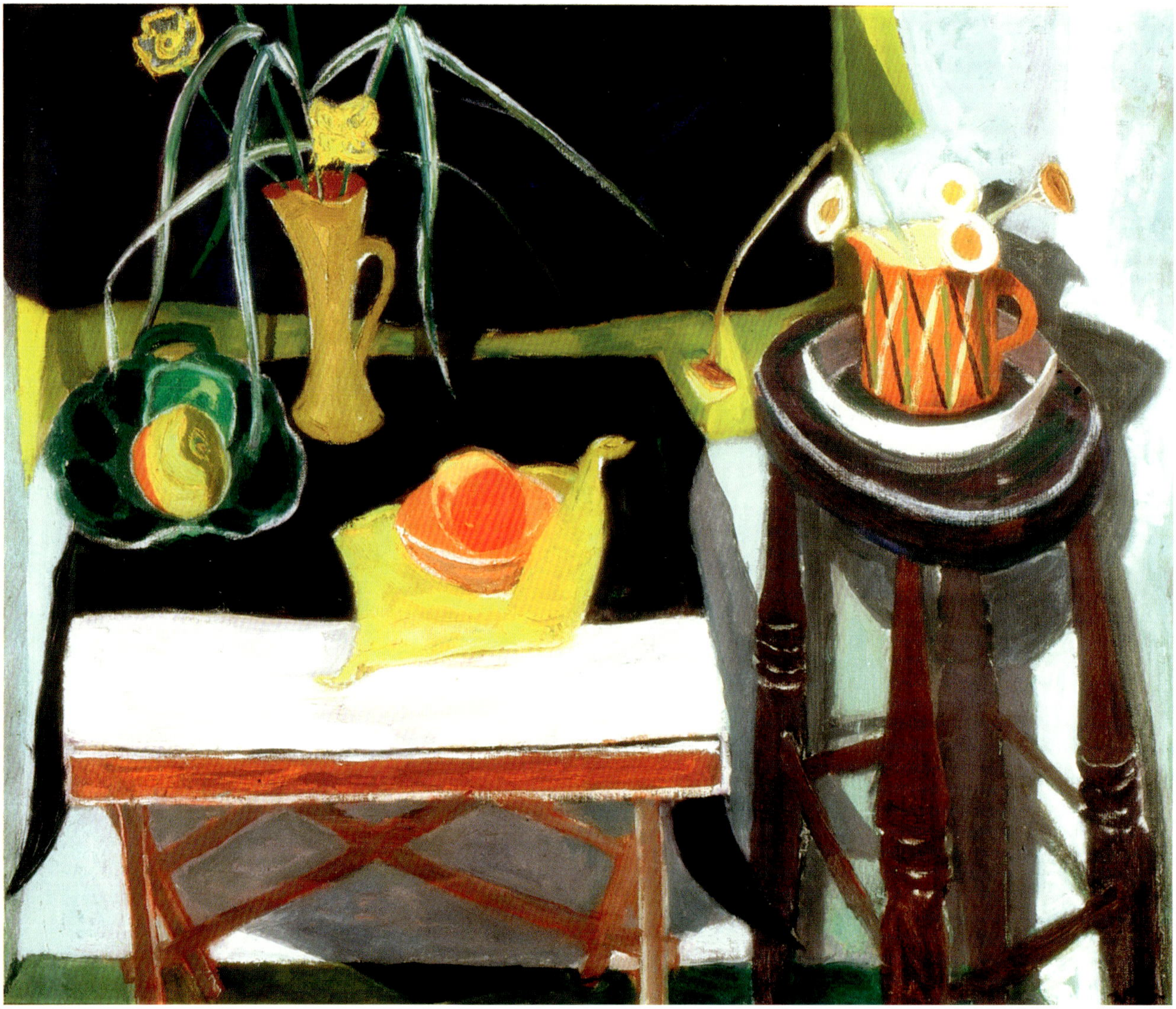

161 *Still Life with Yellow Flowers* (nd, *c.* 1953). Oil, 75.2 cm by 93 cm

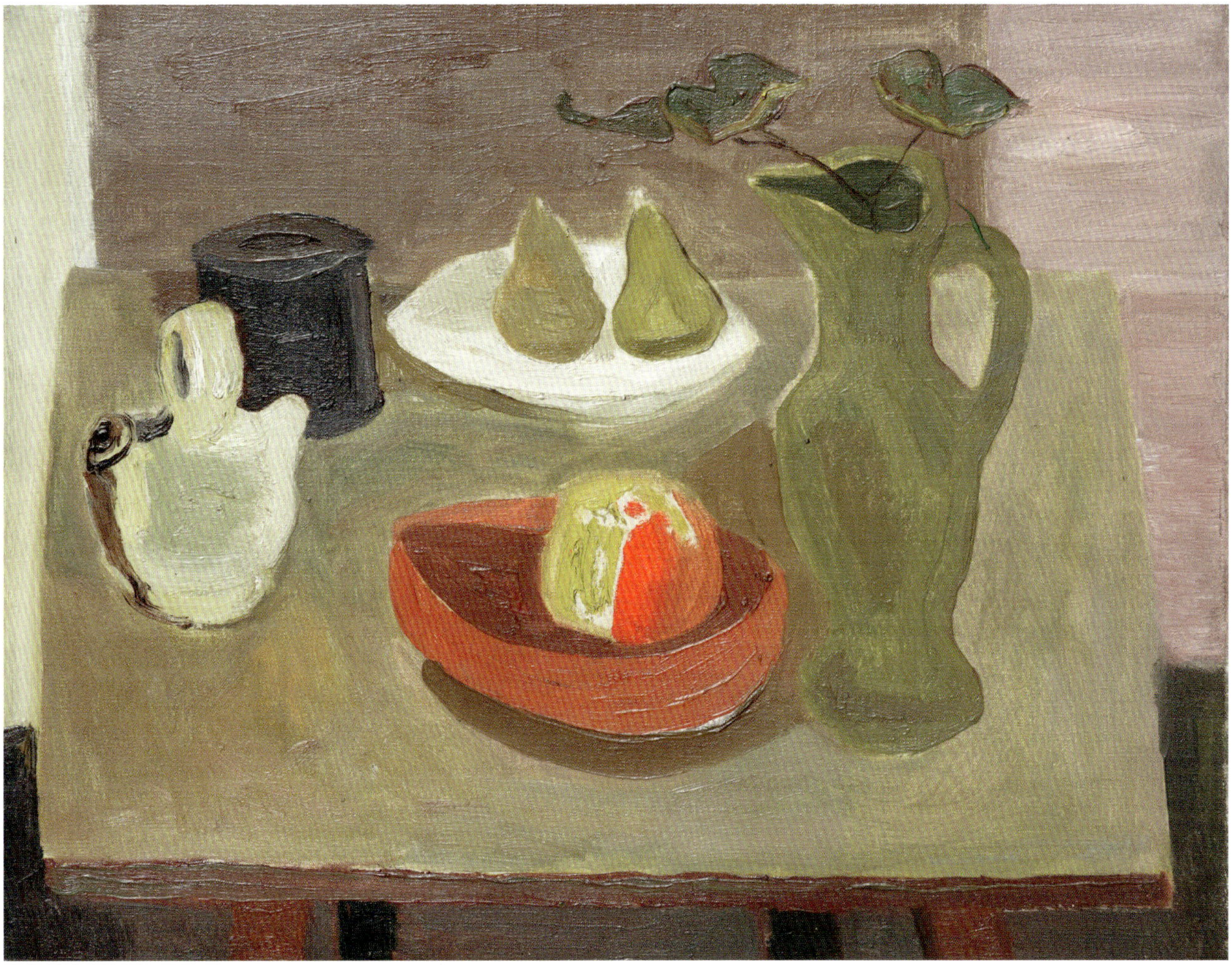

162 *Apple with/on Red Platter* (originally dated 1951 but *c.* 1949). Oil, 43 cm by 53 cm

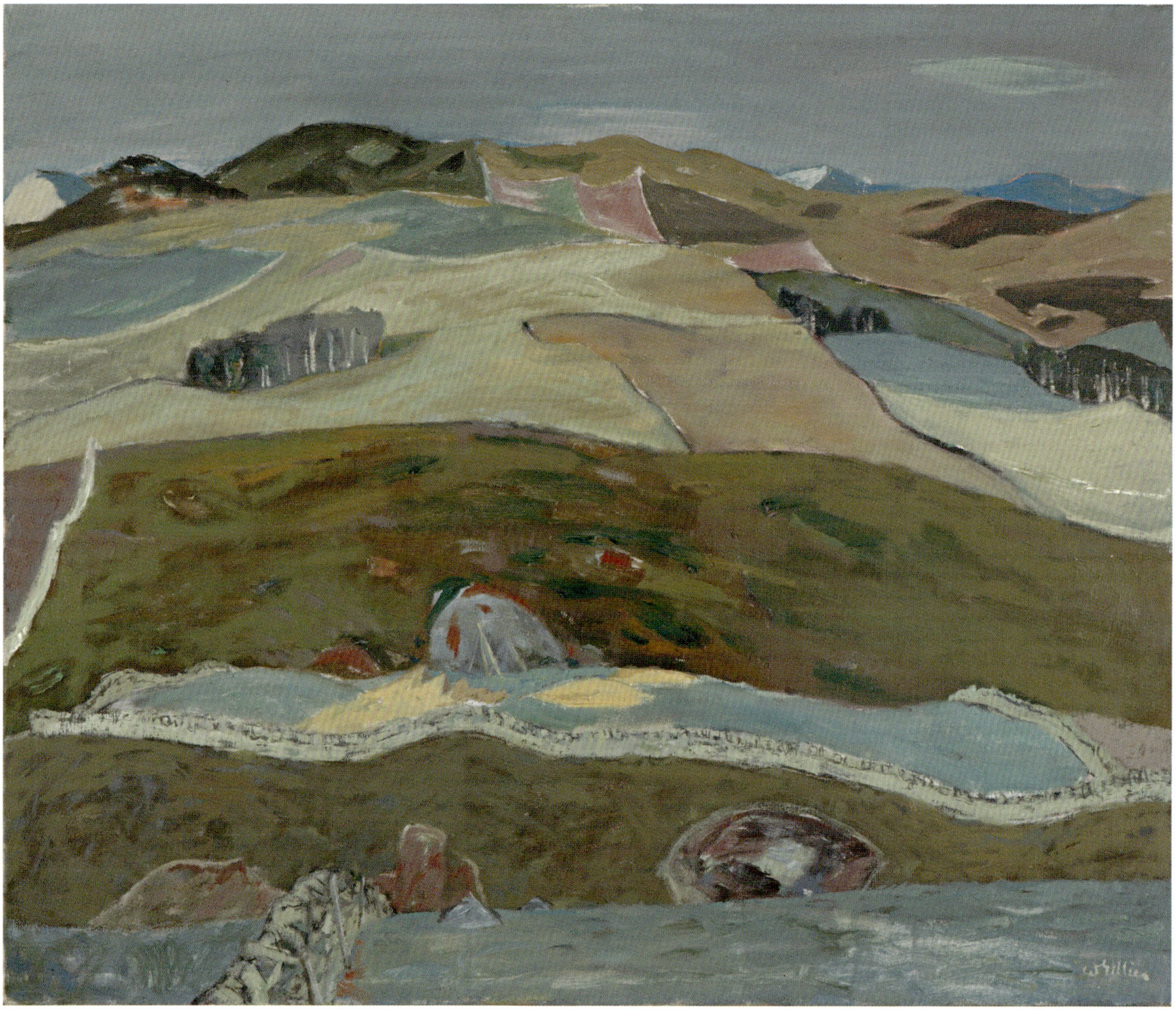

163 *Peeblesshire Landscape* (*c.* 1952). Oil, 69.2 cm by 84 cm

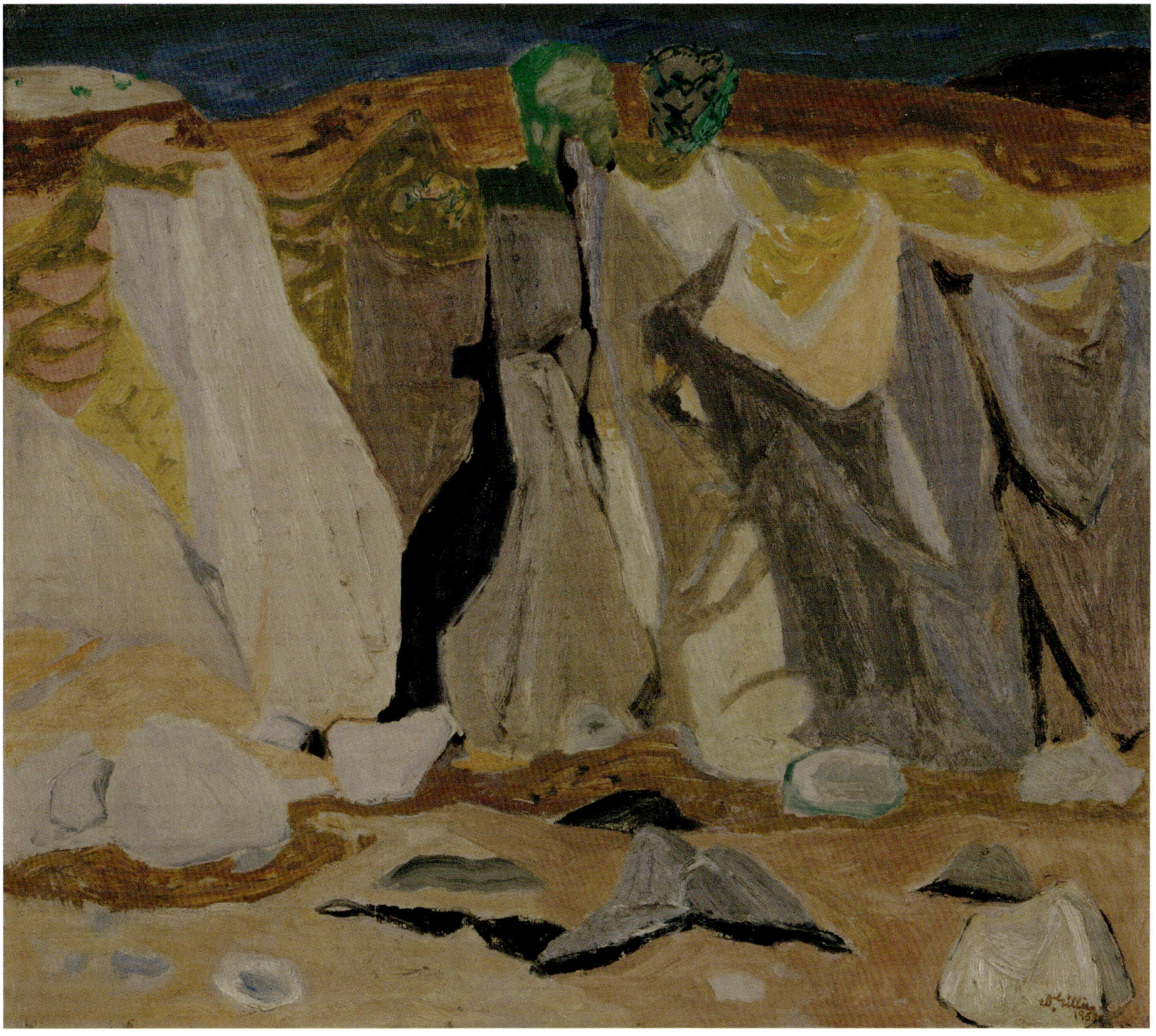

164 *Cliffs, Dalbeattie* (1953). Oil, 63 cm by 74 cm

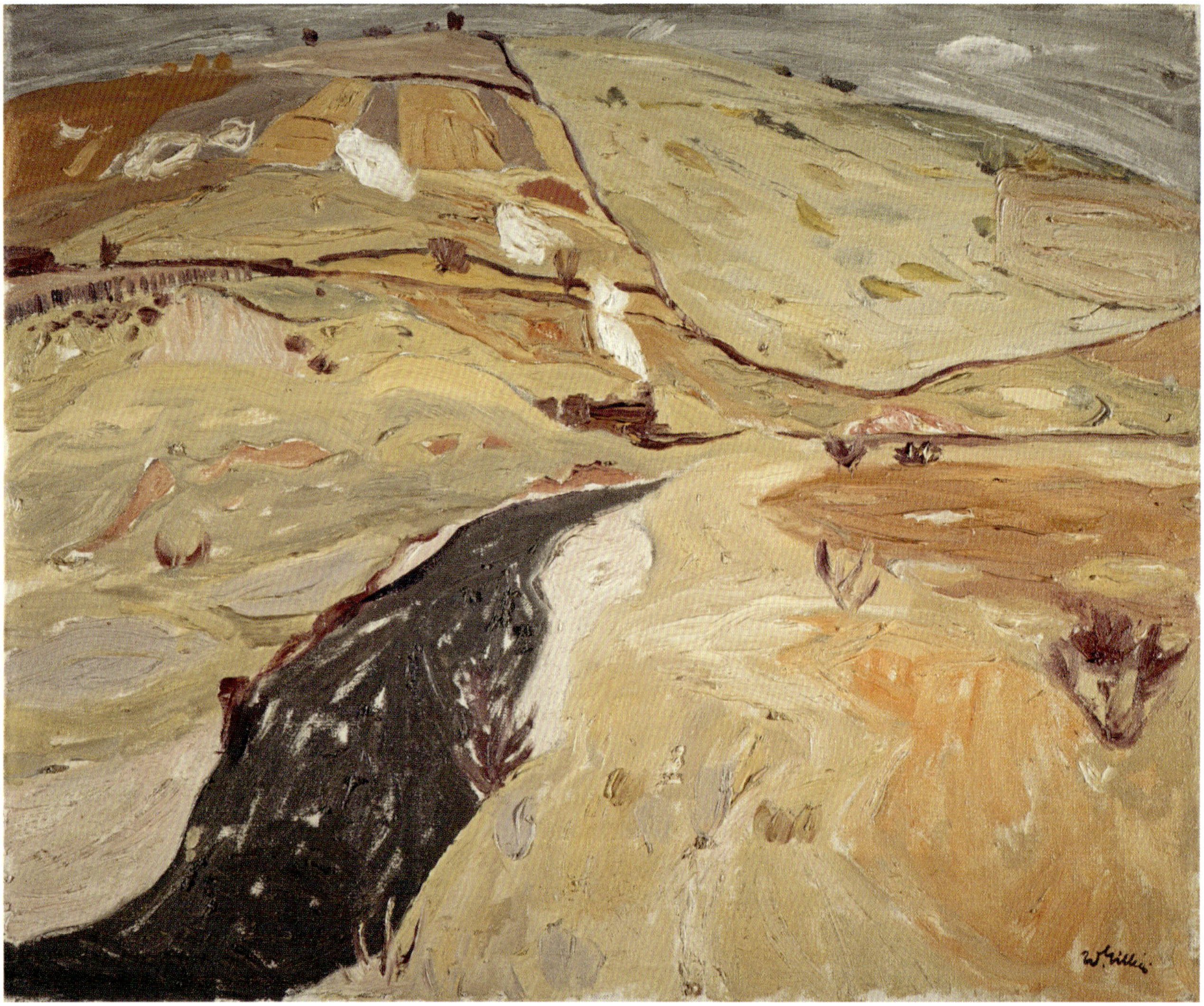

165 *The Peebles Train* (*c.* 1950). Oil, 46 cm by 56.5 cm

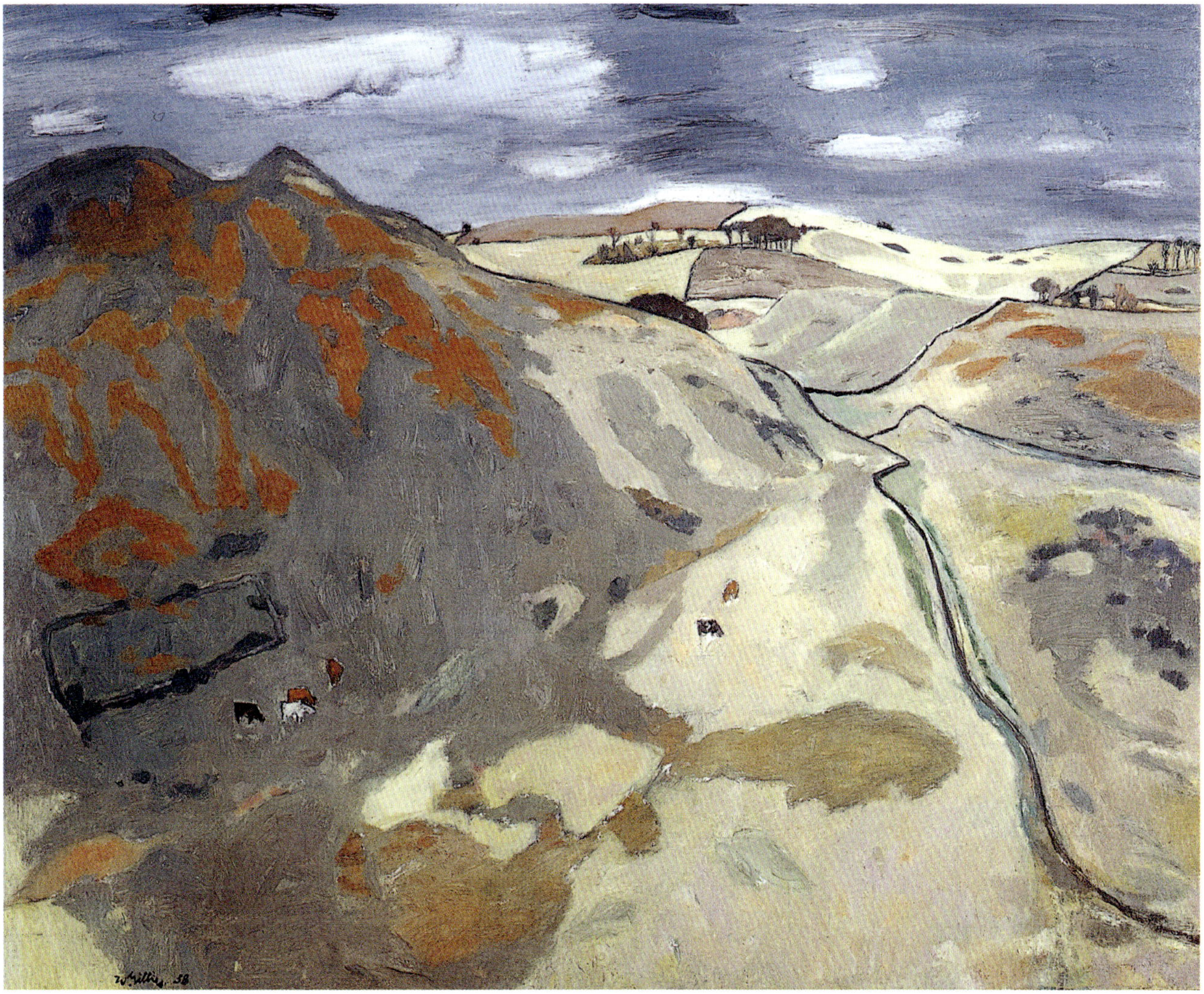

166 *Shadowed Hill* (1958). Oil, 89 cm by 112 cm

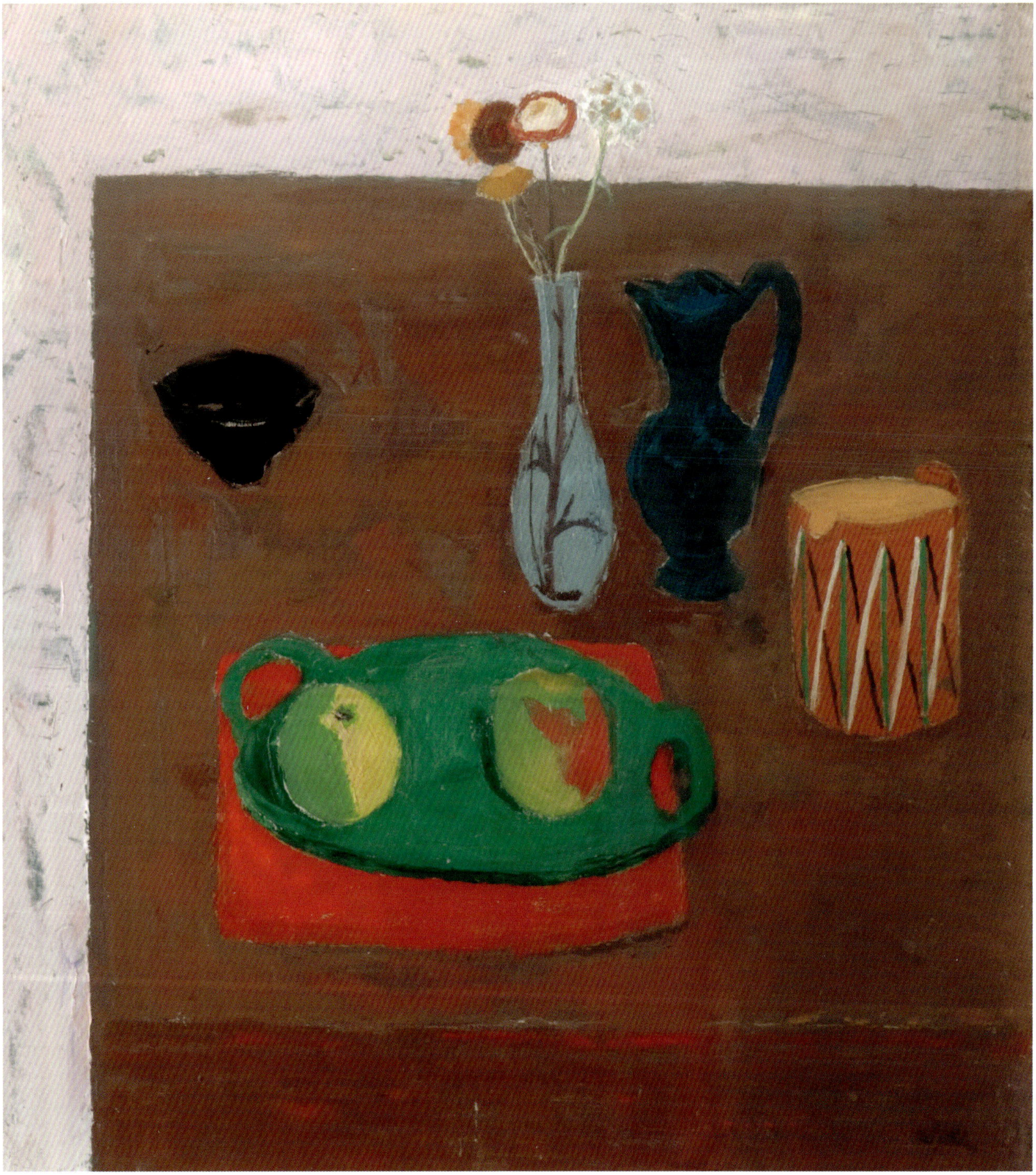

167 *The Green Platter* (nd, *c.* 1956). Oil, 67.7 cm by 65.2 cm

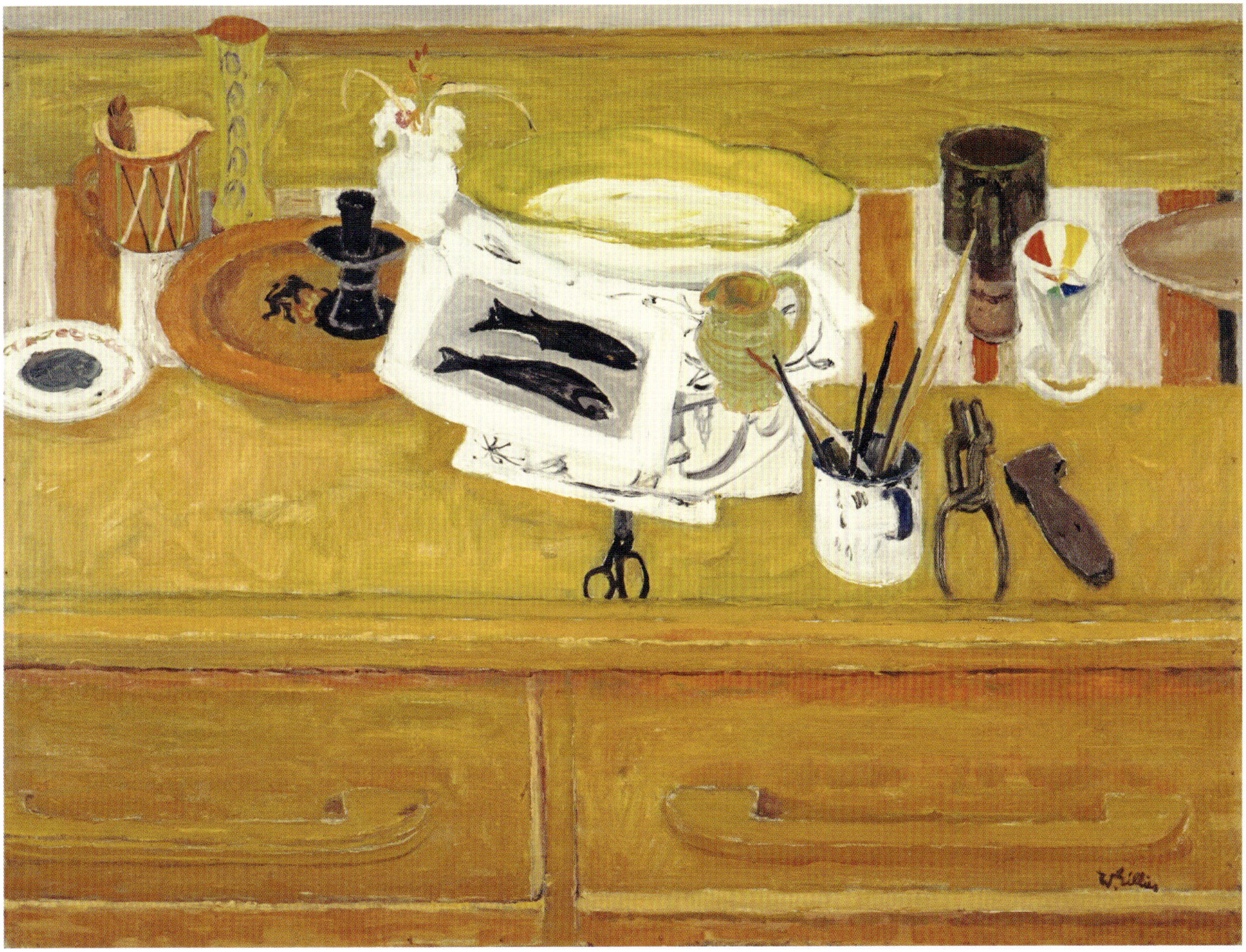

168 *Still Life with Black Fishes* (1965). Oil, 78 cm by 104 cm

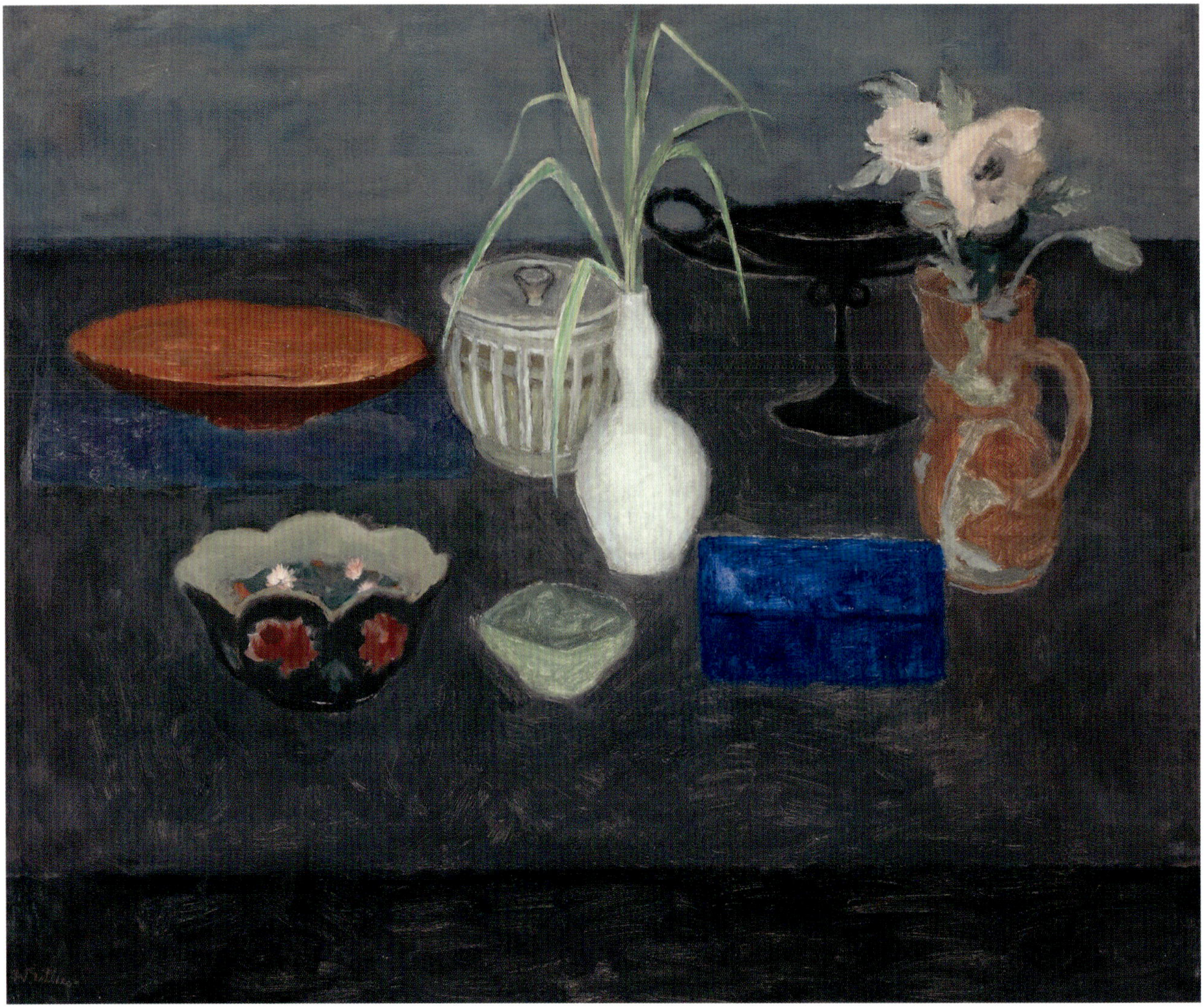

169 *Still Life on a Dark Ground* (*c.* 1971). Oil, 84.8 cm by 105.1 cm

Note on the Dates and Titles of Images

I attribute two dates to some works by Gillies. This arises from the need for date and title to fulfil in combination two functions that sometimes conflict.

One is the function of a label by which a single title and date jointly and uniquely identify a work, or an image thereof, whether in this book or in any source that pre-dates it.

The other function is to convey what I believe to be the correct date of a work (and occasionally, where a title has been transposed, altered or conjectured, the correct title as well).

The two lists, 'Details of Illustrations', and 'Other Visual Works Named', give details of where a work, or an image thereof, can be located, if at all, and a brief indication, where necessary, of my reasons for re-dating.

The first, and often the only, date with which a work is labelled within the brackets for the date is that by which it is already known and by which the work, or an image of it, can be uniquely identified using date and title.

Where a second date follows the first within the brackets, the second indicates a necessary correction to the date by which it is already known. (I allow the first, incorrect or questionable, date to remain so that it can fulfil its necessary function as a label that ensures that the work in question is correctly identified in earlier sources.)

All works are dated. Where a first date is given as 'nd' (no date), then the work or image, as currently known, has hitherto had no date either attributed by others or inscribed by Gillies, and the second date within the brackets is mine. This applies, for example, to some of the images on the <artuk.org> website, and also to some internet images of works that have passed through auction.

It is not always possible to know whether a work carries a date that has been inscribed or supplied by the artist. The absence of 'nd' (no date) should be interpreted accordingly. Where only a single date or date span is given (for example, '1945', or '*c.* 1945', or '1945–7') this means only that any correction or addition is not material to my argument. It does not necessarily mean that the date has been inscribed or supplied by the artist or that this was done correctly or at the time the work was made. Nor does it mean that a date attributed by a third party and that stands alone (is not followed by an amended date of mine within the brackets) is necessarily well based in evidence.

I do not maintain for every work an explicit distinction between the date of making and the first documented date of its existence (often an exhibition catalogue or review), but I do observe this distinction when it is necessary to the argument.

Gillies left many of his works undated at the time of making. Some of the dates he subsequently attributed and/or inscribed (sometimes decades later) are mistaken, for instance when he confused versions of a painting or different visits to the same place. He could also change, transpose and re-use titles. Dates attributed by others to undated works sometimes assume qualitative differences between periods of work. These assumptions, and the periods they imply, are not always correct.

The titles of most works are in italic. Non-italic names are used for works for which the only known designation is not a catalogue or artist's title, but an archival descriptor or a description (i.e. not title) in the source. Such terms are shown within quotation marks. Non-italic descriptors with no quotation marks are the author's.

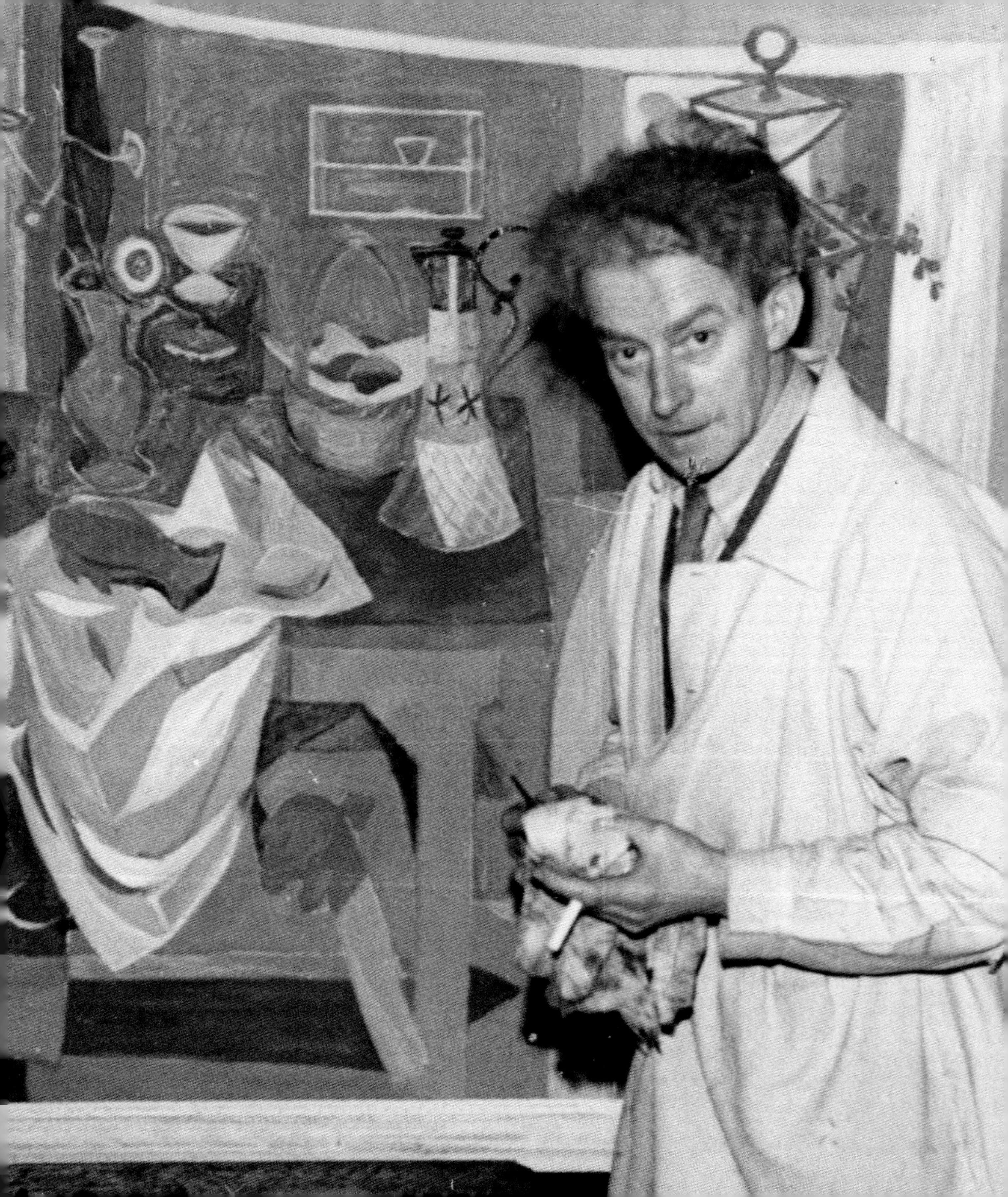

Timeline

1857
Birth of Gillies' father, John Gillies, 24 February, Haddington.

1863
Birth of Gillies' mother, Emma Smith, 27 October, Kirriemuir.

1870
Delirium tremens kills Emma Smith's father, George Smith, aged forty years and proprietor of the Temperance Hotel in Kirriemuir.

1872
Emma Smith's mother Mary (née Dunn), five months pregnant, marries John Mitchell.

1873
Birth of David Mitchell, half-brother to the eight Smith siblings.

***c.* 1877**
Most of the Smith/Mitchell family disperses to Dundee or Tyneside, Northumbria.

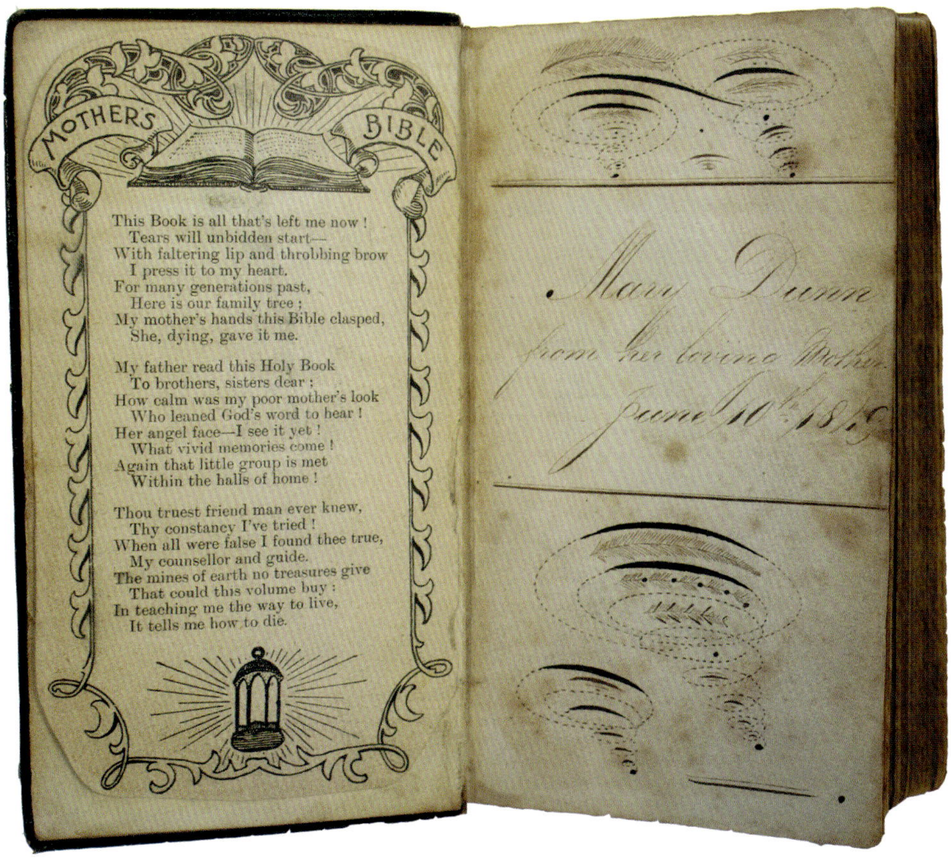

170 Family Bible of Gillies' maternal grandmother, Mary (née Dunn)

Opposite:
Detail from Gillies in 1951 with *Studio Table no. 2* ([179] – see p. 224)

1880

Emma Smith, Gillies' mother, lives and works in the District Lunatic Asylum, Haddington, for the next thirteen years.

1889

First publication of *A Window in Thrums* by J. M. Barrie.

1894

Marriage of Gillies' parents, Emma Smith and John Gillies, in Haddington.

1895

Birth of Gillies' elder sister, Janet Louisa Dunn Gillies, 29 June, Haddington.

***c.* 1897**

Gillies' maternal uncle, William Ryle Smith, made teacher of Drawing (art) at Grove Academy, Broughty Ferry, near Dundee.

1898

Birth of William George Gillies the artist, 21 September, Haddington.

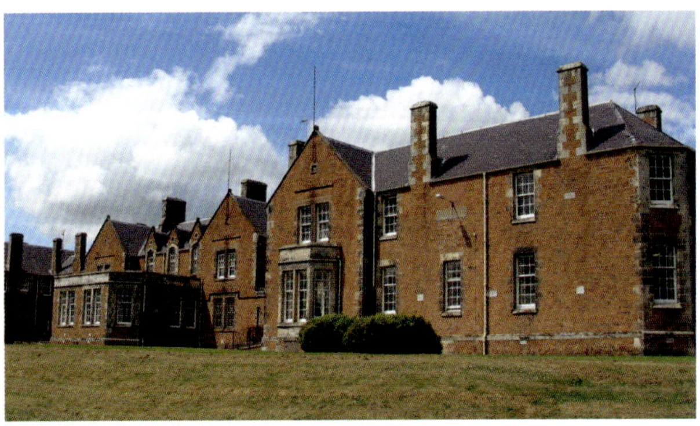

171 The former District Lunatic Asylum, Haddington, in 2009

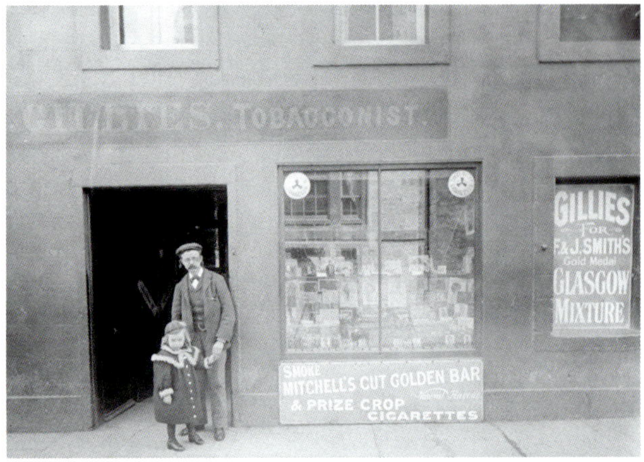

172 John and Janet Gillies outside the family shop, *c.* 1899

1900

Birth of Gillies' younger sister, Emma Smith Gillies, 24 April, Haddington.

Gillies' parents borrow to buy a semi-detached stone villa in Meadow Park, Haddington.

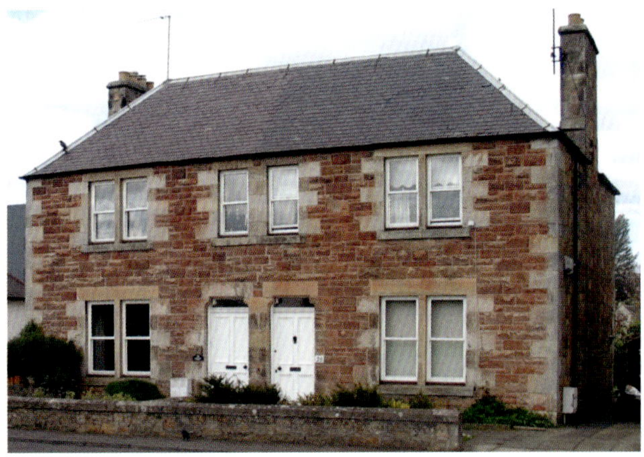

173 Westlea, Meadow Park, Haddington (left) in 2009

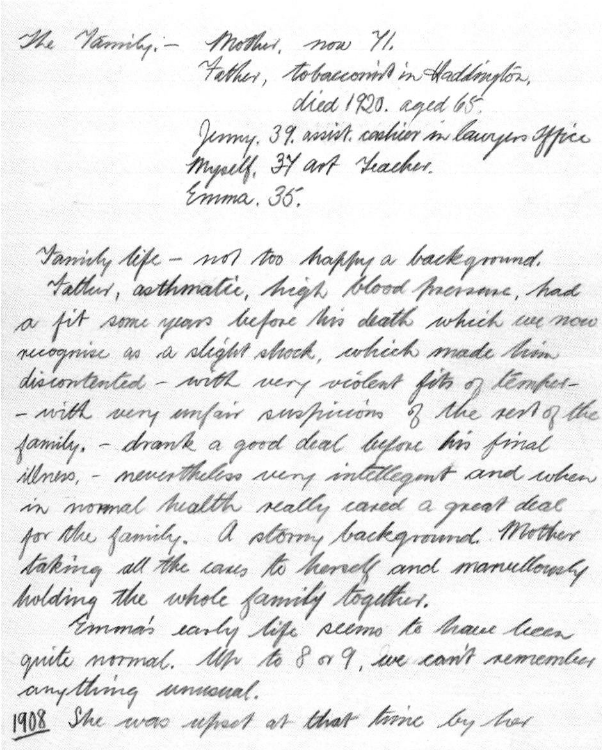
The Family.– Mother, now 71.
Father, tobacconist in Haddington, died 1920. aged 68.
Jenny. 39. assist. cashier in lawyer's office
Myself. 37 art teacher.
Emma. 35.

Family life – not too happy a background.
Father, asthmatic, high blood pressure, had a fit some years before his death which we now recognise as a slight shock, which made him discontented – with very violent fits of temper – with very unfair suspicions of the rest of the family. – drank a good deal before his final illness, – nevertheless very intelligent and when in normal health really cared a great deal for the family. A stormy background. Mother taking all the cares to herself and marvellously holding the whole family together.
Emma's early life seems to have been quite normal. Up to 8 or 9, we can't remember anything unusual.
1908 She was upset at that time by her

174 Opening of Gillies' manuscript account of his family, *c.* 1934

c. 1905

Gillies' father, John, recovers from stroke; onset of John Gillies' abuse of his family.

Marc-André Raffalovich joins Father John Gray in Edinburgh; initiates, and largely funds, the construction of St Peter's Roman Catholic Church, Morningside.

Raffalovich and Gray begin to host a twice-weekly cultural salon, which continues until 1934.

1906–7

Knox Institute cadet force founded [18]; cadets addressed by Haldane, Secretary for War.

William Ryle Smith (Gillies' Uncle Will) serves on a national committee for art education.

1909

Death from exophthalmic goitre of Gillies' paternal aunt, Mary Gillies.

1910

Gillies awarded bursary and enters the Knox Institute for his secondary schooling.

William Ryle Smith ('Uncle Will') begins annual painting holidays in Haddington, joined by Gillies.

1912–13

Gillies gains Intermediate Certificate; enrols as a pupil-teacher; starts Higher Drawing (art) course; with Uncle Will, paints watercolours, visits exhibitions.

1914

Start of First World War.

***c.* 1914**

Gillies begins to work in oils with R. A. Dakers, editor of the *Haddingtonshire Courier.*

1915

Gillies makes *Roll of Honour for Haddington Public School* [19].

1916

Gillies leaves school; conscripted to army; starts four-year Diploma course at the ECA.

A Zeppelin bombs Leith and Edinburgh.

1917

Gillies called up, 5 April, to the 10th Scottish Rifles (Cameronians).

1918

January: Gillies arrives in France.

March: bullet wound in thigh.

May: gassed; makes sketches while convalescing.

July: damaged ankle, possibly in the French Ardennes.

August: repatriated to tented hospital in Glasgow, and Barshaw Hospital, Paisley.

***c.* 1918**

Janet Gillies leaves home to escape her father's abuse.

1919

Gillies discharged after 720 days' war service; returns to second year at ECA.

1920

First of some twenty-five summers up to 1960, many spent under canvas, touring in Scotland and painting with friends.

John Gillies incapacitated by a further stroke.

Family pact sees Gillies' sister Emma take over the family shop.

1921

Death of John Gillies, 16 July, Haddington.

Portrait of Emma (1921) [9].

1922

Gillies graduates, qualifies as teacher of Drawing, begins post-Diploma year at the ECA.

Hugh MacDiarmid (C. M. Grieve) declares a Scottish Renaissance.

1923

Gillies accepts travelling grant and enrols under André Lhote in Paris.

First exhibition of the 1922 Group, Edinburgh.

1924

Gillies leaves Paris, visits Italy with William Crozier and William Geissler.

Returns (May) to teach in Inverness Royal Academy (from August).

Gillies first exhibits with the 1922 Group.

First dated ceramics made and/or decorated by his sister Emma.

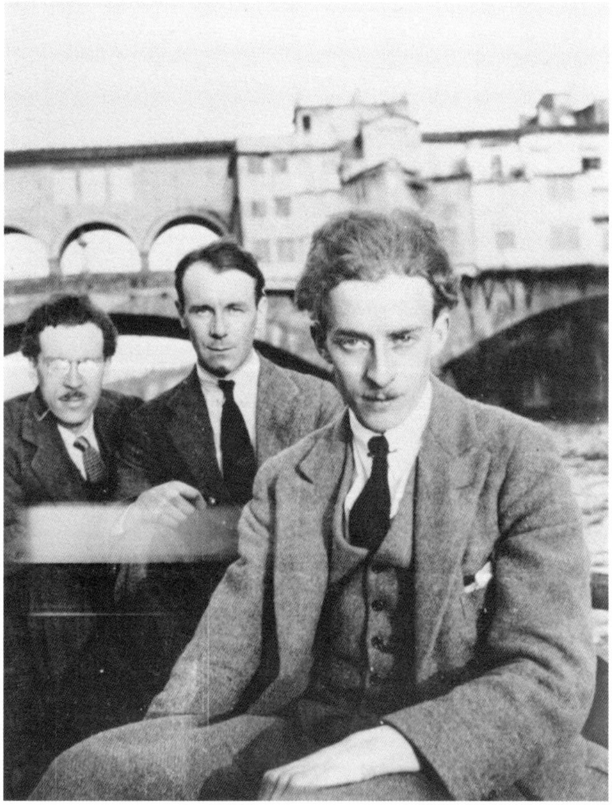

175 Gillies, William Geissler and William Crozier (rear) in Florence in 1924

1925

Gillies starts temporary, part-time, post in the ECA (September).

1926

General Strike.

The White Lodge (1926) [27].

1927

Gillies tours and paints in France with friends.

Fatal ingestion of poison by William Munro, member of the 1922 Group.

1928

First of several showings by Gillies in London, at the St George's Gallery and with the Modern English Water-Colour Society.

The Beeches (1928) [28]; *From Another Window in Thrums* (1928), by William McCance [15].

1929

Gillies, Mrs Gillies, and Janet and Emma Gillies move to 162 Willowbrae Road, Edinburgh.

Emma Gillies begins three-year course in ceramics at the ECA.

Wall Street Crash.

1930

Accidental death of William Crozier, member of 1922 Group (December).

Stanley Cursiter made Director of the National Galleries of Scotland.

1931

National Trust for Scotland founded.

Gillies replaces Crozier in studio he shared with William MacTaggart.

Gillies nominated by S. J. Peploe and F. C. B. Cadell to the Society of Eight.

October: Eighth and final exhibition of the 1922 Group.

Herbert Read becomes Watson Gordon Professor of Fine Art, University of Edinburgh.

Read tours studios with Harry Harvey Wood and gives uproarious parties.

Fanny Aavatsmark brings twelve oils by Edvard Munch to Edinburgh from Oslo.

December: Society of Scottish Artists' annual exhibition opens with the Munch works.

1932

Read generates public debate on Munch, modernism, nationality and decadence.

George Scott-Moncrieff counselled by Father Gray somewhere around this time.

William MacTaggart and Harold Morton in love with Fanny Aavatsmark.

Gillies' sister Emma completes her three-year course in ceramics at the ECA.

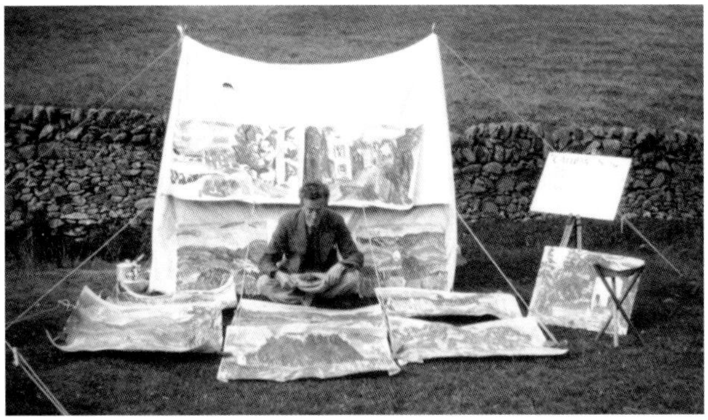

177 Gillies at his Calidon show, *c.* 1933

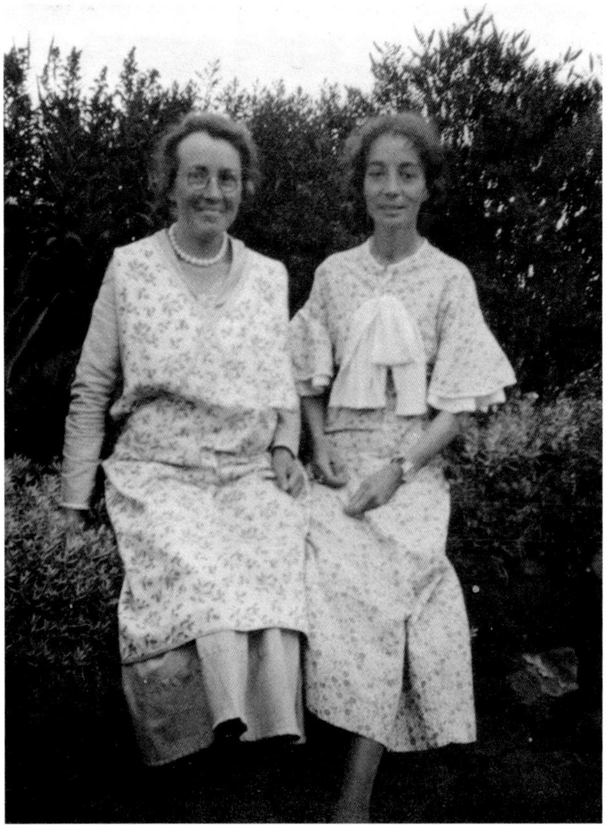

176 Janet and Emma Gillies (right) *c.* 1933

1933

Read resigns university chair over affair with Margaret Ludwig and leaves Edinburgh.

David Talbot Rice appointed to Read's former chair.

Hitler seizes power and pursues German rearmament.

Edinburgh protests against Hitler's persecution of minorities.

Violence against Catholics in Edinburgh by Protestant Action.

Emma Gillies abandons ceramics course at the Royal College of Art under William Staite Murray.

Onset of Janet Gillies' symptoms of Hashimoto's thyroiditis around this time.

Still Life with Chagall Print (1933) [10], *Portrait of Jenny* (*c.* 1933–4) [34].

1934

Eric Gill lectures at the ECA on the holiness of art.

Deaths of Marc-André Raffalovich and Father (Canon) Gray.

Gillies' sister Emma misdiagnosed as 'hysteric' and admitted to psychiatric ward.

Society of Scottish Artists shows twenty-five works by Paul Klee.

Gillies sees Klee's *Drohender Schneesturm* (1927) [63].

Continuing public debate on visual modernism.

Harbour (1934, *c.* 1934) [58 and 64], *The Harbour* (*c.* 1934–7) [59].

1935

Gillies shows abstract oils at the Society of Eight (January).

Society of Scottish Artists shows nine oils by Georges Braque.

Emma Gillies' hospitalisation, misdiagnosis and decline continue.

S. J. Peploe dies after a thyroidectomy.

David Gunn, former member of the 1922 Group, fatally gassed in studio.

David Cleghorn Thomson opens Garret Studio in Edinburgh and shows work by Gillies, Margaret Mellis, Peploe, Cadell, John Maxwell, Matisse, Modigliani, Ben Nicholson, Paul Nash, John Piper and Klee.

In Arniston (1935) [60]; *Marjory Porter 2* (*c.* 1935) [36].

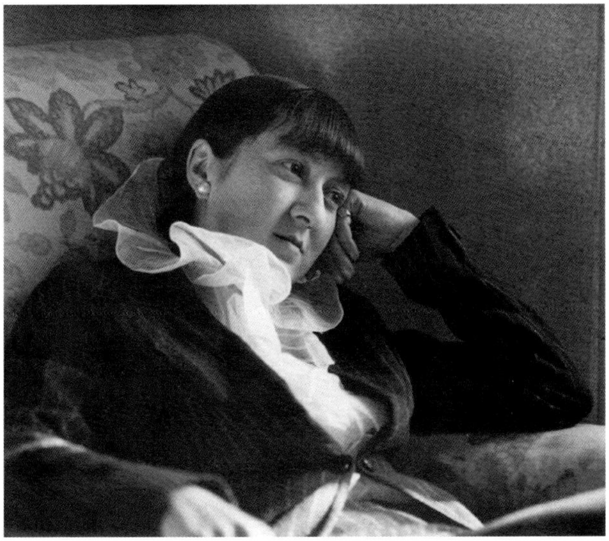

178 Margery Porter, *c.* 1935

1936

Death of Emma Gillies from Graves' disease, recorded as 'asphyxiation'.

La Condition Humaine (1935), by René Magritte, shown at the first annual exhibition of the Fine Art Society of Edinburgh University and Edinburgh College of Art.

Ruthven Todd acts as assistant-secretary to first International Surrealist Exhibition.

George Scott-Moncrieff becomes a founding member of the Saltire Society and buys the future Temple Cottage.

Fanny Aavatsmark and William MacTaggart marry and visit Munch outside Oslo.

In Ardnamurchan (1936) [81].

1937

Gillies joins the Society of Scottish Artists and shows *Family Group* (nd, *c.* 1932–7) [41]; ten works by Max Ernst also shown.

Gillies visits the Exposition Universelle in Paris with John Maxwell, Harold Morton, Margaret Mellis, Wilhelmina Barns-Graham and William Gear; sees Picasso's *Guernica* (1937).

1938

Gillies returns to Paris and paints with friends in St Valéry-en-Caux, Normandy.

Final exhibition of Society of Eight.

Gillies shows *Autumn Moon* (1934, *c.* 1934–7) [84], *Interior* (1938) [42].

1939

First published article on Gillies, by George Scott-Moncrieff in *The New Alliance.*

William Gear co-founds the New Era Group and it exhibits in Edinburgh.

Synoptic retrospective exhibition of Scottish art at the Royal Academy in London.

Talbot Rice questions the quality of Scottish painting.

Cursiter questions Talbot Rice's judgement and experience.

Elder Dickson writes 'In defence of Scottish art'.

Start of Second World War.

Gillies buys Temple Cottage from George and Ann Scott-Moncrieff; moves in immediately.

Studio Interior and Red Poppies (1939) [49].

1940

Gillies retains and lets the Edinburgh family home for the next seven years.

Elected Associate of the Royal Scottish Academy.

Conscripted for war service and becomes Air Raid Precautions warden.

Suspends sociable landscape excursions and holidays.

Robert A. Lillie buys his first work by Gillies.

Harvey Wood made head of British Council in Scotland.

George Scott-Moncrieff works under the Fourth Marquess of Bute.

Self-Portrait (1940) [5].

1942

Gillies' first sales through the Scottish Gallery (Aitken Dott).

Shows in *Six Scottish Artists* at the Reid and Lefèvre Gallery, London.

John Piper publishes *British Romantic Artists.*

Winter Afternoon, Temple (*c.* 1942) [87], *Early Morning, Temple* (*c.* 1942) [91].

1943

Suicide of Ann Scott-Moncrieff, wife of George.

1944

Cursiter enlists Elder Dickson's support for a new gallery of contemporary art in Scotland.

Elder Dickson develops a Scottish version of Read's 'Nordic' sensibility.

Gillies resumes sociable landscape excursions.

1945

Society of Scottish Artists mounts exhibition of contemporary French painting.

1946

Founding of Arts Council of Great Britain, 1945–6.

Gillies appointed Head of School of Drawing and Painting in the ECA.

Takes college students to Paris.

Elder Dickson President of the Society of Scottish Artists (1946–8).

Picasso and Matisse exhibit in Glasgow.

1947

Gillies elected Academician of the Royal Scottish Academy.

Elder Dickson takes the annual exhibition of the SSA to London.

First Edinburgh International Festival.

Dusk at Letterfearn (*c.* 1947) [90].

1948

Mrs Gillies sells 162 Willowbrae Road, Edinburgh.

Lillie exhibits Gillies landscapes in Edinburgh and Aberdeen.

Meningitis kills Margery Porter.

Eight works by Graham Sutherland shown at the SSA.

Elder Dickson restates case for a new gallery of modern art in Scotland.

Still Life, Doyley (*c.* 1948) [96].

1949

Elder Dickson appointed Vice Principal of the ECA.

Inception of the Scottish Covenant.

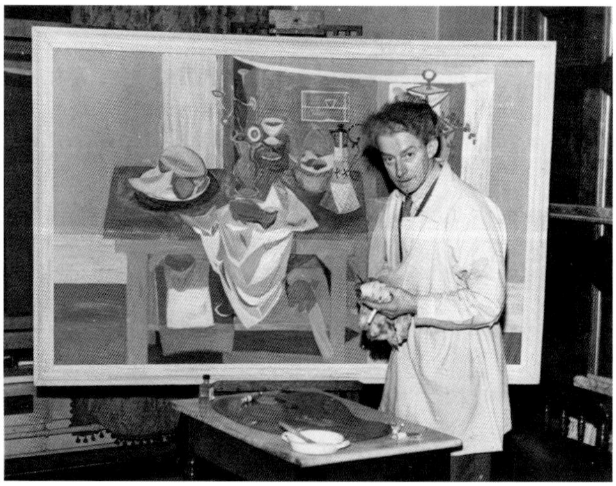

179 Gillies in 1951 with *Studio Table no. 2* (1951)

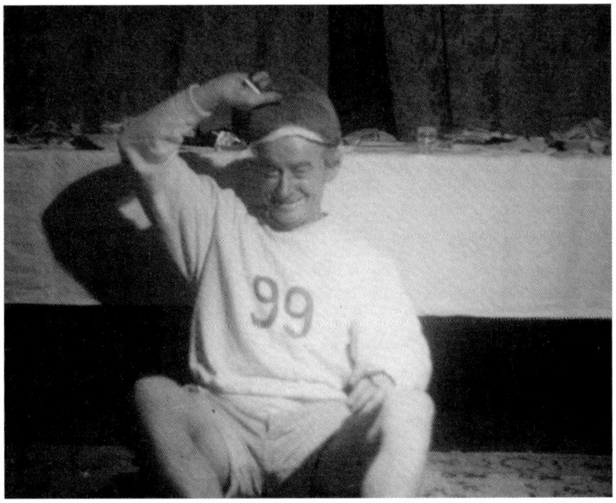

181 Gillies in ECA Revel (fancy dress) as Tour de France cyclist in 1953

1951

Gillies featured in Herbert Read's *Contemporary British Art* (1951).

First Edinburgh People's Festival.

Shows *Studio Table* (1951) [160] in the Festival of Britain.

Interior, Temple Cottage (1951) [159], *Near Howgate* (1951) [103].

1953

Coronation of Sovereign.

National Trust for Scotland shows sixty-eight Gillies landscapes from Lillie's collection in its Edinburgh headquarters, gifted by the Fourth Marquess of Bute; exhibition opened by David Lindsay, 28th Earl of Crawford and 11th Earl of Balcarres; catalogue essay by George Scott-Moncrieff.

Gillies visits Italy.

Mount Lothian (nd, *c.* 1953) [105].

1954

Gillies and Maxwell exhibit in London with the Arts Council of Great Britain.

Still Life (nd, *c.* 1954) [101] and other Gillies works bought by the ACGB.

1955

Diploma work for RSA, *Still Life, Yellow Jug and Striped Cloth* (*c.* 1955) [102].

1956

'Modern Art in the United States' exhibition at the Tate Gallery.

Exhibition of some eighty works by Braque in the Royal Scottish Academy.

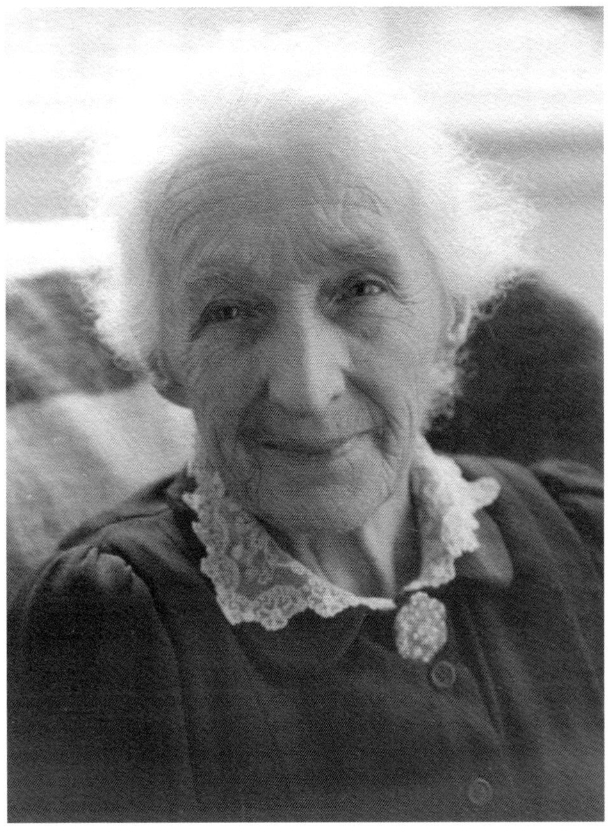

180 Mrs Gillies in her ninetieth year

1957

Gillies made Companion of the British Empire.

1958

Elder Dickson renews call for gallery to show contemporary Scottish art.

First protest march from London to Aldermaston, supported by the Campaign for Nuclear Disarmament [21].

1959

'The New American Painting' exhibition at the Tate Gallery.

Ferniehirst (nd, *c.* 1959) [23].

1960

Gillies becomes Principal of the ECA.

Janet Gillies dies, in Temple, 8 November.

Kenneth Clark opens the Scottish National Gallery of Modern Art.

Elder Dickson publishes his first article on Gillies.

William Johnstone returns to Scotland from London.

Aldermaston Hadeans (nd, *c.* 1960) [22], *Hill Pool* (1960) [112].

1961

Douglas Hall appointed Keeper of the SNGMA.

Studio reports Gillies' criticism of the neglect of Scottish artists by the Edinburgh Festival.

Talbot Rice and William MacTaggart defend Festival policy and practice.

Publication of *The Democratic Intellect* by George Davie.

1962

John Maxwell dies.

Announcement of Lillie's intended bequest of his art collection to the Scottish nation.

1963

Mrs Gillies dies in her hundredth year, in Temple, 15 February.

Elder Dickson, Eric Newton and *Studio* promote the exhibition '14 Scottish Painters' in London.

Douglas Hall condemns the Edinburgh school's 'narrowness of vision'.

Publication of MacDiarmid's *Poems to Paintings by William Johnstone 1933*.

1964

Gillies, John Piper, Robert Colquhoun and Robert MacBryde dropped from revised edition of Herbert Read's *Contemporary British Art*.

1965

Inspired by MacDiarmid, students John Bellany, Alexander Moffat, Alan Bold and Robert Crozier challenge the values and practice of the RSA and the ECA.

Gillies first exhibits as an Associate of the Royal Academy, London.

Interior of Studio, Temple (*c.* 1965) [114].

1966

Gillies retires from post of Principal of the ECA.

1967

Douglas Hall and Elder Dickson clash over the exhibition 'Open 100' promoted by Ricky Demarco.

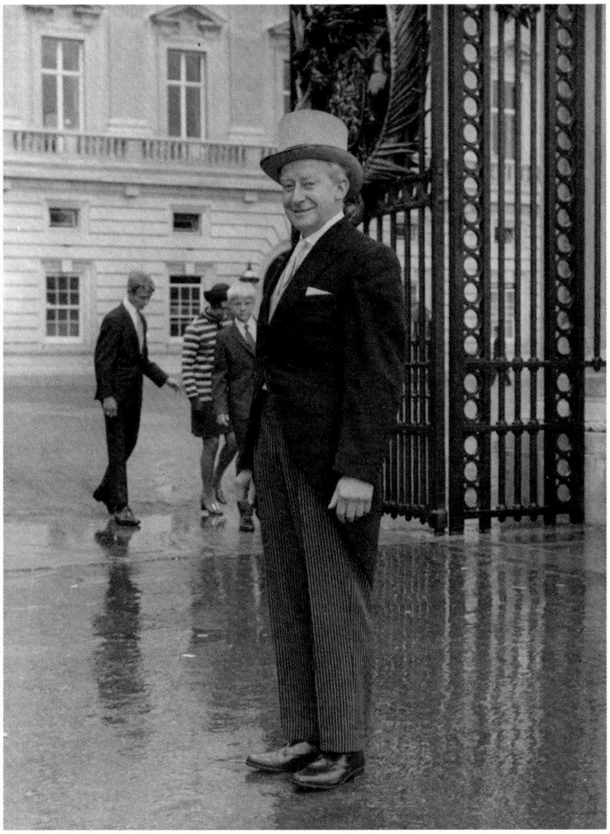

182 The final costume: Gillies at Buckingham Palace in 1970

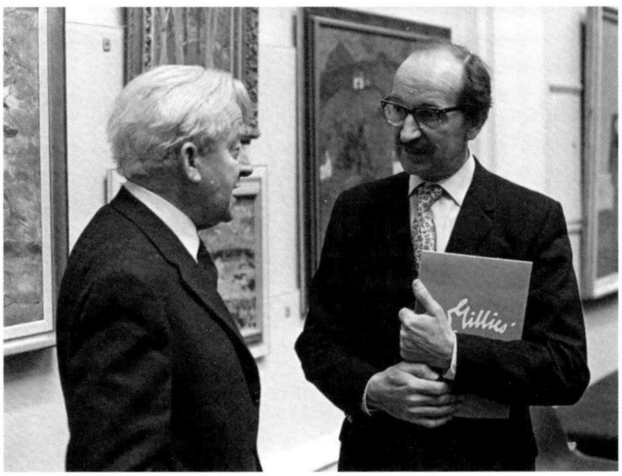

183 Gillies and Sir Norman Reid at the 1970 RSA Gillies exhibition

1968

Scottish Arts Council founded.

Direct action by students in Paris and elsewhere.

1969

The monograph *W. G. Gillies* (1974) commissioned from Elder Dickson.

1970

Direct action by students at the University of Edinburgh.

'Strategy Get Arts' exhibition organised by Ricky Demarco in the ECA.

William Johnstone retrospective at the SNGMA.

Scottish Arts Council shows 221 Gillies works, some not seen since the 1920s and 1930s.

Gillies knighted.

Gillies featured in the film *Still Life with Honesty.*

Nairn Beach (*c.* 1970) [121].

1971

Gillies elected Academician of the Royal Academy, London.

1972

Students elect postgraduate student Gordon Brown, later Prime Minister of the UK, as Rector and *ex officio* Chair of the University Court.

1973

Gillies dies, 15 April, in Temple Cottage; estate bequeathed to the RSA.

Douglas Hall organises William Johnstone exhibition 'Genesis' in the SNGMA.

1974

Publication of the monograph *W. G. Gillies* by Elder Dickson.

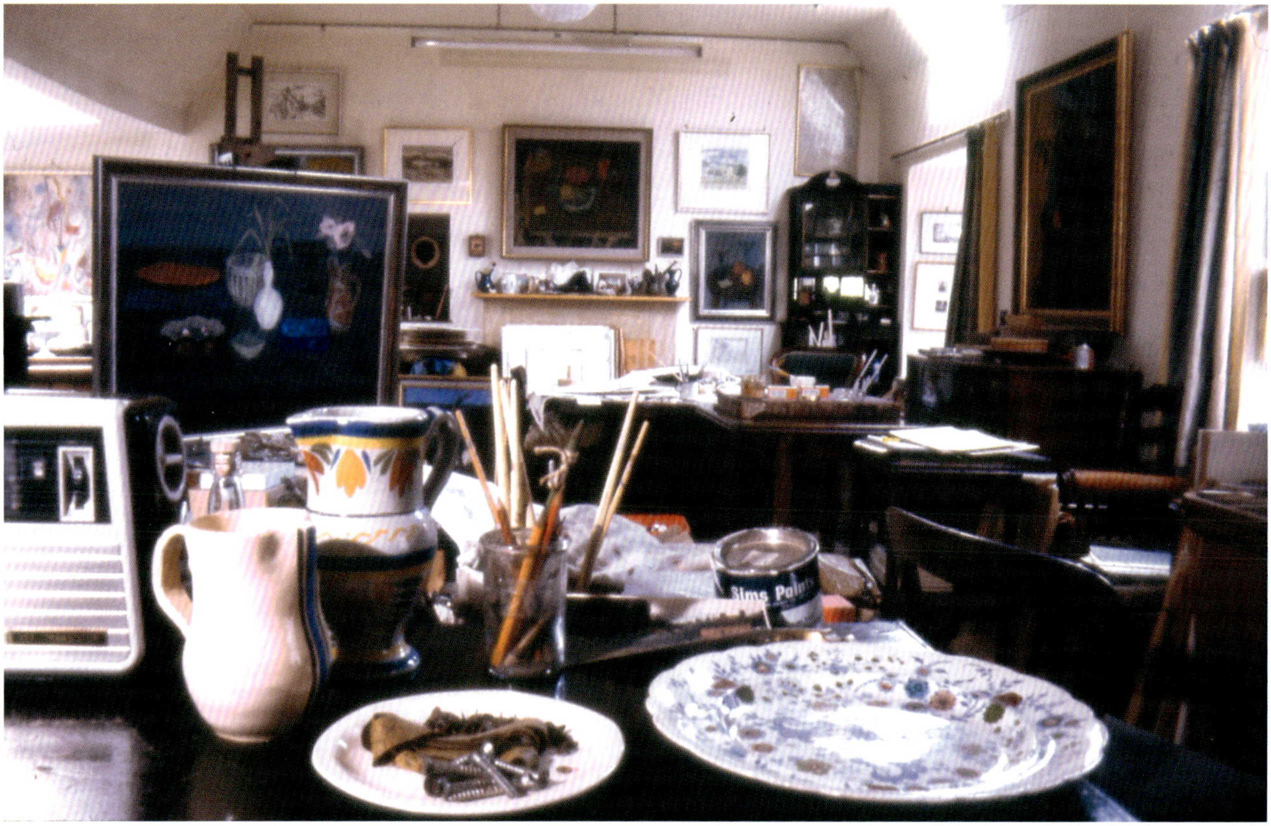

184 Gillies' posthumous studio. Photograph by Robin Philipson

1977

Death of Robert Lillie.

***c.* 1978**

SNGMA accepts 169 of 372 pictures by Gillies in Lillie's estate; others gifted to other Scottish public galleries; the remainder auctioned.

1989

Publication of *Scottish Art Since 1900* by Keith Hartley.

1991

Publication of *W. G. Gillies: A Very Still Life* by W. Gordon Smith.

1994

Publication of *William Gillies: Watercolours of Scotland* by Philip Long.

Publication of *Scottish Art in the 20th Century* by Duncan Macmillan.

1998

Publication of *William Gillies* by Joanna Soden and Victoria Keller.

Royal Scottish Academy shows 216 Gillies works, many not seen since the 1920s and 1930s.

2012

Medical records for Gillies' sister, Emma, become publicly available, including the family history written by Gillies in 1934.

Multiple ceramics by Emma Gillies rediscovered in the Edinburgh College of Art.

Aldermaston Hadeans (nd, *c.* 1960) [22] fails to find a buyer in auction.

2016

A further Gillies manuscript, and papers by Elder Dickson, located in the NLS.

Images of Gillies' oil paintings in public collections made available digitally through ARTUK website.

2018

Further unpublished papers by Elder Dickson accessioned by the NLS.

2020

Images of most of Gillies' works on paper held by the National Galleries of Scotland made digitally available, with the oils, through the NGS website <nationalgalleries.org/art-and-artists/artists/sir-william-gillies>.

2023

RSA collections online database is launched, giving direct access to artwork records and images of the entire Sir William G. Gillies Bequest <collections.royalscottishacademy.org>.

Details of Illustrations

Works are by William Gillies unless stated otherwise. The copyright of all works by William Gillies resides with the RSA. The formats used for artwork titles are explained in the 'Note on the Dates and Titles of Images'. Dimensions are height by width in centimetres to one decimal place as made known to me or measured by me. It is likely that most dimensions refer to the size of the support (paper, board, stretcher) but it is possible that a very small number, individually unknown to me, refer to inner-frame sight-size or to the outer size of the frame. This rider extends to works displayed by the Public Catalogue Foundation (ARTUK). In some entries, details of medium are not exhaustive. Location is the last item in each entry. Internet access to images of works in all media is currently expanding. Almost all works in oil in public collections can already be viewed on the website of ARTUK, and some works on paper. But readers should also consult the websites of local and national institutions, like the RSA and the NGS, where comprehensive coverage of works in all media will continue to spread along with further links to ancillary information to aid interpretation.

1
'Plant Stems II' (nd, 1931–40), pencil
22.8 cm by 17.9 cm
Sir William Gillies Bequest, 1973
Royal Scottish Academy, G.1991.097

2
Moorfoot Hills (1956), watercolour
66 cm by 48 cm
Image courtesy: Fine Art Society
Private collection, untraced

3
The Death of the Queen (1901)
Edinburgh Evening News, Wednesday 23 January
© The British Library Board

4
Gillies in 1949, with *Apple on Red Platter* (1951, *c.* 1949), photograph
Colour added by RSA from the original [162] with Estate's permission
© The Estate of Lida Moser
National Galleries of Scotland, PGP 43.14

5
Self-Portrait (1940), oil
86.9 cm by 71.4 cm
Purchased 1979
NGS, PG 2448

6
Near Durisdeer (*c.* 1932, *c.* 1933), oil
63.4 cm by 76 cm
Date: no visit to Durisdeer is recorded before 1933
Bequeathed by Dr R. A. Lillie, 1977
NGS, GMA 1747

7
Gillies in the uniform of a private in the Scottish Rifles (1917), photograph
Sir William Gillies Bequest, 1973
RSA

8
Our Post Behind Our Wire (1918), 'meant to be Lawton and yours truly', pencil
9 cm by 12.7 cm
Sir William Gillies Bequest, 1973
RSA, G.1991.816

9
Portrait of Emma (1921), oil
76.2 cm by 63.8 cm
Sir William Gillies Bequest, 1973
RSA, G.1991.244

10
Still Life with Chagall Print (1933), oil
56 cm by 45.5 cm
Sir William Gillies Bequest, 1973
RSA, G.1991.069

11
Still Life with Black Jug (1933), oil
56.5 cm by 127.1 cm
Sir William Gillies Bequest, 1973
RSA, G.1991.579

12
Mrs Gillies outside her birthplace in Kirriemuir (*c.* 1930), photograph
Sir William Gillies Bequest, 1973
RSA

13
Frontispiece of the compendium edition of *A Window in Thrums*, by J. M. Barrie (London: Hodder & Stoughton, 1903)
Illustration by W. B. Hole (1846–1917)
Image from Gillies' copy
Sir William Gillies Bequest, 1973
RSA

14
The pre-1947 welfare state: Mrs (Emma) Gillies (back left) and her four sisters, photograph
Title and identities by author
Sir William Gillies Bequest, 1973
RSA

15
From Another Window in Thrums (1928), by William McCance, oil
60 cm by 46 cm
Photograph of lithograph from untraced original
The Modern Scot, volume 1, no. 2, opposite p 16
National Library of Scotland, U.424
© Estate of William McCance
Private collection, untraced

16
Sketch of R. B. Haldane (*c.* 1910), by R. A. Dakers, pencil
27 cm by 20 cm
East Lothian Council

17
Tipperary (*c.* 1915), by Reginald Higgins
Photograph of lithograph from untraced original, dimensions unknown
Colour, May 1915, 14
National Library of Scotland

18
Knox Institute cadets (1907), photograph
Knox Academy, Haddington and East Lothian Council
East Lothian Council

19
Roll of Honour for Haddington Public School (1915), ink, watercolour, gouache
75.5 cm by 54.5 cm
East Lothian Council

20
The War Memorial procession in Haddington (1921), photograph
East Lothian Council

21
Anti-nuclear protestors march on the road to Aldermaston (1958), photograph (detail)
© Henry Grant Collection
Museum of London, 004548

22
Aldermaston Hadeans (nd, *c.* 1960), oil
50.5 cm by 62.5 cm
Date inferred from catalogue description – 'signed W. G. Gillies' and inscribed 'Comp Sketch "Aldermaston" Hadeans' and indistinctly dated on reverse; original uninspected by author
Image courtesy: Bonhams (13 September 2012 catalogue, lot 384)
Private collection, untraced

23
Ferniehirst (nd, *c.* 1959), oil
84 cm by 69 cm
Date from RSA (1970, 46) (see therein, RSA 1959, ce 244)
Reproduced from *The Studio*, January 1960, 15
Private collection, untraced

24
The Little Hut, Eddleston (1958), oil
77.5 cm by 64.5 cm
Date from SAC exhibition label verso
Private collection

25
Sunflower (nd, *c.* 1954), oil
91.7 cm by 76.5 cm
Date from SAC (1970, 45) (see therein, Scottish Gallery Festival Group Show 1954, ce 27)
Image courtesy: Bonhams (12 September 2013 catalogue, lot 74)
Fleming Collection

26
Les Fenêtres Sur la Ville no. 3 (2ème motif, 1ère partie) (1912), by Robert Delaunay, oil
79 cm by 64.5 cm
Dr Emil and Clara Friedrich-Jezler Bequest, 1973
Kunst Museum Winterthur, KV 1169

27
The White Lodge (1926), oil
83.5 cm by 104 cm
Date from SAC (1970, 15, ce 11)
Image courtesy: Sotheby's (L05130, 18 April 2005 catalogue, lot 143)
Private collection

28
The Beeches (1928), watercolour
28.5 cm by 42 cm
Bradford District Museums and Galleries, 1947-017

29
Trees and Coppice (1928, *c.* 1928), oil
89 cm by 124 cm
Possibly not shown until 1930; see the entry in the 'List of Works' in the *LWG* companion volume
Aberdeen City Council, Archives, Gallery and Museums, ABDAG010829 (purchased with assistance from the National Fund for Acquisitions, 1994)

30
Title page of the first British edition of *The Picture of Dorian Gray* by Oscar Wilde (1891)
Image courtesy: Bonhams

31
David Cleghorn Thomson (left) and Ruthven Todd in the Garret Studio, Edinburgh, 1935, photograph
NLS, acc.9234

32
St Sebastian (1920), by Eric Gill, Hoptonwood Stone
100.5 cm by 20.2 cm by 24.7 cm (56 kg)
Commissioned from the artist by André Raffalovich, 1919; bequeathed by him in 1934 to the Reverend Canon John Gray, who presented it in the same year to the Victoria and Albert Museum, in memory of André Raffalovich. Transferred from the V&A in 1983.
Photograph: Tate
Tate, T03745

33
Sisters Emma and Janet (nd, *c.* 1931), oil
76 cm by 60 cm
Also known as *Portrait of the Artist's Sisters, 1932* (SK 1998, illus 55)
Date based on first showing in early January 1932
Fletcher Collection
City Art Centre, Museums & Galleries Edinburgh, CAC1995L2/12

34
Portrait of Jenny (*c.* 1933–4), oil
115 cm by 90 cm
Date based on SK (1998, illus 58); see the entry in the 'List of Works' in the *LWG* companion volume
Photograph: RSA/Andy Phillipson
Private collection

35
Marjory Porter 1 (nd, *c.* 1935), oil
129 cm by 58.5 cm
For the date, see the entry in the 'List of Works' in the *LWG* companion volume
Sir William Gillies Bequest, 1973
RSA, G.1991.581

36
Marjory Porter 2 (*c.* 1935), oil
130 cm by 59 cm
For the date, see the entry in the 'List of Works' in the *LWG* companion volume
Sir William Gillies Bequest, 1973
RSA, G.1991.580

37
Veteran and vamp: Gillies and Margery Porter in *Parisian Café Society* (1938)
DVD of amateur film by unknown maker
<https://media.ed.ac.uk/media/Paris%20Cafe%20Society%20-%20Edinburgh%20College%20of%20Art%20staff%20amateur%20dramatics%201937_38/1_sboalsfz>
Edinburgh University Centre for Research Collections

38
Emma Gillies in parade costume, around 1928, photograph (detail)
Sir William Gillies Bequest, 1973
RSA

39
Portrait [of Emma] (*c.* 1933–4), oil
Dimensions unknown
Image from *The Listener*, 17 January 1934, 107
© Immediate Media
Untraced

40
Out of Great Tribulation (nd, *c.* 1930), by John Duncan, medium unknown
Dimensions unknown
Untraced
Reproduced from bw reproduction (photograph: Violet Banks) in Anon. (1932, 27)
NLS, MMSID: 9917774783804341

41
Family Group (nd, *c.* 1932–7), oil
Dimensions unknown
Known earlier under incorrect title (Portrait of Emma, Mrs Gillies and Janet, c. 1933); author's designation and date following catalogue of work's first exhibition (SSA 1937, ce 236)
Untraced
Image from bw photograph inscribed by Gillies
Sir William Gillies Bequest, 1973
RSA

42
Interior (1938), oil
127 cm by 173.5 cm
Sir William Gillies Bequest, 1973
RSA, G.1991.388

43
Interior (1938), oil (detail)
From [42] above

44
La Toilette de la Mère (1905), by Picasso, etching
23.5 cm by 17.8 cm
Raynal (1922, illus B); Richardson (1992, 335)
©Succession Picasso/DACS, London 2022

45
Still Life with Portrait Postcards (*c.* 1934), oil
82.6 cm by 65.9 cm
Sir William Gillies Bequest, 1973
RSA, G.1991.889

46
Poppies in a Yellow Vase (1934, *c.* 1936?), oil
91.5 cm by 61.5 cm
For the date, see the entry in the 'List of Works' in the *LWG* companion volume
Bequeathed by Dr R. A. Lillie, 1977
NGS, GMA 1821

47
Self-Portrait (1940), oil (detail)
From [5] above

48
Poppies and Cretonne Cloth (*c.* 1937–40), oil
91.5 cm by 71 cm
Bequeathed by Dr R. A. Lillie, 1977
NGS, GMA 1820

49
Studio Interior and Red Poppies (1939), oil
76 cm by 61 cm
Image by the owner
Private collection

50
Winter Landscape (nd, *c.* 1933), oil
85 cm by 101 cm
Auctioned as *Storm over East Lothian* (Christie's, 19 November 2004, lot 70); a photograph in the RSA (Gillies archive) is inscribed in Gillies' hand, 'Winter Landscape East Lothian'; almost certainly identical with 'Winter Landscape' (Society of Eight 1934, ce 66) (*The Scotsman*, 10 January 1934, 13); see the entry in the 'List of Works' in the *LWG* companion volume
Image courtesy: Perth Museum and Art Gallery
Private collection

51
Gardenstown (*c.* 1932, *c.* 1930–2), oil
76 cm by 90.8 cm
Date: possibly painted at the same time and as a variant of *Gardenstown* (*c.* 1930) [ni]
Sir William Gillies Bequest, 1973
RSA, G.1992.040

52
The Red House, Durisdeer (*c.* 1934), oil
76.7 cm by 90.2 cm
Sir William Gillies Bequest, 1973
RSA, G.1991.247

53
River at Cramond (nd, *c.* 1933), pencil
17.7 cm by 22.7 cm
Preparatory drawing for *Cramond* (1934; nd, *c.* 1933) [54 below]. The title is inscribed in Gillies' hand but 'River' has been misread as 'Ruin' in the archival description.
Sir William Gillies Bequest, 1973
RSA, G.1991.455

54
Cramond (1934; nd, *c.* 1933), oil
71 cm by 76 cm
Re-dating from Society of Eight (1934, ce 59)
Image courtesy: Scottish Gallery
Private collection

55
Dark Tree (1934), oil
61 cm by 76.5 cm
Oil version of *Scots Pine* (1934), watercolour [ni]
Image courtesy: Bonhams (3 December 2015 catalogue, lot 41)
Private collection

56
Reisebild[nis] (1918), by Paul Klee (1918, 150), watercolour
PKF 2000 entry 1997, where dimensions are not stated
Reproduced from Gillies' copy of Wedderkop (1920)
Sir William Gillies Bequest, 1973
RSA

57
Sketch for *Harbour* (1934, *c.* 1934) [58 and 64 below] (*c.* 1934), pencil
9 cm by 12 cm
Sir William Gillies Bequest, 1973
RSA, G.1991.820

58
Harbour (1934, *c.* 1934), oil
83.8 cm by 101.6 cm
For the date, see the entry in the 'List of Works' in the *LWG* companion volume
Image courtesy: Bonhams (12 December 2012 catalogue, lot 62)
Private collection

59
The Harbour (*c.* 1934–7), oil
76.5 cm by 91.5 cm
Bequeathed by Dr R. A. Lillie, 1977
NGS, GMA 1766

60
In Arniston (1935), watercolour
48 cm by 62 cm
Image courtesy: Fine Art Society
Private collection

61
Kairuan (1914), by Paul Klee (1914, 38), watercolour
PKF 2000 entry 1147, where dimensions are given as 22 cm by 23 cm
Reproduced from Gillies' copy of Wedderkop (1920)
Sir William Gillies Bequest, 1973
RSA

62
Skye Hills from [near] Morar (*c.* 1931), watercolour and gouache
37.6 cm by 55.8 cm
Bequeathed by Dr R. A. Lillie, 1977
NGS, GMA 1833

63
Drohender Schneesturm (1927), by Paul Klee (1927, 291), watercolour and coloured inks
49.9 cm by 31.6 cm
PKF 2001, entry 4505
Bequeathed by Miss Anna G. Blair in memory of Mr R. K. Blair, 1952
NGS, GMA 1015

64
Harbour (1934, *c.* 1934), oil
83.8 cm by 101.6 cm
For the date, see the entry in the 'List of Works' in the *LWG* companion volume
Image courtesy: Bonhams (12 December 2012 catalogue, lot 62)
Private collection

65
Ascending (1936), oil
98 cm by 74.6 cm
Sir William Gillies Bequest, 1973
RSA, G.1991.578

66
Simultaneous Contrasts: Sun and Moon (1912–13), by Robert Delaunay, oil
134.5 cm diameter
Museum of Modern Art (MoMA), New York (Mrs Simon Guggenheim Fund, 1.1954). Digital image, Museum of Modern Art, New York/Scala, Florence

67
Flags and Bunting (*c.* 1935), oil
76.2 cm by 65.7 cm
Sir William Gillies Bequest, 1973
RSA, G.1991.064

68
Untitled (*c.* 1935), oil
61 cm by 50.7 cm
Possibly titled *Balanced* (*The Scotsman*, 9 January 1935, 10); also known as *Abstract Composition* (*c.* 1935)
Sir William Gillies Bequest, 1973
RSA, G.1991.073

69
Morar Beach around 1998
Photograph by author

70
Rocks, Morar (*c.* 1933–4), watercolour
37 cm by 56 cm
Image courtesy: Scottish Gallery
Private collection

71
Drawing for Rocks and Sea (*c.* 1935) [72 below] (*c.* 1935), pencil
18.1 cm by 23.8 cm
Sir William Gillies Bequest, 1973
RSA, G.1991.102

72
Rocks and Sea (*c.* 1935), oil
64 cm by 76.5 cm
Sir William Gillies Bequest, 1973
RSA, G.1991.573

73
Picnic on the Beach, Morar I (*c.* 1932), pencil
17.9 cm by 22.8 cm
Sir William Gillies Bequest, 1973
RSA, G.1991.095

74
Picnic on the Beach, Morar II (*c.* 1932), pencil
17.9 cm by 22.8 cm
Sir William Gillies Bequest, 1973
RSA, G.1991.098

75
Rocks and Water, Morar (*c.* 1932–4), oil
74.8 cm by 110.8 cm
Sir William Gillies Bequest, 1973
RSA, G.1992.033

76
Highland Landscape [with] Suilven (1936), water-colour
51 cm by 63 cm
Fletcher Collection
Photograph: Antonia Reeve
City Art Centre, Museums and Galleries Edinburgh, CAC1995L2/7

77
West Coast Sunset (nd, *c.* 1936), watercolour
50.4 cm by 63.3 cm
Aberdeen City Council, Archives, Gallery and Museums, ABDAG008125

78
Threatening Storm (1936), watercolour
56.5 cm by 77 cm
Fletcher Collection
Photograph: Antonia Reeve
City Art Centre, Museums and Galleries Edinburgh, CAC1995L2/4

79
Resipol (1938, 1936?), watercolour
51 cm by 64 cm
Possible re-dating based on SSA (1936, ce 53)
Image courtesy: Bonhams (23 April 2009 catalogue, lot 25)
Private collection

80
Wester Ross (*c.* 1934, *c.* 1937?), watercolour
55 cm by 75 cm
Also known as *Laide Looking Towards Ben More c. 1934* and *West Coast 1937*. For possible re-dating, see the entry in the 'List of Works' in the *LWG* companion volume
Blackadder Houston Bequest, 2021
RSA

81
In Ardnamurchan (1936), watercolour
50.6 cm by 63 cm
Bequeathed by Dr R. A. Lillie, 1977
NGS, GMA 1723

82
Achgarve (*c.* 1937), ink and watercolour
56 cm by 77 cm
Perth Museum and Art Gallery, 1988.96

83
Untitled View of the Cleish Hills (nd, *c.* 1932), watercolour
51 cm by 63 cm
Previously known as *Perthshire Croft* (1948) (Lyon and Turnbull, 14 December 1999 catalogue, lot 15). For the new title and date, see the entry in the 'List of Works' in the *LWG* companion volume (and see also *The Cleish Hills near Dunfermline* (1932), by Alan Ronald, under 'Other Visual Works Named' in the present volume)
Image courtesy: Perth Museum and Art Gallery
Private collection

84
Autumn Moon (1934, *c.* 1934–7), oil
71 cm by 82 cm
For the date, see the entry in the 'List of Works' in the *LWG* companion volume
Image courtesy: Christie's (12 December 2014 catalogue, lot 151) ©2014 Christie's Images Limited
Private collection

85
Seifenblasen [Soap Bubbles] (1930), by George Grosz
Reproduced from Gillies' copy of *Das Neue Gesicht der Herrschenden Klasse* (Grosz 1930). © Estate of George Grosz, Princeton, NJ/DACS 2022.
Sir William Gillies Bequest, 1973
RSA

86
Reisende in Friedensourtikeln [loosely, Peace Emissaries] (1930), by George Grosz
Reproduced from Gillies' copy of *Das Neue Gesicht der Herrschenden Klasse* (Grosz 1930). © Estate of George Grosz, Princeton, NJ/DACS 2022.
Sir William Gillies Bequest, 1973
RSA

87
Winter Afternoon, Temple (*c.* 1942), watercolour, gouache, pen and ink
34.2 cm by 51.1 cm
Bequeathed by Dr R. A. Lillie, 1977
NGS, GMA 1873

88
Temple, Midlothian (nd, mid-1940s), oil
44.7 cm by 60 cm
Date based on Scottish Gallery stock number 8670 (label on reverse) which relates to 1946
Museums Sheffield, purchased 1966, VIS.3268

89
Rooks (nd, *c.* 1942), pen and ink
The New Alliance, December 1942, NLS, Y.197

90
Dusk at Letterfearn (*c.* 1947), oil
49 cm by 61.2 cm
Bequeathed by Dr R. A. Lillie, 1977
NGS, GMA 1791

91
Early Morning, Temple (*c.* 1942), oil
54 cm by 69 cm
Bequeathed by Dr R. A. Lillie, 1977
NGS, GMA 1860

92
Temple Village (*c.* 1969, *c.* 1940s), oil
50 cm by 60 cm
Re-dating follows SK (1998, 128)
Bequeathed by George and Isobel Neillands, 1988
Perth Museum and Art Gallery, 1988.93

93
The Red Squirrel (1941), oil
111.8 cm by 114.9 cm
Sir William Gillies Bequest, 1973
RSA, G.1991.387

94
Still Life with Shells and Flowers (Studio Window Still Life) (nd, *c.* 1947), oil
86.6 cm by 114.6 cm
Sir William Gillies Bequest, 1973
RSA, G.1991.267

95
Untitled Still Life (nd, *c.* 1950), oil
Dimensions unknown
Untraced work known only from photograph
Sir William Gillies Bequest, 1973
RSA

96
Still Life, Doyley (*c.* 1948), oil
83 cm by 102.8 cm
Gift from the Trustees of the Stuart Anderson Caird Bequest, 1948
McLean Museum and Art Gallery, 1977.849

97
Still Life (nd, *c.* 1950), oil
41 cm by 73.1 cm
Purchased with help of the Carnegie Dunfermline Trust and Local Museums Purchase Fund
Fife Cultural Trust on behalf of Fife Council, 1983
DUFDM:1983.4

98
Still Life, Lamplight (*c.* 1953), oil
61.5 cm by 73.5 cm
Bequeathed by Dr R. A. Lillie, 1977
NGS, GMA 1845

99
Melon on Platter (1950), oil
67.7 cm by 93 cm
George and Isobel Neillands Bequest, 1988, received 2001
NGS, GMA 4384

100
Two Jugs, Flowers and Conch Shell (*c.* 1952), oil
66.7 cm by 88.9 cm
Sir William Gillies Bequest, 1973
RSA, G.1991.534

101
Still Life (nd, *c.* 1954), oil
58.4 cm by 78.7 cm
Purchased from Aitken Dott and Son, 1955
Arts Council Collection, Southbank Centre, AC 355

102
Still Life, Yellow Jug and Striped Cloth (*c.* 1955), oil
112 cm by 114.7 cm
Diploma Work Deposit, 1956
RSA, 2000.104

103
Near Howgate (1951), watercolour and pencil
25.2 cm by 35.4 cm
Bequeathed by Dr R. A. Lillie, 1977
NGS, GMA 1772

104
The Pentlands, Mount Lothian (*c.* 1948, *c.* 1953), oil
42 cm by 79 cm
For the date, see the entry in the 'List of Works' in the *LWG* companion volume
Scottish Gallery 2003, ce 5
Photograph: RSA/Andy Phillipson
Private collection

105
Mount Lothian (nd, *c.* 1953), oil
61 cm by 113 cm
For the date, see SAC (1970, 44) (see therein, RSA 1953, ce 211) and ACGB (1954, ce 61)
Image courtesy: Lyon and Turnbull (1 December 2010 catalogue, lot 180)
Private collection

106
Empty Fields and Willows (1952), watercolour and pencil
Dimensions unknown
Image courtesy: Hawleys Auctioneers (Beverley) (7 June 2015 catalogue, lot 476)

107
Mauve Landscape (*c.* 1956, *c.* 1952), oil
61.5 cm by 74 cm
Date based on *Empty Fields and Willows* (1952) [106 above]
Sir William Gillies Bequest, 1973
RSA, G.1991.372

108
Fields and River (late 1950s), oil
64 cm by 87 cm
Bequeathed by Dr R. A. Lillie, 1977
NGS, GMA 1755

109
Wooded Hillside (1957), oil
95.7 cm by 80.5 cm
George and Isobel Neillands Collection, presented 1987
NGS, GMA 3326

110
Dusk (1959), oil
74 cm by 94.4 cm
Purchased with income from the Macdonald Bequest, 1959
Aberdeen City Council, Archives, Gallery and Museums, ABDAG 002244

111
Winter Thaw (1962), oil
74 cm by 91.5 cm
Date from photograph of Gillies at work on it (*Scottish Field*, October 1962)
Image courtesy: Perth Museum and Art Gallery
Private collection

112
Hill Pool (1960), oil
76 cm by 101 cm
Photograph: RSA/Andy Phillipson
Private collection

113
Garden, Winter Sunshine (1960), oil
102 cm by 152 cm
Details from Smith (1991, 88–9)
Image courtesy: Fine Art Society
Private collection

114
Interior of Studio, Temple (*c.* 1965), oil
97 cm by 122 cm
Date from SK (1998, illus 88)
Photograph: RSA/Andy Phillipson
Private collection

115
Winter Dusk (1961–3), oil
114.3 cm by 152.4 cm
Purchased 1965
Hunterian Art Gallery, University of Glasgow, GLAHA_43865

116
Still Life with Spider Plant (1966), oil
103.8 cm by 91.6 cm
Diploma Work Deposit, 1971
Royal Academy of Arts, 03/362

117
Still Life with Blue Gloves (1968), watercolour
65.4 cm by 91.4 cm
Presented by the Trustees of the Chantrey Bequest, 1969
Photograph: Tate
Tate, T01126

118
Still Life, Study in Grey (1968), oil
81 cm by 98 cm
Christie's, 31 October 2002, lot 126a, ex-catalogue
Image courtesy: Fine Art Society
Private collection

119
Between Raeshaw and Carcant on Heriot Water (*c.* 1968), oil
83.3 cm by 96.6 cm
Sir William Gillies Bequest, 1973
RSA, G. 1991.582

120
Kitchen Garden in Winter (1968–9), oil
79 cm by 107 cm
Photograph: RSA/Andy Phillipson
Private collection

121
Nairn Beach (*c.* 1970), oil
88.2 cm by 114.8 cm
Sir William Gillies Bequest, 1973
RSA, G.1992.048

122
Pittenweem (1947), watercolour, pen and ink
51 cm by 61 cm
Mundy Fine Art and Scottish Gallery 2016, 3
Image courtesy: Scottish Gallery
Private collection

123
Book launch of *Scottish Country* (1935), photograph
Ink annotation by David Cleghorn Thomson
NLS, acc.9234

124
March, Moorfoot (1951), watercolour and pencil
66.3 cm by 55 cm
Bequeathed by Dr R A Lillie, 1977
NGS, GMA 1806

125
St Monance (1949), watercolour, pen and ink
24 cm by 31 cm
Bonhams, 8 August 2004, lot 148
Image courtesy: Perth Museum and Art Gallery
Private collection

126
Balquhidder (nd, 1950s?), pen, ink and grisaille
55 cm by 77 cm
Dated by style alone
Image courtesy: Lyon and Turnbull (23 May 2003 catalogue, lot 85)
Private collection

127
Arniston Pond (nd, *c.* 1960), pen and ink
21 cm by 35 cm
Image courtesy: Scottish Gallery (2013 catalogue, 26)
Private collection

128
My Mother (1916), oil
34.1 cm by 29.2 cm
Sir William Gillies Bequest, 1973
RSA, G.1991.549

129
The Path by the Beeches, Haddington (1916), watercolour
22 cm by 25 cm
Image courtesy: Scottish Gallery (*Modern Masters* exhibition and catalogue, June 2013, 22–3)
Private collection, untraced

130
Spring (nd, *c.* 1921), oil
Dimensions unknown
Once owned by Gillies' painting companion, William F. Rayner
Image courtesy: Keys Auctioneers, Norwich (12 July 2013 catalogue, lot 193)
Private collection, untraced

131
Life Study (1922), oil
91.5 cm by 61.2 cm
Sir William Gillies Bequest, 1973
RSA, G.1991.065

132
Bathers (*c.* 1924), oil
58.7 cm by 73.8 cm
Sir William Gillies Bequest, 1973
RSA, G.1991.254

133
Inverness (1925), pencil and watercolour
25.4 cm by 35.6 cm
Sir William Gillies Bequest, 1973
RSA, G.1991.795

134
A Highland Farm (nd, *c.* 1925), watercolour
43 cm by 53 cm
Image courtesy: Lyon and Turnbull (4 December 2020 catalogue, lot 106)
Private collection

135
Autumnal Wooded Landscape (1925), pencil and watercolour
25.5 cm by 36 cm
Image courtesy: Lyon and Turnbull (15 January 2020 catalogue, lot 119)
Private collection

136
Trees on the Tyne, Haddington (*c.* 1924), oil
55.8 cm by 64.8 cm
Sir William Gillies Bequest, 1973
RSA, G.1992.028

137
Tréboul (a) (1927), pencil and watercolour
46.1 cm by 54.5 cm
For *Tréboul* (b) and (c), see the *LWG* companion volume
Sir William Gillies Bequest, 1973
RSA, G.1991.774

138
Mallaig (1928), oil
55.9 cm by 65.7 cm
Sir William Gillies Bequest, 1973
RSA, G.1992.031

139
Emma and Janet (*c.* 1925), oil
33.4 cm by 50.4 cm
Also, SK (1998, illus 48 fc, with title *Portrait of Emma and Janet, c. 1925*)
Sir William Gillies Bequest, 1973
RSA G.1991.547

140
Emma (nd, *c.* 1931), oil
60.5 cm by 52.5 cm
For the date, see the entry in the 'List of Works' in the *LWG* companion volume
Fletcher Collection
City Art Centre, Museums and Galleries Edinburgh, CAC1995L2/14

141
Piershill (nd, *c.* 1933), oil
33 cm by 67 cm
Image courtesy: Bonhams (4 December 2014 catalogue, lot 69)
Private collection

142
View from 162 Willowbrae Road, Edinburgh (1932), oil
65.6 cm by 76.1 cm
Sir William Gillies Bequest, 1973
RSA, G.1992.045

143
Landscape with House and Two Heads (*c.* 1930), oil
63.8 cm by 76.8 cm
Sir William Gillies Bequest, 1973
RSA, G.1991.378

144
Edinburgh Abstract (*c.* 1935–6), oil
75.3 cm by 112 cm
Date from SK (1998, illus 111)
Sir William Gillies Bequest, 1973
RSA, G.1991.265

145
The Dark Pond (*c.* 1934), watercolour
50.4 cm by 63.6 cm
SAC (1970, ce 143), where dated 1932
Bequeathed by Dr R. A. Lillie, 1977
NGS, GMA 1818

146
Pampas Grassies, Fearnan, Loch Tay (nd, *c.* 1935), oil
69 cm by 103.5 cm
For the date, see the entry in the 'List of Works' in the *LWG* companion volume
Image courtesy: Bonhams (23 April 2009 catalogue, lot 24)
Private collection

147
Head of the Glen (nd, mid- to late 1930s), watercolour
55.5 cm by 73.5 cm
Bequeathed by Dr R. A. Lillie, 1977
NGS, GMA 1770

148
The Highland Loch (nd, *c.* 1932–50), watercolour
41 cm by 56 cm
For the date, see the entry in the 'List of Works' in the *LWG* companion volume
Image courtesy: Christie's (28 May 1998 catalogue, lot 775) ©1998 Christie's Images Limited
Private collection, untraced

149
Kyleakin (1938), oil
18 cm by 26 cm
Image courtesy: Fine Art Society
Private collection, untraced

150
Summer Harbour (1938), oil
86 cm by 101 cm
Reproduced from Dickson (1974)
Private collection, untraced

151
Harbour, Anstruther (1937–8), watercolour
54 cm by 69 cm
Image courtesy: Scottish Gallery (2013 catalogue, ce 17)
Private collection, untraced

152
Boats at St Valéry en Caux (1938), watercolour
47 cm by 63 cm
Bonhams, 25 September 2014, lot 82
Image courtesy: Fine Art Society
Private collection

153
Flowers on a Sideboard (nd, *c.* 1941), oil
88 cm by 124 cm
Bequeathed by Dr R. A. Lillie, 1977
NGS, GMA 1759

154
The Blue Window (*c.* 1940), oil
122.1 cm by 91.3 cm
Sir William Gillies Bequest, 1973
RSA, G.1991.386

155
Anstruther from the Harbour (1946), oil
46 cm by 56 cm
Image courtesy: Scottish Gallery and Ewan Mundy Fine Art (2018 catalogue, ce 1)
Private collection, untraced

156
Fishing Boats, Anstruther Harbour (*c.* 1945), oil
48 cm by 60.5 cm
Bequeathed by Dr R. A. Lillie, 1977
NGS, GMA 1722

157
Arniston Woods, Midlothian (nd, *c.* 1944), oil
62.5 cm by 76 cm
Date from SSA (1944, ce 186) and *The Scotsman*, 20 October 1944, p. 7
Fletcher Collection
City Art Centre, Museums and Galleries Edinburgh, CAC1995L2/3

158
Sunlit Wood (nd, *c.* 1944), oil
44.7 cm by 85 cm
Purchased by Dumfriesshire Educational Trust, 1944
Gracefield Arts Centre, Dumfries, DGDET 98D

159
Interior, Temple Cottage (1951), oil
117 cm by 168 cm
Fletcher Collection
City Art Centre, Museums and Galleries Edinburgh, CAC1995L2/13

160
Studio Table (1951), oil
118 cm by 187 cm
Fletcher Collection
City Art Centre, Museums and Galleries Edinburgh, CAC1995L2/15

161
Still Life with Yellow Flowers (nd, *c.* 1953), oil
75.2 cm by 93 cm
Purchased from Aitken Dott and Son, 1958
Laing Art Gallery, Newcastle upon Tyne, TWCMS: G528

162
Apple with/on Red Platter (originally dated 1951 but *c.* 1949), oil
43 cm by 53 cm
Re-dating based on *c.* 1949 photo (NGS PGP 43.14), see [4]
Private collection

163
Peeblesshire Landscape (*c.* 1952), oil
69.2 cm by 84 cm
George and Isobel Neillands Collection, presented 1987
NGS, GMA 3327

164
Cliffs, Dalbeattie (1953), oil
63 cm by 74 cm
Image courtesy: Fine Art Society
With Royal Automobile Club in 1991, untraced

165
The Peebles Train (*c.* 1950), oil
46 cm by 56.5 cm
Bequeathed by Dr R. A. Lillie, 1977
NGS, GMA 1811

166
Shadowed Hill (1958), oil
89 cm by 112 cm
Christie's, 26 November 1997, lot 574
Image courtesy: Fine Art Society
Private collection, untraced

167
The Green Platter (nd, *c.* 1956), oil
67.7 cm by 65.2 cm
Gift from Mrs A. F. Stark through the Scottish Arts Council, 1984
Hunterian Art Gallery, Glasgow University, GLAHA 43861

168
Still Life with Black Fishes (1965), oil
78 cm by 104 cm
Scott Hay Collection, presented 1967
NGS, GMA 1039

169
Still Life on a Dark Ground (*c.* 1971), oil
84.8 cm by 105.1 cm
Sir William Gillies Bequest, 1973
RSA, GMA 1991.846

170
Family Bible of Gillies' maternal grandmother, Mary (née Dunn)
Sir William Gillies Bequest, 1973
RSA

171
The former District Lunatic Asylum, Haddington, in 2009
Photograph by author

172
John and Janet Gillies outside the family shop, *c.* 1899
Image: Scottish Photographic Touring Co., Glasgow
Sir William Gillies Bequest, 1973
RSA

173
Westlea, Meadow Park, Haddington (left) in 2009
Photograph by author

174
Opening of Gillies' manuscript account of his family, *c.* 1934
Image courtesy: Lothian Health Services Archive, Centre for Research Collections, Edinburgh University

175
Gillies, William Geissler and William Crozier (rear) in Florence in 1924
Unknown photographer
Image courtesy National Galleries of Scotland. NGS GMA A77/1 & 2

176
Janet and Emma Gillies (right) *c.* 1933
Unknown photographer
Sir William Gillies Bequest, 1973
RSA

177
Gillies at his Calidon Show, *c.* 1933
Unknown photographer
Sir William Gillies Bequest, 1973
RSA

178
Margery Porter, *c.* 1935
Unknown photographer
Sir William Gillies Bequest, 1973
RSA

179
Gillies in 1951 with *Studio Table no. 2* (1951)
Unknown photographer
Sir William Gillies Bequest, 1973
RSA

180
Mrs Gillies in her ninetieth year
Photograph by Paul Shillabeer © Estate of Paul Shillabeer
Sir William Gillies Bequest, 1973
RSA

181
Gillies in ECA Revel (fancy dress) as Tour de France cyclist in 1953
Unknown photographer
Sir William Gillies Bequest, 1973
RSA

182
The final costume: Gillies at Buckingham Palace in 1970
Title by author
Unknown photographer
Sir William Gillies Bequest, 1973
RSA

183
Gillies and Sir Norman Reid at the 1970 RSA Gillies exhibition
Unknown photographer
Sir William Gillies Bequest, 1973
RSA

184
Gillies' posthumous studio
Photograph by Robin Philipson PPRSA
Sir William Gillies Bequest, 1973
RSA

185
'Trees and [with] Dense Foliage' (nd, 1931–40), pencil
22.8 cm by 17.8 cm
Sir William Gillies Bequest, 1973
RSA G.1991.129

Other Visual Works Named

In approximate date order; by William Gillies unless stated otherwise. Dimensions are height by width to nearest centimetre, rounding up. Works from auction or other vendors are presumed to be in private collections unless stated otherwise. Almost all works in oil in UK public collections can already be viewed on the website of ARTUK, as can some works on paper. But readers should also consult the websites of local and national institutions, like the Royal Scottish Academy (RSA) and the National Galleries of Scotland (NGS), where comprehensive coverage of works in all media will continue to spread.

Las Meninas (1656), by Velásquez, oil
318 cm by 276 cm
Museo del Prado, Madrid

The Disasters of War (1810–20), by Francisco Goya, series of 82 intaglios
Various dimensions
Various locations

The Pilgrimage to San Isidro (1819–23), by Francisco Goya, oil
140 cm by 438 cm
Museo del Prado, Madrid

A Corner of Kirrie (1912), by Gillies with William Ryle Smith, watercolour
23 cm by 17 cm
Smith (1991, 12); SK (1998, illus 4)
RSA

Fenêtres Simultanées (1912–14), series of 18 works by Robert Delaunay, oil
Various dimensions
Hughes (2014, illus 1.10–25, 1.28, 1.29)
Various locations

The Bathers (1915), by Edvard Munch, oil
100 cm by 135 cm
Woll (2009, 1151)
Munch Museum, Oslo

Figure Composition (*c.* 1922), medium unknown
Dimensions unknown
SK (1998, illus 49)
Edinburgh College of Art, Prospectus, 1925–6
Untraced

Lady [Woman] in Grey (1924–5), by Edvard Munch, oil
180 cm by 59 cm
Woll (2009, 1507)
Munch Museum, Oslo

Bohemian Wedding (1925–6), by Edvard Munch, oil
138 cm by 181 cm
Woll (2009, 1523)
Munch Museum, Oslo

Hovering Before Rising (1930, 220 (S10)), by Paul Klee, oil
84 cm by 84 cm
PKF 2001, entry 5339
Paul Klee Foundation Art Museum, Berne

Gardenstown (*c.* 1930), oil
24 cm by 36 cm
RSA, G.1991.262

The Cleish Hills near Dunfermline (1932), by Alan Ronald, watercolour
28 cm by 38 cm
Swann and Turner, Jedburgh (22 March 2012 catalogue, lot 9)

Two Pots, Saucer and Fruit (1933, *c.* 1933?), oil
31 cm by 51 cm
The 1933 date in SAC (1970, ce 19) was possibly attributed by Gillies around 1969
RSA, G.1991.546

St Monan's (*c.* 1934), oil
47 cm by 37 cm
Bonhams (20 August 2004 catalogue, lot 1253)

Scots Pine (1934), watercolour
38 cm by 50 cm
Bonhams (25 August 2006 catalogue, lot 1119)

Marjory Porter 3 (*c.* 1935), oil
91.2 cm by 76.5 cm
For the date, see the entry in the 'List of Works' in the *LWG* companion volume
Sir William Gillies Bequest, 1973
RSA, G.1991.845

Landscape with Road and Sun (nd, *c.* 1935), oil
76 cm by 71 cm
RSA, G.1991.256

La Condition Humaine (1935), by René Magritte, oil
Version identified from descriptions in *The Scotsman*, 21 May 1936, 9, and 28 May 1936, 13
54 cm by 73 cm
NWHCM : 1995.88.2 : F
Norfolk Museums Service

Kyleakin (*c.* 1936), watercolour
51 cm by 64 cm
Dickson (1974, illus 22)
Private collection

The Clachan of Laide (*c.* 1930, *c.* 1937), watercolour
55 cm by 76 cm
Kirkcaldy Museum and Art Gallery (1996, 58–9, illus fc)
Kirkcaldy Museum and Art Gallery

Guernica (1937), oil, by Picasso
349 cm by 777 cm
Museo Reina Sofia, Madrid

Harbour with Warning Light (1937), by John Maxwell, watercolour
51 cm by 63 cm
Long (1998, plate 15, illus fc)
Aberdeen City Council, Archives, Gallery and Museums

Acharacle (nd, *c.* 1938), oil and pencil
22 cm by 47 cm
Truncated version of *Acharacle* (1938) [below] from which dating is derived
Phillips (25 August 2001 catalogue, lot 1085, illus fc)

Acharacle (1938), watercolour
53 cm by 74 cm
SAC (1970a, ce 160, illus fc opposite p. 32)
Untraced; possibly destroyed

Highland Hamlet (nd, late 1930s), watercolour
49 cm by 62 cm
Date from style and location
Sotheby's (7 March 2007 catalogue, lot 352, illus fc)

Temple Village (early 1940s), oil
61 cm by 92 cm
NGS, GMA 1870

Landscape, Temple (nd, *c.* 1942), oil
52 cm by 64 cm
Date from Hyslop purchase from Scottish Gallery (stock: 8072)
ARTUK ABDAG010733
Aberdeen City Council, Archives, Gallery and Museums

Temple, Midlothian (1942), watercolour
50 cm by 63 cm
Bonhams (12 December 2012 catalogue, lot 68)

Midlothian Village (*c.* 1944, *c.* 1942–4), oil
62 cm by 92 cm
Date based on features shared with *Landscape, Temple* (nd, *c.* 1942)
NGS, GMA 1803

Still Life with Roses (*c.* 1943), oil
67 cm by 56 cm
NGS, GMA 1849

Temple (mid-1940s), oil
57 cm by 69 cm
NGS, GMA 1858

Thorn Tree (*c.* 1945), by Graham Sutherland, oil
Crucifixion (*c.* 1946), by Graham Sutherland, oil
Deposition (*c.* 1946), by Graham Sutherland, oil
The 1948 SSA Edinburgh catalogue and *The Scotsman* review (8 October 1948, 4) do not uniquely identify the exhibited versions. Possibilities are: *Thorn Tree* (1945–6) (Hammer 2005, Cat. 77; ARTUK P74); *Crucifixion* (1946) (Hammer 2005, Fig. 11); *Crucifixion* (1946) (ARTUK N05774); *Crucifixion* (1947) (ARTUK CHCPH 01555); *The Deposition* (1946) (ARTUK PD.969-1963); *The Deposition* (1947) (ARTUK MCMCA/38)

Still Life in Lamplight (1949), oil
92 cm by 78 cm
RSA, G.1991.570

Eildon (1949), oil
32 cm by 47 cm
Arts Council Collection, South Bank Centre, AC 211

Shiplaw Farm (1950), ink and watercolour
36 cm by 56 cm
Dickson (1974, illus 26, bw)
Scottish Gallery (2013, ce 5), where titled *Shiphorn Farm*

Study for Interior, Temple Cottage (1951) [159 above] (1951), watercolour
25 cm by 32 cm
SK (1998, illus 64)
RSA

Untitled Landscape (nd, *c.* 1952), oil
Dimensions unknown
Un-accessioned photo, GA private collections
RSA

Studio Table no. 2 (1951), oil
Dimensions unknown
Untraced

Still Life, Blue and Brown (1952), oil
99 cm by 137 cm
Accession 2994
Kelvingrove Art Gallery and Museum

Summer Stream (1954), oil
47 cm by 57 cm
ARTUK T00007; no ARTUK image available (as at 15 April 2023)
See Tate website for bw image; also, analogue photo, fc (BAB2/ Box 3 Lillie/3.7, RSA)
Tate, London

The Garden, Temple, Winter Moon (nd, *c.* 1961), oil
94 cm by 121 cm
Date from SK (1998, illus 143)
Paisley Museum and Art Galleries, A0403

The Garden, Temple, Winter Moon (1962, *c.* 1961), pencil and wash
26 cm by 36 cm
Date based on RSA Gillies Picture Lists, 36
Mundy Fine Art and Scottish Gallery (2005, ce 14)

Studio Interior, Dusk (1964), watercolour
66 cm by 102 cm
Lyon and Turnbull (9 June 2016 catalogue, lot 36)

Early Spring (nd, mid-1960s?), oil
97 cm by 123 cm
Fleming Collection, FWAF/RF 153

Bright Little Objects (*c.* 1965), oil
Dimensions unknown
SAC (1970, 48) (see therein, RSA 1965, ce 153)
Untraced

Lit Window, Early Dusk (nd, *c.* 1966), oil
92 cm by 120 cm
Lillie Art Gallery, Milngavie, MINAG: 1987.4

Large Still Life (nd, *c.* 1966), oil
92 cm by 122 cm
Edinburgh College of Art, University of Edinburgh, PCF0072

Interior Winter (nd, *c.* 1966), oil
90 cm by 76 cm
Lillie Art Gallery, Milngavie, MINAG: 1984.31

Still Life on a Cupboard (*c.* 1966), oil
82 cm by 99 cm
Royal Academy of Arts, 03/941

Temple, Dusk (1968), oil
87 cm by 101 cm
City Art Centre, Museums and Galleries Edinburgh, CAC1968/1

Trees Rosebery (*c.* 1970), oil
69 cm by 83 cm
RSA, G.1991.371

References

Ahdémar, Jean (1941) *Goya*, Paris: Bibliothèque Française des Arts [copy in GA].

Anon. (1932) *Contemporary Scots Art* (forty articles reprinted from the *Scots Observer* of 1932), Hamilton: Hamilton Advertiser.

Arts Council of Great Britain (1954) Catalogue for the exhibition 'Paintings, Watercolours and Drawings by W. G. Gillies and John Maxwell', London.

Barns-Graham, Wilhelmina (1994) The British Library Board <http://sounds.bl.uk> C466/34/01 F4747 Side A, transcript.

Barrie, James M. (1903) *A Window in Thrums*, London: Hodder & Stoughton [in a version with Barrie's *When a Man's Single* and *My Lady Nicotine*].

Benjamin, Walter (1936) 'The storyteller', in *Orient und Okzident*, translated in Walter Benjamin (1970) *Illuminations* (edited, and with an introduction, by Hannah Arendt), London: Cape, 83–4.

Colour (1915) London: William Dawson & Sons, May.

Davie, George Elder (1961) *The Democratic Intellect: Scotland and Her Universities in the Nineteenth Century*, Edinburgh: Edinburgh University Press.

Dickson, Thomas Elder (1939) 'In defence of Scottish art', *Scottish Educational Journal*, 5 May, 494–6.

Dickson, Thomas Elder (1960) 'W. G. Gillies', *The Studio*, 159, no. 801, January, 14–18.

Dickson, Thomas Elder (1974) *W. G. Gillies*, Edinburgh: Edinburgh University Press.

Ecob, Russell and Burnhill, Peter (2023) 'Statistical examination of William Gillies' still life paintings', unpublished paper, <royalscottishacademy.org>.

Elder Dickson *see* Dickson

Films of Scotland and Scottish Arts Council (1970) *Still Life with Honesty*, directed by Bill Forsyth and Mark Singleton from an original idea by R. Henderson Blyth in collaboration with Mike Catto; Ogam Films; Scottish Screen Archive (now Scotland's Moving Image Archive), 2686.

Findlay, Jean (2014) *Chasing Lost Time. The Life of C. K. Scott Moncrieff: Soldier, Spy and Translator*, London: Chatto & Windus.

Fussell, Paul (1975) *The Great War and Modern Memory* (25th anniversary edition published 2000), Oxford: Oxford Publishing.

Garlake, Margaret (1998) *New Art New World: British Art in Postwar Society*, New Haven and London: Yale University Press.

Grosz, George (1930) *Das Neue Gesicht der Herrschenden Klasse*, Berlin: Malik Verlag.

Hammer, Martin (2005) *Graham Sutherland: Landscapes, War Scenes, Portraits 1924–50*, London: Scala Publishers and Dulwich Picture Gallery.

Housman, Laurence (1924) *Trimblerigg: A Book of Revelation*, London: Cape.

Hughes, Gordon (2014) *Resisting Abstraction: Robert Delaunay and Vision in the Face of Modernism*, Chicago: University of Chicago Press.

Hyman, Timothy (1994) 'The Scottish Bonnard', *Times Literary Supplement*, 9 September, 17 (issue 4771).

Jones, David (1937) *In Parenthesis*, London: Faber & Faber.

Jones, David (1958) 'The utile', reprinted in David Jones (1973) *Epoch and Artist* (edited by Harman Grisewood), London: Faber & Faber, 180–5.

King, James (1990) *The Last Modern: A Life of Herbert Read*, London: Weidenfeld & Nicolson.

Kirkcaldy Museum and Art Gallery (1996) *Catalogue of the Fine Art Collection*.

Klee, Paul (1969) 'Towards a theory of form-production', in Jürge Spiller (ed.), *Paul Klee Notebooks, Volume 1: The Thinking Eye*, London: Lund Humphries; also <https://www.archive.org/details/paulkleethinking01klee>.

Long, Philip (1994) Catalogue for the exhibition 'William Gillies: Watercolours of Scotland', 7 July – 25 September, National Galleries of Scotland, Edinburgh.

Long, Philip (1998) Catalogue for the exhibition 'John Maxwell 1905–1962', 21 November 1998 – 14 February 1999, National Galleries of Scotland, Edinburgh.

MacDiarmid, Hugh (1930) 'Frae Anither Window in Thrums', in *To Circumjack Cencrastus*, Edinburgh: Blackwood, 91–149.

Mackenzie, Compton (1913) *Sinister Street*, London: Martin Secker.

Maclaren, Ian (1895) 'Domsie', in *Beside the Bonnie Brier Bush* (fourth edition), London: Hodder & Stoughton, 3–53.

Macmillan, Duncan (1998) 'The stillest life', *The Scotsman* (Arts), 3 August, 11.

Macmillan, Duncan (2007) 'George Davie: appreciation', *The Scotsman*, 5 April, 33.

McPherson, Andrew (in press) *The Life, Times and Work of William Gillies 1898–1973*, Edinburgh: Edinburgh University Press.

Mundy Fine Art and Scottish Gallery (2005) Catalogue for the exhibition 'William Gillies and the Edinburgh School', 5–10 June, London.

Mundy Fine Art and Scottish Gallery (2016) Catalogue for the exhibition 'William Gillies and the Edinburgh School', 16–20 May, Edinburgh and London.

Nash, Paul (1922) *Places*, London: Heinemann.

New Alliance (1942) December, Edinburgh: New Alliance.

NIST/SEMATECH (2022) *e-Handbook of Statistical Methods* <http://www.itl.nist.gov/div898/handbook/> consulted 29 December 2022.

Paul Klee Foundation (2000) *Paul Klee: Catalogue Raisonné*, London: Thames & Hudson, vol. 2 (1913–18).

Paul Klee Foundation (2001) *Paul Klee: Catalogue Raisonné*, London: Thames & Hudson, vol. 5 (1927–30).

Proust, Marcel (1941) *Remembrance of Things Past*, translation by Charles Scott Moncrieff of *À La Recherche du Temps Perdu*, London: Chatto & Windus.

Raffalovich, Marc-André (1896) *Uranisme et Unisexualité: Étude sur différentes manifestations de l'instinct sexuel*, Lyon: Storck; Paris: Masson & Cie.

Raynal, Maurice (1922) *Picasso*, Paris: Les Éditions G. Crès & Cie.

Read, Herbert (1951) *Contemporary British Art*, Harmondsworth: Pelican.

Richardson, John (1992) *A Life of Picasso: Vol. I, 1881–1906*, London: Pimlico.

Scott, Sir Walter (1821) *The Monastery*, Paris: J. Smith & D. Glashin, vol. 1.

Scottish Arts Council (1970) Catalogue for the exhibition 'W. G. Gillies Retrospective Exhibition', 7–28 February, Edinburgh.

Scottish Bookman (1935) 1, 1, September, Edinburgh: Scottish Contacts Service.

Scottish Gallery (2003) Catalogue for the exhibition 'Gillies: Paintings, Watercolours and Drawings', 7–30 April, Edinburgh.

Scottish Gallery (2013) Catalogue for the exhibition 'William Gillies: Works on Paper', 5–30 January, Edinburgh.

Scottish Gallery and Ewan Mundy Fine Art (2018) Catalogue for exhibition, 14–18 May, London.

Scott-Moncrieff, George (ed.) (1935) *Scottish Country*, London: Wishart Books.

Smith, Sidney Goodsir (1961) 'Portrait of the artist 2 – W. G. Gillies, Principal of Edinburgh College of Art', *The Scotsman*, 29 April, 5.

Smith, Sidney Goodsir (1965) 'Drawings by W. G. Gillies', *Connoisseur*, vol. 158, no. 636, February.

Smith, W. Gordon (1991) *W. G. Gillies: A Very Still Life*, Edinburgh: Atelier.

Soden, Joanna and Keller, Victoria (1998) *William Gillies*, Edinburgh: Canongate.

Spalding, Frances (2011) *Lives in Art: John Piper, Myfanwy Piper*, Oxford: Oxford University Press.

SSA (Society of Scottish Artists) (1936) Catalogue for exhibition, 28 November 1936–9 January 1937, Edinburgh.

SSA (1937) Catalogue for exhibition, 10 December 1937–22 January 1938, Edinburgh.

SSA (1944) Catalogue for exhibition, 14 October–20 November, Edinburgh.

SSA (1948) Catalogue for fifty-fourth exhibition, 8 October 1948– [closing date not stated], Edinburgh.

Sutherland, Graham (1942) 'Welsh sketch book', *Horizon*, vol. 28, 225–36.

Waugh, Evelyn (1928) *Decline and Fall*, London: Chapman & Hall.

Wedderkop, H. von (1920) *Paul Klee*, Leipzig: Verlag von Klinkhardt & Biermann.

Wilde, Oscar (1891) *The Picture of Dorian Gray*, London: Ward Lock.

Woll, Gerd (2009) *Edvard Munch Complete Paintings: Catalogue Raisonné*, London: Thames & Hudson; vol. 3, 1909–1920; vol. 4, 1921–1944.

Wood, Henry ('Harry') Harvey (2016) *To Make a World*, London: private publication [copies in NLS and SNGMA].

Select Bibliography

Braverman, Lewis E. and Utiger, R. D. (eds) (2005) *Werner & Ingbar's The Thyroid: A Fundamental and Clinical Text*, Philadelphia: Lippincott, Williams and Wilkins.

Dickson, Thomas Elder (1960) 'W. G. Gillies', *The Studio*, 159, no. 801, January, 14–18.

Dickson, Thomas Elder (1970) 'W. G. Gillies', in catalogue for 'W. G. Gillies Retrospective Exhibition', 7–28 February, Scottish Arts Council, Edinburgh, pp. 5–9.

Dickson, Thomas Elder (1974) *W. G. Gillies*, Edinburgh: Edinburgh University Press.

Dilworth, Thomas (2017) *David Jones: Engraver, Soldier, Painter, Poet*, London: Jonathan Cape.

Films of Scotland and Scottish Arts Council (1970) *Still Life with Honesty*, directed by Bill Forsyth and Mark Singleton, from an original idea by R. Henderson Blyth in collaboration with Mike Catto; Ogam Films; Scottish Screen Archive (now Scotland's Moving Image Archive), 2686.

Fussell, P. (2000) *The Great War and Modern Memory* (25th anniversary edition; originally published 1975), Oxford: Oxford Publishing.

Long, Philip (1994) Catalogue for the exhibition 'William Gillies: Watercolours of Scotland', 7 July – 25 September, National Galleries of Scotland, Edinburgh.

McArthur, Euan (2013) *Scotland, CEMA and the Arts Council, 1919–1967, Background, Politics and Visual Art Policy*, Aldershot: Ashgate.

Macmillan, Duncan (1994) *Scottish Art in the 20th Century*, Edinburgh: Mainstream.

Macmillan, Duncan (1998) 'The Stillest Life', *The Scotsman*, 3 August 1998, 11.

McPherson, Andrew (in press) *The Life, Times and Work of William Gillies 1898–1973*, Edinburgh: Edinburgh University Press.

Normand, Tom (2000) *The Modern Scot: Modernism and Nationalism in Scottish Art 1928–1955*, Aldershot: Ashgate.

RSA Collections <collections.royalscottishacademy.org>.

Smith, W. Gordon (1991) *W. G. Gillies: A Very Still Life*, Edinburgh: Atelier.

Soden, Joanna and Keller, Victoria (1998) *William Gillies*, Edinburgh: Canongate.

Strang, Alice (2017) Catalogue for the exhibition 'A New Era: Scottish Modern Art 1900–1950', 2 December 2017 – 10 June 2018, National Galleries of Scotland, Edinburgh.

Indicative Primary Sources

Auction catalogues: Bonhams, Christie's, Lyon and Turnbull, Phillips, Sotheby's and other houses.

Barns-Graham Archive, University of St Andrews: catalogues, photos and papers.

Edinburgh Central Library: catalogues of the SSA and the Society of Eight.

Edinburgh College of Art, Centre for Research Collections, University of Edinburgh: Minutes of the Board of Governors; Annual Reports of the Board of Management; Student Record Books; Diploma examination records and adjudications; returns to the Scottish Education Department; Letter Book; press cuttings; film and ceramics.

Exchanges with some twenty colleagues, students, friends and associates of the artist.

General Register Office (Scotland): <www.scotlandspeople.gov.uk>; Statutory Records of Births, Marriages and Deaths; Valuation Rolls.

Gillies archive, RSA: paintings and drawings, papers, photos, film, ceramics and artefacts; RSA exhibition records and other catalogues <collections.royalscottishacademy.org>.

John Gray Centre, Haddington and East Lothian Council: *Haddingtonshire Courier*; papers and artworks of R. A. Dakers; *Roll of Honour for Haddington Public School.*

Knox Academy, Haddington and East Lothian Council: Log Books, Registers of the Infant, Junior and Secondary departments of the Knox Institute; Log Book, and Register of Admissions and Progress … of the Haddington Public School; photo of cadet corps.

Lothian Health Services Archive, Centre for Research Collections, University of Edinburgh: Gillies manuscript, 'The Family', and records of Emma Smith Gillies (LHB '2 Craighouse Box 5'); records of the Haddingtonshire District (Herdmanflat) Lunatic Asylum.

Munch Museum, Oslo: letters, photos, cuttings for SSA exhibition, 1931–2; artworks.

National Archives of Scotland: Sasines Register; Knox Institute examination records.

National Galleries of Scotland: oil paintings and works on paper <www.nationalgalleries.org>; records of acquisition, holdings and exhibition; Minutes of the Society of Scottish Artists; press cuttings; and papers from GMA A23 (Gillies and MacTaggart), GMA A46 (William Munro), GMA A77 (Crozier), GMA A105 (Firth), and GMA A125 (Gillies and Maxwell).

National Library of Scotland: papers of Thomas Elder Dickson and W. G. Gillies (acc.6308, acc.13859); Robert A. Lillie (dep.316); William MacTaggart (acc.8636), Marc-André Raffalovich (acc.3868, 4112, 4630, 5287, 13342); George and Ann Scott-Moncrieff (ms.26969, mss.26973); David Cleghorn Thomson (acc.9234, 12491); Ruthven Todd (ms.26836, mss.26848); Scotland's Moving Image Archive.

Public Catalogue Foundation: <artuk.org>; oil paintings.

Scottish Gallery (Aitken Dott): Stock Book 1920–45; Picture Stock Book 1946–79; Ledgers; images.

The Scotsman newspaper: digital archive <http://archive.scotsman.com>.

Victoria and Albert Museum: Papers of the Council for the Encouragement of Music and the Arts; papers of the Arts Council of Great Britain and its Scottish Committee.

Image Credits

I am extremely grateful to the following for invaluable assistance with the location and provision of images and for permissions to reproduce them (for acknowledgement of individual images, see Details of Illustrations): Aberdeen City Council, Archives, Gallery and Museums; Arts Council Collection, Southbank Centre; Blackadder Houston Trust; Bonhams; Bradford District Museums and Galleries; British Library Board; Christie's; City Art Centre, Museums & Galleries Edinburgh; East Lothian Council; Edinburgh University, Centre for Research Collections; Edinburgh University Press; Estate of George Grosz, Princeton, NJ/DACS; Estate of Lida Moser; Fife Cultural Trust on behalf of Fife Council; Fine Art Society, Edinburgh and London; Fleming Collection; the family of William Geissler; Gracefield Arts Centre; Hawleys Auctioneers; Hunterian Art Gallery, University of Glasgow; Immediate Media; Keys Auctioneers; Knox Academy Haddington; Kunst Museum Winterthur; Laing Art Gallery; Lyon and Turnbull; the Estate of William McCance; McLean Museum and Art Gallery; Museum of London; Museum of Modern Art (MoMA), New York; Museums Sheffield; National Galleries of Scotland; National Library of Scotland; Perth Museum and Art Gallery; Royal Academy of Arts; Royal Scottish Academy; Scotland's Moving Image Archive; Scottish Gallery (Aitken Dott); Sotheby's; Succession Picasso/DACS, London; Tate; *The Studio*; and ten individual owners who have chosen to remain anonymous. I am also grateful to photographers Chris Park, Andy Phillipson and Antonia Reeve, and to others whom we regret that we have not been able to identify.

Permissions

I gratefully acknowledge permissions to quote extracts from copyright material granted by the following: British Library Sound Collection (Artists' Lives) for W. Barns-Graham interview transcript; Edinburgh University Press for T. Elder Dickson *W. G. Gillies*; Faber and Faber for David Jones, 'The Utile'; Scotland's Moving Image Archive for extracts from Ogam Films, *Still Life with Honesty*; Oxford Publishing for Paul Fussell, *The Great War and Modern Memory*; HarperCollins for *Illuminations* by Walter Benjamin (translated by Harry Zohn, English translation copyright © 1968 by Harcourt Brace Jovanovitch, Inc., originally published in Germany by Suhrkamp Verlag, Frankfurt a.M. copyright © 1955 by Suhrkamp Verlag, Frankfurt a.M., used by permission of HarperCollins Publishers); Christopher Todd for extract from unpublished ms by Ruthven Todd.

Acknowledgements

I am indebted to many individuals and institutions: Griffin Coe, Jennifer Melville, Ann Steed (Aberdeen Art Gallery); Michelle Gait, Olivia McIntosh, Mary Pryor (Aberdeen University); the staff of Angus County Archives; Alessandra Scapin (Arts Council England); Karen Spicher (Beinecke Library, Yale University); the Blackadder Houston Trust; Caroline Speare (Bradford College); Bethany Hamblen (Balliol College, Oxford); Chris Brickley (Bonhams); Camilla MacKay (Bryn Mawr); Wull of the Discussion Forum, Cameronians Museum, Hamilton; Denys Wilcox (Court Gallery); Mr Flett (City Archives, Dundee); the staff of the Wellgate Library, Dundee; Matthew Jarron, Euan McArthur (Dundee University); Sheila Asante, Kate Maynard (East Lothian Council); David Patterson, Helen Scott (City Art Centre, Edinburgh); the late Gordon Brennan, Logan Sisley, Wilson Smith, Marion Watson, Michael Wood (Edinburgh College of Art); Denise Anderson, Tricia Boyd, Laura Brouard, Grant Buttars, Scott Docking, Alice Doyle, Paul Fleming, Rachel Hosker, Stephanie Kelly, Ishbel Mackinnon, Emma Smith, Stephen Willis (Centre for Research Collections, Edinburgh University); Roger Davidson, David McCrone, Duncan Macmillan, Lindsay Paterson, Charles Raab, the late Roger Tarr (Edinburgh University); Ellen McBride (EMB Graphics, Aberfeldy); Laura at Forfar Public Library; Patrick Bourne, Jamie Mackinnon and Emily Walsh (Fine Art Society); the Friends of the RSA; Alistair Tough (Greater Glasgow and Clyde Health Board Archive); the Head Teacher, King's Meadow Primary School, Haddington, 2008; Sarah Rodriguez (Highland Council Archives); Ken Milne, Will Plain (Knox Academy, Haddington); Craig Statham (formerly Local History Centre, Haddington); Aurora Mackintosh, Christine Sharp (Kirriemuir Public Library); Louise Williams of Lothian Health Services Archive; Ken at the Local Studies Centre of Midlothian Council; Terry Humby, Danielle Russell, Terry Tuey (McPherson Library, Victoria University, Canada); the staff of Montrose Public Library; Giorgia Bottinelli (Norfolk Museums Service); Petra Pettersen and Lasse Jacobsen (Munch Museum, Oslo); Stefanie Metze and the staff of the National Archives of Scotland; Kenneth Dunn, Heidi Egginton, Sally Harrower, Diarmid Ross, Robbie Mitchell, Amy Todman and many others (National Library of Scotland); Maria Devaney (Perth Museum and Art Gallery); Jetta Goldie (Registers of Scotland); Sonja Erikssson (Royal College of Art, London); Nicola Ireland, Thom Laycock, Robin Rodger (Royal Scottish Academy); Maia Sheridan (Special Collections, St Andrews University); Christina Jansen, Guy Peploe, the late Robin McClure, Tommy Zyw (Scottish Gallery (Aitken Dott)); Lucy Askew, Catriona Gourlay, Philip Love, Kirstie Meehan, Paul Quast, Ann Simpson, Alice Strang (Scottish National Gallery of Modern Art); Robert Winckworth (Slade School of Art); Sarah Fairclough (Smith Museum and Art Gallery, Stirling); Barrie Duncan (South Lanarkshire Museum Service); Simon Marshall (Stone Gallery); Eva White (Victoria and Albert Museum); and the following individuals: Ivar Aavatsmark, Laila Aavatsmark, Sandra Affleck, Nick Ambrose, Louise Ambrose, George Angus, Simon Aylwin, the late Barbara Balmer, Charles Boyle, Kenneth Brien, Sarah Brownlie, the late William Buchanan, Eileen Burke, the late Derek Clarke, Gail Corbett-Smith, James Coxson,

Betty Douglas, Kenneth and Eve Dingwall, Mike and Evelyn Dunsmore, Richard Ewing, Thelma Ewing, Rob and Roddy Fairley, Kate Fanning, the late Jack Firth, Alan Fraser, Theresa Froehlich and David Godfrey, the late Alison Geissler, Paul and Betty Geissler, Erik Geissler, the late Douglas Hall, Matilda Hall, the late James Henderson senior, the late James Henderson junior, Christine Henderson, Anna Hopkinson, Meaghan Hopkinson, Joan Hughes, Heather Jack, Ronnie Jack, Eleanor John, Victoria Keller, Arabella Lewis, Ken Lochead, Monica Lorimer, Alan Lucas, Hamish McBride, The McCance family, Keith Macdonald, the late George Mackie, Peter Main, Ben McPherson, Alexander Moffat, Duncan Nimmo, Tom Normand, Victoria Peterkin, Diana Lady Philipson, Catherine Pike, the late Perpetua Pope, Martine Foltier Pugh, Gillian Raab, the family of the late Norman Reid, Albert Robson, Eileen Scott-Moncrieff, Robert Smith, Mark Strachan, Keith and Lucy Taylor, Melissa Terras, the late Margaret Thomas, Tony Toft, Tom and Alison Veitch, Selena and Faye Wagenbrenner, Jill Wilkinson, and the late Watty Yellowlees. I thank the several persons among those mentioned above who intervened at one time or another to help the work towards publication, and also the four anonymous reviewers for Edinburgh University Press. I am also hugely grateful to Peter Burnhill and Russell Ecob for the creativity, experience and weeks of hard work they so generously contributed to the statistical modelling of the data on still lifes from the List of Works. My debts to several others were accumulated over decades. I was fortunate to share my early encounters with Gillies with Alison McPherson my late wife. Pauline Turner's enthusiasm and support has been characteristically unwavering over many years. Harriet Harvey Wood pledged her backing in 2006 and renewed it continuously through the indefatigable example of her own authorship. Euan McArthur kindly read and commented on every chapter of a 2017 draft. Joanna Soden was generous from the beginning with her knowledge and advice. She, Kenneth Dingwall and Murdo Macdonald commented on successive drafts of both books. Sandy Wood's guidance was wise and ever ready, often making time that was not really there. I am grateful also to his colleagues at the Royal Scottish Academy, to Past Presidents Arthur Watson and Joyce Cairns, and to members of the RSA Standing Committee and Council. I thank too Ralph Footring for the many improvements his editing made to the text, and Susan Tricklebank for the discrimination and order her index has brought to it. I also thank Carol Macdonald, editor for EUP and her several colleagues for their huge commitment to the publication of both books each in their several forms, Eddie Clark of EUP for ensuring their timely delivery, and the Press Committee of Edinburgh University for their confidence in the project. My elder brother, Ian McPherson, diligently scrutinised every word of many drafts of both works. His sharing with me the erudition, pleasures and insights of his life of scholarship allowed me to inch further out on a limb than my chronic fear of heights would otherwise have allowed. But responsibility for excess and error in whatever form is entirely my own.

Index of Gillies' Artworks

Note: The index is arranged in word-by word order. Page numbers in *italics* indicate pages on which the artworks are shown. Initial definite and indefinite articles are placed at the end of titles.

General Index

Note: The index is arranged in word-by-word order. Page numbers in *italics* refer to illustrations

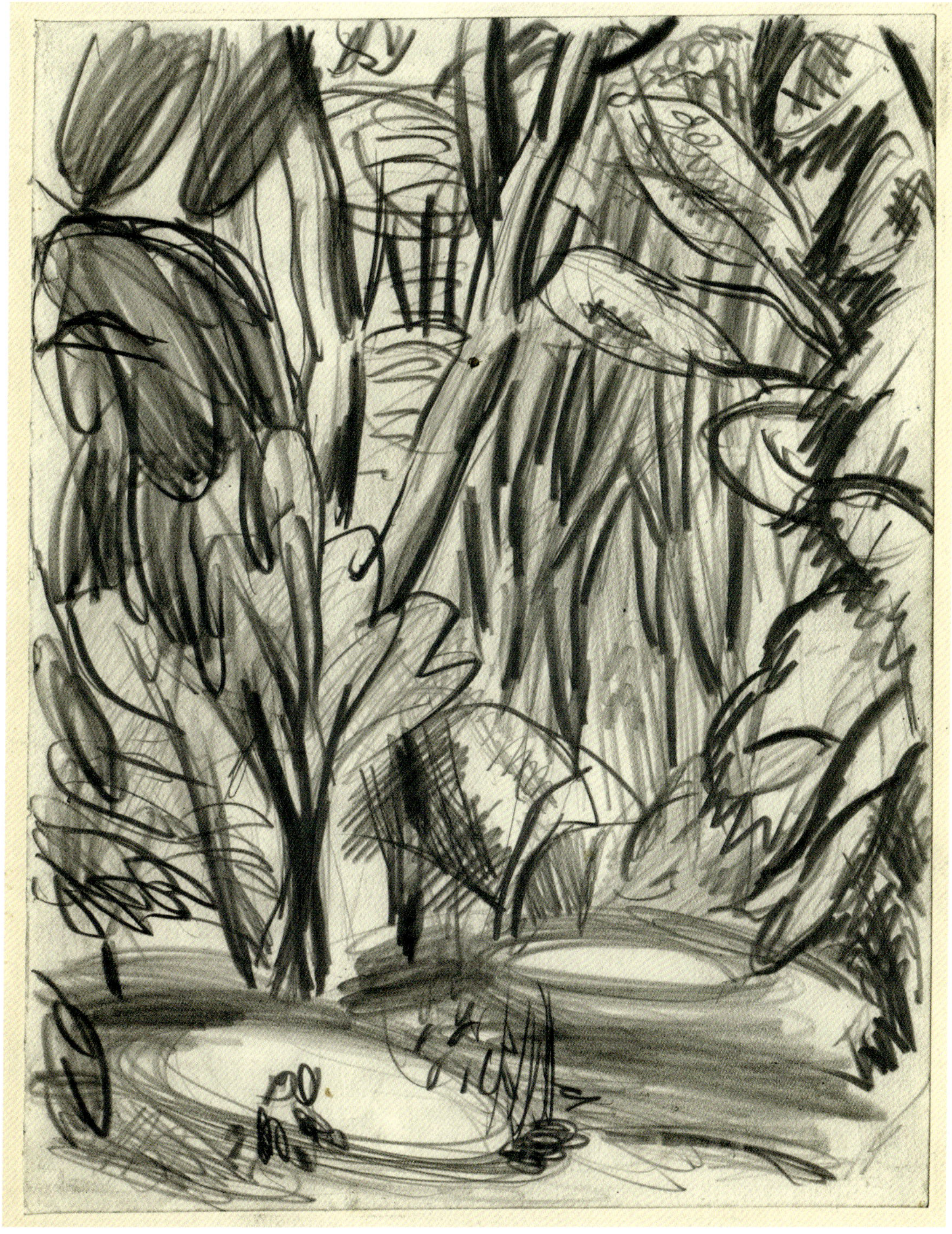

185 'Trees and [with] Dense Foliage' (nd, 1931–40). Pencil, 22.8 cm by 17.8 cm